Creating
Competitive
Markets

Creating Competitive Markets

THE POLITICS OF REGULATORY REFORM

Marc K. Landy
Martin A. Levin
Martin Shapiro
editors

BROOKINGS INSTITUTION PRESS
Washington, D.C.

Copyright © 2007
THE BROOKINGS INSTITUTION
1775 Massachusetts Avenue, N.W., Washington, D.C. 20036
www.brookings.edu

Library of Congress Cataloging-in-Publication data

Creating competitive markets : the politics of regulatory reform / Marc K. Landy, Martin A. Levin, and Martin Shapiro, editors.
    p. cm.
    Summary: "Contributors from academia, government, and the private sector evaluate more than a dozen efforts at market design. Analyzing a broad range of sectors, including airlines, electricity, education, and pensions, authors ask critical questions about developments in Canada, the United Kingdom, and Japan, as well as the United States"—Provided by publisher.
    Includes bibliographical references and index.
    ISBN-13: 978-0-8157-5116-8 (cloth : alk. paper)
    ISBN-10: 0-8157-5116-8 (cloth : alk. paper)
    ISBN-13: 978-0-8157-5115-1 (pbk. : alk. paper)
    ISBN-10: 0-8157-5115-X (pbk. : alk. paper)
    1. Trade regulation. 2. Deregulation. 3. Competition. I. Landy, Marc Karnis. II. Levin, Martin A. III. Shapiro, Martin. IV. Title.
    HD3612.C74 2007
    382'.3—dc22   2006101031

9 8 7 6 5 4 3 2 1

The paper used in this publication meets minimum requirements of the American National Standard for Information Sciences—Permanence of Paper for Printed Library Materials: ANSI Z39.48-1992.

Typeset in Adobe Garamond

Composition by Cynthia Stock
Silver Spring, Maryland

Printed by R. R. Donnelley
Harrisonburg, Virginia

Contents

Part II. Market Design

Part III. Political Sustainability

Part IV. Conclusion

Preface

The four books in *The New Politics of Policymaking* series were written by a national network of more than three dozen scholars affiliated with the Gordon Public Policy Center at Brandeis University.[1] Many of these scholars are or have been affiliated with the Brookings Institution, including Martha Derthick, David Mayhew, Shep Melnick, Jacob Hacker, Paul Pierson, Kent Weaver, Paul Quirk, Eric Patashnik, Thomas Burke, and Adam Sheingate. They reached their conclusions not through abstract theorizing, but through deliberations bringing together scholars and practitioners. Such connections are the raison d'être of both Brookings and the Gordon Center. These institutions seek to bridge the world of ideas and the world of action and help scholars escape their insularity. By paying close attention to what policymakers say about what they are doing, rather than clinging to theoretical predictions, academic experts can become better attuned to what is actually happening.

Focusing on the determinants of public policy in different periods, settings, and policy sectors, these four books go far beyond what "everybody knows" in the academic world about public policy. They consider not only what happened in national policymaking but also why it happened by examining the crucial, though rarely explored, connection between politics and policymaking—the political dynamics of what government does. These books restore the politics of policymaking to the forefront of policy analysis.

As a result, all four books have been sensitive to the unexpected and the unpredicted—in short, the paradoxes of policymaking. *The New Politics of Public Policy* (1995), concentrating on the 1970s and 1980s, argued that major changes in the structure and dynamics of our political system, notably divided government and increasing institutional fragmentation, produced unexpected policy outcomes. In the view of most analysts, these characteristics were—and still are—a recipe for policy gridlock. The conservatism of the presidents of that period was also supposed to incline policymaking toward stasis or conservatism. Paradoxically, however, it took an unexpectedly broad and innovative turn and carried large price tags—distinctly nonconservative. Prominent examples were landmark legislation and precedent-setting executive orders in consumer protection and environmental protection (the creation of the Environmental Protection Agency, the Clean Air and Water Acts, and Superfund), as well as deregulation of airlines, trucking, railroads, telecommunications, and banking. Other innovative policies included the Immigration Reform Laws of 1986 and 1990, the Tax Reform Act of 1986, and the Americans with Disabilities Act of 1990.

The New Politics of Public Policy argued that institutional weakness and policy fragmentation paradoxically helped generate these expansive policies: first by increasing the competition for policy innovation between the parties, then by enhancing the power of strategically placed policy entrepreneurs, and finally by facilitating the breakdown of the defenses against determined policy advocacy. The discipline that used to be provided by stronger parties and institutional checks had weakened considerably. This left a policy vacuum open to the power of strong ideas (often propelled by experts), especially new notions about rights—for the handicapped, the unborn, consumers, and even endangered species—and open to the expertise of economists in the cases of deregulation, immigration, and the 1986 Tax Reform Act.

Similarly, *Seeking the Center: Politics and Policymaking at the New Century* (2000) found paradoxes and ironies in politics and policymaking during the 1990s. This decade was a time of highly partisan political posturing. But unexpectedly, it also produced incremental yet substantial policy innovations. And despite the intense competition between two evenly balanced parties, which alternated in power to a substantial degree, there was no general deadlock in policy. Rather there was a broad consensus regarding the virtues of both the regulated free market and the constrained entitlement state.

The moderate yet innovative policies produced during this highly partisan period included welfare reform (the Personal Responsibility and Work Opportunity Reconciliation Act of 1996, which created Temporary Aid to

Needy Families); the expansion of the federal Earned Income Tax Credit; trade liberalization through the 1994 North American Free Trade Agreement; continual and ultimately successful deficit reduction and reforms in budgeting procedures; and further deregulation in telecommunications, banking, and agriculture.

Seeking the Center argued that these policy outcomes were possible, despite intense partisanship, because the combination of divided government and electoral parity between competitive parties stimulated competition in policy innovation. There was also a politics of credit-claiming and blame-avoidance, which encouraged both parties to avoid being seen as unfair or mean-spirited. The ironic persistence of affirmative action for over twenty years, despite its lack of popular support, illustrates this dynamic at work.

The third book in our series, *Transatlantic Policymaking in the Age of Austerity* (2004), moved beyond the United States to look at policymaking in Europe as well. This book presented a contrarian perspective at a time when most observers predicted policy convergence between the United States and Europe and among the members of the European Union. Instead, it found considerable diversity. Common policy challenges did not yield common policy responses because of national differences in political structure, in the decisionmaking processes that characterize each issue area, and in the initial substance of each policy. Where you end up is shaped by where you start.

In addition, its authors found that policy movement has often taken the form of drift rather than a bold march forward. The public sector has moved very sluggishly and reactively or not at all. Much policymaking has moved by default to the private sector. Often the result has been "reform without change, change without reform."

This pattern is due in large part to the delicate electoral balance that has characterized both sides of the Atlantic since the early 1990s. Parties of the Left have moved toward the center, increasingly acknowledging the virtues of free markets. Parties of the Right, mindful of the huge number of voters in the middle wedded to existing entitlements and also favorably inclined toward further risk regulation, have made a similar shift to the center by acknowledging the welfare state—albeit a constrained one. These political calculations have made bold policy strokes less likely and promoted drift, particularly in a time of private abundance coupled with public austerity.

Like its predecessors, the current volume, *Creating Competitive Markets: The Politics of Regulatory Reform,* is similarly mindful of the unpredicted and the unexpected. The beauty of the market, early deregulation proponents suggested, is that it does not rely on the public sector and therefore can get away from politics. But this book shows that competitive markets are not as easy to achieve as proponents expected. Furthermore, the hope that deregulation would lead to depoliticization has not been realized. Rent-seeking competition in policymaking was not completely displaced by economic competition in the marketplace. Old-fashioned regulation pitted group against interest group, and market design policymaking does the reverse. Since political interference is inevitable, it cannot be wished away. Instead, policy planners must frankly acknowledge and anticipate these political difficulties and take actions before they occur. *Creating Competitive Markets* shows them strategies for doing just that.

Note

1. Marc. K. Landy and Martin A. Levin, eds., *The New Politics of Public Policy* (Johns Hopkins University Press, 1995); Martin A. Levin, Marc K. Landy, and Martin M. Shapiro, eds., *Seeking the Center: Politics and Policy at the New Century* (Georgetown University Press, 2001); Martin A. Levin and Martin Shapiro, eds., *Transatlantic Policymaking in an Age of Austerity: Diversity and Drift* (Georgetown University Press, 2004); and Marc K. Landy, Martin A. Levin, and Martin M. Shapiro, eds., *Creating Competitive Markets: The Politics of Regulatory Reform,* the current volume.

Acknowledgments

The myth of the lone scholar is just that—a myth. Following Plato, we believe that it is impossible to do anything without friends. Research and writing, like most pursuits, are best done in community.

The authors of this book, and the earlier three books in this series, created an interactive conversation from which we all have learned much. Their creative feedback through the long process of preliminary seminars, drafts, conference papers, and then draft chapters produced an illuminating dialogue that broadened our thinking. It transformed a collection of individual works by many authors into a book with coherent themes, arguments, and conclusions. We are grateful to these three dozen or so authors for making these rich products and stimulating journeys. Special thanks to Eugene Bardach, Tom Burke, Jacob Hacker, Robert Kagan, Eric Patashnik, Paul Pierson, Peter Schuck, and Steven Teles, particularly for connecting us to so many fine younger collaborators.

We appreciate the Brookings Institution Press's intelligent, well-managed editorial process in the persons of Christopher Kelaher, Janet Walker, Vicky Macintyre, Susan Woollen, and especially Mary Kwak, who was an ideal acquisitions editor—smart, clever, and wise.

The trustees of the Gordon Foundation—John Adelsdorf, Sanford Bank, Robert Green, and David Silberberg—have our appreciation for their support of this project.

Special tribute goes to Alfred E. Kahn who taught several of us; others were fortunate to serve with him in the public sector. Professor Kahn has probably influenced more government policy in the last fifty years than any other industrial organization economist. A generous teacher, his career has been a unique blend of scholarship and public service, during which he has been a crucial champion and explicator of sound microeconomics, especially the economics of marginal cost. Moreover, he has been an important implementer of those policies, first as chair of the New York State Public Service Commission (electricity and telecommunications) and later at the Civil Aeronautics Board where he gathered and supported economists and lawyers who transformed the deregulation first of air transportation and then of surface transportation, as some associates moved to the Interstate Commerce Commission. Fred has been devoted to market principles but wary of putting the market on autopilot, concerned about real-world outcomes and not economic theology, and always open to argument and evidence.

Creating Competitive Markets

1

Creating Competitive Markets: The Politics of Market Design

MARC K. LANDY AND MARTIN A. LEVIN

*C*reating Competitive Markets should be read, in part, as a cautionary tale. Although we strongly support the use of government to promote market competition, many market reforms we analyze have had checkered results. The privatization of British pension funds launched in 1986, for instance, failed entirely. The U.S. decision to end subsidies for major agricultural commodities under the Federal Agriculture Improvement and Reform (FAIR) Act of 1996 was rescinded after a few years. Changes in telecommunications policy also enacted in 1996 have had at best an ambiguous competitive impact. And the political momentum pushing for greater pro-competitive policy has weakened. The opening up of electricity markets to greater competition in the 1990s, once considered the wave of the future, also met with mixed results. This is in stark contrast to the earlier and highly successful wave of "deregulations" of trucking, airlines, railroads, and telecommunications that took place during the 1970s and early 1980s.

A cautionary tale need not be a pessimistic one, however. Despite the sobering lessons of the second wave of marketization policy reform that our book presents, greater success is possible—but only if policymakers fully appreciate and face up to both the political and analytical difficulties of creating competitive markets.

1

Deregulation and Market Design

For the first two-thirds of the twentieth century, it appeared that the nineteenth-century dream of free markets was being subjected to a rude awakening. Communism had rejected the market throughout much of Asia and Eastern Europe. Government ownership and public provision of goods and services had become a major force in the democratic nations of Western Europe as well—even in the birthplace of free enterprise, Great Britain. Although the United States was less affected by the anticapitalist turn, the dominant trend since the rise of Progressivism in the early 1900s had been toward stricter and more interventionist regulation and control of many economic sectors, including trucking, airlines, telecommunications, banking, power production, agriculture, health, and finance. In the early 1970s there was scant evidence that a worldwide pro-market counterrevolution was about to get under way. Yet by the dawn of the new millennium every alternative to markets—from communism to democratic socialism to command-and-control regulation—was on the retreat around the globe.

In the United States, pro-market public policy took the form of what is conventionally called "deregulation." A wave of deregulation hit aviation, trucking, and telecommunications in the mid-1970s, stimulated by an intellectually powerful and persuasive body of writings from experts in influential economics departments, law schools, and think tanks. In 1985 the Brookings Institution published a seminal account of this phenomenon, *The Politics of Deregulation*, by Martha Derthick and Paul Quirk. During the more than two decades that have elapsed since then, almost every heavily regulated sector of the economy—including banking, agriculture, telecommunications, and energy—has experienced serious reform aimed at improving economic performance by removing the dead hand of regulation and increasing competitive pressure.

Inspired by the pioneering work of Quirk and Derthick, this book takes up where they left off, just as public policy had begun questioning the previous era's rhetoric of disciplining and taming markets. This book examines what is now a thirty-year history of policy innovation dominated by a rhetoric of freeing up competitive forces and replacing flaccid and cumbersome government intervention with the flexibility and creativity that markets are supposed to stimulate.

Central Findings

This book contains seven central findings. First, policy affects market competition on two distinct levels: macro and micro. Second, efforts to create competitive markets do not deregulate; they redeploy regulation. Third, the track record of regulatory redeployments to date is highly uneven, with at least as many failures as successes. Fourth, success can best be fostered if policymakers abide by the following policy design principles: provide risk protection on a *macro* not a micro level, accept the constraints imposed by imperfect knowledge, and limit the ambition of the market design. Fifth, failure to produce more competitive markets is due to complex mixtures of cognitive and political constraints; indeed, the single greatest impediment to successful marketization policy is the sheer amount of political interference in the market design process. Sixth, increased market competition is greatly facilitated by Schumpeterian "creative destruction," which occurs when technological innovations destroy existing oligopolistic barriers and facilitate market entry or when intrusive regulatory agencies are abolished. Whatever the mechanism, creative destruction has positive effects by reconfiguring interest group dynamics to facilitate the formation of a powerful new political coalition that supports the new pro-competitive policy regime. Seventh, the way for policy designers to cope with political constraints and formulate successful policy design is to adopt a more self-consciously political understanding of their roles. To enable the "invisible hand" of the market to gain a foothold and to flourish despite the onslaughts of rent seekers, they need to apply a noninvisible hand—a political hand—that will help them anticipate and stave off political obstacles.

Macro Policy

The role of public policy in promoting competitiveness is by no means limited to intervening directly in the design of particular markets. As discussed in the first part of this book, macro policies that are not market specific may establish or fail to establish the necessary and complementary conditions for sustaining a competitive economic environment. Such macro policies include insurance and other forms of risk amelioration, welfare and health policies that affect labor mobility, corporate reform, and other government policies and programs aimed at creating sufficient levels of security and transparency to encourage individuals and firms to live by market outcomes.

We use the term "macro policy" to draw attention to the broad frameworks in which markets operate. It flags a key question of this discussion: how and why do actors in a particular market system accord it sufficient legitimacy to actually live by its outcomes rather than seek to undermine and destroy it. The term also encourages an appreciation of the relationship between a cultivation of the norms of trust, efficacy, and legitimacy, on one hand, and the design of a particular pro-competitive system, on the other. In this volume, John Cioffi explores that relationship by considering how changes in corporate governance under the Sarbanes Oxley Act of 2002 are likely to affect the public's trust in corporate behavior and thereby its willingness to continue to invest in corporations, whether the reform gives firms relatively free rein to control their own affairs, and to what extent it refrains from interfering in how they compete with one another.

Likewise, Martin Shapiro investigates the dangers that stem from undermining public faith in corporate good behavior. He looks at the relationship between governmental efforts to create greater economic competition and the resulting incentives to both the regulated and the regulator. Shapiro concludes that the doctrine of self-interest central to free market competition does not encourage playing by the rules. Hence a free market economy depends upon rigorous policing to prevent unfair practices. But recent salutary trends in regulatory reform designed to remove the "dead hand" of command and control undermine the government's ability to police the private sector, not to mention itself. Efforts to ease monitoring problems, encourage voluntary compliance, and negotiate settlements of regulatory violations rather than insist on immediate and complete remediation or punishment undoubtedly remove obstacles to greater competition and more efficient operations. By removing a whole series of blunt enforcement instruments, they also make it much easier for the regulated to evade the spirit of a reform. It then becomes easier to cheat, harder for the regulators to catch cheaters, and easier for reluctant regulators to avoid catching them. Further incentives to cheat are provided by the massive amounts of money funneled into corporations by today's highly efficient stock market, bending behavior far beyond the typical levels of corporate fraud. Shapiro's analysis of these dangers speaks to macro policy at the broadest conceivable level—at the interaction between economic efficiency, trust in government, and justice.

This book's discussion of macro policy has its roots in early discussions about the impact of risk protection on economic efficiency and innovation. A positive view, eloquently expressed by the renowned economic anthropologist Karl Polanyi, is that government is the crucial vehicle for tempering and softening the profound dislocations associated with a dynamic economy. In *The Great Transformation,* Polanyi explains how the advent of the welfare state enabled citizens to cope with the destabilizing effects of the Industrial Revolution and its aftermath.[1] Absent government tempering and disciplining, Polanyi claims, the entire capitalist enterprise would have imploded.

Micro Policy

The second part of this book focuses on "micro policy," the specific policy designs created to address perceived inadequacies in the regulatory regimes governing specific economic sectors. The term "deregulatory" does not adequately convey the nature of the micro policies described in this book. A more appropriate term for policies that ostensibly aim to increase private competition in a specific market realm is "market design." This is not merely a semantic quibble. Market design initiatives, successful or not, embody rules and regulations that are often at least as numerous and complicated as those they displace. Indeed, our chapters show a striking interpenetration of politics and markets. The traditional distinctions between government and market and between public and private do not apply to the processes of market design and redesign that we found to be at the heart of creating competitive markets.

The absence of literal deregulation is evident in all of our case studies. Banking, securities, and telecommunications provide especially striking examples of how efforts to stimulate competition result in ever more complex and numerous government strictures. Even if these initiatives have stimulated competition, nothing resembling complete deregulation has in fact taken place. Instead, the government has changed the nature of its involvement in order to make use of laws and policy designs establishing a pro- rather than anticompetitive institutional framework. Rather than deregulating, public policy has been self-consciously fashioning—or as Eric Patashnik puts it, reconfiguring—markets so that they will exhibit particular and contingent features. One of the primary goals of our analysis is to determine the extent to which these frameworks and features promote the pro-competitive goals they were ostensibly designed to foster.

The regulatory redeployments described here come in many guises.[2] Some are fundamental to any effort at market formation, beginning with clearly defined property rights. Likewise, sanctions must be imposed on those who violate the norms of honesty and transparency on which market systems depend. To discourage fraud and deception, measurement must be accurate; information provided by the buyer must be true, and the payment provided by the seller must be genuine and timely. To this end, Cioffi points out, the Sarbanes Oxley Act established new forms of liability for chief executive officers, chief financial officers, and corporate boards of directors. Regulation in the form of antitrust rules and mandated consumer information may also be necessary to cope with certain market imperfections that competition cannot cure and may even magnify. As Frederick Hess shows, state education departments are struggling to make sure parents are adequately informed about the charter schools licensed to compete with ordinary public schools.

Making a new market is a much more subtle and complex regulatory task than maintaining an existing one. More intrusive rules may be needed to stimulate competitive behavior where it did not previously exist—an idea that Steve Vogel captures with the term "asymmetric regulation," in reference to regulations designed to impose restraints on incumbents and give advantages to potential competitors. Alan Jacobs and Steven Teles illustrate this concept in pension privatization in Britain. When privatization began in 1986, there was no market of individualized retirement savings vehicles for workers. The few products that did exist were designed for a small group of the self-employed and wealthy. The government sought to stimulate the creation of a broader market by proposing that holders of personal pensions be given a rebate on their National Insurance contributions (which then flowed into their occupational scheme, if they had one), and that contributions to personal pensions be deferred, just like contributions to occupational schemes. In addition, the government boosted returns on privately purchased pensions above the actuarial baseline.

Any such changes in the rules of the competitive game, despite the fact that they are meant to improve efficiency, will inevitably punish some competitors or some consumers, or both. Therefore new rules are likely to include some form of direct compensation, grandfathering, or other means of benefiting those who have been harmed. If benefits are difficult to define, Darius Gaskins notes, market designers may face great political obstacles, as those in the electricity sector do because they cannot guarantee in advance that the changes they propose will always produce lower prices. In the airlines case discussed by Michael Levine and Eric Patashnik, Congress had to establish a program of side payments in the form of regional and other subsidies to those interests whose opposition had to be neutralized if the reform was to be adopted.

Technological Innovation, Government, and Competitive Success

Our studies focus largely on micro efforts to create competitive markets and macro efforts to undergird and sustain them. But we recognize that in some instances the most important influences on particular markets may not be those micro or macro policies, but rather an exogenous force such as technological innovation. Regulation has repeatedly proved unable to stifle innovation. For example, tight regulation of railroads by the Interstate Commerce

Commission (ICC) may have slowed the growth of competition in the transport sector but did not prevent it. Technological innovation in the form of trucks, automobiles, and airplanes placed relentless pressure on railroads to lower rates and improve service.

The best example of the impact of technological change is in telecommunications, which has seen greater price declines over time than any other economic sector discussed in this book. As Andrew Rich explains, telecommunications competition increased *despite* the Telecommunications Act of 1996, as a result of a technological development ignored by the act—cellular telephony. This technology dates back to the 1970s, when new telecommunications entrants such as MCI and Sprint developed novel alternatives to AT&T's reliance on landlines.

Although such innovation is exogenous to the policies this book considers, its success was dependent on prior government action. Neither Sprint nor MCI could have entered the long-distance phone market if not for the successful suit brought by the Justice Department to end AT&T's monopoly. The settlement forced AT&T to allow competitors to purchase space on its landline facilities. Without this court-imposed toehold, these dynamic innovators would not have had the chance to explore the technological alternatives to landlines that proved to be the precursors to the cell phone industry.

Successes

As mentioned at the outset, public policy's performance in creating competitive markets has been quite mixed.[3] Among the successes, deposit insurance has had a very salubrious effect on the efficiency of banking, as Jonathan Macey shows. Although the returns are not yet in, innovations under the Sarbanes Oxley Act emphasizing structural reform rather than litigation-driven enforcement are expected to diminish accounting and securities fraud and enable the capital markets to function more efficiently, says Cioffi. In transportation, airline and railroad regulatory policy changes were instrumental in increasing competition in the American market, as noted in the chapters by Darius Gaskins, Michael Levine, and Eric Patashnik. Edward Iacobucci, Michael Trebilcock, and Ralph Winter found similar results in Canada. In electricity, reforms adopted by the Pennsylvania, New Jersey, and Maryland Regional Electricity Pool (PJM) worked to decrease electricity rates, report Richard O'Neill and Udi Helman. And in agriculture, the 1996 FAIR Act gave farmers greater freedom to decide what and how much to plant, Patashnik points out.

Failures

Cioffi describes a failure that predates the Sarbanes Oxley Act: Congress's failure to protect the integrity of the private auditing process led to flagrant fraud, which in turn caused the collapse of Enron and other major corporations. Vogel discusses how the Japanese practice of employment security diminishes labor market mobility. As Shapiro shows, recent trends in regulatory reform designed to remove the "dead hand" of command and control, such as negotiation and soft law, have in some cases undermined the government's ability to police both the private sector and itself. In the examples he cites—including railroads—this resulted in less efficient and less safe market behavior. Some other failures are Congress's inability to sustain the abolition of farm price subsidies, passed in1996 (see Patashnik's discussion); the weak outcome of school choice proponents (described by Hess); and California's failed effort to create a competitive electricity market (see the chapter by O'Neill and Hellman). In Canada, as Iacobucci and his colleagues point out, the effort to open up Ontario's electricity market was short-lived, and the marketizing of telephony throughout the country, though by and large successful, ran into problems when the regulatory commission tried to maintain price floors for certain services. In the United States, the 1996 Telecommunications Act left the marketplace unimproved for consumers, concludes Rich, and eliminating certain forms of regulation led to the very costly savings and loan (S&L) debacle, argues Macey.

As noted earlier, a particularly striking failure befell the British experiment in privatizing pensions, which began in 1986. Its threefold objective was to protect the public purse, reduce collectivism in the public sphere, and increase labor mobility in the private sphere. But as Jacobs and Teles show, the outcome was rampant "mis-selling"—fraudulent or nearly fraudulent representations—of private pensions. In response, the government passed the Pensions Act of 1995, which imposed unprecedented regulation on the private pensions market.

As also pointed out, the sparse success of marketization during the late 1980s and 1990s stands in stark contrast to the virtually uniform success of the 1970s and 1980s. This contrast suggests that the earlier successes may relate to "low-hanging fruit": government-created oligopolies were ripe for the plucking because the rationale for suppressing competition had long since disappeared, and new entrants were available that were both able and eager to compete once regulatory barriers were removed. The question remains, however, as to why they were harder to marketize in the later period. Our ambitious task is to answer this question.*

The Politics of Market Design

Clearly, competitive markets are not as easy to achieve as proponents suppose. The hope was that once a policy realm was "deregulated," it would become permanently depoliticized as rent-seeking competition in the political realm would be largely displaced by economic competition in the marketplace. Nor does a neutral set of competitive rules necessarily mean that self-interested parties will rest content to play by the rules. To be sure, the first wave of deregulation provided some support for proponents' expectations. In *The Politics of Deregulation,* Quirk and Derthick found that in the policy spheres of trucking and airlines, at least, old-fashioned rent-seeking politics had been blunted by a new politics dominated by congressional and bureaucratic policy entrepreneurs and academic experts. And in our earlier book, *The New Politics of Public Policy,* we extended this insight to such diverse policy arenas as taxes, the environment, and immigration.

By contrast, *Creating Competitive Markets* finds that old-fashioned group-based politics never died away. Indeed, political interference of that nature—and policymakers' failure to anticipate it—is probably the strongest single reason that policy reform failed to promote competition. For example,

---

*As Peter Schuck suggests in the last chapter in this volume, the conditions associated with these successes and failures are manifold, the phenomena analyzed "are dauntingly complex" and at times even opaque. Of the many conditions that Bardach finds associated with these outcomes, he explores only one: "when policymakers have high stakes in deregulation . . . , their actions often lead, directly or indirectly, to failure." Similarly, Schuck only comes up with one generalization: "politics pervades not only the forms of market design . . . , but also the[se reforms'] substantive content. . . . Beyond this . . . each of our case studies reveals a stubborn singularity." Schuck concludes that this will be frustrating to "lumpers" yearning for theoretical elegance and predictive power, because we are left "without powerful predictive formulas . . . [and are reminded that] a satisfying explanation of public policy outcomes depends on many factors that are difficult to characterize and highly specific to the individual case. Once again, the splitters win." Thus both eschew our more ambitious mission. While we agree that political factors are the most powerful condition shaping these outcomes, additional crucial conditions must also be taken into account, particularly the extent of political interference in the market design process; the extent of the presence or absence of government institutions that regulate, subsidize, or directly provide services; the nature of the interests involved and the extent to which they have been reconfigured in a direction that supports the new deregulatory regime; the extent to which market forces induce creative destructiveness; and the extent of technological innovation in the particular broad business sector.

according to a prominent participant, the designers of airline deregulation in the 1970s did not anticipate that a decade later the Reagan administration would, in effect, "close down the Anti-Trust Division of the Justice Department," permitting airline firms to indulge in anticompetitive behavior (predatory pricing, mergers), which led to overconcentration and inefficiency in the industry. This otherwise sagacious policymaker had unrealistically assumed that opening up markets would be a game played according to Marquis of Queensbury rules. In fact, players always feel free to change the rules to their advantage.

Thus market design reform did not mark the "beginning of the end" of governmental involvement and political conflict over economic regulation. Rather, to borrow from Winston Churchill, it marked the "end of the beginning" of a new twist on the old politics. Efforts to gain competitive advantage now have to be cloaked in new and subtle free market rhetorical and institutional garb. But rent-seeking objectives remain very much the same.

Not recognizing that the politics of rent seeking was still in full swing, marketization advocates failed to adequately understand the political implications of and political influences on their policy reform objectives. They were too apt to view marketization in principle as marketization in practice, expecting the magic of the market not only to reconcile supply and demand but also to turn nasty rent-seekers into fierce but punctilious competitors cheerfully abiding by market rules. One is reminded of the old Soviet-era joke that capitalism is the exploitation of man by man and communism the reverse. In the world of regulatory politics, that translates as old-fashioned regulation pits interest group against interest group while market design policymaking does the reverse.

Ronald Coase once observed that the real choice in determining how best to achieve economic efficiency is between imperfect markets and imperfect regulators. Friedrich Hayek, champion of free markets, argued further that it is very hard for markets and regulators alike to attain efficiency, but harder for regulators. Our chapters force market advocates to squarely face the significant political obstacles to designing market mechanisms that actually live up to the theoretical potential to which the likes of Coase, Hayek, and Charles Schultze aspire.

The cases described in this book are political in every sense: they stir partisan passions, spark intense ideological struggles, involve complex bargains and compromises, and mobilize diverse political coalitions. And they show that rent seeking is more cleverly disguised in today's world. Thus it might be better to reword Coase's adage: the choice is no longer between imperfect markets and imperfect regulators, but between imperfect regulation and imperfect deregulation.

The new version of rent seeking is evident in many of our cases. Congress, Patashnik points out, was eager for political advantage in 2002 when it reinstated the price subsidies so popular with most farmers and their trade associations. California's effort to deregulate electricity discussed by O'Neill and Helman demonstrates that even if experts help design policy, they may not be impartial. The consultants and expert witnesses in this case were chosen for and by a state legislature that had been successfully lobbied by Enron and various other energy and investment companies. By cloaking their preferred policies in the free market rhetoric of hired experts, these rent seekers promoted inefficient market design that maximized their capture of transaction cost profits. Significantly, many economists who were not asked to testify before the legislature were skeptical of the market design proposals precisely because of their flaws.

Another flawed market design with political roots, described by Macey, was that advocated by the "Keating Five": Senators John McCain, Alan Cranston, John Glenn, Dennis DeConcini, and Don Reigle, who all received large campaign contributions from S&L executive Charles Keating. As Rich points out, the passage of the Telecommunications Act of 1996 was yet another throwback to the "old" politics of public policy. The "Baby Bells," facing the loss of their oligopolistic rents, aggressively lobbied Congress and the Federal Communications Commission (FCC) to preserve their advantages. Their champions, such as Senate Majority Leader Robert Dole and Senator Ernest Hollings, vociferously defended policies designed to insulate companies based in their home states from competition. Cloaked in the language of marketization, the resulting legislation placed barriers in the path of new entrants, especially smaller, more technologically oriented companies.

Consumers, argue Iacobucci and his colleagues, can also play a strong political role in blunting competitive market design. When electricity marketization in Ontario failed, consumer backlash was instrumental in bringing about re-regulation. Their Canadian analysis as well as that of Jacobs and Teles on U.K. pension reform and Vogel's on marketization in Japan demonstrate that much is to be learned from comparing policies across countries.

Until recently, however, many U.S. analysts ignored this broader perspective and "comparativists" ignored the United States. This tendency was due in large part to the organization of political science. For a long time, "comparative politics" referred less to a method of inquiry than to a category of study, namely, the politics of some country other than the United States.

Since the late 1990s, however, "comparative" has come more often to be taken seriously and refer to inquiries into the ways that different countries, including the United States, respond to similar policy problems. We include this kind of discussion in the hope of stimulating both Americanists and comparativists to widen their intellectual and empirical horizons, in the tradition of our earlier *Transatlantic Policymaking in an Age of Austerity* and that of other truly comparative policy analyses, such as Pierson's, Hall's, David Vogel's, and Steven Vogel's.[4]

Of course, the role of the government itself in marketization must not be overlooked either, as Eugene Bardach emphasizes. The depth of governmental organizations' and actors' stakes in the outcome of market-oriented reform vary from policy to policy. Bardach argues that, perversely, the greater the government's perceived stakes in a particular innovation, the more likely that design is to fail.

Eric Patashnik's fine chapter, "The Day *after* Market-Oriented Reform," reveals today's rent-seeking dynamic—"what happens when economists (reform ideas) meet politics." Much of this book centers on what occurs when economists' ideals meet the realities of the highly political market design process.

Cognitive and Political Constraints

In *Transatlantic Policymaking in an Age of Austerity,* Martin Levin and Martin Shapiro underlined the great importance of cognitive constraints in limiting policy success. They found that for many of Europe's and America's complex socioeconomic problems, no expert consensus existed for solutions.[5] Health care, for example, is rife with severe disagreements about how to resolve the tensions between cost containment and adequate access to care. Describing these cognitive complexities, Jacob Hacker observes: "Medical industrial complex leaders are caught between fiscal constraints and public demands . . . with competing evaluations and prescriptions, and embroiled in bitter struggles in which questions of equality, justice, professional sovereignty, the role of markets, and indeed life and death are never far beneath the surface."

Regulatory policies, including regulatory redeployments, are inherently more difficult to conceive and implement than distributive policies (building a highway, for example) or redistributive ones (transfer payments, for example). In the regulatory realm, policymakers cannot act directly to hire building contractors or write a check to recipients. Instead, they must cause others to act, often through indirect means. When British policymakers privatized their pension system, they were well aware that few private suppliers were poised to provide pension schemes. But because they *needed* such suppliers for the reform to work, they assumed that once erected, a private scheme, like the mythical baseball stadium in *Field of Dreams,* would bring many in.

Cognitive difficulties can compound political problems, as is vividly illustrated by California's experience with electricity. From the outset, policy designers faced imponderable or at least uncontrollable factors, such as the price of oil and the amount of rainfall, on which hydroelectric power production depends. To add to their concerns, political factors suggested that a truly free market in electricity might create prices that consumers would consider too high. Citizens and legislators alike so mistrusted the utilities that when the latter sought to have consumers pay for the billions of dollars of "stranded costs" due to failed or incompetent construction of generating facilities, the state legislature agreed to this bailout only in exchange for a cap on retail rates, even though wholesale rates were allowed to float with the market. When wholesale prices rose unexpectedly, electric utilities, unable to raise retail rates, spiraled into bankruptcy. The inability to predict wholesale prices, a cognitive constraint, combined with the political constraint on raising prices, produced an energy policy fiasco.

Fostering Success

Despite all the problems that our cases depict, many positive lessons emerge about how to foster success at both the macro and micro levels. A particularly important one is that policymakers must pay close attention to the political sustainability of efforts at regulatory reform.

Coping with Risk through Macro Policy

The analysis of macro policy in part one of this book tends to support Polanyi. For example, Vogel's observations on Japanese social policy support the Polanyian belief that governments need to keep individual risk levels to manageable proportions in order to sustain markets. One large obstacle to marketization in Japan, many argue, is its poor unemployment insurance system, which would be unable to cope with the politically unacceptable labor dislocation and unemployment likely to ensue from increased competition. In other words, says Vogel, "in the Japanese context anticompetitive regulation *is* a critical component of the social safety net."

Because Japan provides such meager social insurance, its citizens look to specific sectors of the private economy for job and income security. This stultifies the labor market and makes it very difficult to introduce competitive principles into these sectors. Perhaps the most effective means of increasing their competitive efficiency would be to decouple social insurance policy from employment and thus enable the labor market to function more freely.

Macey's finding suggests an important refinement to the Polanyi-Vogel argument in banking, where an additional concern is how protection is provided. Two forms of risk protection are available to banks—deposit insurance and bailouts of failing banks—and both create moral hazard. If a depositor is insured, that individual has no incentive to exercise oversight over how his or her money is being lent or otherwise invested. Likewise, if a bank has a reasonable hope of being bailed out if its loans go bad, it has a greater incentive to make high-risk, high-return loans. However, these two forms of moral-hazard-inducing risk protection do not produce the same result. Bailouts, Macey shows, have a far more deleterious effect on banking efficiency than does deposit insurance.

Although economic theory suggests that competitiveness and efficiency should be addressed separately from fairness and equity, in the political world all these issues are inevitably conflated. Those who find themselves worse off in a competitive environment fight for assurances of protection. For the public, fairness and equity generally have a higher value than the promise of efficiency does. Therefore the critical policy design question regarding equity and efficiency relates to how, not whether, it is provided. Indeed, one of the most critical determinants of regulatory success or failure is whether equity and risk protections are part of macro policy or are directly incorporated into market-oriented policy reform. Equity remedies that are built into market design—such as price controls and rate-setting regulations for electricity and telephone services or Lifeline policies designed to help low-income and elderly citizens with the cost of utilities—distort market outcomes. Not only do they create inefficient levels of production and distribution of the service per se, but they can also lead to inflation, inefficient distribution of labor, poor quality in products, shortages, and queuing.

As several of the chapters—especially Hess's on education—indicate, markets often hurt when they work. The adjustments they force in supply and demand risk pricing poorer consumers out of crucial markets (such as those for health care, higher education, and private pensions) and marginal producers out of the market for their product. Railroad marketization, recounts Gaskins, is still haunted by the passionate opposition of Dakota grain shippers, who saw shipping rates rise dramatically as a result of price deregulation and then could no longer keep their prices competitive. Likewise, state attempts to allow competitive rate setting for retail electricity have foundered on opposition from representatives of the poor and the elderly.

On the other hand, macro policies that broadly subsidize those adversely affected by freer market competition—the elderly, the poor, and the isolated—need not distort market outcomes. Such policies address inequalities and income maldistribution apart from the market transactions that produce them. Thus they do not distort the transactions themselves, as do price controls and rate-setting regulations. Policies that perform this function include income transfers that range from Social Security to the Earned Income Tax Credit and Temporary Assistance for Needy Families; the progressive income tax; voucher programs such as food stamps and virtual ones such as Medicare and Medicaid; the direct provision of services (for example, by Veterans Administration hospitals); and subsidized goods and services such as public transportation and the Section 8 housing program. Such welfare state policies soften the market's less desirable impacts.

We draw support for our view of macro policy from Vogel's fine discussion of Japan, but we differ on how to best reconcile micro and macro policy. Vogel favors pro-competitive regulation and planning, strengthened by institutions and institution building. But as he himself recognizes, business can be quite skillful at evading the spirit of such reform efforts, as in the case of Japan. Its firms, he points out, often respond to government efforts to liberalize markets by insulating themselves in some way from the full force of competition. When the government removed capital controls in the 1960s, for instance, corporations increased their cross-shareholdings to protect themselves from foreign takeovers. And when trade was liberalized in the 1970s, some industries replaced tariffs and quotas with private sector substitutes, including preferential procurement practices.

Japan's across-the-board liberalization policies could be compared to the U.S. antitrust policy approach, notorious for its ineffectiveness and deleterious latent consequences. By contrast, we favor policies that foster equity and security at a macro level—such as bank deposit insurance, single-payer health care, child care and transportation subsidies for the poor, and job training—but that do not affect the inner workings of any particular market.

Coping with Cognitive Constraints through Macro Policy

Some regulatory policies may be intrinsically easier to design than others and therefore make fewer demands on the skills and wisdom of regulators. At the same time, some objectives, even if they are not logically inconsistent, may simply be too difficult to reconcile in practice. A key finding of this book is that market design efforts that are limited to constructing a framework for market activity, by establishing property rights and removing regulatory impediments, have proved more successful than those that intervene in specific aspects of market operations or that try to simultaneously establish and constrain markets. This is largely because such frameworks are easier to understand and easier to design. They impose a lighter cognitive burden on their designers and on their implementers.

Market designs range from least to most intrusive and complex. Pro-competitive results, on the whole, are most likely to occur where policy does not intrude inordinately and does not pursue a panoply of goals. As Peter Schuck discusses in a concluding chapter, even the most unregulated markets need rules in order to define property rights and proscribe force and fraud. We call this basic form of public intervention "market framing." "Market-perfecting rules"—such as antitrust law, information requirements, and taxes on externalities—may also be needed to remedy any defects that competition cannot cure and may even magnify. Evidence from the cases indicates that designs for competitive markets are most successful when limited to market framing and market perfecting.

Other forms of market design (Schuck describes eight categories) are far more ambitious and intrusive. One form seeks to induce market entry, as in the case of British pension reform. Another simultaneously promotes and constrains competitive behavior through "strings" that ensure the market rewards efficiency yet does not undermine other desirable objectives. School reform proposals, Frederick Hess points out, invariably include provisions designed to prevent competition between schools from placing other crucial values, notably equity, at risk. Such ambitious goals as inducing entry and simultaneously pursuing other objectives, no matter how worthy, turn out to be very difficult to achieve and may well put the entire effort to enhance competition at risk.

Political Sustainability

In most instances of competitive reform, as already mentioned, the prevailing political dynamic favors the status quo. Therefore, as Patashnik argues, market-oriented reforms can only prevail and survive when they reconfigure that political dynamic. Durable reforms do not merely destroy an existing policy subsystem, they generate a self-reinforcing process in which the identities and organizational affiliations of relevant interests change and key social actors adapt to the new regime. Schumpeterian "creative destruction" is central to the creation of politically sustainable circumstances.[6] It does so by eliminating or substantially reducing the power of obstructionist government entities and private firms. In the first case, the destruction is through conscious and targeted reform efforts. In the second, it is the product of the impersonal forces of the market, which have little respect for a corporation's political power or previous large market share and prestige.

Obstructionist government entities take a variety of forms. Some are regulatory agencies, such as the FCC or former Civil Aeronautics Board and ICC. Some subsidize as well as regulate, as in the case of the Department of Agriculture (DOA). Others are direct service providers, like the nation's public school systems. They obstruct competition because it threatens their institutional maintenance and enhancement. To increase their strength, they ally with interest groups that share their anticompetitive objectives; the two, in Patashnik's words, "develop a powerful symbiotic relationship."

Abolishing such government institutions—as was done in airlines and trucking, but not in telecommunications, agriculture, or education—is a vital aspect of market reform because it deprives losers of a useful arena for revisiting their setbacks and creating new forms of regulatory complexity with which to obstruct new competitors. Now that the FAA, ICC, and CAB are extinct, the airline and trucking industries thrive. By contrast, those who would interject greater competition into telecommunications, agriculture, and education continue to be foiled by the FCC, the DOA, and the public school systems, all of which are very much alive and wield more political power and resilience than ever.

From Patashnik's and Levine's investigations, it is clear that pro-competitive airline policy reform was politically strengthened not only by the abolition of the CAB but also by a shift in the interest group dynamics surrounding the airlines. This reconfiguration through the creative destructiveness of a competitive market freed up the air transport market quickly and led to the demise of politically powerful but competitively weak carriers such as Pan Am and Eastern Airlines. At the same time, it facilitated the emergence of new low-cost entrants such as Southwest, Midway, and Jet Blue and persuaded legacy carriers such as United and Delta, along with their unionized workforce, that they were better served by a pro-competitive environment. This new coalition of new and old competitors proved too strong for opponents to the reforms. As Levine concludes, the market forces unleashed by competition destroyed the interest group cohesion created by regulation. As a result of this political transformation, the competitive principle became so deeply engrained that it even stymied later efforts at rent seeking by members of the new coalition. Speaker of the House Dennis Hastert, for one, proved unable to exploit his position to obtain a government-backed loan for the once-powerful legacy carrier United Airlines, headquartered in his district. His appeal was rejected because the administration and most of Washington's political establishment now saw the airlines industry operating in a competitive market system, which they agreed should not be subject to political manipulation.

It should be emphasized, however, that the benefits of abolishing governmental entities do not run counter to those of government-provided risk protection. Rather, they indicate that the government performs a variety of functions and that it does some better than others. It is good at enhancing security, particularly when it does so according to universalistic principles that do not affect competition between firms. It is not so good at regulating individual markets, because its own institutional maintenance needs are likely to cause it to intrude in market operations, to the detriment of competition.

Since political interference is inevitable, it cannot be wished away. If policy planners could frankly acknowledge this political difficulty, they would be less innocent about their function and obliged to plan for political interference well before it takes place. They would see their role in a new light, outside of their comfort zone as calculators of economic efficiency whose purity of heart exempts them from the need to think and act politically. This would force planners to anticipate political problems and cope with them when they are still of manageable proportions. They might anticipate the counterattacks of rent seekers and their bureaucratic and congressional allies by including proposals to abolish intrusive government entities and to alter congressional committee jurisdictions in their initial policy designs.

Policy Implications

The findings of the specific cases in this book and the generalizations we have drawn from them have important policy implications. They give evidence of what markets have done well (fly planes) and what they have not, so far at least, done well (run schools); what markets should do (grow food) and what roles they should divest (compensating "losers"). We also show what government has done well (enabling transport competition) and what it has failed to do well (privatize public pensions); what government should do (provide macro-level risk protection) and what it should not do (intervene in markets at a micro level).

Our findings with regard to risk protection, market design, and political sustainability shed light on three critical policy issues: health care, social security, and food. Health care fits our definition of an appropriate subject for macro policy. It insures individuals against the economic risks of illness. But it is not immune to moral hazard: individuals might well invest more in their well-being and reduce their consumption of health care if they were not insured and therefore had to bear the full cost of their own illnesses and of their medical care choices.

But the public is unwilling to trade the peace of mind that health insurance offers for a diminution of moral hazard. Therefore the relevant policy question is how best to provide such insurance. Currently, in the United States, health insurance for the non-elderly and non-poor is handled more or less as employment security is handled in Japan, by individual firms rather than by the government. And it has the same deleterious economic effects. Firms that are generous in providing health care suffer an economic handicap in comparison with firms that do not or with international competitors whose workers are covered by their governments. Workers, for example, sometimes resist testing the labor market for fear of jeopardizing their health insurance. Thus shifting the burden of providing health care insurance from firms to the government, regardless of the content of that insurance, would improve the competitiveness of American companies and the efficiency of the American labor market.

This example is intended to be merely suggestive. This is hardly the place to try to elaborate a full-fledged health policy framework. Such an effort would begin with the recognition that policymaking for health care is a question of market design as well as of risk protection. And as we suggest throughout this book, its design aspect in particular requires attention to the whole panoply of political and technical design issues involved. Here we limit ourselves to pointing out the business and labor efficiency advantages of a single-payer approach. We are well aware that a full health policy proposal would have to account for the strong interests of doctors, pharmacists, hospitals, insurance companies, and medical schools.

Social Security is the quintessential macro policy, providing all workers with financial protection against the financial risks of old age. But its future must also be considered a market design question, particularly in light of recent proposals for privatization. Like the privatization scheme in Great Britain, they are built on the expectation that new entrants will materialize to offer private plans, even though no one yet knows whether such plans will prove profitable.

As emphasized throughout this and many of our other chapters, this type of cognitive constraint is often exacerbated by a political one. What if the capital markets in which private pension schemes invest suffer a prolonged downturn? The experience in energy markets is instructive. Price increases after privatization made it difficult for energy privatization to survive in Canada or in California. Consumers were simply too resistant to paying more when they had understood the promise of marketization to be that they would pay less. Moreover, for any given consumer, the economic significance of higher energy bills is far less than a loss of a significant part of one's retirement savings resulting from the fact that markets go down as well as up. If workers feel that the viability of their retirement is being threatened, they will demand that the government make up the difference between what they expected to receive and what the private market has delivered.

Faced with these difficulties, policy planners should think like statesmen, not merely technicians, and follow more the dictates of Machiavelli than Adam Smith. They should recognize that incantations about how, in the long run, the capital markets outperform treasury bonds will not placate an insecure citizenry. They should anticipate the political resistance they will face rather than decrying it. Any effort to add a greater private element to Social Security must include credible evidence that everyone will be held harmless by the reform—in short, it must guarantee that they will be at least as well off as if the existing system remained in place. This is an extremely expensive proposition—political resources are as scarce as economic ones. The inglorious defeat of President George W. Bush's Social Security reform effort means that a future president is far less likely to risk political capital on such reform. If providing greater access to the capital markets is indeed a vital way to cope with the realities of an aging population, then his politically shortsighted effort may well prove more costly than a more expensive program guaranteeing pensioners against loss would have been.

In the case of agricultural commodity price deregulation, if farmers are always poised to oppose price deregulation when commodity prices decline, the key to sustainable reform lies in binding the government's hands so as to make price re-regulation almost impossible. This might be done by shifting the farm issue from the domestic to the foreign policy realm, where it is very hard for a government to renege on its treaty obligations. If bound by treaty to allow commodity prices to fluctuate, it would be unable to respond to demands for price supports despite the ability of farmers to mobilize politically. Consequently, perhaps would-be price deregulators should not fritter away their political resources in fighting for a new farm bill unless it is part of a treaty-making process.

Conclusion: The Noninvisible Hand

Our findings have important implications not only for the format and content of public policy but also for the roles and responsibilities of policy planners, entrepreneurs, and analysts. Many cases in this book reveal the deleterious impact of political interference, whether that interference is instigated by producers, consumers, or governmental actors. The greater the access of these groups to key congressional players or to the surviving regulatory agencies, the more likely they are to stymie market competition.

These political realities have great bearing on policy planning, policy leadership, and policy analysis. Above all, political interference is best addressed by political foresight. To reiterate, policy designers must anticipate the likely political objections to proposed policy reform and figure out how best to meet those objections in a manner that is both politically viable and does not unduly interfere with market operations.

Effective public policies are not discovered; they are constructed. Creating competitive markets is a process of market design, not merely deregulation. Markets do not magically spring to life when the government has gotten out of the way, or a thoughtful, well-crafted policy is initially put in place. Furthermore, policies of this kind not only need to be well constructed, but also must be adequately maintained to guard against powerful rent-seeking interests that surround newly established markets. Almost every chapter in this book shows that policymaking pertaining to the design of new markets pits interest group against interest group just as much as old regulatory policymaking did. There are "alligators" on both sides of the river and they never sleep.

In neoclassical economic thought, coordination can occur in the market without a coordinator—under the market's invisible hand. But when markets are created and sustained through policymaking, there needs to be a *political hand* to chart a proper course and steer through the dangerous political shoals.[7] The political mind guiding that hand must be capable of anticipating political obstacles and developing proactive strategies to circumvent and stave off these obstacles.[8] Good policy is better served by the politically savvy opportunistic spirit of a Joseph than by the pessimism of a Jeremiah.

Notes

1. Karl Polanyi, *The Great Transformation* (Boston: Beacon Press, 1944; repr. 1971).

2. Other important ways apart from regulatory redeployment include "soft law," negotiations, and other corporatist approaches adopted by the Bush administration. See chapter 14 by Shapiro.

3. We rely much here on Eugene Bardach's thoughtful description in chapter 15 of the success and failure patterns in these cases.

4. See, for example, Paul Pierson, *Dismantling the Welfare State? Reagan, Thatcher and the Politics of Retrenchment* (Cambridge University Press, 1994); Stephen Leibfried and Paul Pierson, eds., *European Social Policy: Between Fragmentation and Integration* (Brookings, 1995); Peter Hall, *Governing the Economy: The Politics of State Intervention in Britain and France* (Oxford University Press, 1986); Peter H. Hall and David Soskice, *Varieties of Capitalism: The Institutional Foundations of Comparative Advantage* (Oxford University Press, 2001); Steven Vogel, *Japan Remodeled: How Government and Industry Are Reforming Japanese Capitalism* (Cornell University Press, 2006); Steven Kent Vogel, *Freer Markets, More Rules: Regulatory Reform in Advanced Industrial Countries* (Cornell University Press, 1998); David Vogel, *Trading Up: Consumer and Environmental Regulation in a Global Economy* (Harvard University Press, 1995); David Vogel, *National Styles of Regulation: Environmental Policy in Great Britain and the United States* (Cornell University Press, 1986).

5. Martin A. Levin and Martin Shapiro, *Transatlantic Policymaking in an Age of Austerity: Diversity and Drift* (Georgetown University Press, 2004).

6. Joseph A. Schumpeter, *Capitalism, Socialism, and Democracy* (New York: Harper & Row, 1976).

7. For a more detailed discussion of this concept and how policymakers can provide the public sector's missing "political hand," see Martin A. Levin and Barbara Ferman, *The Political Hand: Policy Implementation and Youth Employment Programs* (New York: Pergamon Press, 1985).

8. For an in-depth discussion of how proactive strategic skepticism can help implement a potential AIDS vaccine and treatment program, see Martin A. Levin and Mary Bryna Sanger, *After the Cure: Managing AIDS and Other Public Health Crises* (University of Kansas Press, 2000). Levin and Sanger discuss a strategy for political executives and policy designers of such programs that anticipates the inevitable management conflicts and delays and then takes action in advance to ameliorate and head them off.

PART I

Metapolicy

2

Why Freer Markets Need More Rules

STEVEN VOGEL

According to many political economy scholars, modern market systems are not natural phenomena that arise spontaneously but complex institutions that must be created and sustained by the visible hand of the government. Scholars apply this precept to three types of market transitions: from feudalism to market society in the West, from communism to capitalism in Eastern Europe and East Asia, and from poorly developed to viable market systems in developing countries.[1] For the most part, however, they have not applied it to the more subtle transition toward more competitive market systems in the advanced industrial countries. But if markets are institutions, market reform should consist of building institutions more than of removing constraints, and this principle should apply to more developed market systems as much as to less developed ones.

There is no controversy on this point in its most stripped-down form: namely, that markets are institutions. Yet scholars diverge considerably in what they mean by this. Classic liberals acknowledge that the government must establish and enforce basic property rights; design the essential infrastructure for a modern economy, such as a monetary system; and provide

The author is grateful to Roselyn Hsueh and participants in this project for valuable feedback on an earlier draft.

certain public goods, such as national defense.[2] Institutional economists identify a much broader range of market institutions, including the modern corporation, corporate governance systems, and long-term business contracts. They view transaction costs (such as information and enforcement costs) as the "friction" in the market system and property rights, broadly defined, as the institutional mechanisms for reducing these transaction costs.[3] Economic sociologists define market institutions even more broadly, including social networks and market cultures. They emphasize that market systems are inherently embedded in society itself, not only in formal structures but also in standard practices and social norms.[4]

Markets as Institutions: Some Implications

If markets are institutions, this quickly leads to some rather profound implications for market reform in the advanced industrial countries, both in theory and in practice. I use the term "market reform" here to refer to a wide range of measures that enhance the role of markets in society.

1. *There are no "free" markets.* Economists often assume perfect markets for the purposes of devising a model or making an argument, and there is nothing inherently wrong with that. They have made some of their greatest theoretical breakthroughs and presented some of their most useful prescriptions through precisely this sort of simplifying assumption. But one should not forget that these frictionless markets—in which buyers and sellers are seamlessly matched without any transaction costs whatsoever—do not really exist. In the most basic case of two people exchanging goods, the rules governing their transactions may be very simple. In real-life market systems in advanced industrial countries, however, the institutions that structure markets are extremely complex. They consist of intricate networks of laws, practices, and norms. This first point may not be particularly controversial in itself, but it logically leads to the following propositions, which challenge the prevailing discourse on the relationship between governments and markets.

2. *There is no such thing as a disembedded or even a less embedded market system.* Scholars have developed various typologies to identify the varieties of national market systems, such as liberal market economies versus coordinated market economies.[5] Some of these designations imply that liberal market systems are less embedded in politics and society than other systems.[6] Yet an American-style liberal market economy is not disembedded from society, nor is it even less embedded than a Japanese-style coordinated market economy.

An American-style external labor market, for example, is not any less embedded than a Japanese-style internal labor market, an American equity-based financial system is not any less embedded than a Japanese credit-based system, and an American antitrust regime is not any less embedded than a Japanese corporate network (*keiretsu*). That is, an American-style liberal market economy is embedded in its own specific matrix of policies, practices, and norms. The Japanese labor market, for example, is embedded in a political-economic system in which government policies discourage labor mobility, large firms favor new graduates over midcareer hires, employees are reluctant to defect from large firms to their competitors, and social norms place a premium on employment stability and employee loyalty. But the American labor market is embedded in its own system, in which government policies encourage labor mobility, firms embrace midcareer hires, employees commonly defect to competitors, and prevailing norms encourage firms to lay off workers and employees to offer their services to the highest bidder.

3. *Market reform involves changes at every level of a political-economic system: government policies, private sector practices, and social norms.* Most scholars focus on government policy as the primary locus of the market reform process. This is natural, for government policy is the component of a market system that is most amenable to conscious reform. But one must keep in mind that government policy affects market outcomes only in *interaction* with private sector behavior. The government might liberalize a particular sector, for example, but this does not automatically mean new entrants will emerge or firms will begin to compete on price. Economists differ on whether they view competition as more fragile or more robust, and this in turn affects their views on how far the government must go to generate competition. As Adam Smith himself attests, most businessmen would prefer the comfort of collusion over the challenge of competition.[7] So in many cases businesses must not only be allowed to compete but also be forced to do so.

Even if one accepts that individuals and businesses do have some natural propensity to engage in market activity (without the government forcing them to do so), social relations and prevalent norms still shape *how* they do so. For example, policymakers might give employers greater flexibility to dismiss workers, but this policy change may not result in more competitive labor markets if managers decide not to resort to dismissals because of the nature of their relations with workers or broader societal norms.

4. *The regulation-versus-competition dichotomy that animates most debates about market reform is fundamentally misleading.* The conventional use of the term "deregulation" reflects this misperception, referring to less regulation

and more competition, as if these two developments were naturally associated. In fact, generating more competition usually requires more regulation, not less. Thus the dominant trend in advanced industrial countries has not been one of deregulation (less regulation), but rather liberalization (more competition) combined with re-regulation (more regulation)—or "freer markets and more rules."

That is to say, whereas popular discourse presupposes a negative relationship between regulation and competition, it is actually more positive than negative. More precisely, it varies across time and across sectors and subsectors. It may be more positive at an early stage, when the government has to create the basic infrastructure to support market competition, and more negative at a later stage, when an incremental increase in the government's role would be more likely to impede than to enhance competition. Or it may be more positive in sectors that are particularly conducive to monopoly (network industries) and more negative in sectors where competition is more likely to evolve naturally (retail). In reality, of course, the relationship is even more complex than this. Some regulations enhance competition, while others impede it. The process of liberalization consists of increasing regulations that enhance competition, such as antitrust rules, and removing regulations that impede it, such as price and entry restrictions. Yet the story does not end there: policies that enhance competition are almost always accompanied by corollary regulations designed to facilitate the competition (as with financial disclosure requirements), protect society from negative side effects (as with environmental regulations), or compensate the potential losers from these policies (as with welfare policies).

5. *The government-versus-market dichotomy that animates most debates about economic policy is also misleading.* As one moves from a thin definition of market institutions (the minimal rules of the game) to a thicker one (a broad range of laws, practices, and norms), the relationship between government and market becomes more positive and less negative. This is not simply because competition requires regulation (as point 4 indicates), but because market competition is not incompatible with a substantial government role in the marketplace beyond that of a referee. The government is the largest consumer, employer, lender or borrower, insurer, and property owner in market economies.[8] Moreover, the government can still manipulate the terms of competition to favor certain marketplace outcomes even if it allows or promotes competition.

Pushing this argument further would require refining language to differentiate between the government's role in creating and sustaining markets and its role in impeding or crowding out markets. The more common analytical distinctions in the literature—such as the government as a referee versus the government as a player, passive regulation versus active intervention, or setting the rules versus shaping outcomes—provide a useful start, but they do not settle the issue. Indeed, all governments are by definition market players as well as referees, all passive regulation entails some active intervention, and all rule setting has some ramifications for outcomes.

6. *Market reform is primarily a creative process, not a destructive one.* Given points 4 and 5, market reform implies not the dismantling of institutions that impede competition so much as the creation of institutions that sustain it. One cannot simply get the government out of the way and expect greater competition to arise naturally. As already mentioned, scholars have gone further in fleshing out the implications of this principle for transitional economies and developing countries than for advanced industrial countries. If market reform is considered a negative process, then shifting from a command economy to a market system should be easy: just dismantle the command system and let markets flourish. Fostering markets in developing countries should be equally straightforward: just get interventionist governments to back off, and then markets will take over. If market development is considered a constructive project, however, the transition will entail a complex process of building new market institutions. In the next section, I apply this basic logic to the more subtle transition involved in market reform in advanced countries via an extended example from Japan.

How to Make a Market: Evidence from Japan

The debates over market transition in post-communist and developing countries boil down to a simple question relevant to all countries: how does a society make a market? These cases are especially illuminating because the countries are attempting a wholesale transition from planned to market economies or from primitive markets to a functioning national market system. Yet the same insights apply to advanced industrial countries that already have market systems but are attempting a more modest transition toward significantly enhanced markets.

The United States and other advanced industrial economies depend on a market infrastructure—a complex web of government policies, corporate practices, and social norms—that continuously evolves over time. Current-day Japan provides an especially vivid example to illustrate this point, because reformers have been striving to shift the Japanese economic system from a coordinated market architecture to a more liberal one.[9] They have been striving not simply to liberalize specific industrial sectors (via "deregulation," the topic addressed in the next section) but to enhance competition by altering the overall governance of the economic system, including its labor and capital markets.

Japan already has a well-developed legal system that defines and enforces property rights, a modern financial system, and a regulatory bureaucracy. Yet its labor and capital markets differ fundamentally from those of the United States. For example, Japan lacks a "real" labor market in the sense of an active labor market for the core employees of large corporations. Scholars refer to this arrangement as an "internal" labor market, in contrast to the American "external" labor market. What they mean by this is that Japanese companies rotate their core employees across functions, divisions, and locations within the firm or corporate group, but they do not poach employees from competitors, and employees do not defect to competitors. Thus companies do not compete for workers on the basis of wages, and workers do not compete for outside offers.[10]

Likewise, Japan lacks a "real" capital market in the sense of an active market for corporate control.[11] Industrial corporations and banks maintain a substantial proportion of their shares in friendly hands via cross-holdings of shares within business groups, thus insulating firms from the threat of hostile takeover. Although the Japanese government has gradually eased regulations that impede corporate takeovers and introduced policies to facilitate them, the mergers and acquisitions market has only recently begun to emerge—but it is from a very low base compared with that in the United States.

What, then, would it take for Japan to develop a real labor market or a real capital market? This is where the logic of post-communist transition and the creation of market institutions in developing countries outlined earlier can be applied to an advanced industrial economy. From a classical liberal perspective, this should be a relatively simple, primarily negative process, in the sense of removing constraints rather than building institutions. Regulating markets requires hard work, but liberating them should be easy. Since Japan already has a basic system of property rights, then just get the government out of the way, and more active labor and capital markets should emerge spontaneously. From an institutionalist perspective, however, this should be an exceedingly complex, primarily constructive process, in the sense of creating new market institutions and transforming old ones.

To develop a real labor market, the Japanese government would have to remove constraints on employers and nurture the infrastructure for a more

active labor market (see table 2-1). For example, it would have to give
employers more flexibility in setting wages, benefits, hours, and working
conditions and ease restrictions on hiring nonregular workers, but it would
also have to strengthen organizations to match employers with workers and
disseminate more information to both employers and workers. In addition, it
would have to make changes in areas outside of labor policy itself—including
financial regulations, accounting standards, and commercial law—that
would encourage firms to be more responsive to shareholders and less
beholden to their workers. And it would have to promote portable pension

Table 2-1. *What Would It Take to Turn Japan into a Liberal Market Economy?*

Government policy	Corporate behavior
Labor	
Laws	Practices
Labor market reform	Lay off workers when necessary
Changes in case law doctrine	Do not favor new graduates over
Corporate governance reform	midcareer hires
Pension reform	Shift from seniority to merit-based pay
Financial reform	Introduce stock options
Norms	Norms
The government should not use	Companies should not preserve
regulation to preserve employment	employment at the expense of profits
Net result: an active external labor market	
Finance	
Laws	Practices
Financial reform	Sell off cross-held shares
Banking crisis resolution	Banks make lending decisions and price
Corporate governance reform	loans on the basis of risk
Pension reform	Corporations choose banks on the
Tax reform	basis of price
	Banks stop lending to insolvent firms
Norms	Norms
The government should not protect	Companies should maximize shareholder
banks or manipulate financial	value
markets	
Net result: a market for corporate control	

Source: Steven K. Vogel, *Japan Remodeled: How Government and Industry are Reforming Japanese Capitalism* (Cornell University Press, 2006), p. 6.

plans, such as 401(k) plans in the United States, so that employees who switch employers would not sacrifice their retirement benefits.

Over the past decade, the Japanese government has made considerable progress on a package of reforms that might promote a more active labor market, but it has watered down some measures and failed to complete others. In any case, government policy by itself is not sufficient to transform corporate practices. For a true labor market to emerge, companies would have to renegotiate their compacts with their workers and redesign their systems of employee representation. They would have to become less loyal to their workers, and the workers would have to become less loyal to them. And there would need to be sufficient numbers of employers looking for workers and workers looking for new employers to provide ample liquidity in the market.

Likewise, to cultivate a real capital market, the government would have to enact substantial reforms in financial regulation and corporate governance, as well as in areas less directly related to capital markets, such as pensions, antitrust, and taxation. Here again, the Japanese government has made substantial progress on this agenda, but it has not completed the full slate of reforms that would be required. To create a market for corporate control, it would have to abandon its propensity to protect domestic financial institutions and corporations and to manipulate financial markets. Corporations would have to go even further in unwinding cross-shareholdings, become less loyal to members of their corporate group, and embrace a philosophy of maximizing shareholder value. Shareholders would have to become more assertive in pressing managers to maximize returns. And banks would have to stop protecting their main bank clients from takeover bids.

Deregulation and Variations across Sectors

I now turn from market reform in the broadest sense, the enhancement of the basic market infrastructure of an economy as a whole, to market reform in a narrower sense, as it is more commonly studied in advanced industrial countries—that is, regulatory reform designed to promote competition in specific sectors. Both of these types of reform require "more rules," but they do so in a slightly different sense. In the first case the government and the private sector enhance the basic institutions that govern markets, whereas in the second the government intervenes more actively to create or to sustain competition in sectoral markets in which private actors are prone to collude or competition is not likely to emerge on its own. Here the analyst needs to pay greater attention to cross-sectoral variation.

Given the argument presented thus far, one must be wary of making a simple dichotomy between "regulated" and "unregulated" sectors. All sectors are governed in the sense that they rely on a common market infrastructure; all sectors are subject to social regulations such as health, safety, and environmental codes; and all sectors are subject to economic regulations in that "unregulated" sectors are inevitably linked to "regulated" sectors. In fact, some of the most heavily regulated sectors—such as finance, energy, transport, telecommunications, and retail—constitute the core infrastructure for the rest of the economy. These caveats aside, there is a qualitative difference between sectors that are subject to direct economic (price and entry) regulation, such as the infrastructure sectors just listed, and those that are not, such as most manufacturing sectors.

The deregulation movement that began in the United States in the mid-1970s and spread to all advanced industrial countries (first to Britain and Japan and then Western Europe) sought to curtail both economic and social regulation, but with the emphasis on the former.[12] A driving force behind the movement in the United States was an unusual bipartisan coalition that included academics and business and consumer groups. Economists challenged the public interest rationale for regulation, arguing that policymakers should not assume that any market failure requires government regulation as a response but should carefully weigh the costs and the benefits of regulation. Furthermore, they contended that technological change and market dynamics had undermined the original rationale for regulation in many sectors.

Yet as noted earlier, the movement achieved little true deregulation, but rather a combination of liberalization with re-regulation. Of course, liberalization does not *always* beget more rules, as Peter Schuck points out in chapter 16 of this volume. I would add, however, that it usually does. The U.S. government came closest to true deregulation (freer markets and *fewer* rules) in the airline industry, where it eliminated an entire regulatory agency (the Civil Aeronautics Board) and abandoned economic regulation. Even in this case, it coupled deregulation with a substantial strengthening of safety regulation.[13] By contrast, other deregulation programs have been accompanied by an explosive proliferation of rules. Britain's Thatcher reforms of the 1980s, for example, led to the creation of no less than twelve new regulatory agencies. Most notably, its "Big Bang" financial liberalization of 1986 coincided with the passage of the Financial Services Act, which ushered in a far more extensive, intrusive, and legalistic regulatory regime. In the one country with hard data on the actual numbers of regulations—Japan—an explicit goal of regulatory reform was to reduce their number. In utter frustration, officials saw the number increase instead. For every regulation they eliminated, another would somehow emerge.[14]

The logic by which liberalization drives re-regulation varies according to the nature of the preexisting regime and the character of the transition toward greater competition. A shift from monopoly to competition typically requires pro-competitive regulation to jump-start competition (see the discussion of telecommunications in the following paragraphs). A transition from public to private provision of services often requires new regulation to mandate public service requirements (such as universal access or interoperability) that were previously met directly by the public corporation. An increase in the number and diversity of market players generally demands a more codified regulatory regime ("more rules" in the literal sense). And an intensification of competition may spur companies to behave worse (to produce greater externalities), therefore requiring more social, environmental, or other types of protective regulation.

When British authorities launched a bold telecommunications reform program in the early 1980s, advocates recognized that they would need to increase regulation in order to generate competition, but they believed that this would be a temporary phenomenon: as competition took hold, they expected regulation to wither away.[15] To the contrary, regulation of telecommunications has turned out to be an ongoing necessity to sustain and govern competition. In every case of telecommunications reform, the government initially had to confront the monopoly power of the incumbent service provider. The incumbents held an overwhelming advantage because they owned and operated the national infrastructure, possessed access to all existing customers, dictated technical standards, and commanded the relevant technical knowledge and expertise in the sector. So the government could not simply allow competition—it had to *create* it. It usually did this with some form of "asymmetric" regulation: imposing restraints on the incumbent and giving advantages to the competitors. It could break up the incumbent into multiple companies (divided along functional or regional lines, or both), force the incumbent to reduce charges in noncompetitive areas (such as local service), prohibit the incumbent from lowering charges in competitive areas (such as long distance), restrain the incumbent from introducing new services, and require the incumbent to lease its lines at reduced rates. This last measure was critical, because the incumbent carrier controlled the phone lines, so creating competition meant forcing the incumbent to lease lines to its competitors. The regulatory battle then hinged on the rate of the interconnection charge the incumbent would levy on its competitors. In many cases, the incumbent and the competitors devised complex rationales to justify their own position (incumbents favor "historic" cost calculations whereas challengers prefer "incremental" costs), yet these debates essentially concerned political judgments about how far to favor the incumbent versus the challengers. This is a never-ending process because the incumbent never completely loses its structural advantage, and technological and market changes require constant recalibration of the regulatory balance.

Given the growing complexity of the telecommunications sector and the interrelationships between its many lines of business (land-based telephony, mobile communications, satellite communications, cable television, Internet services, and so on), the overall level of regulation is more likely to increase than to decrease. Mobile technology has altered the dynamics by allowing new carriers to challenge incumbents without relying as heavily on the incumbents' land-based network. Yet to the extent that mobile customers call other customers on the incumbent's land-based network, the mobile carriers still face the issue of interconnection charges. Ongoing market developments are bound to change this further, but regulators are not likely to reach a point in the foreseeable future where they can simply withdraw and let free and fair competition take over (see chapter 11).

Other network industries share some common features with telecommunications. For one thing, they are natural monopolies since the network infrastructure is so costly that duplication would be inefficient. Hence liberalization takes the form of fabricating competition over a common infrastructure. Governments strive to achieve this in a variety of ways. They can opt for franchising, whereby they grant monopoly franchises to operators for a limited period via competitive bidding. They can adopt a highway model in which the government runs the infrastructure and allows operators (such as trucking companies) to compete freely using that infrastructure, but this is more difficult in other sectors (railways, telecommunications, energy). The British government tried this approach for railways, creating a single public rail track authority and auctioning franchises to service providers, with problematic results.[16] In energy sectors, governments have generally separated generation from distribution, allowing competition in generation while restricting it for distribution. They have also distinguished between large corporate users and household consumers, allowing more competition in the industrial sector (see chapters 6 and 7).

In many cases, decreases in economic regulation are accompanied by increases in social regulation. Regulators typically fear that companies faced with greater competition will be more likely to compromise health, safety, or environmental standards. Trucking companies might push their drivers to work too hard, airlines might take shortcuts on safety codes, or utility companies might lower standards for pollution emissions. To compensate, governments strengthen regulations in these areas. Many of the old licensing regimes fused economic and social regulations: the same licensing system served to limit entry and to maintain standards of conduct. So the task of regulatory reform is to separate economic regulation from social regulation and to reduce the former while increasing the latter.

In finance, the connection between liberalization and re-regulation is particularly striking. In chapter 3, Jonathan Macey describes this logic persuasively in relation to the banking sector, so I shall not present the case here. The need for perpetual regulation is equally compelling on the securities side, but the rationale is different. In order for capital markets to operate properly, investors must have accurate information about the financial circumstances of publicly listed firms. Insiders must be prohibited from taking advantage of information available to them at times but not to the broader public, and managers and large investors must be prohibited from manipulating share prices for short-term gain. Moreover, corporate boards must be required to serve the interests of the shareholders as a whole. In recent years, governments have responded to various scandals by substantially strengthening regulations on securities transactions and corporate governance (see chapter 4).

Across subsectors and countries more broadly, the general trend has been toward not only greater competition but also massive expansion of financial regulation. Governments have eliminated many forms of price regulation, such as regulations on deposit interest rates and stock commissions, and lowered barriers between business lines within finance (banking versus securities, for example). At the same time, they have substantially augmented and codified other types of regulation, such as prudential supervision and disclosure requirements. There is a logical connection between these two facets of reform, because intensified competition begets greater incentives for risky behavior, which requires tougher regulation, and brings in new players who are less likely to play by informal rules, which spurs further codification.

Ultimately, as noted at the outset, scholars need to develop language to move beyond the presumption of a negative relationship between regulation and competition by recognizing the government's various roles in the market. In an earlier work, I proposed four categories of regulatory reform that strive to create more competition yet entail more regulation, not less.[17] *Pro-competitive re-regulation* offers regulatory advantages to competitors or imposes disadvantages on incumbents in a market where competition is not likely to arise naturally, such as basic telephone service. *Juridical re-regulation* adds more detail to existing regulations, by putting tacit rules into written form or by putting administrative rules into legal form. *Strategic re-regulation* favors particular firms, often national champions, within a newly opened market. And *expansionary re-regulation* creates new regulations to prevent the loss of bureaucratic authority that can accompany the liberalization process, or to simply take advantage of the process to expand administrative powers.

Alternatively, one might devise analytical categories specifying the varieties of market reform rather than the (related) varieties of re-regulation. For example, market reform might be divided into two broad categories—primary and corollary measures—and each of these subdivided further. Primary measures would include (1) enhancing the basic infrastructure of a market economy, such as the financial and legal systems; (2) strengthening related policies that sustain competition, such as disclosure requirements and corporate governance codes; (3) tightening antitrust policy and pro-competitive regulation; (4) removing or relaxing anticompetitive regulations; and (5) reducing the government's role in functions that could be performed by private actors. Corollary measures would include policies that tend to accompany the market reform process and facilitate it for functional or political reasons. For example, governments typically couple reductions in economic regulation with increases in health, safety, and environmental regulations for the functional reasons outlined earlier. They also couple liberalization with politically motivated adjustments, such as compensating social groups for the costs of increased competition via subsidies, insurance, or welfare policies.

The Market Reform Process

Thus far I have argued that a sophisticated understanding of the relationship between regulation and competition, and between governments and markets, is a prerequisite for understanding the market reform process in advanced industrial countries, which is the primary concern of this volume. While I have introduced various examples to illustrate this point, let me conclude by recapitulating the argument, with special attention to its implications for the market reform *process*.

1. *Market reform is a highly complex process precisely because it entails building new institutions and not simply removing barriers.* The standard government-versus-markets rhetoric is misleading particularly because it implies market reform should be easy: just get the government out of the way and markets will flourish. In this view, the only reason things do not work out

this way is political opposition: vested interests that benefit from protection and regulation block liberalization. But this argument misses a critical part of the story: it is actually not easy to enhance market systems or to make them more competitive. In other words, the challenge of market reform is functional as well as political, and the political difficulty is compounded by the functional complexity. As stressed throughout this volume, this implies that market reform requires considerable attention to the specifics of *market design*.

2. *Market reform often requires not just one policy change but a wide range of interrelated measures.* This reflects policy linkages, or "macro-macro" links. As Japanese labor and capital markets demonstrate, reform in one area might only have its intended effect if combined with related measures in other areas. Linkages across policy areas may be political as well as functional. For example, many argue that Japan cannot fully liberalize service sectors because it lacks a sufficient social safety net in the form of a well-developed unemployment insurance system. That is, policymakers recognize that more competition would mean greater labor dislocation and unemployment, and they judge that this would be politically unacceptable because they do not have sufficient policies in place to cope with such dislocation.[18] I would put this slightly differently: in the Japanese context anticompetitive regulation *is* a critical component of the social safety net. Once this connection becomes clear, the Japanese government's response to its long-standing economic malaise makes more sense. The government has been slow to liberalize service sectors in order to avert labor dislocation, and it has been slow to develop a more standard social safety net in order to avoid greater liberalization of service sectors.[19]

These policy linkages also shed light on the failings of partial reform. Many reforms do not achieve the expected results because they have enacted one part of a policy package but not another. Or even worse, they have generated or exacerbated major crises via incompatible combinations of policies or poor sequencing. In the case of the U.S. Savings and Loan (S&L) crisis, which some blame on financial liberalization and others on too little liberalization, it would be more accurate to blame the particular combination of policies in place at the time. The government had deregulated deposit interest rates, liberalized the S&Ls' use of funds, and maintained deposit insurance—giving the S&Ls both the freedom and the incentive to take greater risks. But it did not increase prudential regulation (see chapter 3).[20] A decade later, Japan triggered a full-fledged banking crisis by combining poor macroeconomic management, financial liberalization, and a tacit guarantee to bail out failing banks with lax banking supervision.[21] Likewise, poor policy coordination played a major part in the California energy crisis of 2000–01 (see chapter 7).

3. *Market reform is not simply a process of policy change, but a combination of policy change and societal response.* This reflects public-private linkages, or "macro-micro" links. Any account that focuses on only the public side risks missing the essence of what is happening. Market reform often means replacing existing market institutions with alternatives. This includes not only switching from one type of government regulation to another but also switching modes of governance, replacing government regulation with private sector regulation and vice versa. Market reform often requires a broader transformation of social norms as well.

This interaction can take many forms. In Japan, government policies to liberalize markets have often been accompanied by private sector efforts to insulate businesses from the full force of competition.[22] When the government removed capital controls in the 1960s, corporations responded by substantially increasing their cross-shareholdings to protect themselves from foreign takeovers. When the government moved forward with trade liberalization in the 1970s, some industries replaced tariffs and quotas with private sector substitutes, including preferential procurement practices, exclusive dealerships, and cartels. Kodak argued this point in its case against Fuji Film before the World Trade Organization, contending that Japan's Ministry of International Trade and Industry worked with Fuji to establish exclusive dealer networks that effectively shut out foreign suppliers. And when the government implemented sector-specific liberalization (deregulation) in the 1980s, the removal of government regulation sometimes failed to spur competition or was replaced with outright collusion among producers. The liberalization of deposit interest rates, for example, led to very little actual competition for deposits based on price.[23] More recently, Prime Minister Junichiro Koizumi pledged to double foreign investment into Japan by 2008, particularly through measures to facilitate foreign mergers with and acquisitions of Japanese companies. At the same time, the government enacted corporate law reforms for corporate takeover defenses and issued guidelines to clarify what defense strategies would be legal and appropriate. In response, companies rushed to prepare defenses to insulate themselves from foreign takeovers.

For a different example of public-private linkages, I turn to labor market trends in the United States, Germany, and Japan. I cannot capture the full complexity of this story here, but a stylized interpretation should illustrate the general point that government reforms and private sector developments do not necessarily coincide. I would characterize the broad trends as liberalization without policy change in the United States, policy change without liberalization in Japan, and partial liberalization via policy change in Germany.[24] Over the past two decades, the U.S. government has made no major changes to labor law, but adjustments in policy implementation and corporate practices have combined to produce more competitive labor markets. The Japanese government has enacted considerable policy reforms, as already discussed, yet corporate practices have not been greatly transformed. After years of stalling, Germany moved forward with substantial reforms beginning in 2003, which had more impact than in Japan because the legal framework plays a greater role in structuring labor markets.

4. *There is no single equilibrium for optimal market reform.* Perfect markets do not exist, but they can serve as a useful fiction for analytical purposes. Many experts also assume that they provide an optimal target against which to assess reform progress. But the positive relationship between regulation and competition complicates this exercise. Market reform advocates themselves are divided over the merits of the laissez-faire variant of liberalism as opposed to a more pro-competitive approach. The former are more skeptical of the benefit of government action to generate or enforce competition, while the latter are more favorable toward aggressive antitrust policy and pro-competitive regulation. This philosophical difference is at the heart of many policy debates, such as those surrounding the Microsoft antitrust case or rulings by the Federal Communications Commission.

5. *Market reform is inherently a political process.* This final point may be the most obvious one of all, but points 1–4 help to explain *how* and *why* this is so. It is not simply that government regulation generates winners and losers, and therefore regulatory decisions involve political battles. Market reform is inherently so complex, with linkages across policy arenas and combinations of government policy and private sector response, that the process is bound to be more political than it would be if it were just a matter of repealing a specific regulation. Moreover, because there is no agreed-upon target for market reform, even among its advocates, the political process inevitably involves a contest of ideas as well as a clash of interests.

Notes

1. On the historical evolution of markets, see Karl Polanyi, *The Great Transformation: The Political and Economic Origins of Our Time* (Boston: Beacon Press, 1944); and Douglass C. North, *Structure and Change in Economic History* (New York: W. W. Norton, 1981). On post-communist transition, see Stephen Cohen and Andrew Schwartz,

"Deeper into the Tunnel," in *The Tunnel at the End of the Light: Privatization, Business Networks, and Economic Transformation in Russia,* edited by Stephen Cohen, Andrew Schwartz, and John Zysman (University of California, Berkeley, 1998), pp. 1–23; and Joseph Stiglitz, *Globalization and Its Discontents* (New York: W. W. Norton, 2002). On development, see Kiren Chaudhry, "The Myths of the Market and the Common History of Late Developers," *Politics and Society* 21 (September, 1993): 245–74; and World Bank, *World Development Report 2002: Building Institutions for Markets* (Oxford University Press, 2002).

2. Adam Smith, *The Wealth of Nations* (University of Chicago Press, 1976), especially bk. 5; Milton Friedman, *Capitalism and Freedom* (University of Chicago Press, 1962), pp. 22–36.

3. Ronald Coase, "The Nature of the Firm," *Economica* 4 (November, 1937): 386–405; North, *Structure and Change in Economic History;* Oliver Williamson, *The Economic Institutions of Capitalism* (New York: Free Press, 1985).

4. Polanyi, *The Great Transformation;* Mark Granovetter, "Economic Action and Social Structure: The Problem of Embeddedness," *American Journal of Sociology* 91 (November, 1985): 481–510; Neil Fligstein, *The Architecture of Markets: An Economic Sociology of Twenty-First Century Capitalist Societies* (Princeton University Press, 2001).

5. Peter Hall and David Soskice, eds., *Varieties of Capitalism: The Institutional Foundations of Comparative Advantage* (Oxford University Press, 2001).

6. Colin Crouch and Wolfgang Streeck, eds., *Political Economy of Modern Capitalism.* (London: Sage, 1997).

7. Smith, *The Wealth of Nations.*

8. Charles E. Lindblom, *Politics and Markets: The World's Political-Economic Systems* (New York: Basic Books, 1977), pp. 107–14.

9. This section builds on Steven K. Vogel, *Japan Remodeled: How Government and Industry Are Reforming Japanese Capitalism* (Cornell University Press, 2006).

10. Japan's "lifetime" employment system for core employees at large companies is complemented by more flexible employment relations for noncore employees. "Permanent" employees, mostly men, enjoy higher status, salary, benefits, and job security than "temporary" workers, mostly women.

11. On this point, the United States is more the outlier than Japan. While some European countries have more active mergers and acquisition markets than Japan, none have a market for corporate control comparable to that of the United States. For that matter, the United States only developed an active market for corporate control in the 1980s. See chapter 4 in this volume.

12. This section builds on Steven K. Vogel, *Freer Markets, More Rules: Regulatory Reform in Advanced Industrial Countries* (Cornell University Press, 1996).

13. Martin A. Levin, *Making Government Work: How Entrepreneurial Executives Turn Bright Ideas into Real Results* (San Francisco: Jossey-Bass, 1994), pp. 45–47.

14. The number of regulations increased from 10,054 in 1985 to 12,376 in 2005. (Ministry of Internal Affairs and Communications data).

15. Stephen Littlechild, *Regulation of British Telecommunications Profitability* (London: Department of Industry, 1983).

16. Vogel, *Freer Markets, More Rules,* pp. 124–25.

17. Ibid., p. 17.

18. Jonah Levy, Mari Miura, and Gene Park, "Exiting *étatisme?* New Directions in State Policy in France and Japan," in *The State after Statism: New State Activities in the Age of Liberalization,* edited by Jonah Levy (Harvard University Press, 2006).

19. In other words, the government does not have an easy way to move from one political equilibrium (employment maintenance, or anticompetitive regulation as social protection) to another (employment adjustment, or more competition coupled with unemployment insurance as social protection).

20. Levin, *Making Government Work,* pp. 42–43.

21. Ryoichi Mikitani and Adam S. Posen, eds., *Japan's Financial Crisis and Its Parallels to U.S. Experience* (Washington: Institute for International Economics, 2000).

22. On the trend toward private sector governance in Japan since the 1980s, see Ulrike Schaede, *Cooperative Capitalism: Self-Regulation, Trade Associations, and the Antimonopoly Law in Japan* (Oxford University Press, 2000).

23. Vietor argues that U.S. incumbents responded to deregulation not by outright collusion but by devising market strategies to impede new entry, including market segmentation and manipulation of distribution channels. Richard H. K. Vietor, *Contrived Competition: Regulation and Deregulation in America* (Cambridge, Mass.: Belknap Press, 1994), pp. 320–21.

24. In chapter 5, Hacker elegantly describes how U.S. policy drift has led to substantial changes in the pension regime in the absence of major policy change.

3

Regulation in Banking: A Mechanism for Forcing Market Solutions

JONATHAN R. MACEY

S tate regulatory autonomy masquerading as "deregulation" sometimes distorts the operation of markets in ways that threaten to create crises with national consequences. Examples of banking regulation and deregulation indicate that regulation, contrary to common opinion, can actually foster markets, while deregulation tends to be successful only when coupled with a strong guiding hand from government.

In the case of the United States, banking regulation often is suboptimal because states are subject to a variety of moral hazard problems that weaken their incentives to regulate effectively. In particular, when states regulate banks, they have incentives to create rules that promote excessive risk taking, because the states disproportionately benefit when banks are successful but share losses with other states through the U.S. system of national deposit insurance when banks fail.

Banking: Economic and Political Theory

Three core structural features distinguish banks from other sorts of business in the economy.[1] First, banks are much more highly leveraged. Well-capitalized banks have debt-equity ratios around 10:1, as opposed to the 1:1 debt ratios typical of nonfinancial firms.

Second, the balance sheets of banks indicate a severe disparity in the characteristics of their assets and liabilities with respect to liquidity and transparency. Their assets (commercial and home mortgage loans) tend to be highly illiquid and opaque, while their liabilities tend to be highly liquid and transparent (transaction accounts, particularly checking accounts and short- and medium-term certificates of deposit).

Third, their balance sheets are unusual because of the mismatch in the term structures of their assets and liabilities. Bank assets tend to be invested in long-term instruments (loans to commercial and residential borrowers), while their liabilities take the form of deposits, most of which are available on demand (demand checking accounts) or in the extremely short term (federal funds and short-term certificates of deposit). While the precise relationships change over time, it is not unusual for a bank's liabilities to mature in only six months but its assets to mature in six years.

These core characteristics appear to be endogenous. Specifically, they predate exogenous regulatory events such as the introduction of government-issued currency to replace bank-issued specie, and, of course, the more recent introduction of deposit insurance. These fundamental, defining characteristics of banks are due to the existence of economies of scope that are generated when lending and deposit taking are combined: lending requires close monitoring of borrowers, and deposit taking facilitates such monitoring by giving bankers accurate, real-time information about borrowers' cash flows.

The core characteristics of banks make them particularly susceptible to runs and panics because depositors have access to banks' liquidity on a first-come, first-served basis. This means that if depositors experience an unexpectedly large demand for liquidity, banks will encounter a "run," as word of the liquidity demand spreads and depositors attempt to protect themselves by cashing in their accounts.

In other words, bank depositors face a collective action problem. The best strategy for depositors as a group is to refrain from withdrawing their funds precipitously and to base withdrawal decisions not on what other depositors do, but on their own, endogenous need for liquidity over their life cycles. By contrast, the safest strategy for depositors as individuals is to withdraw their funds the moment they hear the slightest rumor of financial weakness within the bank or even unusual activity among depositors. Banks, in the absence of a creditable deposit insurance regime, are extremely unstable creatures.

Government regulation of some kind is necessary to prevent bank failure. Such regulation might take the form of deposit insurance, which operates ex ante to prevent bank runs and panics, or it could operate ex post by using monetary policy orchestrated by the central bank to inject money into the system and provide liquidity for banks that were the subject of runs and panics.

There is another explanation for deposit insurance in democracies. Irrespective of one's *philosophical* preference for a libertarian state, the regulation that one actually observes will be determined by the necessity for political actors (politicians and bureaucrats) to maintain a certain level of political support in order to remain in office. Thus at times, particularly during periods of economic crisis, deregulation simply may not be a viable survival strategy for political actors.

Once one admits the inevitability of certain governmental action, one must similarly acknowledge the desirability of regulation where such regulation can affect future political responses to perceived crises. Thus the question is not whether to regulate, but how to regulate most effectively.

Where there have been large or systemic banking failures in industrialized democracies, there have been bailouts. In the United States, Russia, the Czech Republic, Israel, Argentina, Japan, Israel, Sweden, Finland, Norway, the Netherlands, and France, the government response to bank crisis has been to bail out, at massive government expense, most, if not all, of the banks' creditors.

The bailouts have taken one of two forms. In countries with de jure deposit insurance regimes, such as the U.S. regime established under the Federal Deposit Insurance Corporation (FDIC) Act of 1933, the nature and limits of the government's exposure are set ex ante, that is, before a banking crisis has manifested itself. In other democracies that have experienced banking crises without the existence of FDIC insurance (Israel, Czech Republic, Sweden), the absence of deposit insurance has been viewed ex post (after the banking crisis has manifested itself) as a regulatory failure. To cope with this failure, the government has acted as though it were responsible for meeting the liabilities of the failed bank. In other words, where no de jure deposit insurance regime exists, there has been a de facto deposit insurance regime, as the government has stepped in after the fact and made good on claims of depositors and others.

Regulatory theory and practice should take note of this political reality. Politicians' survival instincts lead them to engineer bailouts even in the absence of explicit deposit insurance protection. Consequently, the real-world policy choice in banking is between a regulatory regime characterized by de jure (explicit) deposit insurance protection and a so-called nonregulatory regime characterized by de facto deposit insurance in the form of gratuitous government bailouts of failed banks.

De facto deposit insurance regimes impose uncertainties: although it is clear that the government will be responsible for bank failures to some extent, the nature and limits of that responsibility are not transparent to investors in such regimes. Inefficiencies will then arise because creditors will demand compensation for the lack of information and certainty concerning the nature of the governmental guarantees.

The advantage of de jure deposit insurance is that it allows governments to commit to a relatively low level of protection, thus capping their liability at the amount specified in the deposit insurance regime. In addition, de jure deposit insurance limits the economic waste associated with rent seeking by reducing the rent seeking that occurs in anticipation of, and in the wake of, bank failures by creditors seeking recourse to the government.

Case Study 1: The Savings and Loan Crisis

If regulation is needed to maintain the stability of the banking industry, a critical question is how to make it work.[2] To illustrate, I draw on the lessons of the savings and loan (S&L) crisis in the United States, which developed because deregulation permitted banks to engage in excessive amounts of risk taking. In a particularly striking example, in 1967 the state of Texas approved a major liberalization of S&L powers that, among other things, permitted S&Ls to make loans on undeveloped property, regardless of the lack of income generated by such property, in amounts up to 50 percent of its appraised net worth. Then the Financial Institutions Regulatory and Interest Rate Control Act of 1978 allowed S&Ls to invest up to 5 percent of their assets in each of the following types of loans: development, construction, and education loans. This put an S&L's entire equity at risk, not from fluctuations in the relatively stable home mortgage market, but from fluctuations in the notoriously volatile real estate development and construction markets.[3]

During the period 1980–82, the pace of deregulation quickened even further. Statutory and regulatory changes permitted S&Ls to enter new areas of business in order to promote greater profitability. For the first time in history, the government approved measures aimed at improving S&L profitability rather than at promoting the traditional, fiscally conservative goals of promoting broader access to housing and home ownership.

The Depository Institutions Deregulation and Monetary Control Act (DIDMCA) of March 1980, promulgated during the Carter administration, removed interest rate ceilings on deposit accounts and expanded the ability of federally chartered S&Ls to make loans for corporate acquisitions and commercial development and construction projects. The DIDMCA also raised the ceiling on government deposit insurance from $40,000 to $100,000, without any additional restraints to diminish moral hazard, such as regulations linking insurance premiums to risk.

In November 1980, the Federal Home Loan Bank Board (FHLBB) reduced the minimum capital requirements for federally insured S&Ls from 5 percent of total deposits to 4 percent of total deposits. It also reduced curbs on risk taking by removing regulatory limits on the amount of brokered deposits (hot money) that S&Ls could hold.[4] These reforms were followed by the Tax Reform Act of August 1981, which provided powerful tax incentives for real estate investment by individuals, helped to create a strong demand for real estate loans, and led to extensive overbuilding.

In September 1981, the FHLBB permitted troubled S&Ls to meet their recently reduced minimum capital requirements by issuing "income capital certificates," which were included as equity capital on S&L balance sheets. The effect of these certificates was to make insolvent financial institutions appear, for regulatory accounting purposes, as though they were solvent. These certificates did not comply with generally accepted accounting principles (GAAP), either for banks or for any other type of business. Such certificates, if issued by private firms, would have constituted securities fraud.

These deregulatory efforts were followed by significant reductions in the FHLBB regulatory and supervisory staffs during the period 1982–85, when the industry was growing by leaps and bounds. During the same period, S&L industry assets (loans) increased by 56 percent. Forty Texas S&Ls tripled in size, and many S&Ls in California and Texas grew at rates in excess of 100 percent a year.

Like much of S&L "deregulation" of the era, these regulatory changes are better described as "de-marketization" or "dis-incentivization" because of the perverse incentives they created. For example, in January 1982 the FHLBB reduced net worth requirements for insured S&Ls from 4 percent to 3 percent of total deposits. S&Ls were allowed to depart from GAAP still further through the introduction of new, so-called regulatory accounting principles (RAP), which only applied to S&Ls, were inconsistent with GAAP, and permitted banks to artificially pad their balance sheets, claiming that they had far more capital than was, in fact, the case.

In April 1982, the FHLBB issued new regulations that made it much easier for risk-taking speculators to purchase S&Ls. These new regulations eliminated restrictions on the minimum number of S&L shareholders. Previous regulations had required that each S&L have at least 400 stockholders, with at least 125 of them from the "local community." Also, no individual could own more than 10 percent of the stock of an S&L, and no "controlling group" could own more than 25 percent of an S&L's stock. The new regulations permitted single owners for S&Ls, thus reducing market monitoring and creating incentives for excessive loan concentrations among borrowers. In particular, these regulations made it easier for individuals to buy S&Ls by allowing them to put up land and other hard-to-value real estate assets, as opposed to cash, when purchasing ownership interests in a thrift institution.

It was in late 1982, however, that the real "race to the bottom" began among regulators. In December 1982, Congress passed the Garn–St. Germain Depository Institutions Act, a Reagan administration initiative designed to give even broader powers to federally chartered S&Ls with a view to making them more profitable as well as more diversified. Its major provisions eliminated the ceilings on interest rates paid on deposits; eliminated the previous statutory restrictions on loan-to-value ratios; and expanded the power of federal S&Ls to invest in assets unrelated to the business of making home mortgages by permitting those with federal charters to put up to 40 percent of their assets in commercial mortgages, up to 30 percent in consumer loans, up to 10 percent in commercial loans, and up to 10 percent in commercial leases.

Garn–St. Germain caused immediate, massive defections of state-chartered banks to the federal system so that bank equity holders could avail themselves of the expanded powers permitted under the act. Soon thereafter, California, followed closely by Texas and Florida, passed state laws permitting state-chartered (but federally insured) S&Ls to invest 100 percent of their deposits in any sort of venture whatsoever. Within a year, 10 percent of all S&Ls were insolvent as measured by standards consistent with GAAP but were permitted to remain open because they were not insolvent when the artificial equity permitted under RAP was included in their balance sheets. They retained their ability to attract additional liquidity to meet current financial obligations because the liquidity came in the form of federally insured deposits, which they could attract by offering depositors slightly higher rates of interest or other inducements (toaster ovens, televisions, and the like).

By 1983, 35 percent of all S&Ls were losing money. Such a result, along with the high number of bank failures (10 percent), is consistent with the conclusion that banks were taking advantage of their new powers by engaging in excessive risk taking of the "heads-I-win, tails-the-taxpayer-loses" variety. Shareholders, as equity claimants, benefited from the higher returns garnered when excessive risks paid off. The government and, ultimately, taxpayers bore the brunt of the burden when the heavily leveraged banks became insolvent.

The deregulatory process just described had a profound effect on the risk-taking proclivities of S&L owners. Once the regulatory constraints were removed and government-sponsored deposit insurance was still available at low, fixed cost (that is, not adjusted for risk), acute moral hazard emerged in the form of extremely strong perverse incentives for S&L shareholder-owners to engage in excessive risk taking. This had significant consequences for U.S. taxpayers, compounded by the lack of incentives for fixed claimants to monitor banks' excessive risk taking because of the protection afforded by deposit insurance.

Without government regulation to substitute for the market discipline typically supplied by contractual fixed claimants, disaster ensued. In other words, supporters of deregulation of the S&L industry failed to perceive that government regulation in an environment of insured depository institutions is necessary for the stability of the financial system. Such regulation serves as a necessary substitute for the restrictions that private sector creditors would place on risk taking by borrowers.[5]

It has been suggested that the debacle of the S&L de-marketization resulted "not so much from poor policy choices as from flawed management of the deregulation process."[6] It is certainly true that the disaster was not simply due to poor policy choices or a failed ideology, also that loosening government constraints on banks required more rather than less regulatory oversight. But the better explanation is rent seeking. These so-called deregulatory policies, which enriched equity owners of S&Ls, sprang from a desire to garner political support from politically powerful bankers, particularly in the key election states of California, Florida, and Texas. For example, in April 1987, shortly before he was forced to resign as chair of the FHLBB, Edwin Gray was summoned to the office of Senator Dennis DeConcini, who along with four other senators (John McCain, Alan Cranston, John Glenn, and Donald Riegle) questioned Gray about the appropriateness of FHLBB investigations into Charles Keating's Lincoln Savings and Loan. All five senators, who later came to be known as the "Keating Five," received campaign contributions from Keating. The subsequent failure of Lincoln Savings and Loan was estimated to have cost the government more than $2 billion.[7]

This case study shows that rent seeking and other forms of abuse of the government decisionmaking process manifests itself in the form of so-called deregulation as readily as it manifests itself in the form of regulation. This is a straightforward application of an accepted insight: like the power to regulate, the power to deregulate and the power to refrain from regulating are tempting sources of rent for governmental actors and thereby provide valuable rent-seeking opportunities for interest groups.[8]

Case Study 2: Lender Liability and Environmental Protection

Lender liability refers to civil liability for money damages and other relief that may be imposed on banks and other lenders that cause damages or act in bad faith, either to borrowers or to third parties outside of the debtor-creditor relationship. If, for example, a bank makes explicit or implicit promises to extend credit and then imposes harm on a client by reneging on the promise, the lender is likely to be liable to the client. Similarly, when a particular lender takes actions that impose harm on third parties, such as other creditors, by improperly diverting assets of the debtors to itself, the third party can bring a lawsuit against the lender. Suppose that a bank has loaned a client money and uses its influence or its access to the client's transaction accounts to benefit itself at the expense of other, similarly situated or senior creditors. Those creditors could then seek civil remedies against the bank for damages.

An area of intense uncertainty in lender liability that involves very high stakes claims pertains to environmental damage on the debtor's property. The problem begins with the so-called Super Fund statute, also known as the federal Comprehensive Environmental Response, Compensation and Liability Act (CERCLA).[9]

CERCLA imposes cleanup costs on "owners" or "operators" of hazardous waste sites, without regard to fault. The problem, a common one when borrowers become financially distressed, is that large bank lenders, which often have a security interest in all of the borrower's assets, will actually take over the day-to-day operation of the debtor's plant after a default. If hazardous waste is present on the site and the bank is now deemed an "operator" of the facility as defined by CERCLA, then it will be strictly liable for the costs of cleaning up the facility, regardless of when the damage occurred.

In order to protect banks and other secured lenders from the broad liability of CERCLA, the statute contains a specific exemption for a person who "without participating in the management of a facility holds indicia of ownership primarily to protect his security interest in the facility."[10] However, the contours of the statutory exemption for secured lenders is a bit vague, since it leaves open to (statutory) interpretation the question of what it means to participate in management, or to hold indicia of ownership "primarily to protect" one's security interest. Of course, there is no problem as long as the borrower is making timely payments of principal and interest. Once a borrower defaults, however, and the lender takes possession of the collateral, it is difficult to avoid the argument that the bank is participating in management, where the collateral is the entire facility.

The potential for CERCLA to impose millions of dollars in liability on banks, despite the statute's exemptive language, manifested itself in the early 1990s when judges began interpreting the meaning of the "operator" language in CERCLA. In particular, in *United States* v. *Fleet Factors Corp.,* the court held that

> a secured creditor may incur [strict liability for the costs of an environmental cleanup under CERCLA] by participating in the financial management of a facility to a degree indicating a (mere) *capacity to influence* the corporation's treatment of hazardous wastes. It is not necessary for the secured creditor actually to involve itself in the day-to-day operations in order to be liable—although such conduct will certainly lead to the loss of the protection of the statutory exemption. Nor is it necessary for the secured creditor to participate in management decisions relating to hazardous waste. Rather, a secured creditor will be liable if its involvement with the management of the facility is sufficiently broad to support the inference that it could affect hazardous waste disposal decisions if it so chose.[11]

This opinion sent a wave of shock through the financial community as banks and other secured lenders fretted that they would have to choose between the unattractive alternative of relinquishing their ability to take possession of their collateral in case of default and the even worse alternative of taking action that might lead to potentially devastating claims for cleanup costs under CERCLA.

In the wake of the decision in *Fleet Factors,* lawyers for secured lenders began advising their clients how to avoid liability under CERCLA should their borrowers default. Some suggested that their clients stop such common, and socially desirable, activities as monitoring facility operations, monitoring compliance with legal requirements of federal and local environmental codes, and providing strategic and financial advice to borrowers in distress, all because such activities would make the lenders strictly liable as operators of a facility if construed as "participation in management," either generally or with regard to environmental issues.

To illustrate, before the misguided decision in *Fleet Factors,* it was common for lenders to inspect the property of prospective borrowers for environmental problems and to demand that these problems be corrected before making a loan. It was also common for secured lenders to protect their investments in the borrower by requiring periodic reports from borrowers on compliance with applicable environmental regulations, and by making regular environmental inspections of the borrower's facilities to make sure that the reports were accurate. In the wake of *Fleet Factors,* these sorts of lender activities, however socially desirable, risked the imposition of strict liability for environmental claims under CERCLA if there was a suspicion that lenders had the "capacity to influence" the treatment of hazardous wastes. Hence well-advised lenders were reluctant to agree to maintain environmental safeguards as part of any credit transaction.

Environmental activists and the professionals at the U.S. Environmental Protection Agency (EPA) naturally wanted to restore lenders' incentives to proactively manage environmental risk. In response, the EPA enacted a detailed new rule, clarifying lender liability under CERCLA.[12] It overruled the Eleventh Circuit decision in *Fleet Factors* by stipulating that the "mere capacity to influence or the ability to influence, or the unexercised right to control" does not constitute control of a nature to trigger liability under the strict liability provisions of CERCLA. Also, to encourage monitoring, the rule provides that liability will not result where lenders impose contractual or other documentary requirements that force borrowers to maintain certain environmental standards. Similarly, no liability will result where lenders require, as a condition for a loan, that the borrower make representations, warranties, covenants, or other promises to maintain environmental quality.

The EPA regulation modifying *Fleet Factors* to avert its unintended consequence is a clear example of "marketization" by a regulatory agency. *Fleet Factors* had removed the incentives of an important class of market participants, banks, to engage in the socially desirable activity of monitoring and controlling their borrowers' disposal of hazardous waste. By crafting a clear rule protecting banks from CERCLA liability if they made sure that their clients complied with the environmental laws, the EPA, by regulation, corrected a market distortion caused by a poorly reasoned judicial decision.

The EPA arrived at its rule after extensive consultation with banks, environmental groups, and other affected parties. Political pressure by banking interests may have played a role but in itself is a simplistic and unconvincing explanation of the EPA's action. For one thing, banks are not repeat player constituents of the EPA and are therefore not likely to be interested in spending the resources necessary to "capture" the agency, even if they could. Moreover, environmental groups, which are, of course, repeat players before the

EPA, also favored amending the rule: they, like the banks, favored creating a "safe harbor" from CERCLA liability for bank monitoring of environmental hazards. Finally, firms themselves were not averse to this rule, because the potential liability imposed by the Eleventh Circuit decision in *Fleet Factors* raised the cost of capital and made banks unwilling to lend at a competitive rate to financially precarious firms with potential environmental issues that needed close monitoring.[13] Thus, in this example, the solution maximizing political support for the regulators at the EPA was also the efficient and socially optimal solution.

Case Studies 3–5: Marketization and Federal-State Relations in Banking

U.S. banks operate under a dual system of state and federal chartering and safety and soundness regulation. The "dual banking system" has long enjoyed significant political support. It ostensibly allows banks operating in any state to choose between two sets of primary laws to define their powers and to regulate their activities and investments. Banks may opt for a national charter, and be regulated by the Comptroller of the Currency, or they may pursue a state charter, in which case their primary regulator will be the banking regulator of the chartering state.

It was once thought that the dual banking system created good incentives for regulators, resulting in "the maximum freedom from regulation consistent with a safe and sound banking system."[14] Indeed, it "has long been a sacred cow in the American political tradition."[15] Many argue that it causes state and federal regulators "to compete for bank charters in order to retain market share," and that this competition reduces the arbitrary or abusive use of regulatory discretion.[16] Critics, on the other hand, believe the system leads to a destructive "race to the bottom" among regulators who compete to attract chartering business from banks.

Neither of these arguments gives proper credit or respect to the reality of post-Roosevelt-era constitutional interpretation. The federal government can—and does—invoke the Commerce and Supremacy clauses of the U.S. Constitution to preempt state laws whenever state laws give state-chartered banks a meaningful advantage over federal banks. Even if that were not true, as a matter of both legal compulsion and competitive necessity, all banks must obtain deposit insurance from the federal government, and the FDIC requires that banks obtaining such insurance comply with its uniform regulations regardless of contrary provisions in the laws of individual states.

Two related points about regulation in general and state-federal relations in particular should also be mentioned. First, the competition between the states and the federal government in the domain of banking law and regulation is more imagined than real. Second, the paucity of meaningful competition within the U.S. federal system is socially desirable because competition between the states and the federal government in the realm of banking regulation would not produce beneficial results if it were to occur.

Reserve Requirements

The history of reserve requirement regulations for state-chartered and federally chartered banks provides a prime example of states' perverse incentives to regulate their domestically chartered banks in an optimal way. Reserve requirements consist of bank assets that must be held in the form of vault cash or non-interest-paying deposits with one of the regional Federal Reserve banks or with banks approved by the Board of Governors of the Federal Reserve System. Because banks do not generate any interest or other income on these reserves at the central bank, they would prefer reserve requirements to be kept as low as possible. From a financial perspective, reserves are viewed as a tax on banks' operations.

Before 1980, national banks and state banks that had elected to be members of the Federal Reserve System were subject to reserve requirements established by federal regulation. State-chartered banks that were not members of the Federal Reserve System were not subject to these federal regulations. To avoid reserve requirements, which cut into banks' profitability, some state banks left the Federal Reserve System. In response, bank regulators passed the Depository Institutions Deregulation and Monetary Control Act of 1980, which extended the reach of the Federal Reserve requirements to state non-member banks.

This federal statute eliminated a major dimension of the competition within the dual banking system by imposing standardized minimum reserve requirements. This decision was clearly inconsistent with the idea of competition in the dual banking system. The harder question to address is the normative one: whether competition between state and federal chartering agencies and regulators would be beneficial in banking. The problem, as the reserve requirement controversy illustrates, is that states have no _incentive_ to enact laws that constrain banks' proclivities toward excessive risk taking.

To the extent that lax state laws permit banks to engage in excessive risk taking, the benefits from such risk taking fall on certain local borrowers (who would be unable to obtain credit under a more prudent regulatory regime) and often on local shareholders (only a small percentage of banks are publicly held), who, as residual claimants, benefit if the risks pay off. By contrast, the costs of such risk taking are borne not by private sector creditors of the state-chartered banks, and not by the banks' state regulators, but by the federal government (and depositors and taxpayers in all fifty states), which bears the costs of administering and funding the federal deposit insurance funds.

In 1991 Congress passed the Federal Deposit Insurance Corporation Improvement Act (FDICIA) to respond to this problem. This statute prevents state banks insured by the FDIC from engaging in any activity that is not permissible for a national bank unless a federal agency determines the activity would pose no significant risk to the deposit insurance fund.[17] The legislation strengthens the argument, originally set forth by Henry Butler and myself, that the dual banking system is, and should be, a myth.[18] More important, the interplay between the states and the federal government provides another example of both "illusory deregulation" and the related phenomenon, incentive-enhancing regulation that either encourages or replaces market-driven responses to public policy problems.

The elimination or reduction of reserve requirements by a state banking regulator is not deregulation. Rather, it reflects an effort by local regulators to export the costs of tolerating excessive risk taking by bankers to the national level. This enables the local regulators to enjoy greater political support from bankers, while transferring the costs of their "deregulation" to the general population. State-reserve-requirement "deregulation" was really incentive-destroying regulation. Preemption and reregulation by Congress restored the proper incentive structure for banks, because it reduced banks' proclivity to succumb to the moral hazard of excessive risk taking.

Bank Closure Policy

The entire administrative scheme of regulation and enforcement in the banking industry is based on the need to protect against bank failure. This is a concern of public policy in ways that the failure of other business is not. First, and most obviously, the failure of an FDIC-insured depository institution places the assets of the government's insurance fund at risk. In addition, bank failures impose losses, anxiety, and inconvenience on depositors. And third, the failure of one bank may spread to others, creating the danger of generalized banking panics.[19]

One of the more startling historical attributes of the dual banking system is that the power to cause the appointment of a receiver for a financially distressed bank, that is, the power to close a bank, was vested in the bank's chartering agency. Thus the Comptroller of the Currency has the power to close national banks, and, at least until 1991, state banking agencies had the exclusive power to close state-chartered banks, including federally insured banks and thrift institutions. The problem with this allocation of regulatory power was that state banking regulators had no incentive to close failed state-chartered banks as long as those banks continued to employ people and as long as those banks continued to make loans to local borrowers. Another disincentive is that bank closures lead to rashes of foreclosures of delinquent loans by the receiver of the failed banks, not to mention other events, such as strict adherence to debt covenants, which, from a macroeconomic perspective, are highly deflationary to local economies.

Thus, as with reserve requirements, recalcitrant state bank regulators, particularly in Arizona, California, Florida, and Texas, were able to transfer wealth to themselves from the federal deposit insurance fund in that administrative delay increased the ultimate costs of resolving bank failures of state-chartered banks. As the costs of bailing out the insurance fund soared in the 1980s, the issue of bank failure became politically salient. Congress finally responded with the Federal Deposit Insurance Company Improvement Act of 1991, which gave the FDIC the power to close state-chartered insured banks if their closure is necessary to avoid or mitigate losses to the insurance fund.

FDICIA allocates regulatory responsibility over bank closure to the regulator with the greatest stake in implementing optimal closure policy. Thus the provisions of FDICIA wresting regulatory authority over the timing of bank closures away from state regulators are an example of market-based, incentive-compatible regulation.

Minimum Capital Requirements

For the purposes of this discussion, the term "capital" refers to the amount by which a business's assets exceed its liabilities.[20] The regulatory issues associated with minimum capital requirements are nicely summarized in a U.S. Treasury report:

> In a private, competitive market economy, the primary purpose of capital is to cushion both equity holders and debt holders from unexpected losses. Debt holders are protected by the equity cushion that must be exhausted before the firm's losses eat into their principal. Equity holders are protected in the sense that, in a world where bankruptcy is costly, substantial equity reduces the probability that bankruptcy will occur.

The existence of the federal safety net for depository institutions [notably federal deposit insurance and access to the Federal Reserve discount window] increases the importance of capital, since the safety net adds taxpayers to private debt holders as potential losers if an institution fails. Adequate capital holdings by depository institutions . . . lower[s] the probability of bank failure; reduces the incentive to take excessive risk; acts as a buffer in front of the insurance fund and the taxpayer; and increases long-term competitiveness.[21]

Stunningly, there was a time when state regulators could set minimum capital requirements for state-chartered banks. But state regulators lacked the incentive to establish capital requirements for state-chartered banks that provided adequate protection for the federal deposit insurance fund.

Conclusion

The preceding case studies concerning reserve requirements, bank closure policy, and minimum capital requirements all represent situations in which the states, under the guise of deregulation, inject market distortions into the regulatory system by relaxing rules that contribute to bank safety and soundness. However, the existence of federal deposit insurance requires that bank safety and soundness regulation be dealt with at the national not the state or local level. The debacle of the S&L crisis and the concomitant insolvency of the Federal Savings and Loan Insurance Corporation were due in large part to the misallocation of regulatory responsibilities between the states and the federal government.

The broader theme of this chapter is that regulation at the appropriate level is often necessary to cause the market to function effectively. Banks are very efficient at allocating capital, but they are very fragile economic entities. Without government intervention in the form of deposit insurance and access to emergency loans, banking crises of the kind that occurred during the Great Depression would be regular occurrences. Thus banking is a paradigmatic example of an industry in which regulation is necessary in order for a market, indeed for an entire industry, to function efficiently. Deposit insurance in particular is a necessity. Not only does deposit insurance prevent bank runs and panics; it can also serve the valuable end of putting a ceiling on the extent to which the government will be expected to respond in case of a systemic banking crisis.

Notes

1. Financial intermediaries come in many forms, the subset known as "banks" being those that combine commercial lending with transaction services, particularly demand deposits. See Jonathan Macey, Geoffrey Miller, and Richard Carnell, *Banking Law and Regulation,* 3rd ed. (Gaithersburg: Aspen Law & Business, 2002).

2. For an excellent earlier treatment of the same subject in this context, see Martin A. Levin and Mary Bryna Sanger, *Making Government Work: How Entrepreneurial Executives Turn Bright Ideas into Real Results* (San Franciso: Jossey Bass, 1994).

3. This history draws heavily on the Federal Deposit Insurance Corporation's monograph "The S&L Crisis: A Chrono-Bibliography" (www.fdic.gov/bank/historical/s&l).

4. The term "brokered deposits" refers to blocks of funds pooled by securities broker/dealers and then placed in depository institutions offering the highest (federally insured) yield. During the thrift crisis of the 1980s, many failing institutions used brokered deposits to "gamble on resurrection." As a result, supervisors now closely monitor institutions that rely heavily on this type of funding. See http://www.stlouisfed.org/publications/cb/2003/d/pages/cedars_deposits.html.

5. Clifford C. Smith, and Jerold C. Warner, "On Financial Contracting: An Analysis of Bond Covenants," *Journal of Financial Economics* 7 (June 1979): 117–61.

6. Levin and Sanger, *Making Government Work,* p. 42.

7. See FDIC, "The S&L Crisis."

8. The notion of using regulation to benefit private parties rather than to serve the public interest was first developed formally by the University of Chicago's George Stigler, who modeled the regulatory process as a function of the government's ability to benefit private parties by restricting entry into markets, policing cartels, and legitimizing various price-fixing strategies. These devices, Stigler showed, make it possible for private firms able to galvanize into effective political coalitions to earn supercompetitive returns called economic rents. In a nutshell, Stigler showed how regulation can benefit the regulated, rather than the public. According to Stigler, the market for regulation consists of the provision of value to politicians in the form of campaign contributions, efforts to organize voting, intimations of future jobs, and occasional outright bribes in return for favorable regulation. Major research advancing the "rent-seeking" (also known as the "public choice") approach to regulation has been carried out by James Buchanan, Sam Peltzman, Robert Tollison, and Gordon Tullock. Consistent with one of the principal insights of this school of thought, this chapter models politicians, bureaucrats, and others involved in the policymaking process as rational economic actors who, subject to a variety of constraints, act in their own self-interest rather than some vaguely defined conception of the private interest. Students of public policy and others interested in improving the quality of regulation and policy formation should understand the incentive structure under which policymakers and regulators operate. For a description of the political payoffs from declining to regulate, see Fred S. McChesney, *Money for Nothing: Politicians, Rent Extraction and Political Extortion* (Harvard University Press, 1977).

9. 42 U.S.C. 9601–9657.

10. 42 U.S.C. 9601(20)(A).

11. 901 F.2d 1550 (11th Cir. 1990), *cert. denied,* 498 U.S. 1046 (1991).

12. Environmental Protection Agency, "National Oil and Hazardous Substances Pollution Contingency Plan: Lender Liability under CERCLA," 57 Fed. Reg. 18,344 (April 29, 1992).

13. The history of this controversy subsequent to the implementation of the EPA rules is fascinating. After the EPA issued its rule, the U.S. Court of Appeals for the District of Columbia Circuit rejected it on the constitutional ground that it was beyond the EPA's statutory authority to implement a rule construing the statutory provisions of CERCLA. This created tension between the executive branch and the judicial branch, as both the EPA and the Department of Justice publicly announced that they would follow the EPA rule anyway as a matter of their own administrative discretion to pick and choose cases for enforcement action. This controversy was resolved when Congress, as part of a Defense Department appropriations measure, reincarnated the EPA's rule and forbade further judicial review, finally making it clear that the EPA rule is the authoritative interpretation of the statutory-secured lender exception to CERCLA.

14. George J. Benston and others, *Perspectives on Safe and Sound Banking: Past, Present, and Future* (Cambridge, Mass.: MIT Press, 1986), pp. 276–78; Robert Scott, "The Dual Banking System: A Model of Competition in Regulation," *Stanford Law Review* 20, no. 1 (1977): 1.

15. Geoffrey P. Miller, "The Future of the Dual Banking System," *Brooklyn Law Review* 53 (1987): 1.

16. Jonathan R. Macey, Geoffrey P. Miller, and Richard S. Carnell, *Banking Law and Regulation,* 3rd ed., p. 115.

17. 12 U.S.C. 1831a.

18. Henry N. Butler and Jonathan R. Macey, "The Myth of Competition in the Dual Banking System," *Cornell Law Review* 73 (June 1988): 677.

19. Macey, Miller, and Carnell, *Banking Law and Regulation,* p. 723.

20. The terms "equity" and "net worth" also are used to describe this differential.

21. U.S. Department of the Treasury, *Modernizing the Financial System: Recommendations for Safer, More Competitive Banks* II-1 (Government Printing Office, 1991).

4

Revenge of the Law? Securities Litigation Reform and Sarbanes-Oxley's Structural Regulation of Corporate Governance

JOHN W. CIOFFI

T he Sarbanes-Oxley Act of 2002 is the most significant reform of American securities and corporate governance law since the New Deal.[1] It is part of a long history of political struggle over the form, power, and legitimacy of the corporation and financial capital. Yet the act also represents a break with nearly two centuries of American federalism and established forms of corporate governance regulation. The central puzzle of American corporate governance reform is how and why Congress passed such significant reform during a politically conservative era in which corporate and managerial power were at a zenith, and why it took such a novel form. The answer to both parts of the puzzle is contextual and historically contingent. First, extraordinary conditions of stock market crashes and corporate financial scandals temporarily disrupted interest group politics and partisan divisions

I would like to thank Neil Fligstein, Peter Gourevitch, Darius Gaskins, Bob Kagan, Mark Landy, Bronwyn Leebaw, Martin Levin, Jonathan Macey, Ulrike Schaede, Peter Schuck, Martin Shapiro, Steven Teles, Steven Vogel, Graham Wilson, and Nick Ziegler for their comments and encouragement. I would also like to thank Bill Frenzel and Pietro Nivola of the Brookings Institution and Thomas Richardson for their help in facilitating research for this chapter. All errors are my own. I would also like to thank the Academic Senate of the University of California, Riverside, and the Gordon Public Policy Center at Brandeis University for financial support for this research.

to allow substantial legal and institutional change. Second, political constraints on the use of litigation as a means of addressing managerial financial fraud and abuse impelled legislators to embrace alternative mechanisms of regulation as part of the reforms. Financial crisis and political constraints provided the conditions for regulatory innovation.

The internal structure and governance of the corporation in the United States has long been defined by detailed prescriptive transparency and disclosure regulation under federal securities law, as well as minimal mandatory legal requirements concerning the internal form and operation of the firm under state corporation law.[2] This established pattern began to change with the federal corporate governance reforms precipitated by the wave of financial scandals that began with the collapse of Enron in 2001. In view of the veto-prone political structure of the United States, some political theories of regulation would have predicted either that powerful interest groups would block significant legal and regulatory reforms or, alternatively, that reforms would remain within the established trajectory of increasingly detailed prescriptive (or proscriptive) legal rules reinforced by additional litigation-driven remedies.[3] Other theories of regulation and economic governance would have anticipated new forms of law and regulation but overlooked the political dynamics capable of producing such regulatory innovations. This chapter takes issue with such perspectives.

The stock market crashes of 2001–02, dot.com failures, and seemingly endless disclosures of financial fraud and manipulation, accompanied by the largest corporate bankruptcies in American history, represented massive failures of market, corporate, and regulatory institutions. A crisis of investor confidence and, ultimately, of the broader legitimacy of the American political economic order compelled Congress to act quickly to pass reform legislation that could never have been passed under ordinary conditions. Significant reforms *did* follow in the wake of the post-Enron corporate governance crisis, but they *did not* expand or create new avenues for litigation. Instead, many of the Sarbanes-Oxley reforms and those later adopted by the Securities and Exchange Commission (SEC) took a strikingly different path—one that I label *structural regulation*. In contrast to prescriptive regulation and litigation-backed liability rules, structural regulation restructures institutional and organizational arrangements within the private sphere to alter behavior with minimal, if any, recourse to further formal legal enforcement. The regulatory politics of the corporate governance reform drove policymakers to use this mode of regulation to improve corporate governance, managerial accountability, and financial market legitimacy.

In this sense, recent corporate governance reform in the United States, unlike deregulation or reregulation, has sought to restore and maintain both the efficiency and legitimacy of national securities markets. In the post–New Deal era, American capital markets, and securities markets in particular, came to be widely regarded as some of the most developed and efficient in the world. In part, the success of American securities markets—and related financial services—derived from the fact that they were well regulated. Financial actors gradually fashioned ways around regulatory restrictions or violated legal rules outright, putting great strain on both the regulatory regime and the market, which resulted in the worst financial crisis since the Great Depression. Corporate governance reform at the federal level was a deliberate response to shore up that regulatory regime and restore investor confidence on which the markets relied—all within more narrow political constraints than had existed in prior decades. These objectives reflect regulation's central functions: the narrow and enormously important economic function of providing for market competition and efficiency, and an equally vital legitimation function that maintains popular belief in the integrity of a market. Reform may be embodied in law or regulation, but it is the product of politics rather than economic optimality. If this is a story that supports the argument that freer markets require more rules, to paraphrase Steven Vogel, it also reveals that we only get the rules the political system can deliver.

This chapter asks how and why corporate governance reform in the United States overrode interest group and partisan politics, departed from the established forms of regulation, yet remained cabined by powerful political constraints that could limit the effectiveness of regulatory innovations. Those constraints pertained to the use of private litigation to curb managerial financial misconduct. During the mid-1990s, hostility toward litigation as a mechanism of legal and regulatory enforcement culminated in the passage of federal securities litigation reform laws and since then has become an entrenched feature of federal legislative politics. Unable to use traditional litigious mechanisms of enforcement to protect shareholder interests, congressional proponents of reform pursued an incremental *federalization of the structural components of corporate law* to achieve their ends, as demonstrated by the Sarbanes-Oxley's nonlitigious, self-executing mechanisms of regulation.

The exigencies of recent corporate governance reform and the political legacy of antilitigation politics produced a paradox: the political constraints on the use of litigious enforcement mechanisms led to even more extensive and intensive forms of governmental regulatory power over corporate affairs. Ultimately, this encroachment on the institutional bases of managerial power and autonomy, and attempts to build upon it by the SEC, led business to resist further reforms and lash out against parts of Sarbanes-Oxley itself. Three basic observations inform this analysis: (1) faced with crisis conditions, state actors marshaled the political forces driving reform to increase regulatory intervention in the private sphere; (2) clashing partisan political agendas induced policymakers to embrace the use of structural regulation in corporate governance; and (3) Congress, and later the SEC, failed to alter the way in which directors are nominated and elected because the prevailing conditions of American politics limited the extent of reform through structural regulation. The broader historical context of corporate governance reform elucidates its political dynamics. Three temporal phases merit particular attention: the politics of securities litigation reform of the mid- to late 1990s, the legislative and regulatory corporate governance reforms of 2001–04, and the business backlash against reform that facilitated the restoration of politics as usual.

The Politics of Securities Litigation Reform in the 1990s

Litigation has played a uniquely prominent role in American securities regulation and corporate governance. Securities fraud suits have long served as a major, if controversial, mechanism for defining and enforcing shareholder rights in the United States. Criticism of securities litigation began to intensify during the merger and acquisition boom of the 1980s and the subsequent recession and bankruptcies of the early 1990s.[4] From the 1970s to the 1990s, firms were sued with greater frequency.[5] This was due in part to the development of a sophisticated plaintiff-side securities litigation bar (its activities produced a veritable litigation industry, which provided substantial financial backing to the Democratic Party), and to the increased use of sophisticated and often manipulative financial practices. In response to the rising securities litigation rates, the antilitigation coalition expanded in size and its opposition intensified. The supporters of securities reform legislation included not only corporate managers, the traditional foes of securities litigation, but also securities firms and accounting firms, as well as the economically ascendant Silicon Valley firms that depended upon equity financing.

By the early 1990s, these critics found both political parties increasingly congenial to their pleas for legislative relief from lawsuits. In 1993 and 1994, as part of a more business-friendly political strategy and policy agenda, the Democrats sought to neutralize the issue by drafting more moderate reform legislation that balanced the interests of corporations, shareholders, and plaintiffs' attorneys.[6] Driven by interest group loyalties, political calculation, and an increasingly hard-line ideological approach to policy, the Republican Party pushed for more substantial legal change. In 1993 the Republicans made securities litigation reform a component of their "Contract with America" campaign platform. After the 1994 "Republican Revolution," in which the right wing of the Republican Party took control of Congress under the leadership of Newt Gingrich, the party made good on its promise.

Neoliberalism and Structural Experimentation: The Private Securities Litigation Reform Act of 1995

After three years of fierce political conflict and an epochal shift in the control of Congress, conservative congressional Republicans spearheaded the passage of the Private Securities Litigation Reform Act of 1995 (the PSLRA) over President Bill Clinton's veto—the only time Congress overrode a veto by President Clinton during his two terms in office.[7] Intended to curtail the use of the courts and litigation for the prosecution of securities fraud claims, the PSLRA placed more stringent pleading requirements on securities fraud suits in an attempt to streamline the procedure for dismissing these suits before they entered the expensive discovery phase.[8] Its proponents hoped that the law would reduce the settlement value of, and thus the incentive to file, weak or meritless suits. The PSLRA reflected a sea change in American politics and policy characterized by a hardening of Republican opposition to and erosion of Democratic support for private litigation as an enforcement mechanism.

The PSLRA also reflected the struggle to find alternative enforcement mechanisms to replace private litigation. Its measures provided for three such alternatives: (1) the use of institutional investors to monitor plaintiffs' attorneys on behalf of all shareholders; (2) reliance on certified public accountants as informational intermediaries and monitors of corporate finances and performance; and (3) litigation by the SEC rather than private plaintiffs and attorneys. By highlighting the role of institutional investors and external auditors, the act represented a nascent structural turn in securities and corporate governance law based on the hope that private actors would perform governance and enforcement functions through the design of institutional relationships and incentives under law. The growing importance of institutional investors was reflected in the PSLRA's creation of a "lead plaintiff" position (generally the shareholder with the largest stake) to police shareholder securities litigation, promote the swift disposition of meritless suits, and prevent collusive settlements.[9] The provision legally empowered institutional investors to act as a counterweight to the power of both plaintiff attorneys and corporate managers. Congress wishfully saw institutional investors as a less disruptive, adversarial, and litigious means of controlling conflicts of interest. This image of self-regulation by rival capitalists appealed to policymakers and managerial interests alike.

However, the PSLRA's lead plaintiff provision produced unintended and paradoxical results. Institutional investors initially had little interest in intervening to terminate lawsuits.[10] The expense and unpredictability of litigation and the fear of potential liability to other shareholders displeased with their conduct as lead plaintiff discouraged deep-pocketed institutional investors from curbing securities litigation. Instead, they used this new power to intervene with growing frequency in securities litigation to prevent plaintiffs' counsel from cutting opportunistic settlement deals with managers in meritorious cases, thereby *prolonging* litigation and *increasing* the amount of final settlements and damage awards.

The PSLRA's use of auditors to detect fraud and the SEC civil actions to enforce the securities laws proved even less effective. In hindsight, Title 3 of the PSLRA, which contains the auditing and auditor disclosure provisions, failed to address the basic conflicts of interest in the management-auditor relationship and did not provide a functional means of enforcement. Instead, during the late 1990s, auditing firms became—knowingly or unknowingly—instrumental in the manipulation or outright misrepresentation of corporate finances. Auditor responsibilities under the PSLRA were enforceable by the SEC alone, not by private litigation, and only when auditors filed a report of suspected illegal activity. The act was insufficient to alleviate the conflicts of interest entrenched within the accounting industry and auditor-client relationships. More generally, SEC civil and criminal actions authorized under the PSLRA failed to fill the enforcement gap left by securities litigation reform, as the stock market boom of the late 1990s sent the agency's workload spiraling upward, with its budget lagging far behind.[11] Although the PSLRA's experiments with structural regulation were disappointing, they reflected a clear and potent political realignment antagonistic to securities litigation.

Neoliberalism through Centralization:
The Securities Litigation Uniform Standards Act of 1998

The antilitigation realignment became even clearer several years later. The federal character of American law and regulation raised the specter of a massive loophole for plaintiffs' attorneys. Critics of litigation asserted that any reduction in federal securities suits would be offset by the number filed in state courts. Spurred on by arguments—and at best ambiguous evidence[12]—that the PSLRA had pushed securities litigation into state courts, Congress passed the Securities Litigation Uniform Standards Act of 1998 (SLUSA) to close the alleged loophole by preempting state securities fraud laws and granting federal courts exclusive jurisdiction over securities lawsuits brought under federal law.[13] This time the Republicans had support from a majority of Democrats in Congress, especially those within the California delegation, who were eager to cultivate high-tech industry support. Chastened by the PSLRA veto override and acutely sensitive to the political trends supporting litigation reform, the Clinton administration also signed on in support of the legislation.

The SLUSA centralized regulatory authority over securities markets in striking fashion. The political potency of the securities litigation reform agenda and the growing political power of antilitigation constituencies overrode the sentiments and rhetoric of conservative neofederalism. Despite their centralizing effect, however, the PSLRA and SLUSA preserved the autonomy of state corporate law, including fiduciary law and related derivative suits. Federal securities litigation reform thus generated opposing policy incentives: on one hand, it invited further fragmentation of corporate governance law by inducing increased reliance on state corporate law; on the other hand, it promoted even more radical intrusion of federal law into the traditional core areas of state corporation law.

The Sarbanes-Oxley Reforms: Corporate Governance Reform and Constrained Autonomy in Policymaking

This tension between the fragmentation and federalization of corporate governance law heightened as American finance capitalism became enveloped in controversy fueled by scandals and systemic crisis in the aftermath of the late 1990s stock market bubble. The combination of irresistible forces pressing for legislative and regulatory change and inescapable political constraints on policymaking that persisted even through the nadir of the crisis prompted the structural character of reforms but also produced their substantial flaws.

The Legitimacy Crisis of Finance Capitalism and the Politics of Reform

The euphoric dot.com bubble of the 1990s died a painful death, as bubbles always do. The Dow Jones Industrial Average fell by 25 percent between March 19, 2000, and July 19, 2002. Standard & Poor's 500 Index lost nearly 28 percent during the same period.[14] The Wilshire 5000 Index, among the most comprehensive of American stock indexes, fell by over 40 percent, from a peak of $17.25 trillion on March 24, 2000, to $10.03 trillion on July 18, 2001.[15] The bursting of the stock market bubble and the sustained impact of corporate scandals and bankruptcies after the collapse of Enron in December 2000 wiped out approximately $7 trillion of market capitalization. According to one estimate, 17 percent of these losses were attributable to the wave of corporate finance scandals.[16]

The crash not only destroyed investors' portfolios, but it also revealed the manipulative and often outright illegal financial conduct of corporate managers, accountants, financial institutions, and attorneys. The collapse drained a swamp of misconduct, bringing into full view the prevalence and severity of the fraud, financial engineering, earnings management, creative accounting, and other dubious financial practices of the boom years. In response, public confidence in the reliability of accounting and financial disclosure reached a new low, and the entire financial system came under suspicion of insider conflicts, fraud, and manipulation.

The mass shareholding that had developed in the United States during the 1980s and 1990s, once a key societal support for pro-market policies, now fueled pervasive cynicism, resentment, and finally fury against business, financial, and political elites. Business and neoliberal deregulation lost their luster in both ideological and political terms. The legitimacy of finance capitalism itself appeared to teeter as the prestige and reputations of principal political and economic actors plummeted. Investor confidence in the securities markets collapsed along with stock prices. Massive finance scandals at Enron, Tyco, WorldCom, Global Crossing, Adelphia, and other major corporations, along with the enormous market losses, stoked the public's resentment against corporate and financial elites. Revelations of managerial fraud, looting, and empire building punctured the inflated cult of the chief executive officer (CEO). The abuses and improprieties of corporate managers also revealed the inadequacies of corporate boards of directors, auditors, and other informational intermediaries, as well as government regulation and regulators. In the harsh light of hindsight, boards of directors of defrauded, looted, and bankrupt firms appeared at best negligent and at worst corrupt.

Key informational intermediaries, particularly accountants and stock analysts, failed to protect the public interest and appeared mired in conflicts of interest. If Enron symbolized the culture of corporate fraud and board failure during the 1990s, its auditor, Arthur Anderson, represented the spread of corruption to the self-regulating professionals entrusted to protect the public interest in transparency. Likewise, stock analysts were unveiled as shills for the investment banks that employed them, and their stock ratings exposed as largely worthless and often deceptive. The government did not escape the public's corrosive skepticism. Securities regulators and prosecutors had failed to deter, detect, or punish managerial misfeasance and malfeasance. Congress's litigation reform legislation had intensified the pressures on the SEC while the agency was starved of resources. The SEC itself was chaired by an avowed skeptic of regulation, Harvey Pitt, known for his representation of accounting firms in private practice. During the 1990s, congressional opposition in both parties had also rolled back a proposal by the Financial Accounting Standards Board (FASB) to require expensing of stock options and an effort by the SEC to compel the separation of auditing and consulting services by accounting firms. Boards turned out not to be watching the CEOs, and no one was watching the watchers. The wave of corporate finance scandals and bankruptcies had frayed public confidence in the soundness, stability, and fundamental integrity of the financial and corporate governance systems.[17]

By the spring of 2002, some political and economic leaders had begun to fear that the American financial system as a whole might collapse. By late June, some were also worrying that an international financial contagion had taken hold, in view of the double-digit losses sustained in the first half of 2002 by the American, British, French, and German stock markets. "Investor confidence" became a de facto metric of political economic legitimacy. Perhaps for the first time in American history, the interests and perceptions of the investor class were viewed (questionably) as largely coterminous with those of the electorate at large. The idea that the backlash in response to scandal and financial crisis had been driven, or at least colored, by antifinancier populism is a recurrent theme in American political and legal history.[18] Yet the post-Enron politics of reform was not so much antimanagement or antifinancier as it was *pro-shareholder*. This reflects a substantial shift in the politics of corporate and financial regulation in the United States. Integrity and fairness of the markets, the adequacy of financial disclosure, and conflicts of interest in corporate governance were increasingly judged by the criteria of shareholder interests rather than those of consumers, local communities, workers, unions, or small business. The post-Enron corporate governance crisis made clear that the legal rules, market and corporate structures, and regulatory enforcement that buttress shareholder interests and investor confidence had become crucial to the legitimation of the political economic order. Consequently, *corporate governance reform was designed to restore and reinforce the structural features of the American political economy,* with its market-centered financial system, preoccupation with shareholder value, and financially driven managerial style. From this perspective, corporate governance reform was an essentially conservative, not a radical, response to crisis in a conservative era.

The Relative Autonomy of Reform Politics

Paradoxically, these overwhelming external forces and events endowed policymakers with a rare and short-lived period of relative autonomy from established interest group politics. The most severe legitimacy crisis of the American financial and corporate governance systems since the Great Depression disrupted the grip of a conservative coalition that favored minimal regulation and had blocked pro-shareholder reforms during the 1990s. Yet public support for reform remained unfocused and detached from any specific concrete proposal, program, or policy agenda. Crisis conditions loosened the constraints of interest group politics while increasing the autonomy of policymakers in fashioning a response to the crisis. That response became the Sarbanes-Oxley Act of 2002.

Sarbanes-Oxley was the product of a political struggle between Democrats using financial scandals against the Republicans, on one hand, and Republicans seeking to delay or dilute the legislation in keeping with their loyalty to corporate supporters and their antiregulation ideological policy agenda, on the other hand. Given the Republican Party's control of the presidency and House of Representatives, and its greater unity and discipline within the veto-prone structure of the federal government, substantial reform was only possible under crisis conditions that weakened interest group influence and made resistance to reform intensely unpopular. Congressional Democrats took advantage of this opportunity. Corporate governance reform in the United States was as much a product of historical contingency as of underlying structural changes in the economy. This outcome can only be understood in the context of an unusual—and temporary—interregnum of interest group politics.

Opponents of reform among interest groups and in the Republican Party hoped to ride out the scandals without any major legislative or regulatory initiative. Sensing political vulnerability from the spreading scandals, the Bush administration announced a ten-point plan to combat corporate corruption in early March of 2002. House Republicans led by Michael Oxley, chairman of the House Finance Committee, quickly submitted a bill patterned after the Bush plan. The bill garnered little praise from commentators and the public, and derision from congressional Democrats, for its support by, and relatively weak restrictions on, the accounting industry. The Republicans pressed forward with Oxley's bill as a way to frame the legislative debate and establish the party's bargaining position against the Democrats.[19]

Shortly after the Republicans began work on their bill, Senate Democrats, led by Banking Committee chairman Paul Sarbanes, began hearings on the scandals and potential legislative responses to the crisis. Because they were completely shut out of the Republican-dominated House legislative process, the Democrats' policy positions could only be channeled through the Senate, where they held a short-lived one-vote majority following Senator James Jeffords's defection from the Republican Party.[20] Of the numerous committees that held hearings on Enron and the unfolding corporate governance crisis, however, the staid Committee on Banking, Housing, and Urban Affairs, with jurisdiction over securities law and accounting issues, took the lead on accounting and corporate governance reform.[21]

The rhetoric of shareholder value filled the chambers of Congress. In the more ideologically driven and rhetorically astringent House, representatives sought to outdo one another in their denunciations of greed and corporate fraud and malfeasance. Democrats sought to seize the political mantle of reform and capitalize on the scandals by denouncing Republican neoliberalism and systemic flaws in securities regulation and corporate governance. The Republicans set out to neutralize these attacks by adopting the rhetoric of shareholder value and confidence while framing the scandals as a matter of a few "bad apples" rather the product of structural flaws in regulation and corporate governance. Similar language permeated the Senate debates over corporate governance reform. A number of Democrats sharpened this general argument into a slashing attack on the Republicans' domestic policy agenda, including litigation reform, which they presented as pro-management, anti-investor, and increasingly dangerous to economic stability. Republicans sought to neutralize the Democrats' attacks by using the same language of trust and investor confidence—though in more muted terms.

Legislative results accompanied this rhetoric of shareholder interests and investor confidence only because the corporate governance crisis had generated conditions that suspended interest group politics as usual. In the reform politics of 2001–02, Congress saw the disintegration of interest group influence and the rise of entrepreneurial political actors.[22] Tainted by scandal, corporate managers, accounting firms, and investment banks were weakened within the legislative process. Corporate managers, in particular, lost prestige and influence in the wake of successive corporate scandals and the popular perception that they, as a class, had looted American corporations and stolen from their shareholders.

The institutional investor community remained split over legislative and regulatory reforms. Corporate pension funds and most mutual funds, which are either controlled by or beholden to corporate managers, did not press for reform. Large public employee and union pension funds, long involved in a largely nonregulatory and voluntarist form of corporate governance activism, shifted their policy preferences dramatically in support of increased regulatory stringency and intervention in corporate governance. The AFL-CIO and its member unions strongly supported corporate governance reforms that would help protect their members' private pension investments, provide them with more information regarding the financial health of businesses, and curtail managerial power. Like other interest groups, however, institutional investors and organized labor wielded minimal influence on the content of the reforms.

Business interests were also deeply divided over reform. The financial services sector could not agree on the proper extent of corporate governance reform and government regulation of business and markets. Its members depended on public faith in the integrity of the securities markets, but as privileged insiders they benefited from the status quo. Financial institutions and service providers were politically weakened not only by intrasectoral divisions but also by their alleged roles in numerous scandals—such as dishonesty and conflicts of interests in stock analysis, initial public offering and stock market manipulation, and the aiding and abetting of dishonest corporate executives.

The business community's divisions only widened as the corporate scandals deepened. Leading investment firms understood the depth and seriousness of the crisis, and they had an enormous stake in ensuring that it was contained—by regulatory reform if necessary. Likewise, the New York Stock Exchange came out in support of reform, also in order to calm investors and restore confidence. The leading business lobbying groups, the Business Roundtable and the Chamber of Commerce, took opposing positions. The Chamber of Commerce, historically more ideological in its intense opposition to government regulation, fought a rearguard battle against the reforms. The Business Roundtable, whose membership of the CEOs of large public corporations had long been opposed to government intervention into corporate governance, remained moderately opposed, but in the end supported the Sarbanes-Oxley reforms.

The accounting industry, having much to answer for and fearing even more to lose from reform, fought strenuously against the legislation—even at the risk of further antagonizing public opinion—but was in no position to stem the tide of popular opinion and political momentum. The large accounting firms—down to the Big Four of PricewaterhouseCoopers, Deloitte Touche Tohmatsu, Ernst & Young, and KPMG after the indictment, collapse, and conviction (later reversed) of Arthur Anderson—and the accounting industry's trade association (the American Institute of Certified Public Accountants) were tainted by association with scandal, fraud, and conflicts of interest. Each of the Big Four was implicated in scandals. The industry had lost its legitimacy as a profession. As the legislative process moved forward, some Republican staffers on Capitol Hill even told accounting industry lobbyists to stay away—their very presence was politically damaging.[23]

With the discrediting of and divisions among economic elites and interest groups, the autonomy of policymakers increased. This left the reformers in the Democratic Party remarkably unconstrained by interest group politics and free to capitalize on the public's outrage in pushing the reform legislation. In contrast to the Republicans in both the House and Senate, Paul Sarbanes and a majority of his fellow Democrats were favorably predisposed toward reform. The Democrats' slim Senate majority gave Sarbanes the institutional power to frame and advance a specific and technical legislative agenda. The Democrats draped their concerns and proposals in the rhetoric of pro-shareholder fairness and regulatory reform that was overwhelmingly supported by public opinion. The Senate Banking Committee moved deliberately through the winter, and more quickly during the late spring and early summer of 2002, as the scandals and the sense of financial crisis among the public and the political economic elite escalated.

By June 2002, the reform politics had taken on a life of its own beyond the control of interest groups and even congressional party leaders. After cooling somewhat during the spring of 2002, the sense of panic and outrage spiraled upward again as the corporate financial and accounting scandals culminated in late June with the multibillion-dollar collapse of WorldCom, following disclosure of a multibillion-dollar accounting fraud. The WorldCom collapse finally broke Republican resistance to Democratic legislative reforms. Public demand for securities law and corporate governance reform had become irresistible. The Bush administration and much of the congressional Republican leadership sought to neutralize the scandals as a potent November 2002 election issue by supporting corporate governance reform and accepting only minor compromises from the Democrats as the price.[24]

Structural Regulation: The Politics of Constraints and Regulatory Innovation

The corporate governance crisis revealed the necessity of strong legal rules and regulatory institutions as the foundation of functional, efficient private economic institutions—including both markets and the non-market hierarchical organization of the corporate firm.[25] Significantly, however, the law and the regulation it enabled did *not* loosen legislative restrictions on securities litigation, let alone create new causes of action. Instead, the Sarbanes-Oxley Act relied on a combination of governmental enforcement and structural regulation to carry out its reforms. Political dynamics and constraints drove the legislation in these directions.

Even at the height of the corporate governance crisis, two fundamental constraints of partisan politics remained intact. The first was the Republicans' intransigence over adding or expanding any new shareholder rights enforceable through litigation. Second, members of both parties recognized that reforms giving shareholders a more direct and enhanced role in nominating and electing corporate directors were off-limits. Preservation of securities litigation reform was a nonnegotiable item for congressional Republicans and the Bush administration.[26] As a result, Sarbanes did not even raise the issue of private causes of action when drafting legislation. Nor did the legislative debate present a serious effort, let alone a credible threat, of rolling back the 1990s' legacy of restrictions on securities suits. The Republicans did not even have to fight over such issues.

Driven by intense and rapidly shifting political pressures for reform, yet still constrained by the antilitigation politics of the 1990s, the Sarbanes-Oxley reforms were in effect forced to experiment with structural regulation. This followed not only from the political logic of the situation but also from policymakers' practical assessment of the unfolding corporate governance crisis in 2002. Sarbanes and many of his Democratic colleagues believed that this was a structural crisis, rooted in accounting and conflicts of interest, and they fashioned, in part, a structural solution to it.[27]

Sarbanes-Oxley imposed a welter of new regulatory requirements and prohibitions on publicly traded corporations, directors, corporate managers, accountants, securities analysts, and attorneys. This discussion focuses on the most important and innovative provisions: the creation of the Public Company Accounting Oversight Board (the PCAOB) and the reform of internal corporate board and management structures to institutionalize improved corporate governance within the firm.[28] The PCAOB was a new private regulatory body, appointed by and under the oversight of the SEC, charged with regulating the accounting industry. The creation of the PCAOB federalized accounting regulation and displaced the self-regulatory character of the accounting profession

The more innovative and path-breaking provisions of the Sarbanes-Oxley Act are those using structural regulation to intervene in the *internal* structure and affairs of the corporation. Whereas the PCAOB extended traditional transparency and disclosure regulation to the accounting industry, the structural regulation provisions of Sarbanes-Oxley represent the first time that federal law and regulation directly intervened in the composition, structure, and operation of corporate boards.[29] These issues had been within the traditional preserve of state corporation law. Public firms are now required to appoint an auditing committee comprised *entirely* of independent directors, and at least one member must be qualified as a financial expert under new SEC rules. The audit committee now has direct responsibility for the appointment, compensation, and oversight of the outside auditors. The auditors report directly to the audit committee, which must approve all auditor services and resolve any disputes between management and the auditors concerning financial reporting. Likewise, the boards of public firms must now put in place independent compensation committees that set managerial pay. Sarbanes-Oxley also enhances the more general institutional capacities of the board by giving it the legal authority to hire independent counsel and consultants. Finally, the law requires CEOs and chief financial officers to certify the accuracy of the firm's accounts. Section 404 of Sarbanes-Oxley also requires that CEOs certify the firm's internal monitoring and risk management systems as adequate to prevent accounting manipulation and fraud. In practice, this provision compelled the thoroughgoing restructuring of intrafirm managerial, monitoring, and reporting structures and practices.[30]

Together, these regulatory reforms represent not only a potentially vast expansion of federal regulatory power but also a substantial centralization of regulatory authority. By encroaching on the traditional subjects of state corporate law, the Sarbanes-Oxley reforms centralized and federalized key aspects of corporate governance. This unprecedented federalization of corporate law represents a break with nearly two centuries of American federalism.[31] This departure from such a long-established allocation of policymaking power indicates the growing practical import and policy salience of corporate governance issues, along with the extraordinary political impact of the financial and governance scandals of 2001–02.[32] Federal law and regulation have begun to displace traditions of federalism and the private managerial autonomy that had characterized much of American corporate governance. Sarbanes-Oxley thus represents both a stunning reversal of the antiregulation agenda of the 1990s *and* a continuation of the skepticism toward private litigation as a mode of regulatory enforcement.

The result has been an innovative expansion of structural regulation. Members of Congress were aware of the innovative nature of the corporate governance reforms. They were also aware that the use of structural regulation afforded them a solution to the rapidly eroding legitimacy of American corporate governance institutions as well as the problem of enforcement. These structural fixes would be "self-executing" with no need (or option) for litigation.[33] The operation of the institutional arrangement itself would be the enforcement.

The importance of structural regulation and board reform implicates the second powerful political constraint on the politics of corporate governance reform. Despite the significance and sweep of the reforms, Sarbanes-Oxley did not reform how directors are nominated and elected. The act left the very foundation of corporate governance and managerial power largely under the control of managers. In a statute that relies to such a degree on structural regulation utilizing board independence, this is a striking omission. There are only intermittent references to the subject in the legislative record. Surprisingly, given its importance, there were but a few passing statements on the subject by witnesses, and congressional Democrats were almost entirely silent on the matter. The question of board nominations and elections was simply too explosive to broach.[34] Any attempt to reform board nomination and election rules would have mobilized the American managerial elite against the Democratic Party and shifted its support even more disproportionately toward the GOP. Because the Democratic Party has become increasingly reliant on the support of at least sections of the managerial class, this threat precluded a fundamental challenge to the institutional bases of its power. If a litigation provision would have killed it, so too would a foundational reform of the corporate power structure.

The Business Backlash: Return to Politics as Usual?

Ultimately, the SEC, under the chairmanship of Pitt's successor, William Donaldson, advanced a rather weak proposal in October 2003 to reform corporate proxy voting on board nominations and elections. This proposal triggered a backlash by business against Sarbanes-Oxley and the regulatory reforms that followed; it vindicated the Democrats' reluctance to address the issue in the first place. This backlash and the election of November 2004 would bring the post-Enron reform era to a virtual end. The Sarbanes-Oxley reforms were the product of exceptional, and by definition temporary, circumstances that short-circuited interest group and institutional politics as usual. With the ebbing of the corporate governance crisis, the dynamics and interest group balances of "normal" politics were restored.

The hostility of managers to the Sarbanes-Oxley Act had been simmering almost since its passage. By Sarbanes-Oxley's first anniversary, one year after the peak of the accounting scandals, a former head of the American Institute of Certified Public Accountants fumed that Sarbanes-Oxley represented "the criminalization of [corporate] risk taking, which is the same as criminalizing capitalism."[35] A growing number of business representatives and neoliberal commentators had begun to voice what would become an increasingly familiar litany of complaints about the reforms:

—Compliance costs, including increased audit fees and "directors and officers" insurance premiums, were too high.

—The reforms reduced the number of qualified people willing to serve on boards.

—Domestic firms were discouraged from going public and public firms were induced to go private.

—Foreign firms were discouraged from listing on American stock exchanges.

—The reforms slowed investment and growth.

—They encouraged excessive risk aversion by management.

With the exception of increased directors and officers insurance and auditing fees, empirical and anecdotal evidence did not support these criticisms. One leading corporate governance consultant ridiculed the complaints as a bunch of "urban myths," and Treasury Secretary John Snow dismissed them out of hand.[36] Even the increased auditing fees did not appear to be significant in the broader context of corporate cost structures. Even so, polls of corporate executives revealed growing managerial skepticism and outright hostility toward corporate governance reform and regulation.[37] Managers found two other issues particularly objectionable: (1) the expensing of stock options under newly proposed accounting rules, and (2) the difficulties and expense of complying with the internal control certification requirements of Section 404 of Sarbanes-Oxley. However, neither triggered broadly based resistance to corporate governance reform.[38]

The political terrain shifted dramatically in mid-2003. The SEC's proposal to change proxy rules to give shareholders the (very limited) ability to nominate and elect corporate directors transformed passive resentment into a potent managerial backlash. The proposed rules would have allowed institutional investors access to corporate proxies mailed to all shareholders only after substantial delays and under exceptional conditions.[39] Because structural regulation under Sarbanes-Oxley depends on improving the functioning of boards, the proposed proxy rule amendments went to the very foundations of corporate governance and managerial power in the United States. Following the passage of Sarbanes-Oxley, the SEC engaged in a historic run of rulemaking, covering an array of subjects, including mutual and hedge funds, financial and proxy vote disclosure, accounting rules, and stock exchange regulation. None of these initiatives proved as controversial as the board nomination rules proposed by the SEC.[40] The reaction was immediate. Hundreds of comments poured in from business groups, professional associations, corporate attorneys and law firms, institutional investment funds, and shareholder advocates. By the time the comment period closed on the proposed rules, the SEC had received over 13,000 letters, by far the largest number regarding any rule in the commission's history.[41]

The ferocity of opposition to the SEC's modest proposal indicates the extraordinary sensitivity of board nomination and election rules and the strength of the gathering managerial backlash. Whereas interest groups became enfeebled by the divisions during the debate over Sarbanes-Oxley and policymakers empowered, the former were now far more unified—and polarized. Managers, business groups, and allied organizations attacked the proposed rules as destructive of corporate efficiency and an invitation to public and union pensions to use their vast holdings to conduct divisive campaigns and pursue special interest agendas. Both the Business Roundtable and the Chamber of Commerce publicly opposed the rules, with the Chamber threatening to sue if they were adopted. Unions, shareholder and consumer advocates, many institutional investors, and a number of state treasurers publicly supported the changes, but some argued that the proposed rules were *too weak* to make a practical difference in who oversees the country's largest corporations.

The conflict escalated in the runup to the 2004 presidential election. Opponents intensified their attack on the proposed proxy rule while the Bush administration reportedly weighed in against it behind closed doors. The SEC commissioners themselves split over the issue, with the Democratic and Republican commissioners bitterly divided at 2-2, and Chairman Donaldson seeking a compromise that neither side supported. By July 2004, he conceded that the SEC was deadlocked over the board nomination proposal. Its fate would turn on the election. As soon as the November 2004 election ended in a Bush victory and a restored Republican majority in the Senate, postmortems for the board nomination proposal started appearing in the news. By January 2005, news items reported that the plan was dead. Corporate governance reform had reached its high-water mark. The failure of the SEC's proxy rule proposal brought a brief era of reform to a close. The structure of corporate governance was left in a state that preserved the institutional foundations of managerialism. Under intense pressure from administration and congressional conservatives, under fire by business groups, and his reform agenda criticized and blocked by increasingly hostile Republican SEC commissioners, Donaldson faced a deteriorating and untenable political position. He resigned in early June 2005. Within hours of Donaldson's resignation, President Bush nominated Representative Chris Cox—the principal author of the House draft of the PSLRA in 1995 and a vocal critic of regulation—to replace him.

Conclusion

The narrative of corporate governance reform and the failure of either Congress or the SEC to carry it to its logical conclusion by giving shareholders a meaningful role in nominating and electing directors highlights some basic characteristics of policymaking and reform politics in the United States. First, the very structure of the federal government and pluralist interest group politics makes it exceedingly difficult to pass major reform legislation under ordinary political and economic conditions. Second, crises provide the conditions that allow critics and reformers to break through the bottlenecks and veto points of politics as usual, but only for the usually brief duration of perceived emergency. Accordingly, reform and institutional development proceeds in a pattern of punctuated equilibrium, with periods of sudden, episodic, and crisis-driven reform led by state actors. Third, even under crisis conditions, structural and political constraints on policymaking do not disappear. Markets and the institutions on which they depend may fail, at times spectacularly, but the underlying dynamics of institutionalized interests and political constraints persist. Established patterns of interest group politics usually swiftly reassert themselves. Knowing this, politicians internalize political constraints on policymakers for fear of antagonizing potent constituencies. This renders nonnegotiable matters implicating the fundamental interests of powerful groups—even when they are politically weakened.

Corporate governance reforms in the United States exemplify this pattern of punctuated change within powerful, implicit, and largely unchallenged constraints. Senate Democrats never openly challenged the premises or policy of securities litigation reform or managerial control over board nominations and elections. Hostility toward private litigation may have begun on the Republican right, but it achieved bipartisan support that placed firm political limits on any advances in regulatory policymaking. Because of the enforcement problems created by this aversion to litigation, the trend toward structural regulation accelerated. Paradoxically, this emphasis on structural regulation led policymakers to tinker with some of the most basic and sensitive power relations in any capitalist society. In turn, this regulation of the structure of the corporate form triggered resistance that revealed the political limits of reform. Even at the height of the corporate governance crisis, the fundamental reform of corporate power structures, such as that implied by the SEC's proxy reform proposal, was politically impossible. By failing to address how boards are actually nominated and elected, the corporate governance provisions of Sarbanes-Oxley, which rely so heavily on the independence of directors and board committees, were left with a weak foundation. The struggle over board nomination and election rules illustrates that corporate governance has become an important policy arena and partisan political issue. It also shows that politics is back to normal.

Notes

1 . P. L. 107-204, 116 Stat. 445 (July 30, 2002).

2. John W. Cioffi, "Building Finance Capitalism: The Regulatory Politics of Corporate Governance Reform in the United States and Germany," in *The State after Statism: New State Activities in the Age of Globalization and Liberalization,* edited by Jonah Levy (Harvard University Press, 2006); John W. Cioffi, "The State of the Corporation: State Power, Politics, Policymaking and Corporate Governance in the United States, Germany, and France," in *Trans-Atlantic Policymaking in an Age of Austerity,* edited by Martin Shapiro and Martin Levin (Georgetown University Press, 2004).

3. Consider George Tsebelis, "Decision-Making in Political Systems: Veto Players in Presidentialism, Parliamentarism, Multicameralism and Multipartyism," *British Journal of Political Science* 25 (July, 1995): 289–325; Robert A. Kagan, *Adversarial Legalism: The American Way of Law* (Harvard University Press, 2001).

4. See Janet Cooper Alexander, "Do the Merits Matter? A Study of Settlements in Securities Class Actions," *Stanford Law Review* 43 (February, 1991): 497–598; Joel Seligman, "The Private Securities Reform Act of 1995," in *Symposium: Securities Litigation: The Fundamental Issues: Supplemental Paper, Arizona Law Review* 38 (summer, 1996): 717.

5. The rate and significance of the increase in securities litigation has been, and continues to be, hotly debated. See Alexander, "Do the Merits Matter?"; Seligman, "The Private Securities Reform Act of 1995"; also U.S. Senate, *Private Litigation under the Federal Securities*

Laws: Hearings before the Subcommittee on Securities of the Senate Committee on Banking, Housing, and Urban Affairs, 103rd Cong., 1st sess. (1993).

6. Seligman, "The Private Securities Reform Act of 1995," pp. 717–19.

7. P.L. 104-67 (December 22, 1995)

8. "Congress Overwhelmingly Passes Bill to Reform Private Securities Litigation," *Securities Regulation* and *Law Reporter* (BNA) 27 (1995): 1899.

9. PSLRA, sec. 27(a)(3)(A) & (B), 15 U.S.C.A. secs. 77z-1(a)(3)(A) & (B); 78u-4(a)(3) (A) & (B) (procedure and substantive criteria for appointment of "lead plaintiff"). This provision was inspired by an inventive 1995 law review article. Elliott J. Weiss and John S. Beckerman, "Let the Money Do the Monitoring: How Institutional Investors Can Reduce Agency Costs in Securities Class Actions," *Yale Law Journal* 104 (June, 1995): 2053.

10. Joseph A. Grundfest and Michael A. Perino, "Securities Litigation Reform: The First Year's Experience: A Statistical and Legal Analysis of Class Action Securities Fraud Litigation under the Private Securities Litigation Reform Act of 1995," unpublished report (February 27, 1997); Securities Litigation Reform: The First Year's Experience, *Annual Institute on Securities Regulation* 29 (Winter 1997): 241–95.

11. See 15 U.S.C. sec. 77t(f) (authorizing SEC actions for "aiding and abetting liability"), and 15 USC 78j–1(d) (SEC has exclusive authority to enforce auditor's duty to disclose fraud and penalize violations).

12. See Eugene P. Caiola, "Comment: Retroactive Legislative History: Scienter under the Uniform Security Litigation Standards Act of 1998," *Albany Law Review* 64 (2000), nn. 186–90 and accompanying text.

13. P.L. 105-353, 112 Stat. 3227.

14. Carol Graham, Robert E. Litan, and Sandip Sukhtankar, "Cooking the Books: The Cost to the Economy," Brookings Policy Brief 106 (August 2002), p. 3.

15. Joel Seligman, *The Transformation of Wall Street,* 3rd ed. (New York: Aspen, 2003), p. 624.

16. Graham and others, "Cooking the Books," p. 2.

17. Enron collapsed just after the terrorist attacks of September 11, 2001; the succession of post-crash scandals unfolded in the aftermath of that catastrophe. The combination of the terrorist attacks and pervasive financial scandals led policymakers in and out of Congress to fear the possibility of a general collapse of the American and international financial systems. This perception was repeatedly stated in my interviews with congressional aides from both parties.

18. Mark J. Roe, "A Political Theory of American Corporate Finance," *Columbia Law Review* 91 (January, 1991): 10; Mark J. Roe, *Strong Managers, Weak Owners: The Political Roots of American Corporate Finance* (Princeton University Press, 1994).

19. Interviews with members of the U.S. House of Representatives and Senate, and with former congressional staffers, Washington, March 2004.

20. This majority was precarious, and the public's attention to and memory of financial scandals was short. Following losses in the November 2002 midterm elections, both the Democrats' control of the Senate and the public's fixation on corporate finance scandals were gone.

21. The Senate Judiciary, Commerce, Labor, Tax, and Investigations committees held hearings on issues raised by Enron and the crisis of corporate governance, but their jurisdictional competence was either too narrow or comparatively peripheral to frame a comprehensive policy response.

22. This analysis was originally developed in John W. Cioffi, "Building Finance Capitalism: The Regulatory Politics of Corporate Governance Reform in the United States and Germany," in *The State after Statism: New State Activities in the Age of Globalization and Liberalization,* edited by Jonah Levy (Harvard University Press, 2006); see also Cioffi, "The State of the Corporation: State Power, Politics, Policymaking and Corporate Governance in the United States, Germany, and France."

23. Former senior Republican staff member, House Finance Committee, interview, March 2004.

24. The Democrats gave up a potent campaign issue out of a combination of idealism and calculation. In part, the Democrats chose to pursue good public policy over tactical expediency. In interviews (Washington, March 2003, March 2004), Republicans as well as Democrats described the motivations for passing the act in these terms. They also needed to insulate themselves from charges of obstructionism and from appearing to play politics with the American economy. Even at the height of the scandals, the Democrats received little credit from the public for their corporate reform efforts. The corporate financial scandals fostered an all-embracing public cynicism toward American economic and political institutions and elites that extended to both parties. Either party would have faced intense public hostility, and likely electoral losses, if it appeared to have obstructed reforms or foiled the progress of the legislation.

25. Steven K. Vogel, *Freer Markets, More Rules: Regulatory Reform in Advanced Industrial Countries* (Cornell University Press, 1996); Cioffi, "Building Finance Capitalism."

26. Senior Treasury Department official, interview, Washington, March 2004. Sarbanes needed the support of Republican senator Michael Enzi to report his bill out of committee, and the Democrats knew any attempt to expand the use or availability of private litigation was a "deal killer" for the Republicans. Interviews, Washington, March 2003, March 2004. There were two modest exceptions to this political rule. One was a private cause of action under section 306 against officers to recover profits from illegal insider trading of company securities during pension fund "blackout periods" (during which beneficiaries are not allowed to sell shares). The other was an extension of the statute of limitations for securities fraud claims, which had been substantially shortened by the Supreme Court. Republicans could live with these exceptions so long as the PSLRA's restrictions remained intact.

27. Senate Banking Committee staff, interviews, Washington, March 2004.

28. One important regulatory change that does not neatly fit into the analysis developed here is Sarbanes-Oxley's mandatory separation of auditing and consulting services. Although this could be considered a form of structural regulation, it is more accurately described as enforced market segmentation to reduce conflicts of interest.

29. Federal law had placed some rather minor restrictions on boards, such as the ban on interlocking directorates under the Clayton Antitrust Act and the composition of mutual fund boards under the Investment Company Act of 1940, but nothing approached those imposed by Sarbanes-Oxley. Although New York Stock Exchange listing rules, adopted under SEC pressure, had already imposed board independence and committee requirements, Sarbanes-Oxley represented a new level of federal intervention in intracorporate affairs.

30. No provision of the Sarbanes-Oxley Act has sparked more criticism than Section 404 on internal risk-management certification. Ironically, this provision has also been a boon to accountants, who audit, assess, and sometimes consult on the design of risk-management

systems. The law that targeted the accounting industry has in at least one way enriched it significantly.

31. Members of Congress understood that the reforms ran counter to the established federalist allocation of corporate law to the states. Indeed, Oxley discussed the issue with his staff repeatedly (interviews, Washington, March, 2004). However, even a majority of Republicans believed that the securities markets, and thus corporate governance framework that underpinned them, were national in scope and importance (ibid.). Federalism was again jettisoned when it got in the way of practical politics.

32. John W. Cioffi, "Irresistible Forces and Political Obstacles: Securities Litigation Reform and the Structural Regulation of Corporate Governance," Research Paper 7/2006 (York University, Osgoode School of Law, May 2006); Roberta Romano, "The Sarbanes-Oxley Act and the Making of Quack Corporate Governance," Working Paper 04-37 (Yale University, International Center for Finance, 2004).

33. Interview, Washington, March, 2004.

34. This assessment was confirmed by a former senior Republican congressional aide. E-mail communication, February 1, 2005.

35. Michael Schroeder, "Corporate Reform: The First Year: Cleaner Living, No Easy Riches; Critics Say Sarbanes-Oxley Law Hobbles Stocks, Chills Risk Taking, But Upshot Is Far Less Dramatic," *Wall Street Journal,* July 22, 2003, p. C1.

36. Ibid.

37. PricewaterhouseCoopers, "Senior Executives Less Favorable on Sarbanes-Oxley, PricewaterhouseCoopers Finds," *Management Barometer,* July 23, 2003 (www.barometer-surveys.com/).

38. Complaints that Sec. 404 imposed excessive compliance costs on small and medium-size public firms are well taken. However, repeated delays in applying the provision to these companies rendered much of the criticism speculative. Significantly, larger firms accepted Sec. 404 with little protest, and many found it useful in streamlining their internal operations. Therefore opposition to Sec. 404 did not trigger a broadly based managerial backlash against Sarbanes-Oxley and corporate governance reform, though attacks on the provision on the ostensible behalf of smaller firms became a potent rhetorical strategy.

39. The proposed rules would have created a two-step, multiyear process to place shareholder board nominations on the corporation's formal proxy ballots. First, at least 35 percent of voting shareholders would have to withhold their support for a company's director candidate in an annual board election. If this criterion was satisfied, a group representing at least 5 percent of shares would be able to nominate and run its own nominee(s) on the corporate proxy the following year. Even then, the proposed rules would have allowed dissident shareholders to elect no more than a minority of three directors in this fashion. This was almost certainly insufficient to substantially strengthen boards as checks on managerial power.

40. Securities and Exchange Commission, "Proposed Rule: Security Holder Director Nominations," 17 CFR PARTS 240, 249 and 274, Release 34-48626, IC-26206, File S7-19-03, RIN 3235-AI93, October 14, 2003 (modified October 17, 2003).

41. Securities and Exchange Commission, "SEC Comments on Proposed Rule: Security Holder Director Nominations," Release 34-48626, IC-26206, File S7-19-03, January 7, 2004.

5

The Politics of Risk Privatization in U.S. Social Policy

Jacob S. Hacker

When President George W. Bush was reelected in 2004, he declared that his signature policy goal would be to incorporate "private accounts"—or, as advocates soon insisted they be called, "personal accounts"—into America's popular retirement program, Social Security. The details of Bush's plans were hazy, but the aspiration was clear: to transform Social Security from a single program with benefits defined in law into something closer to a 401(k) plan, in which a large chunk of workers' Social Security taxes are invested in private investment accounts from which they (or their heirs) alone benefit.

A year later, President Bush's hazy plan was dead, and leaders of the Republican-controlled Congress were scrambling to distance themselves from it. Polls showed that Americans preferred the security of Social Security to a more individualized framework.[1] Social Security, it seemed, was still the "third rail of American Politics"—touch it and die. The American welfare state had survived yet another assault.

Although Social Security survived intact, other once-secure benefits were unraveling, largely outside the public eye—namely, the employment-based private benefits on which Americans so heavily rely.[2] Between 2000 and 2005, the number of Americans lacking health insurance climbed to more than 46.6 million, an increase due entirely to a fall in the proportion of Americans covered by employment-based health plans.[3] The number without coverage at some point over a two-year period was even higher: some 80 million, or 1 out of 3 non-elderly Americans (nearly all lived in working families, and almost two-thirds were uninsured for six months or longer).[4] Roughly half of the 1.5 million personal bankruptcies in the United States in 2001, according to one estimate, were caused in part by medical costs and crises.[5]

Families have not been the only ones facing bankruptcy. As President Bush called on the private sector to rescue Social Security, key corporations called on the public sector to rescue them from their mounting private benefit costs. The financial meltdown of companies like United, Delta, Delphi, Ford, and GM, and the decision of otherwise healthy companies like Verizon, IBM, and Motorola to phase out their traditional pensions, threw into the spotlight the growing precariousness not just of company health benefits but also of so-called defined-benefit pension plans that offer a guaranteed benefit in retirement. An entire structure of benefits constructed in a more stable business climate was under siege.

These two sets of events—the continuing political strength of America's largest social insurance program and the continuing erosion of its uniquely extensive system of private workplace benefits—form the backdrop for this chapter. The welfare state and the market are my twin subjects. A key contention of this chapter, however, is that the sharp line often drawn between the two is much fuzzier and more contested than commonly believed. Alongside the public social programs typically identified with U.S. social policy lies a massive system of *private* social benefits that are regulated and subsidized by the government. When these private benefits are included in tallies of social spending, U.S. after-tax expenditures are as high (as a share of the economy) as the spending of many European nations.[6] Yet these private benefits are distributed in distinct ways, and they have distinctively shaped the evolution of U.S. social policy since the 1970s.

The now conventional view of this evolution can be summed up in a single world: *resilience*. Even before President Bush's Social Security plan went down in flames, analysts by and large agreed that the welfare state was the toughest of nuts for conservatives to crack. Despite intense strain and cuts around the margins, according to this conventional account, existing social policy frameworks were essentially secure, anchored by their enduring popularity, their powerful constituencies, and their centrality within the postwar order.

This chapter tells a different story. Although most U.S. public social programs have indeed resisted radical retrenchment, the American social welfare framework has also offered increasingly less protection against the key economic risks that confront Americans. As a result of both large-scale social changes and the ground-level transformation of America's public-private system of social benefits, individuals and families now face many of the most potent threats to their income on their own, rather than with the help of collective intermediaries, such as employers and the government. The American welfare state has not been privatized. Economic risk increasingly has.

This momentous transformation has not occurred naturally. Sweeping changes in the economy and family have propelled it. Yet, political leaders could have responded to these forces by reinforcing the buffers that protect families from risk. Instead, critics of the welfare state have attempted to trim these buffers back, with considerable, and largely unrecognized, success.

Today, however, the movement to privatize risk is running headlong into a nasty reality: many economic risks cannot be effectively dealt with in the private market. Ironically, the future of U.S. social policy—and, indeed, of America's dynamic and flexible free market more generally—may hinge on the rediscovery and reformation of the government's special role in softening the sharp edges of a competitive market economy.

Dismantling the Welfare State?

The privatization agenda in social policy has four main priorities: (1) to scale back direct government action so as to encourage self-reliance and private provision; (2) to expand subsidies for private insurance, savings, and charitable activities; (3) to expand government contracting with voluntary organizations and for-profit service providers; and (4) to infuse into established programs vouchers and other mechanisms that allow (or require) recipients to opt out of these programs and obtain benefits from the private sector instead. None of these strategies eliminates the government's role. Rather, they shift the emphasis from direct state action to private action under the management and oversight of government.

After two decades of debate, judgments still differ on how far the privatization agenda has progressed. In most rich nations, it is fair to say that the agenda itself never had much backing. But even where the ideology of privatization gained committed support, notably in Britain and the United States, achievements unquestionably fell short of ambitions. Some cutbacks have occurred. Some programs have been eliminated. But if the question is whether major retrenchment has occurred, the answer appears to be no. As Paul Pierson puts it in one of the earliest and most influential assessments,

"Economic, political, and social pressures have fostered an image of welfare states under siege. Yet if one turns from abstract discussions of social transformation to an examination of actual policy, it becomes difficult to sustain the proposition that these strains have generated fundamental shifts."[7]

The reason for this is simple—at least in the view of Pierson and others who have followed his lead. Cutting back the welfare state is much harder than building it up. Social programs are popular, and they give rise to powerful constituencies well positioned to fight retrenchment. To buttress this simple but powerful argument, scholars of retrenchment have extensively examined efforts to introduce cutbacks into existing programs, using both qualitative case studies and multivariate statistical techniques.[8] Their main findings confirm Pierson's initial claim: dismantling the welfare state is a nonstarter.

For all its virtues, this argument has real limits. The first and simplest is its emphasis on authoritative change in existing programs. Although this may seem an obvious approach, it excludes from consideration a host of subterranean means of adjustment that can occur without formal policy change, from "bureaucratic disentitlement" caused by the decisions of front-line administrators to decentralized cutbacks in benefits caused by the actions of private benefit sponsors and providers.[9]

Perhaps more important, in emphasizing affirmative decisions, the conventional approach also excludes from consideration a wide range of agenda-setting and blocking activities that may well be crucial in shaping the welfare state's evolution. Most critical in this regard are deliberate attempts to prevent the updating of policies to reflect changing social circumstance. In the early 1990s, for example, the United States hosted a bitter debate over the future of American health insurance. Advocates of expanded government responsibility, led by Democratic president Bill Clinton, embarked on an ambitious campaign to extend health coverage to counteract the declining reach of private benefits. Their efforts, in turn, fell victim to a concerted countermobilization among affected interests and conservatives, who denied that government should step in to deal with the increasing hardships caused by skyrocketing costs and dwindling protections. Whether the campaign for universal health insurance was necessary or unnecessary, poorly executed, or simply doomed to fail, its defeat had enormous implications for the scope and character of U.S. social protection. Yet from the standpoint of the conventional approach to retrenchment, the failure of health care reform is a nonevent.

This example only hints at the broad range of processes and outcomes that a single-minded focus on formal policy change occludes. Historically, welfare states have been directed not just at ensuring protection against medical costs but also at providing security against a number of other major life risks: unemployment, death of a spouse, retirement, disability. Yet the incidence and extent of many of these risks have changed substantially over the past three decades, leading to potentially significant transformations in the consequences of social policies, even without formal changes in public social programs.

Furthermore, even within the relatively narrow conception of the welfare state that most research employs, some important policies routinely get left out. Notable here are two overlapping policy realms that are central to the U.S. social policy framework: tax breaks with social welfare purposes and regulatory and tax policies governing privately provided social welfare benefits.[10] Controlling for tax burdens, for example, private workplace benefits constituted more than a third of U.S. social spending in 2001—by far the highest level in the advanced industrial world.[11] In 2006 the cost to the federal treasury of subsidizing these benefits through the tax code exceeded $300 billion, about what is spent on the Medicare program.[12] Moreover, these benefits have changed dramatically in the past generation, as corporations have unilaterally cut back benefits or shifted toward less secure income guarantees. Thus leaving policies that govern private benefits out of the analysis entirely, as nearly all retrenchment studies do, misses a critically important dimension of social policy change, particularly in the United States.

Private benefits are provided at the discretion of employers within a framework of government inducements and constraints. As a result, most changes in such benefits occur without formal policy revision. Like the other less visible sources of change just discussed, therefore, the evolution of private benefits calls for an analysis that is attuned to the internal reworking of otherwise stable policies and to the shifting interaction of policies and their environment.

This is, of course, a formidable challenge. Researchers are a long way from having good data on shifts in benefit rules, much less on how these rules are implemented or actually affect citizens. Still, the shortcomings of the conventional approach to retrenchment suggest some straightforward prescriptions. First, attention should focus not only on the structure of policies but also on their effects—not only on the rules governing benefits or eligibility but also on the outcomes that those rules produce as they are carried out by front-line policy actors in the context of shifting social conditions. Second, and no less important, *explanations* must take seriously the possibility that those who wish to change policies will seek to do so without formal revision, attempting instead to alter policies through less visible means.

Such strategies of stealth can follow three main courses: (1) "convert" existing policies by changing the way they are carried out on the ground, (2) "layer" new policies on top of old ones so as to change the operation of the old, and (3) abet the "drift" of policies away from their original purposes by blocking attempts to update existing policies to new social circumstances.[13] In an environment of new or worsening social risks, opponents of expanded state responsibility do not have to enact major policy reforms to move policy toward their favored ends. Merely by delegitimizing and blocking compensatory interventions designed to ameliorate intensified risks, they can gradually transform the orientation of existing programs, allowing these programs to drift away from their original mission. Each of these forms of subterranean change—conversion, layering, and drift—has been on vivid display in the post-1970s privatization of risk in U.S. social policy.

The Welfare State Confronts New (and Newly Intensified) Social Risks

The constellation of risks citizens face has changed significantly in the past three decades, owing to linked changes in work and family. One set of changes has occurred in the labor market, which has become both more unequal and more uncertain, with cyclical unemployment gradually giving way to structural employment. In cyclical unemployment, workers are laid off or lose jobs when the economy sours but are able to return to work at a similar job in the same industry, and sometimes even with the same employer, when the economy improves. Today, however, job loss is more likely to be persistent. Workers are less often able to return to a similar job in a similar industry, so unemployment frequently ends only when workers accept a new job that requires major cuts in pay, hours, or both.

This trend shows up in a number of places. Although the unemployment rate has remained historically low in recent years, the rate of involuntary job loss (defined as "worker terminations as a result of business decisions unrelated to the performance of the particular employee") has actually been rising.[14] In the 2001 recession, the rate of involuntary job loss rivaled the levels reached in the early 1980s, during the deepest recession since the Great Depression.[15] The last two recessions, of 1990–91 and 2001, also featured historically high levels of unemployment lasting six or more months. Traditionally, long-term unemployment has peaked six to eight months after a recession ends. In the recession of the early 1990s, however, long-term unemployment peaked nineteen months into the recovery. After the 2001 recession, long-term unemployment peaked twenty-nine months in.[16]

The consequences of job loss are also more severe than they once were. More than a third of workers involuntarily displaced between 2001 and 2004 (notably a period of economic recovery) failed to find employment, and 13 percent found only part-time work. Even full-time workers who found full-time jobs—the best-case scenario, as it were—ended up earning around 17 percent less than they would have had they not been displaced, a bigger loss than recorded during the early 1980s.[17]

A major reason for the discrepancy between the unemployment and job-loss figures is that many of those displaced from the labor market are not "actively seeking work" and hence are not formally unemployed. Yet there is good evidence that many of these potential workers would be in the labor force were the opportunities for them greater. In 2005, according to Katharine Bradbury of the Federal Reserve Bank of Boston, the total labor force "shortfall"—compared with similar points in the business cycle in the past—was as high as 5.1 million men and women.[18] This amount would raise the official unemployment rate to 8.7 percent, a level not seen since the steep recession of the early 1980s.

The second major shift that appears responsible for increasing family economic volatility is the transformation of the family—most notably the dramatic movement of women into the workforce.[19] This may come as a surprise. Much of what economists write about the family assumes that increasing workforce participation by women serves as a form of private risk sharing, in that it allows families to better deal with shocks to income.

Although two-earner families do enjoy special advantages when it comes to private risk sharing, they can scarcely eliminate economic risk—and in some important ways, two-earner families face special risks of their own. This is partly because the world has not stood still as women have entered the workforce. In the idealized view of two-earner families, couples "diversify" risk by deciding to jointly enter the workforce and then purchase private substitutes for the previously unpaid labor provided by stay-at-home moms. In reality, the choices of two-earner families have not been as unconstrained as this idealized picture suggests. To most families today, a second income is not a luxury but a necessity in an era in which wages have been relatively flat and the cost of basic expenses has been rapidly rising.[20] In time-use surveys, both men and women who work long hours indicate they would like to work fewer hours and spend more time with their families—which strongly suggests they are not able to choose the exact mix of work and family they would prefer.[21]

Moreover, although two-earner families are less likely to experience a catastrophic drop in income, they are more likely to experience smaller fluctuations in income. After all, if every worker has an equal chance of experiencing a drop in income, a family with two workers has a substantially greater chance of experiencing an income shock. To be sure, the drop in family income is smaller than it would be if the worker experiencing it were the sole breadwinner. But it is still a more likely occurrence. A person may never lose all of his or her eggs when they are in more than one basket, but the likelihood of losing at least some of them is greater.

In addition, two-earner couples are often parents as well as workers, making the tradeoffs even starker. If both parents work, who stays home when a child gets sick? If both parents work, what happens to family finances when one leaves the workforce to raise a new baby or care for young children or elderly parents? In short, when both parents work, events within the family that require the love and care of family members produce special demands and strains that traditional one-earner families did not generally face.

Finally, women's movement into the workforce has changed not just the character of parenting but also the economic relationship between spouses, encouraging greater equality within the household and increasing the ability of women to support themselves and children outside of marriage (despite the endurance of a substantial gender gap in earnings). Across the Western world, divorce has become more common precisely when and where women's participation in the labor force has expanded.[22] This is not to suggest that law and culture are immaterial, only that the increased instability of American families has important roots in the expansion of female economic autonomy.

One sign of these changes can be gleaned from the characteristics of people in poverty. Although poverty rates dipped in the strong economy of the late 1990s, they rose over the 1970s and 1980s and are rising again. No less striking than the overall rise is the change in the characteristics of those affected: poverty among the elderly fell sharply in the 1970s and has remained relatively low since, while a sizable and increasing portion of the poverty population is made up of parents with young children.

A similar but in many ways more nuanced portrait is provided by the number and characteristics of Americans filing for bankruptcy. As is well known, personal bankruptcy has risen sharply, with filings increasing more than fivefold between 1980 and 2002, to more than 1.5 million. (In 2005 the total topped 2 million, though many of these filings represented the rush to file before the new bankruptcy law passed by the Republican Congress and signed by President Bush in early 2005 tightened the rules for filing.) Meanwhile, the mortgage foreclosure rate has increased fivefold since the early 1970s, and levels of personal debt have risen to record levels.[23]

It is less well known that the characteristics of bankruptcy filers have also changed dramatically. Women, for example, have emerged as the largest single group of filers, their share of filings rising eightfold between 1981 and 2001. Although unmarried women with children are the most likely household type to file, married couples with children are not far behind, with filing rates more than twice that of men and women without children (married or not). Revealingly, half of filers cite health problems, childbirth, a death in the family, or substantial medical bills as a prime reason for filing.[24] By comparison, a 1970s study found just 11 percent of filers citing one or more of these reasons in 1964.[25]

The rise in economic inequality and the changing character of the poor and bankrupt are each strongly suggestive of the changing composition of social risks that citizens face. Perhaps the most telling evidence of increased economic insecurity is the growing *volatility* of family incomes. Along with Nigar Nargis of the University of Dhaka, I have examined the variability of family incomes using the Panel Study of Income Dynamics (PSID), a data set managed by the University of Michigan that has been tracking a nationally representative group of households since the late 1960s. The PSID data are valuable because most government statistics—such as the unemployment rate, the poverty level, and the distribution of annual income—are "snapshots" of what people are experiencing at a given time rather than "moving pictures" of what happens to people over a period of several years. Because the PSID tracks families over time, it provides a true dynamic record of the up-and-down trajectory of Americans on the economic ladder over the course of their lives.

What this picture shows is that families are not merely pulling apart economically—as the well-documented rise in inequality shows. They are also experiencing greater income instability *over time*. Since the early 1970s, as figure 5-1 shows, family incomes in the United States have become much more volatile. Volatility is higher for women than for men, higher for blacks and Hispanics than for whites, and higher for less educated Americans than for more educated Americans. Furthermore, volatility has risen across all these groups and almost as quickly among the educated as among the less educated. It has also risen faster than economic inequality over the past generation.

Figure 5-1. *Increasing Instability of American Family Incomes, 1974–2002*[a]

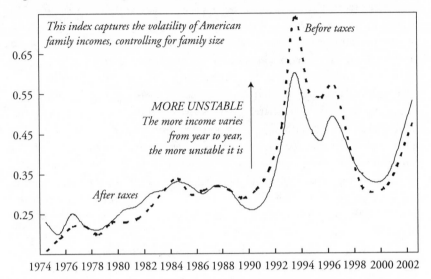

Source: Panel Study of Income Dynamics, University of Michigan; Cross-National Equivalent File, Cornell University.

a. In all the analyses, family income includes taxable income received by the head of the household, the wife, or the spouse of the head, and other members of the family unit; cash public benefits received by family members; and private transfers, such as alimony. Family income is adjusted for changes in family size by dividing by the square root of family size—a common equivalence scale. This allows family-level income to be converted to individual-level income for the purposes of variance estimation. All the income variables are adjusted to account for inflation. In all the analyses, families with zero or negative income are dropped. All the analyses are also restricted to families whose heads were aged twenty-five to sixty-one in the year under study.

Drops in family income provide an even better sense of the serious economic risks that rising volatility represents. About half of all families in the PSID experience a drop in real income over a two-year period, and the number remains fairly steady. Yet the median drop—larger than half of drops and smaller than half—has risen from a low of around 25 percent in the 1970s to around 40 percent. A more precise multivariate regression shows the probability of at least a 50 percent drop in family income for individuals with average characteristics. As figure 5-2 shows, this predicted probability was 7 percent at the beginning of the 1970s. By the early 2000s, it had more than doubled, to around 17 percent.

To be sure, greater instability could reflect increased social mobility, or it could represent a largely benign side effect of rapid increases in family

Figure 5-2. *Predicted Chance of a 50 Percent or Greater Income Drop for Average Americans, 1970–2002*[a]

Chance for average person

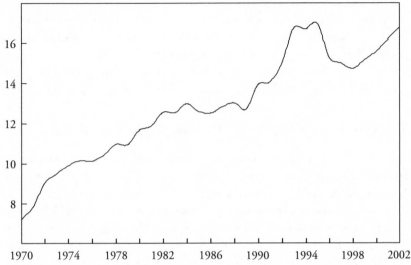

Source: Panel Study of Income Dynamics, University of Michigan; Cross-National Equivalent File, Cornell University.

a. Probabilities are based on the time trend from a logistic regression, with all other variables set at their annual means. Variables include age, education, race, gender, income (mean of five prior years), and a series of events (such as unemployment and illness) that affect income. The time trend is highly significant and robust to the inclusion of fixed effects; all standard errors are robust and adjusted for clustering.

incomes. Unfortunately, neither of these sunny interpretations of rising income volatility is warranted. The extent of social mobility in American society remains a subject of heated dispute, but analysts generally agree that social mobility is no higher today than it was a generation ago, and perhaps lower. Nor does it appear higher in the United States than it does in other advanced industrial nations. Quite the opposite: among nations for which good comparative evidence exists, only South Africa and Britain have experienced a little upward mobility across generations.[26]

On the other hand, family incomes *have* certainly increased since the late 1970s—particularly at the top of the economic ladder. Yet in the middle of the economic ladder, the average rise has been surprisingly modest: median family incomes increased by about 15 percent between 1979 and 2000. Furthermore, about three-quarters of the rise in median family income can be accounted for by the increasing work hours of women. Median families are richer.[27] But they are richer not mainly because workers are earning more but because they are working more hours than they used to.

In short, the high levels of economic instability seen today are not the result of massively improved social mobility or runaway prosperity for the middle class. Instead, they appear to result from the complex interaction of rising job instability and the transformation of the American family, which have together increased the risks to income faced by most Americans.

Public Inaction—and Private Retreat—in the Face of Rising Risk

What can be said with certainty is that existing public and private policies are not adequately protecting families against economic instability in a new era of work and family. One revealing piece of evidence is provided by the PSID data just discussed: whereas family income drops were substantially cushioned by government taxes and transfers in the 1970s, that is far less so today. To be sure, this may partly reflect the growing role of in-kind benefits, which are not included in the PSID. But it seems clear that, at least when it comes to income protection, the government is not doing as much as it once did to help families that experience economic shocks.

In principle, U.S. social policy could have adapted to changing realities. In recent decades, some nations have increased their provision of services that help families balance work and child rearing. Many of these same nations have also tackled the new realities of the labor market with active employment and training polices. Putting aside some exceptions, however, the United States has clearly not followed this path. Increases in the Earned Income Tax Credit for low-wage workers, shifts of money from cash assistance to child care and job retraining, and new family leave legislation were all steps toward a response. But low-wage workers continued to receive only meager public supports. Family leave rules did not apply to small employers and did not provide income support to leave-takers. Government assistance for child care remained scant and frequently unavailable, even for eligible families. Despite newly intense job insecurity, unemployment insurance contracted. And while failing to uphold the direst predictions, the welfare reform legislation of 1996 removed important elements of the safety net for the most disadvantaged. Perhaps most striking was a massive decline in employment-based health and pension protections among lower-wage workers—which was only weakly offset by public coverage expansions.

A partial glimpse into these trends is provided by the cross-national measures of redistribution provided by the Luxembourg Income Study (LIS).[28] The LIS statistics show that inequality before taxes and transfers rose sharply during the 1980s and 1990s in the United States, which has the highest levels of inequality among nations in the LIS. Yet compared with other nations, the United States appears to have done much less to offset the rise in inequality that many nations experienced during this period. Averaging across the thirteen other nations for which LIS data exist, for example, the reduction in inequality created by taxes and transfers increased 4.5 percent over the 1980s and 1990s. In the United States, by contrast, taxes and transfers reduced inequality 4.4 percent less by the end of the series (2000) than at the outset (1986).

This is an incomplete measure, of course. But its message is confirmed by the review presented in the next two sections, which takes a closer look at recent developments in the two largest areas of U.S. social policy: health insurance and pensions. These policy areas not only account for the majority of social spending in the United States (and, indeed, in all affluent democracies). By virtue of their size and unambiguous popularity, they are also widely seen as the most resilient components of the postwar welfare order. Yet in both these bedrock areas, relative stability in public programs has masked major declines in the ability of social policies to provide inclusive risk protection. Social risks have shifted from collective intermediaries—government, employers—onto individuals and families. Efforts to address new and newly intensified risks have failed. New policies sharply at odds with established ones have been created and expanded. Although the paths of health and pension policy differ in revealing ways, their overarching trajectories appear to be moving in the same direction: toward a significant privatization of risk.

The Unraveling of American Health Insurance

By the 1970s, the basic structure of American health insurance was firmly in place. For most Americans—more than 80 percent by the mid-1970s—private health insurance provided the first line of protection against the risks of medical costs. Employment-based health protection was (and is) heavily subsidized through the tax code, which treats virtually all workplace health benefits as exempt from taxation as compensation. (The revenue loss created by this tax break was roughly $188.5 billion in 2004.)[29] From 1965 on, the federal Medicare program provided public coverage for the elderly—and, later, the nonworking disabled—and the joint federal-state Medicaid program covered poor people on public assistance, the working disabled, and the indigent aged.

Since the 1970s, the private foundation of this system has undergone a radical contraction—in what amounts to a textbook case of drift within the bounds of stable formal policies. From a peak of more than 80 percent of Americans, private insurance coverage fell during the 1980s and early 1990s to less than 70 percent. Employment-based protection was the biggest casualty: Between 1979 and 1998, the share of workers who received health insurance coverage from their own employers fell from 66 percent to 54 percent.[30] At the same time, employers have grown less willing to cover workers' dependents, and they have required workers to pay a larger share of the cost of coverage, which has discouraged some from taking coverage even when it is offered. The result has been a marked rise in the number of Americans without health insurance.

The gravest effects have been felt by those most disadvantaged by the economic trends of the past three decades. The share of workers in the lowest 20 percent of the wage spectrum receiving health insurance from their employers, for example, fell from almost 42 percent to just over 26 percent between 1979 and 1998.[31] These trends reflect multiple factors, including declining unionization and changing employment patterns. But above all, they mirror the simple reality that medical costs have risen much faster than median wages, outstripping the ability of workers and their employers to finance protection. With employers free to drop coverage, and workers under financial pressure to decline it even when it is offered, the risk of medical costs is being shifted from insurers and employers onto workers and their families.

This view is reinforced by one of the most fundamental transformations in American health insurance since the 1970s: the rise of "self-insurance" among employers. As already discussed, corporate self-insurance—the paying of medical claims directly—was encouraged by the 1974 Employee Retirement Income Security Act (ERISA), in that its so-called preemption clause protects self-insured health plans from most state insurance regulations and lawsuits in state courts.[32] But an additional crucial underlying motive for self-insurance has been the desire of larger employers to limit the cross-subsidization of the medical expenses of workers outside their own employment pool. Self-insurance has thus seriously worsened the situation of smaller employers, whose employment groups are too small to self-insure safely, while encouraging private insurers to weed out subscribers with high expected costs. The chronically ill, near-elderly, and those with expensive conditions have all faced increasingly serious barriers to obtaining insurance as a result.

Meanwhile, employers (and in some cases unions, which jointly manage many self-insured plans) have worked with conservative politicians to beat back any attempt to revisit the provisions of ERISA that exempt self-insured health plans from regulation. The ERISA Industry Committee, an organization of large employers created in 1976, has been perhaps the most vociferous champion of the preemption clause, supporting "legislation that preserves and strengthens ERISA preemption and reduces government interference with employers' efforts to provide cutting-edge, comprehensive health care benefits to their employees."[33] As a consequence, government regulation of private health plans has changed relatively little since the mid-1970s, despite a massive swing away from inclusive risk protection in the private sector.

Although Americans' prime source of health protection is eroding, public programs have by and large failed to fill the gap. Medicare—a centerpiece of U.S. social insurance—has essentially been caught in a holding pattern. Its popularity and the veto-ridden American political structure have prevented radical retrenchment, but it has grown increasingly inadequate as costs have rapidly outstripped the program's constrained spending. In a striking demonstration of the program's drift, Medicare beneficiaries pay more for medical care today than they did at Medicare's passage. At the same time, employment-based coverage for retirees and supplemental private benefits have been in a tailspin, as insurers and employers find that they cannot bear the risks Medicare does not cover. These risks are thus shifting by default to beneficiaries and their families.

Medicare has not been static, of course, and in 2003 prescription drug coverage was added to the program. The Medicare drug plan will reduce the total out-of-pocket spending of Medicare beneficiaries, but the effects are likely to be quickly swamped by rising drug costs, in part because the plan features substantial gaps and in part because it relies on private health plans that will have limited market reach (and indeed explicitly forswears using Medicare's concentrated purchasing power to hold down costs).

Medicare contracting with private health plans may eventually represent a threat to Medicare's broad risk pooling. Since contracting's origins during the Reagan administration, conservatives have aggressively pushed to transform it into a full-fledged system of competing, risk-bearing private plans, which they hope will undermine the unified constituency that has blocked direct benefit cuts in the past. Although studiously careful not to challenge Medicare head-on, the strongest advocates of a competitive system clearly believe that the traditional program should, as Republican House Speaker

Newt Gingrich infamously put it in 1995, "wither on the vine." (Gingrich was, in fact, unusually candid about Medicare reformers' covert strategy, noting that "we don't get rid of [Medicare] in Round One because we don't think it's politically smart.")[34]

Another potential threat to broad risk pooling in American health insurance—and a classic example of the "layering" of new benefits onto existing options—is the move toward so-called health savings accounts (HSAs, also known as medical savings accounts). A darling of conservative policy advocates since the early 1990s, HSAs are high-deductible "catastrophic" insurance policies that are coupled with tax-favored savings accounts in which patients save for routine medical expenses. In his 2005 State of the Union Address, President Bush called for a major expansion of federal tax breaks for such accounts, calling for substantial spending on top of the $16 billion over ten years that was devoted to expanding enrollment in HSAs for the non-elderly in the 2003 Medicare prescription drug legislation. While enrollment has historically been low, it rose from roughly 1 million to about 3 million between March 2005 and January 2006, and some projections suggest it will reach 15 million by 2010, or a tenth of the insured. A 2005 survey of employers found that 40 percent of large employers not currently offering an HSA are "somewhat" or "very" likely to offer one in the next year.[35]

HSAs are a threat to broad risk pooling because they are likely to be most attractive to healthier and wealthier individuals. Both existing research and surveys of employers suggest that HSAs will disproportionately attract healthy, higher-income workers who are already insured in the private, employment-based insurance market (most of the uninsured, in contrast, are unlikely to receive any tax benefits for establishing an HSA). The movement of such workers into HSAs would undermine employment-based plans, leaving them with a less healthy mix of workers. HSAs are thus another vehicle for privatizing risk without directly confronting existing benefit programs

At the same time, coverage of the poor has unquestionably grown: first, with federally mandated extensions of Medicaid in the 1980s; and second, with the creation of the state-federal Childrens' Health Insurance Program (CHIP) in 1997. These were important expansions, all the more remarkable because they occurred in such a hostile climate. Before ending the story, however, I should emphasize three points. First, the expansion of Medicaid has only partly offset the decline in private coverage. Second, the trend toward expanding coverage appears to have run its course: even before the 2001 economic downturn, enrollment in Medicaid had slowed dramatically. And third, the 1996 welfare reform bill has created a massive exodus from the welfare rolls, with those who leave moving into the low-wage employment sector, where private coverage is rare. Millions eligible for CHIP and Medicaid are not enrolled, and this is likely to become truer as time limits on welfare kick in. Overall, the share of children who are uninsured has remained remarkably constant in the face of public coverage increases.[36] In sum, Medicaid and CHIP appear more like band-aids on a festering wound than an inexorable expansion of public protection.

In strategic terms, critics of Medicaid have been greatly aided by the joint federal-state structure of the program, which has facilitated cutbacks by fostering interstate competitive pressures in favor of budgetary stringency while making cutbacks more difficult to identify and assign responsibility for. Since 2000, the Bush administration has aggressively used federal waivers to encourage state-based program restructuring and to shift from the current guaranteed matching formula to so-called block grants, in which the states are provided a fixed amount of funds. Like Medicare reform, Medicaid block grants last became a major issue in the mid-1990s. Then, as now, advocates of block grants espoused "an ideological commitment to shrink the welfare state and return power to states from Washington."[37]

No discussion of the recent evolution of U.S. health insurance is complete without mention of the stunning defeat of the Clinton health plan—arguably the most dissected legislative failure in modern history. Rather than rehash the saga, I wish simply to emphasize that its defeat represents perhaps the best evidence of politically mediated policy drift. The Clinton health plan and its major competitors reflected a belief that the American policy of relying on voluntary employer provision of health benefits was increasingly unworkable as a secure foundation for risk pooling. The opposition to the plan, centered among hard-core political conservatives, employers, insurers, and private medical interests, in turn reflected not simply the recognition that many of these groups would be immediately hurt by the plan but also the awareness that its passage would create a new and valued entitlement for anxious middle-class and working-class voters whose long-term political allegiances were very much up for grabs. Thus conservative activist William Kristol warned that the Clinton plan would "relegitimize middle-class dependence for 'security' on government spending and regulation" and "revive the reputation of . . . the Democrats . . . as the generous protector of middle-class interests."[38] On the other side, Clinton explicitly cast his crusade as an effort to undo the policy drift of the past two decades—drift that had created, in the words of the White House's *Health Security* report, "growing insecurity." "From the 1940s through the 1970s," the report explained, "the

United States made steady progress toward broader health care coverage. . . . Beginning in the 1980's, however, the number of Americans lacking health insurance has increased steadily—while health care costs have increased at ever-rising rates."[39]

In the end, the Clinton plan was brought down by much the same dynamic that stymied conservatives' efforts to dismantle public programs: the easily ignited fears of Americans that reform would compromise the social protections on which they relied—in this case, private insurance. But what is crucial is that U.S. leaders debated whether social policy would adapt to the changing job market and declines in private protection. Although the privatization of risk in American health insurance occurred without major policy reforms, it was very much a matter of political struggle.

In sum, when one considers the broader framework of U.S. risk protection in health care, the direction of change is clearly toward a marked narrowing of the bounds of collective protection, driven principally by the politically mediated drift of policies away from their original scope and purpose. To be sure, major public programs have been preserved. The demise of conservative efforts to scale back Medicare and Medicaid in 1995 is a powerful illustration of the hurdles thrown up by American political institutions and the enduring popularity of established programs. But resilience in the overall framework of American health insurance has not prevented a major shift in the distribution and intensity of the risks faced by citizens. The Medicare program has stagnated in the face of rapidly rising costs. The Medicaid program has expanded, but not nearly enough to offset the implosion of private coverage. There has been a massive decline in private health protection, which has increasingly ceased to be available or affordable for lower-wage workers. Serious efforts to deal with this have been effectively blocked by a formidable constellation of ideologically committed opponents and vested interests, which have pushed for individualized private accounts instead. The outcome has been a significant privatization of risk.

Individualizing Retirement Security

The American approach to retirement security is also a public-private hybrid, blending public social insurance and employment-based benefits—and, increasingly, tax-favored savings accounts. But pension policy differs crucially from health policy in the respective roles of public and private benefits. Whereas Medicare and Medicaid emerged after the large-scale development of private health insurance, private retirement pensions were by and large built on top of the public foundation of Social Security.[40] This supplementary role was embodied most concretely in the practice of "integration," in which employers that qualified for tax breaks for their private retirement plans were allowed to reduce pension benefits sharply for lower- and middle-income workers to reflect expected Social Security benefits. It was also embodied in the 1974 ERISA statute, which regulated private plans to ensure that they would be secure counterparts to the public foundation established by Social Security.

This vision of the division of labor between public and private still has relevance, but it is much less accurate or widely shared than in the past. First, since the 1970s, Social Security has been under serious financial pressure. Slower wage growth and increases in the ratio of retirees to workers precipitated the passage of two major legislative overhauls, in 1977 and 1983. While preserving the program, albeit at reduced levels, these reforms have effectively ended its expansion.

Second, employers have rapidly shifted away from the traditional "defined-benefit" plans that were the subject of ERISA. Instead, they have adopted so-called defined-contribution plans that are not tied to Social Security and, unlike defined-benefit plans, place most of the risk of investment onto workers themselves. Although this momentous transformation is mostly a case of conversion, in which employers have restructured their plans within relatively stable federal guidelines, it is important to note that defined-contribution plans were enabled and greatly encouraged by new and expanded federal tax subsidies layered onto the existing retirement system during periods of conservative ascendance. As in the health insurance field, there has also been a major decline in employer support for retirement benefits and, in tandem, a major privatization of risk.

As employers have moved away from defined benefits and decreased their commitment to pensions since the 1970s, their pension contributions have significantly decreased as a share of pay. Like the decline in private health insurance, the fall in pension contributions is symptomatic of the broader reversals in the economic outlook of less-educated workers. Between the early 1980s and the mid-1990s, the value of pension benefits to current workers dropped in every income group, but by far most rapidly among the lowest-paid workers, who already had the lowest coverage levels. In addition, tax breaks for private pensions and other retirement savings options heavily favor better-paid employees: two-thirds of the more than $120 billion in federal income tax breaks for subsidized retirement savings options accrue to the top 20 percent of the population.[41]

Although the post-1970s economic transformation was the underlying spur for these changes, its impact has been deeply mediated by politics. The 1980s signaled the beginning of an ongoing tug-of-war between two increasingly homogenized and polarized parties, with Republicans seeking to create and liberalize individual retirement options and Democrats fighting to place new restrictions on existing pension tax subsidies and to limit the top-heavy skew of individual accounts. The overall thrust of policy has nonetheless been in the more conservative direction—toward the expansion of tax-favored plans and toward the loosening of restrictions both on eligibility for them and on the purposes for which they can be used.

The path of individual retirement accounts (IRAs) illustrates the overall pattern. Included in ERISA as a retirement savings device available only to workers without private coverage, IRAs were expanded and made available to all workers in the early 1980s. In 1997 and 2001, they were liberalized again: permissible uses of the accounts were broadened to include education and housing expenses, and a new plan—called "Roth IRAs"—was created that would require account holders to pay taxes up front and then avoid all future taxes on their accounts (including estate taxes). Since, at the time, the vast majority of Americans already could establish traditional IRAs, the main effect of these changes has been to make tax-favored accounts more available and attractive to upper-income households.

The story of so-called 401(k) plans is different but similar. The 401(k) plan is a defined-contribution plan that operates under section 401(k) of the tax code—a provision added with little debate in 1978. In 1981 a private benefits expert pressed the IRS to rule that the provision extended to pensions in which workers put aside their own wages, much as in an IRA. The Internal Revenue Service under Ronald Reagan agreed, and corporate sponsorship of 401(k) plans exploded. In 2001, as part of that year's tax reduction plan, Republicans successfully pressed for liberalization of 401(k)s and IRAs, and for the creation of "Roth 401(k)s" similar to Roth IRAs.

Behind the explosive growth of 401(k) plans and IRAs over the past decade lies a new conception of pensions, for these retirement accounts have few of the characteristics of either Social Security or older defined-benefit plans. These accounts are voluntary for individual workers, participants have a significant degree of control over investment choices, and benefits are often paid as a lump sum upon employment separation or achievement of a specific age and, increasingly, can be accessed for purposes besides retirement. Because they are voluntary, many younger and poorer employees who are offered them choose not to participate or contribute little. And the risk of

poor investment decisions or bad financial luck falls entirely on participants—as became painfully clear in the wake of the recent stock market
downturn.

The strength of the stock market in the 1990s obviously helps explain the
enthusiasm for individualized investment accounts. But the shift must also
be seen as rooted in linked economic and political developments of the past
two decades. By the 1980s, defined-benefits pensions no longer offered the
attractions to employers that they had in the more stable employment climate of the 1950s and 1960s, with its strict managerial hierarchies and large,
unionized manufacturing firms. Nor, as Social Security's tax-to-benefit ratio
grew less favorable, did employers have a strong incentive to set up integrated
plans whose expense would be partly offset by the federal program.

No less important are the political motives that lie behind the expansion of
private accounts. For years, conservatives despaired of ever effectively challenging Social Security. Even at the height of Reagan's influence, the conservative push for reform was quickly crushed by the weight of past programmatic
choices. However, these past defeats fostered a new awareness on the part of
critics that Social Security could be fundamentally reformed only if there
existed a "parallel system" of private individual accounts that could eventually
be portrayed as a viable alternative to the public program. Conservatives
therefore retooled their strategy to encourage private retirement savings
through ever more flexible and individualized means, acclimating Americans
to private accounts and layering the institutional infrastructure for a full-
fledged private system on top of the core public program of Social Security.

The strategic assumptions behind this approach have been carefully analyzed by Steven Teles, who argues that "conservatives have slowly built up
counter-institutions, counter-experts, and counter-ideas . . . [in] an attempt
to solve the political problem of social security privatization." The core of
this strategy, Teles concludes, was to "carve out a competing policy path, one
that would slowly undermine support for Social Security and preserve the
idea of privatization for the day when it was politically ripe."[42]

Whether the day will ever be ripe remains a very open question. As President Bush's dismal experience in 2005 suggests, the reluctance of elected
politicians to consider plans for even partial privatization of Social Security is
overwhelming—all the more so in light of the federal budgetary turnaround.
The difficulty of reforming mature pay-as-you-go-pensions, which stems
from the massive expectations and accumulated fiscal commitments they
embody, stands out as the ultimate example of programmatic path dependence and policy feedback. Nonetheless, these barriers should not distract our

eyes from the significant change that has already occurred. With corporations and individuals shifting to more individualized plans, the explicit links between the public and private systems have steadily eroded, undermining some of the self-reinforcing mechanisms that previously secured Social Security's privileged position. And most American employers have lost their direct stake in the program's health, as their own plans have broken off from the public pension core around which they previously revolved. These transformations are perhaps most visible in the growing role of tax-favored retirement accounts linked to the stock market and in the changing balance of public and private pension benefits—a balance that tilted toward the private side of the scale for the first time in the 1980s. Whatever else these momentous shifts foretell, they clearly signal a major privatization of risk.

Economic Insecurity in an Age of Market Triumphalism

When Hurricane Katrina ripped through the Gulf Coast in September 2005, leaving death, grief, and wreckage in its wake, Americans were reminded that risk is an integral element of everyday life. For a moment, a sense of shared fate linked the nation, just as it had after the terrorist attacks of September 11, 2001. Money poured forth to charities. Volunteers inundated the area. Tears were shed over the plight of strangers. The issue was not one of personal responsibility; it was one of national responsibility.

When it comes to economic risk, Americans have, for almost a century, responded in the same way. The Great Depression of the 1930s—which left "a third of the nation," in FDR's famous telling, "ill-housed, ill-clothed, ill-nourished"—was widely seen as a natural disaster beyond the control or responsibility of the Americans it struck. In its wake, and especially after World War II, political and business leaders put in place new institutions designed to spread broadly the burden of key economic risks. These public and private institutions did not ignore personal responsibility. They required work, ongoing contributions, and proof of eligibility. But they were based on the ideal of "social insurance"—the notion that certain risks can only be effectively dealt with through inclusive institutions that spread costs across rich and poor, healthy and sick, able-bodied and disabled, young and old.

Today, however, this public-private framework is coming undone. As a new century begins, Americans are witnessing a major transfer of economic risk from broad structures of insurance onto the balance sheets of families. This transformation is reworking Americans' relationship to their government, their employers, and each other, with consequences for politics and society that promise to be profound.

The privatization of risk has implications not just for America's future, but also for the recent evolution of its social policy. As I have shown, public social programs have by and large resisted direct attacks in recent decades. Yet that does not mean they have continued to play the role they once did. Instead, critics of these programs have transformed them indirectly, through three primary means: "drift," the obstruction of efforts to recognize and respond to changing social risks; "conversion," shifting the ground-level operation of social programs in directions at odds with their initial goals; and "layering," the supplementation of existing programs with new policies that subvert or threaten older policies. The result has been a significant erosion of U.S. social protection, despite the absence of many instances of major policy reform. Since the American experience is widely considered to be the strongest evidence of welfare state resilience in the face of conservative opposition, this is a notable finding in itself. But it also sheds some light on welfare state restructuring in other nations, and on the character, cause, and consequence of policy reform more generally.

In extreme form, American developments provide a window into transformations taking place in many affluent democracies, as fiscally constrained welfare states confront new and newly intensified social risks. As the sociologist Gosta Esping-Andersen argues, the rise of such risks has strained the capacity of existing social welfare frameworks.[43] Yet, unlike Esping-Andersen and others who have examined the "new social risks," I have argued that this growing gap between risks and benefits is not simply a result of exogenous shocks to stable welfare states, but that it grows directly out of the politics of welfare state reform. By reframing debates, blocking new initiatives, and creating parallel policy paths that undermine existing programs, opponents of the welfare state have transformed U.S. social policy, even without achieving the large-scale reforms that retrenchment studies have searched for (and mostly found lacking). For all the reasons that retrenchment scholars have highlighted—the status quo bias of political institutions, public attachment to existing programs, the powerful constituencies that broad government action creates—the privatization of the welfare state has largely proved a nonstarter. The privatization of risk, however, has proved much more politically feasible, and it must be counted as a major victory for those who believe the welfare state is an outmoded and inefficient institution whose role should be reduced.

The ultimate irony is that in the new climate of economic and family risks, the case for a robust framework of risk protection is stronger than ever—and the case for thinking that this framework must have a central role for the government just as powerful. Today, America's public-private framework of risk protection is under strain, and most of that strain is coming from the erosion of private workplace benefits. It was once argued that the government was not needed to provide basic risk protection—that private insurers could take care of health care, that private employers would ensure that everyone had a good pension. No one can confidently hold that view today. The only question is whether the government should step in to assume the growing risks of America's flexible, dynamic economy, or whether Americans should be left to cope with these uncertainties largely on their own.

The argument for having the government pool these risks is powerful: enhanced social insurance could provide all Americans with the financial security they need to survive and thrive in a highly uncertain economy, encouraging workers to accept the downs as well as the ups of a largely unfettered free market. Without basic risk protections, workers and families may be tempted instead to support intrusive restraints on commerce and production, undermining the dynamic economy that the project of market reform was supposed to bring about. Moreover, social insurance programs like Medicare and Social Security feature low administrative costs and broad public acceptance and popularity. And because of the public sector's formidable bargaining power and unmatched standard-setting capacity, Medicare is also arguably better poised than private sector benefits to control health spending and encourage cost-effective medical utilization in the future.

But these arguments are hardly universally accepted. For those who believe that risk protection interferes with the free play of competitive forces, for those who believe that government insurance merely coddles people who make the wrong choices, the only solution is to shift even more risk onto Americans' shoulders. The great debate of the twenty-first century will be whether the privatization of risk should be halted or hurried. And the outcome may well determine not just the future of U.S. social policy, but that of the American model of capitalism as well.

Notes

1. Pew Research Center for the People and the Press, "Bush Failing in Social Security Push" (March 2, 2005) (http://people-press.org/reports/pdf/238.pdf).

2. Jacob S. Hacker, *The Divided Welfare State: The Battle over Public and Private Social Benefits in the United States* (Cambridge University Press, 2002).

3. U.S. Bureau of the Census, *Income, Poverty, and Health Insurance Coverage in the United States: 2004* (Government Printing Office, August 2005), p. 17 (www.census.gov/prod/2005pubs/p60-229.pdf).

4. Families USA, *One in Three: Non-elderly Americans without Health Insurance, 2000–2003* (Washington, 2004) (www.familiesusa.org/assets/pdfs/82million_uninsured_report6fdc.pdf).

5. David U. Himmelstein and others, "Illness and Injury as Contributors to Bankruptcy," *Health Affairs,* Web Exclusive (2005), pp. 65–73 (http://content.healthaffairs.org/cgi/reprint/hlthaff.w5.63v1.pdf).

6. Hacker, *The Divided Welfare State.*

7. Paul Pierson, "The New Politics of the Welfare State," *World Politics* 48, no. 2 (1996): 173. See also Paul Pierson, *Dismantling the Welfare State? Reagan, Thatcher, and the Politics of Retrenchment* (Cambridge University Press, 1994).

8. The studies employing this approach are too numerous to list but include Karen M. Anderson, "The Politics of Retrenchment in a Social Democratic Welfare State," *Comparative Political Studies* 34, no. 9 (2001: 1063–91; Giuliano Bonoli, Vic George, and Peter Taylor-Gooby, *European Welfare Futures* (Cambridge, U.K.: Polity Press, 2000); Gosta Esping-Andersen, *Social Foundations of Postindustrial Economies* (Oxford University Press, 1999); Evelyne Huber and John D. Stephens, *Development and Crisis of the Welfare State* (University of Chicago Press, 2001); and Duane Swank, "Political Institutions and Welfare-State Restructuring: The Impact of Institutions on Social Policy Change in Developed Democracies," in *The New Politics of the Welfare State,* edited by Paul Pierson (Oxford University Press, 2001). For a recent literature review, see Peter Starke, "The Politics of Welfare State Retrenchment: A Literature Review," *Social Policy & Administration* 40, no. 1 (2006): 104–20. Starke observes (p. 113) that in most studies "retrenchment is studied as a discrete policy change, traceable to intentional decisions by political actors."

9. The term is Michael Lipsky's; see his "Bureaucratic Disentitlement in Social Welfare Programs," *Social Service Review* 58 (March 1984): 3–27.

10. Hacker, *The Divided Welfare State;* Christopher Howard, *The Hidden Welfare State: Tax Expenditures and Social Policy in the United States* (Princeton University Press, 1997).

11. The details of these calculations are provided in Hacker, *The Divided Welfare State,* appendix; updated OECD data are available, in spreadsheet form, at www.oecd.org/dataoecd/56/21/35632949.xls.

12. U.S. Office of Management and Budget, *Budget of the United States Government, Fiscal Year 2006: Analytical Perspectives* (GPO, 2005), table 19-1 (www.whitehouse.gov/omb/budget/fy2006/pdf/spec.pdf).

13. For further elaboration of this theoretical framework, see Jacob S. Hacker, "Privatizing Risk without Privatizing the Welfare State," *American Political Science Review* 98, no. 2 (2004): 243–60. See also Kathleen Thelen, "How Institutions Evolve: Insights from Comparative Historical Analysis," in *Comparative Historical Analysis in the Social Sciences,* edited by James Mahoney and Dietrich Rueschemeyer (Cambridge University Press, 2003); Eric Schickler, *Disjointed Pluralism: Institutional Innovation in the U.S. Congress* (Princeton University Press, 2001).

14. Henry Farber, "What Do We Know about Job Loss in the United States?" (Federal Reserve Bank of Chicago, 2005), p. 13.

15. Ibid., p. 23.

16. Stacey Schreft and Aarti Singh, "A Closer Look at Jobless Recoveries" (Federal Reserve Bank of Kansas City, 2003), pp. 45–73.

17. Farber, "What Do We Know about Job Loss?" p. 23.

18. Katharine Bradbury, "Additional Slack in the Economy: The Poor Recovery in Labor Force Participation during This Business Cycle," Public Policy Briefs (Federal Reserve Bank of Boston, July 2005) (www.bos.frb.org/economic/ppb/2005/ppb052.pdf).

19. Elizabeth Warren and Amelia Warren Tyagi, *The Two-Income Trap: Why Middle-Class Mothers and Fathers Are Going Broke (With Surprising Solutions That Will Change Our Children's Futures)* (New York: Basic Books, 2003).

20. Ibid.

21. Jerry A. Jacobs and Kathleen Gerson, *The Time Divide: Work, Family, and Gender Inequality* (Harvard University Press, 2003).

22. Torben Iversen and Frances Rosenbluth, "The Political Economy of Gender: Explaining Cross-National Variation in the Gender Division of Labor and the Gender Voting Gap," *American Journal of Political Science* 50, no. 1 (January 2006).

23. Jacob S. Hacker, *The Great Risk Shift* (Oxford University Press, 2006), pp. 13–15.

24. Elizabeth Warren, "What Is a Women's Issue? Bankruptcy, Commercial Law, and Other Gender-Neutral Topics," *Harvard Women's Law Journal* 25 (spring, 2003).

25. Melissa B. Jacoby, Teresa A. Sullivan, and Elizabeth Warren, "Rethinking the Debates over Health Care Financing: Evidence from the Bankruptcy Courts," *New York University Law Review* 76, no. 2 (2001): 375–417.

26. "Ever Higher Society, Ever Harder to Ascend," *Economist,* December 29, 2004 (www.economist.com/world/na/displayStory.cfm?story_id=3518560).

27. Jared Bernstein and Karen Kornbluh, *Running Faster to Stay in Place: The Growth of Family Work Hours and Incomes* (Washington: New America Foundation, June 2005).

28. Timothy Smeeding, "Globalization, Inequality, and the Rich Countries of the G-20: Evidence from the Luxembourg Income Study (LIS)" (Syracuse University, Maxwell School of Citizenship and Public Affairs, 2001).

29. Jon Sheils and Randall Haught, "The Cost of Tax-Exempt Health Benefits in 2004," *Health Affairs* 106, no. 1 (2004): 106.

30. James L. Medoff and Michael Calabrese, *The Impact of Labor Market Trends on Health and Pension Benefit Coverage and Inequality* (Washington: Center for National Policy, 2001).

31. Ibid.

32. Marie Gottschalk, *The Shadow Welfare State: Labor, Business, and the Politics of Welfare in the United States* (Cornell University Press, 2000).

33. ERISA Industry Committee (ERIC), *Who We Are* (2003) (www.eric.org/public/who/overview.htm).

34. Adam Clymer, "Of Touching Third Rails and Tackling Medicare," *New York Times,* October 27, 1995, p. D21.

35. Jonathan Cohn, "Crash Course," *New Republic,* November 7, 2005, pp. 18–23; Cybele Weisser, "A Health Revolution in Slow-Mo," *Money,* July 2005, p. 28.

36. Janet Currie, *The Invisible Safety Net: Protecting the Nation's Poor Children and Families* (Princeton University Press, 2006), p. 45.

37. R. Kent Weaver, "Deficits and Devolution in the 104th Congress," *Publius* 26, no. 3 (1996): 45–86.

38. Theda Skocpol, *Boomerang: Clinton's Health Security Effort and the Turn against Government in U.S. Politics* (New York: W. W. Norton, 1996).

39. White House, Domestic Policy Council, *Health Security: The President's Report to the American People* (GPO, 1993).

40. Hacker, *Divided Welfare State.*

41. Peter Orszag and Jonathan Orszag, "Would Raising IRA Contribution Limits Bolster Retirement Security for Lower- and Middle-income Families or Is There a Better Way?" Center on Budget and Policy Priorities, May 2000 (www.cbpp.org/4-12-00tax.htm).

42. Steven M. Teles, "The Dialectics of Trust: Ideas, Finance, and Pension Privatization in the U.S. and U.K.," paper presented at the Annual Meeting of the Association for Public Policy Analysis and Management, New York, October 29–31, 1998, pp. 14–15.

43. Esping-Andersen, *Social Foundations of Postindustrial Economies.*

II

Market Design

6

The Success and Limits of Deregulation in Network Industries: Freight Railroad and Electricity

DARIUS GASKINS

Throughout history, network industries have been either heavily regulated or owned directly by the state, largely because of their inherent characteristics. First and foremost, most networks exhibit declining marginal costs throughout the scope of their operation. In other words, the cost of serving an additional customer or providing an additional unit of service costs less than the average cost of service. This simple fact leads both to an inherent instability when networks compete for customers and substantial pressure from customers for lower prices (that is, closer to marginal costs) either through secret concessions or regulatory fiat when the network is controlled by a monopolist.

Second, most networks frequently need some form of government assistance to establish themselves. In the case of railroads, both eminent domain and land grants aided the early development of most large rail systems. This dependence on government seems to inevitably lead to more regulatory oversight than in the case of less politically connected industries.[1]

In the United States, the predominant form of control has been regulation of privately owned networks. Recently, major attempts have been made to partly or fully "deregulate" the country's network industries. Airlines, railroads, natural gas pipelines, trucking companies, electric utilities, and communication companies have all experienced deregulation to some extent.

Figure 6-1. *Chronology of Railroad and Electric Utility Regulation*

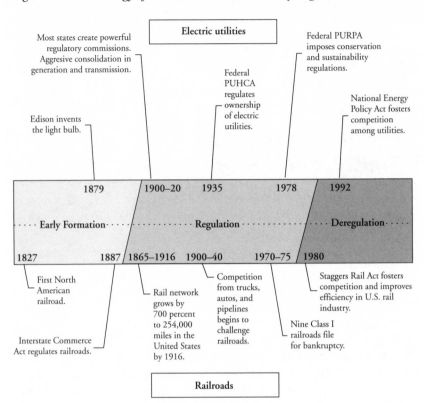

Freight railroads and electric utilities provide particularly interesting cases of deregulation for analysis, because the work is still in progress and there seems to be a residual core of regulation necessitated by politics and economics. Furthermore, the economics and history of regulatory policy of U.S. freight railroads and electric utilities are strikingly similar (figure 6-1).

Both industries were invented and rose to prominence in the nineteenth century. Both exhibit strong declining marginal costs, which means that if prices (rates) are driven toward marginal costs, the producers will fail to cover their full costs.[2] And both were deemed early on to be too powerful to operate without public oversight.

At the same time, the two industries differ in several important respects. First, freight railroads have declined in economic importance much more rapidly than electric utilities.[3] Trucking, barges, and airfreight have become effective competitors for much of the freight once handled by railroads. Second, the financial issues the two industries face are quite different. Railroads have been struggling with inadequate financial returns for the past fifty years, whereas electric utilities are financially robust. The problem for utilities is that the pattern of their investments has been harshly criticized by the public, which believes the utilities have wasted billions of dollars on nuclear power plants while underfunding transmission lines.

The Railroad Experience

Several aspects of U.S. railroads led to their economic regulation. First, declining marginal costs forced railroads into financially debilitating rate wars when they competed head to head. Second, being the dominant form of transportation, particularly in the West, they were deemed too powerful to be operating without regulatory checks. Third, railroads provided lower rates and rebates to large shippers, typically in "secret" deals that threatened smaller rail shippers. Thus railroads came under increasingly intensive regulation until they were taken over by the government during World War I.

After the war, operational control returned to the private sector, but strict regulation of rail rates had been established. The railroads then began a long, gradual economic decline as trucking competition increased all over the country. The regulatory apparatus expanded in response to this new competition, in part as a means of "protecting" railroads from new competition from trucks and airlines.

Regulation seemed to satisfy public policy objectives concerning railroads for more than fifty years. By the 1950s, however, the regulatory rationale and tools had become outmoded as the interstate highway system and the growth of trucking had eroded the railroads' market power for many shippers. Regulators limited the railroads' flexibility to respond to the changing environment in terms of setting rates, entry and exit of geography, capacity rationalization, and merger activity. The lack of competition stifled innovation and cost management. By 1970 the rail industry's return on equity was less than 3 percent, and the return on sales was only 4 percent.[4] Between 1970 and 1975, nine Class I railroads (the largest railroads) filed for bankruptcy.[5]

By 1980 the federal government had almost run out of options for saving the freight railroads. Several legislative attempts to liberalize rail regulation had not achieved their objective.[6] Direct operating subsidies to Conrail and the Rock Island railroad had not made either property economically viable.[7]

Lacking other palatable alternatives, Congress chose to deregulate the railroads to a large extent, in the form of the Staggers Act of 1980.

Why Did Railroad Regulation Occur When It Did?

After nearly a century of increasingly tight regulation, the nation's railroads were near collapse. The final gasp of the old political regime was epitomized by the appearance of Senator Warren Magnuson before the then Interstate Commerce Commission (ICC) in 1980, pleading for financial aid to save the Milwaukee Railroad. Congress was no longer willing to spend more money propping up failing railroads and had few alternatives other than to rely on the market to save some remnant of the freight railroads. These circumstances were the primary factors behind the design of the Staggers Act. The path chosen was supported by rail labor, railroad management, and shippers who were most dependent on railroad transportation. All parties were convinced that economic freedom would probably mean higher rail rates, and indeed, the Staggers Act allowed rates to rise to some extent.[8]

The Staggers Act allowed railroads to raise and lower rates freely and prohibited collective rate making via rate bureaus. It authorized and encouraged the use of confidential contracts between railroads and their customers. While it did provide some prospective rate protection for captive shippers (those bulk shippers served by a single railroad), it depended on competition to protect the interests of most rail shippers.

The ICC and its successor, the Surface Transportation Board (STB), played a vital role at this stage. They served as a safety valve by providing some limited intervention as political forces rose in protest to the railroads' rates, service problems, and proposed mergers. Like any good referee, they tried to be impartial in rate proceedings, which meant that neither the railroads nor the shippers were continually pleased by their decisions. A major intervention by the STB was its moratorium on rail mergers imposed in 2000, when the rail industry seemed on the verge of a final merger wave that would have produced two or three transcontinental rail systems.

The consequences of the Staggers Act have been truly amazing. Over the past twenty-five years, the railroads have been revitalized. They have dramatically improved their profitability and greatly rewarded their stockholders.[9] The most surprising part of this story is that the railroads have also lowered their rates, both in nominal and real terms. The industry's financial success resulted primarily from the railroads' aggressive cost reductions in the competitive environment created by the deregulation of both railroads and the

Figure 6-2. *Sustained Cost Reductions in the Rail Industry, 1975–2002*

1982 dollars per RTM

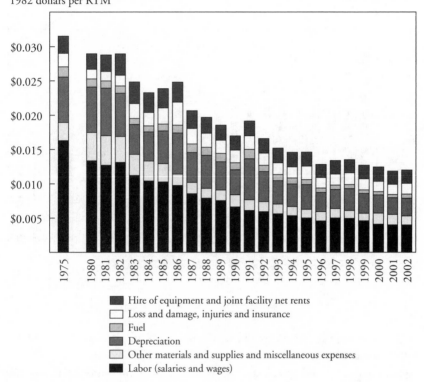

Hire of equipment and joint facility net rents
☐ Loss and damage, injuries and insurance
▨ Fuel
▨ Depreciation
☐ Other materials and supplies and miscellaneous expenses
▨ Labor (salaries and wages)

Sources: Association of American Railroads, *Analysis of Class I Railroads,* Washington, DC, 1981 (p. 13); Association of American Railroads, Railroad Ten Year Trends 1982–1991, Washington, DC (p. 72); Association of American Railroads, Railroad Ten Year Trends 1982–1991, Washington, DC (p. 72); Association of American Railroads, Railroad Ten Year Trends 1993–2002, Washington, DC (p. 68).

trucking industry. Since 1980, railroad costs in all cost categories—from labor, equipment, and fuel to loss and damage—have declined on a ton-mile basis (figure 6-2).

The cost reductions have been achieved through productivity gains and other efficiencies. Labor and fuel efficiency illustrate the productivity improvement. From 1982 to 2002, revenue ton-miles per employee-hour increased more than 320 percent. Gallons of fuel per revenue ton-mile dropped 41 percent during that same time period.

Figure 6-3. *Railroad Revenue per Revenue Ton-Mile, 1980–2001*

1982 dollars per RTM

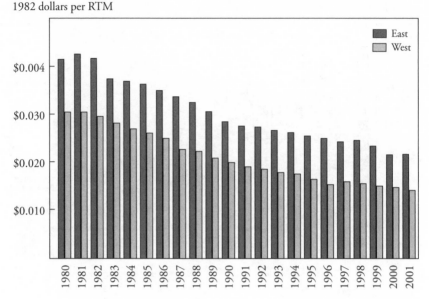

Source: Surface Transportation Board data.

Competition has also brought new service offerings to customers. Many of the innovations address the need for the railroads to compete with trucks. Intermodal shipping (trailers and containers moving on railroad flatcars) has become the fastest-growing segment of railroad traffic. Railroads have found their niche in this very competitive sector through lower-cost line-haul economics. Ironically, trucking companies—long-time competitors of railroads—have become major railroad customers. Railroads are also entering the arena of logistics services to increase their ability to compete with trucks. For example, railroads are developing logistics parks that integrate rail, truck, and transload services with warehousing capabilities to serve major markets.

Perhaps the greatest surprise of rail deregulation is that much of the cost savings has been passed on to customers. As figure 6-3 illustrates, rates have declined steadily since the Staggers Act was promulgated in 1980. The reductions have occurred across a range of commodities, from coal to chemicals. The steep reduction in coal rates (figure 6-4) is particularly noteworthy because only one or two carriers generally serve coal customers.

The competition between rail carriers hauling coal rose in 1984, when the ICC permitted a second railroad to serve the Powder River Basin (PRB), the

Figure 6-4. *U.S. Class I Railroad Coal Rates, 1982–2002*

1982 dollars per RTM

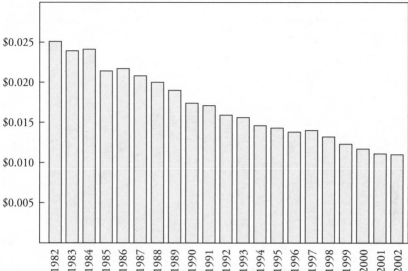

Source: Surface Transportation Board data.

largest coal-producing region in the world. Head-to-head competition not only lowered coal rates to existing customers but also drove PRB coal into eastern markets. A lesson of rail deregulation is that it only takes two carriers to generate competition.[10]

The overall result of railroad deregulation is that competition dramatically increased productivity and lowered the cost of transportation for customers. One hundred years of regulation had made the railroads inefficient. Deregulation let the market drive decisionmaking. The railroads responded to market-based competition by racing to reduce costs. The savings have allowed railroads to reinvest in their infrastructure and reduce rates charged to shippers. Twenty-five years later, the benefits are still flowing.

Limits to Railroad Deregulation

Railroad deregulation is neither complete nor universally beloved. High-volume shippers (predominantly coal-burning utilities) do have protections under the Staggers Act, in that they can apply to the STB for rate relief under the STB's Coal Rate Guidelines. This process has been successful for some

Figure 6-5. *U.S. Railroad Cost of Capital and Returns on Investment,*
1980–2003

Percent

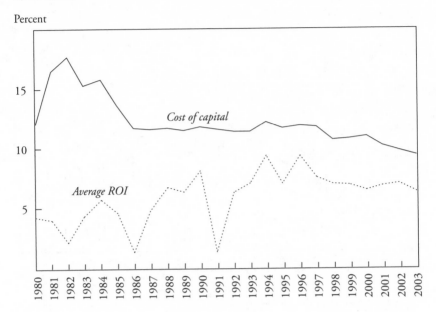

Source: American Association of Railroads and Surface Transportation Board data.

applicants; but it is quite expensive (a rate case costs several million dollars) and not available to shippers served directly by two or more railroads. The cost of these rate cases leaves small "captive" shippers (such as North Dakota grain shippers) with no obvious remedy to high rates.[11]

The provision of rate relief for shippers unable to afford a rate proceeding under the existing guidelines is complicated by the fact that no railroad has been able to earn the cost of capital on its whole system for any sustained period since the passage of the Staggers Act.[12] With the decline in cost structure, some rail rates must exceed marginal costs in order to achieve adequate revenues to cover full costs. The central question for railroads is how far can they go beyond marginal costs in their charges to a captive shipper? As figure 6-5 shows, the railroad industry has failed to earn its cost of capital since deregulation in spite of substantial financial progress.

The regulatory dilemma is therefore how to provide real relief to low-volume captive shippers without greatly reducing railroads' profitability. The existing regime has allowed railroad profitability to rise, but the northern-tier grain shippers remain very unhappy with the status quo.

Electricity "Deregulation"

Over the past decade almost half of the country's states have attempted to restructure their regulation of electricity markets. Although they have differed in detail, all these efforts have been motivated by concern about prior investment decisions by regulated utilities (such as nuclear generating facilities) and by a desire to reduce electricity rates. These restructuring efforts have all attempted to introduce competition into the generation sector of the industry.

For California, one of the first states to restructure its electric utility sector, the result was a debacle that bankrupted one of its utilities, cost the taxpayers $13 billion in electric subsidy payments, and surely contributed to the recall of its governor. Its experience is a cautionary tale for the future of electricity deregulation elsewhere. First, California forced its vertically integrated utilities to sell off all of their generating facilities. The state also required them to buy all of their power from the spot market by prohibiting the use of long-term power contracts. The restructuring straw that broke the camel's back was California's freeze of retail electricity rates, which meant that any shortfall between historic electricity rates and spot prices had to be borne first by the shareholders of the electricity utilities and ultimately by the taxpayers, after bankruptcy.

The immediate cause of the crisis was a dearth of hydropower related to several years of low snowfall and rapidly rising prices for natural gas, which fueled most of the power plants selling into the California market at the margin. California was now heavily dependent on both sources of power, especially since no new sources had been developed in the state for a decade. Hence California's economic growth and burgeoning population had to be served by power produced beyond its borders.

This crisis was probably exacerbated by deliberate price manipulation by certain electricity sellers, such as Enron.[13] The spot price in the newly restructured California market was set by the plant selling the most expensive power into the electricity grid. By shutting down large units during periods of peak demand, owners of multiple power sources could drive up the spot price. During the crisis, spot prices peaked at $450 to $500 per megawatt hour, compared with $50 per megawatt hour in the spring before the crisis.[14]

This crisis, the August 2003 blackout, and the demise of energy traders such as Enron have led policymakers to reconsider the concept of restructuring. In fact, six states—Arkansas, California, Montana, Nevada, New Mexico, and Oklahoma—have repealed, suspended, or delayed their proposed restructuring. At the same time, seventeen states have continued with their experiments in restructuring the wholesale market for electricity. Most of these states are in the Northeast and Midwest. The experiments so far lend credence to the notion that power generation should be separated from distribution, and that competition should be allowed between wholesale electricity suppliers in order to improve economic performance—through more efficient production and lower rates.

Another facet of electricity deregulation is the growing significance of regional transmission organizations (RTOs) stimulated by the Federal Energy Regulatory Commission (FERC). RTOs such as the Pennsylvania, New Jersey, and Maryland Interconnection (PJM) have become an integral part of the deregulation of wholesale electricity. An RTO provides access to the wholesale market for all the generating units on its grid. In the PJM system, actual authority to dispatch all generating assets is turned over to the RTO.

A particular form of restructuring in which wholesale power is procured through a competitive process has shown substantial promise. Competitive procurement seems to have led to lower rates in the three states that had adopted it by 2003. As figure 6-6 shows, restructured states with competitive procurement achieved greater rate reductions than states without competitive procurement. The benefits of this practice have been seen in residential, commercial, and industrial sectors.

One notable example of competitive procurement is the auction conducted for New Jersey electric customers, which establishes a "market" price for wholesale power. Structured to be as competitive as possible, the New Jersey descending clock auction is said to have produced lower rates than would have occurred under the prior regulatory system. A descending clock auction works in stages and relies upon *sellers* instead of buyers to bid on products. New Jersey's descending clock auction has achieved more savings for residential and commercial customers than programs in states with other procurement systems (see figure 6-7). The New Jersey model has the added benefits of being straightforward and transparent.

Yet another benefit is that the range of price volatility, a common feature of competitive markets, can be managed (see figure 6-8). A large, diverse RTO can help smooth wholesale prices over time and space, and a mix of

Figure 6-6. *Retail Electricity Changes in Restructured States, 1995–2003*[a]

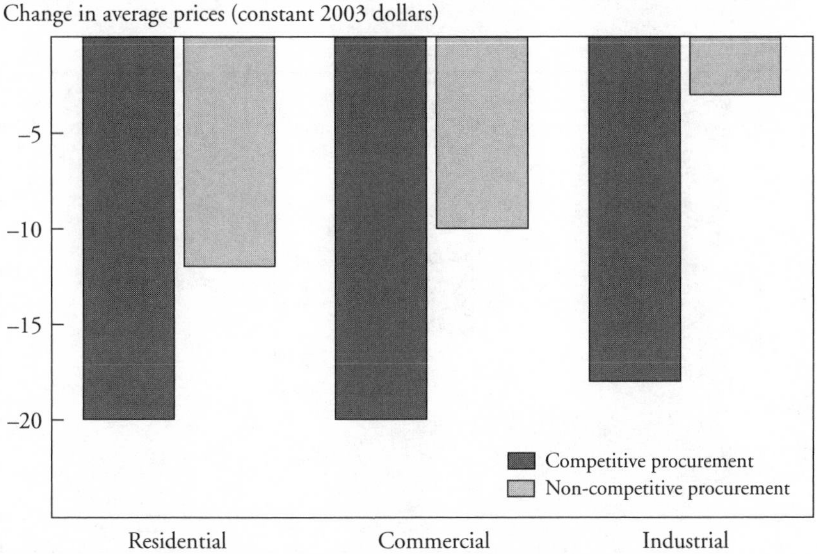

Change in average prices (constant 2003 dollars)

Source: Energy Information Administration.

a. A state's procurement is considered "competitive" if it met its standard offer demand with either an auction or a competitive RFP in 2003 and if its standard offer customers paid fully deregulated rates. Maine, New Jersey, and Rhode Island fit this definition in 2003. Average prices are demand weighted and are adjusted for inflation using the GDP (chained) price index.

contract lengths can dampen volatility. In addition, it is important to recognize the need for market intervention and to act accordingly—a lesson painfully learned in California.

Because the cost of wholesale electric power represents approximately two-thirds of the existing retail price of electricity, effective deregulation of the wholesale market promises major benefits. The impact on this market remains unclear, however, because deregulation is a complicated process and also has had to contend with the secular increase in natural gas prices in recent years (see figure 6-9). An objective evaluation of deregulation should adjust for changing fuel prices since power plants burning natural gas frequently provide the marginal electricity supply for most electricity markets. Rising gas prices therefore lead directly to higher retail electricity prices and consumer distress.

Figure 6-7. *Average Retail Electricity Changes in States with Competitive Procurement, 1995–2003*[a]

Change in average prices (constant 2003 dollars)

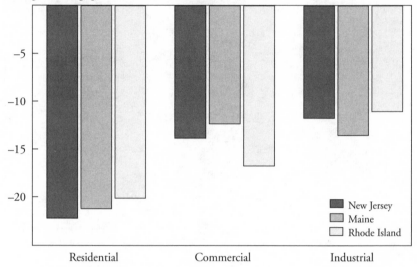

Residential   Commercial   Industrial

Source: Energy Information Administration.

a. A state's procurement is considered "competitive" if it met its standard offer demand with either an auction or a competitive RFP in 2003 and if its standard offer customers paid fully deregulated rates. Maine, New Jersey, and Rhode Island fit this definition in 2003. Average prices are demand weighted and are adjusted for inflation using the GDP (chained) price index.

Limits to Electricity Deregulation

There is substantial unfinished business in the restructuring of electricity regulation. Major decisions need to be made about who provides and controls transmission capacity. The FERC has proposed new rules partly in response to the general view that inadequate transmission capacity is limiting the effectiveness of the wholesale market.

A second and potentially more difficult dilemma is that there is no obvious way to eliminate regulation of the distribution of electricity. Unfortunately, residential customers are universally served by only a single distribution company. Direct competition for residential customers would entail a wasteful duplication of existing wires. As a result, residential electricity customers are akin to the railroads' "captive" shippers. But the central problem is that rate-of-return regulation seems to have inhibited productivity and innovation in electricity distribution.

Figure 6-8. *Price Volatility in California and in Pennsylvania, New Jersey, and Maryland Interconnection, 1998–2001*

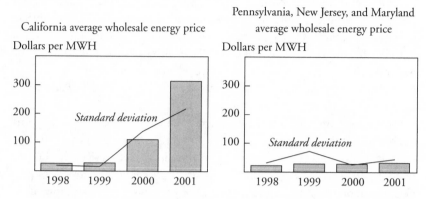

California average wholesale energy price
Dollars per MWH

Pennsylvania, New Jersey, and Maryland
average wholesale energy price
Dollars per MWH

Source: University of California Energy Institute and Pennsylvania, New Jersey, and Maryland Interconnection.

Figure 6-9. *Natural Gas Price Trends, January 1980–2005*[a]

Average wellhead price

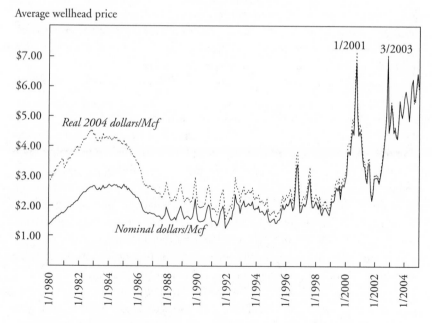

Source: Energy Information Administration.
a. Real values generated using the GDP (chained) price index.

States can and probably will continue to use competition in the wholesale market to improve the economic performance of the generation of electricity. The railroad experience strongly suggests that the economic performance of electric distribution could be improved as well under a more appropriate incentive structure. What states really need is a system of regulation that will put significant "competitive-like" pressure on costs while rewarding the development of new products and services. Politically more important, they need a regulatory system that will minimize retail price volatility and avoid dramatic short-term price increases.

As is clear from the railroad experience, competition can have an enormous effect on costs and productivity. In the long run, an even bigger benefit may accrue from the development of new products and services. In the case of electricity, this might include the use of the distribution network to provide broadband communications services or to facilitate the development of demand-side management of electricity. It is essential that the local distribution company be given appropriate incentives to pursue these and other future alternatives.

The Probable Future of Railroad and Electricity Deregulation

Regulatory reform in electricity and freight railroads addresses the perceived problems with basically the same remedy—more explicit competition. Indeed, competition seems to have been a powerful tool where it has been applied in both industries. However, the existence of "captive" customers served by a single network seems to preclude complete deregulation of both industries.

For the foreseeable future, the path of electricity deregulation may differ substantially from that taken by the rail industry, which employed competition to govern railroad markets with the aid of substantial and sustained rate reductions. The concerns of the naysayers and remaining captive shippers could never gain traction against declining rail rates.

In the case of electricity, the modest progress made in introducing competition in electricity generation may not spread beyond the existing restructured states. Current attempts to restructure the transmission of electricity are embroiled in debate, with the proponents of the status quo on one side and the promoters of the FERC's proposed new rules on the other. Moreover, no steps have yet been taken to implement any real reform in the regulation of electricity distribution. It will take a major success for competition in generation (that is, substantial and sustained lower rates) to drive restructuring to other states and into the distribution sector.

Notes

1. Some observers note that the land-grant system overstimulated the building of rail-roads in the United States. The Great Northern Railroad was the only railroad built in the West that did not avail itself of land grants, and it was the only western railroad to avoid bankruptcy throughout its history.

2. It is important to note that rates may be driven toward marginal cost either by onerous regulation or by fierce competition. Some observers think that competitive pressures gave impetus to the early regulation of railroads. See, for example, Gabriel Kolko, *Railroads and Regulation 1877–1916* (Princeton University Press, 1965), pp. 7–44.

3. They currently handle only 16 percent of all freight in the United States measured by tonnage. American Association of State Highway and Transportation Officials, *Freight—Rail Bottom Line Report* (Washington, 2003).

4. American Association of Railroads, *Railroad Facts* (Washington, 2004), pp. 12, 17, and 21.

5. American Association of Railroads, *Chronology of U.S. Railroading* (Washington, July 2006).

6. Specifically, the 3R and 4R acts were passed to speed up the regulatory process and to focus the Interstate Commerce Commission's attention on the financial health of the railroads.

7. By 1980 the government had spent $7 billion in direct subsidy to Conrail, the surviving remnant of the New York Central and Penn Central railroads. A last-gasp subsidy was granted in 1979, when the government spent $275 million to directly operate the bankrupt Rock Island railroad.

8. The major rate-controlling mechanism was the jurisdictional threshold specifying that rates below 180 percent of variable costs could not be challenged by shippers.

9. Railroad stocks have outperformed the Standard &Poor's 500 since 1980. See Jeremy Siegel, *The Future for Investors: Why the Tried and the True Triumph over the Bold and the New* (New York: Crown Business, 2005), p. 62.

10. This phenomenon is reminiscent of the notorious rail rate wars of the nineteenth century. Kolko, *Railroads and Regulation,* p. 19.

11. The political outcry from grain shippers from Montana and North Dakota is very prominent in any public hearing involving the STB.

12. This fact seems startling, given the increased profitability and good investment returns enjoyed by the railroads since 1980. As Jeremy Siegel points out, profitability more than expectactions is the driver of financial return for investors. The railroads confounded the financial community with the steady improvement in their profitability. Siegel, *The Future for Investors.*

13. Richard Pierce, "Market Manipulation and Market Flaws," *The Electricity Journal* 16, no. 1 (January): 39–46.

14. James Sweeney, *The California Electricity Crisis* (Stanford, Calif.: Hoover Institution Press, 2002), p. 110.

7

Regulatory Reform of the U.S. Wholesale Electricity Markets

Richard O'Neill and Udi Helman

In the mid-1990s, the United States began undertaking major regulatory reforms to promote competition in the electricity industry. The Federal Energy Regulatory Commission (FERC) fostered competition at the wholesale level by establishing an open-access regime for the transmission network, promoting the development of regional power markets, and allowing the partial liberalization of wholesale power sales.[1] These policies, in turn, provided the foundation for retail competition, which is under state regulatory control.[2]

Many of the states implementing retail competition encouraged or required substantial divestiture of generation assets by investor-owned utilities; some utilities also made such decisions voluntarily in anticipation of industry restructuring.[3] The recovery of some of the resulting "stranded costs"—investments in generation made with the guarantee of a regulated rate of return that were not financially viable under market competition—

The views presented in this chapter do not necessarily represent those of other staff or commissioners of the FERC, nor the commission itself. The authors would like to thank Rob Gramlich for suggesting that we write this chapter; David Mead, William Meroney, and the book editors for their comments; and the workshop participants for their feedback.

were typically factored into regulated utility retail rates for a period of several years going forward. Elsewhere in the country, the industry remained largely vertically integrated, but with increasing entry by nonutility generators (which include independent power producers and "merchant" suppliers).[4]

These reforms became controversial during the electricity shortages and spikes in wholesale power prices (and retail power rates in some areas) that affected California and other western states in 2000–01. They received further notoriety with the collapse of Enron, a firm thought by many until just weeks before its demise to be a leader in developing innovative energy market products and risk-management strategies. We argue that these events, while representing regulatory and market design (and business) failures whose lessons need to be learned, are not indicative of a broader failure of competitive reforms in this sector. The transformation of this industry has required specific market designs and regulatory safeguards tailored to the public policy goals of reliable customer service and economic efficiency. Indeed, the electricity markets that have emerged over the first decade of competitive reforms are highly rule-bound and explicitly regulated economically in certain ways (although now under market-based regulation rather than cost-based regulation). Although the market designs fell short in some cases, as in California, they have been put in place elsewhere to positive effect. But there has also been a price to pay—a growing complexity to the market rules that, at least in some regions, appears to be proving difficult to balance with market development. That part of the story is still unfolding.

Politics and Economics of Electricity Markets and Regulation

As pointed out in chapter 6, electricity is a "network" industry. The transmission network, or grid, connects the plants that generate electricity to consumers, or "load." The grid is subdivided into a higher-voltage network, which includes the facilities over which open access is required and wholesale power is traded, and the lower-voltage network, called the distribution network. Generation plants are classified by fuel source (for example, nuclear, coal, gas, hydro, wind) and by capacity (measured in megawatts). Large plants (usually nuclear or coal) run almost all the time and hence serve the "base" load; smaller plants run for a few hours a day or even more intermittently and hence serve the "peak" load. The reliable operation of an electricity system is technologically challenging, requiring, among other things, the instantaneous (that is, second-by-second) balancing of energy demand and supply. The coordination of transmission network flows and the balancing of demand and supply are undertaken by a centralized entity, known generically as a system operator. It is able to monitor all the inputs, outputs, and network flows and has sufficient control to enforce system constraints and take actions in the event of an emergency. Before the recent restructuring, the system operator was generally the local, vertically integrated utility, although in some parts of the country utilities had jointly given a fair degree of operational control to "power pools."

Following a period of sometimes intense competition among electricity companies in the latter decades of the nineteenth century, cost-based regulation of franchised monopolies dominated electric utility regulation for most of the twentieth century—owing in part to the high up-front costs and revenue requirements of building and maintaining large, long-lived generation and transmission facilities. During much of this period, state regulatory authorities played the leading role in setting rates for cost recovery. The federal role began in 1935, when, because of the growth in the interstate transmission grid, the Federal Power Act (FPA) gave federal regulators jurisdiction over transmission and wholesale power rates. (The Federal Power Administration, an independent government agency, administered the FPA and later became the FERC.) Although this federal role remained fairly marginal in electric utility regulation until the recent competitive reforms, the FPA established standards that continue to be influential in the design and regulatory oversight of new markets for electric power. In particular, the rates set by utilities under the FERC's jurisdiction must be judged "just and reasonable" before they are charged or be subject to refund.[5] Under this standard, cost-based rates must give utilities the opportunity to earn at least normal profits for prudent investments. In addition, the FERC must prevent "monopoly profits." In the market context, this same standard gives the FERC the authority to cap offers into the market and undertake other market design measures that affect product pricing, as discussed in the next section.

Revival of Competition

Over the decades of cost-based regulation, evidence accumulated that many electric utilities were not making efficient investment decisions and were also missing opportunities for short-term trading that could lower costs. Regulatory reforms to reintroduce competition in electric power began in the wake of the energy crises of the 1970s. The first federal attempt to promote competition in generation was the Public Utility Regulatory Policies Act of 1978 (PURPA). PURPA required utilities to buy power from "qualifying" independent power producers, which could be small renewable generators or co-generation plants (that jointly produce heat and power). This legislation led to an initial period of growth in independent generation capacity, but over the course of the 1980s and early 1990s, declining fossil fuel prices, reductions in renewable energy subsidies, and more stringent qualifying tests, among other factors, precipitated the decline of PURPA-driven investments, and this phase of market development subsided.

One factor limiting the development of robust power markets under PURPA was access to the transmission network. Before 1980 in most of the country, economies of scale and scope and the limitations of the technology for controlling power systems argued for weak connections between contiguous networks operated by large electric utilities. These weak connections created a physical barrier to potential competition. However, as system control technology improved and concerns over reliability and economics grew, so did transmission interconnection. Over the 1980s, the combination of PURPA reforms and efforts by industrial customers and municipal utilities to purchase cheaper power from regulated utilities in lower-priced areas, or simply to build their own plants in those areas, among other factors, greatly increased the demand for transmission service within and across the service territories of transmission-owning utilities. The rates for this service differed across utilities, and obtaining transmission service on acceptable terms could entail years of bargaining, legal action, and sometimes political effort.

The FERC tried to promote open access to transmission through the regulatory levers at its disposal. For example, it conditioned approval of several mergers in the 1980s and early 1990s on agreement by the merged firm to provide open access to its grid. For the most part, however, the electric utilities remained opposed to such measures.

Despite this opposition, by the early 1990s market developments and technology innovations prompted a renewed push by the U.S. Congress and the FERC to promote competition in generation and open access. Influential factors included massive cost overruns in the nuclear generation sector, cost overruns and inefficiencies in other generation business, overbuilt generation capacity in many markets owing to poor forecasts of demand, a recognition that some utilities were more efficient at building and operating generation, long-term PURPA contracts at above-market prices, a reduction in the scale economies of generation, a decline in the economies of reliability and coordination due to advances in computing and information technology, and the commission's experience in achieving open access to natural gas pipelines in the late 1980s. In addition, by this time a number of groups had emerged as strong advocates for competition and open access, including industrial customers in high-price states (particularly California and the northeastern states) that were seeking access to cheaper power in neighboring regions, smaller utilities that were seeking to break the larger utilities' stranglehold on transmission access, and prospective entrants into the ostensibly deregulated markets, such as nonutility power producers and financial traders.

The Energy Policy Act of 1992 sought to encourage competition at the wholesale level by creating a class of wholesale generators that was exempt from certain utility regulation and by promoting access to transmission. Following its passage, the state of California was the first, in 1994, to contemplate a substantial reorganization and restructuring of its electricity sector around market competition. As wholesale market activity increased, both in California and elsewhere, the FERC moved in 1996 to launch a series of regulatory and market design reforms.[6]

Why Design Electricity Markets?

All markets for commodities are subject to market rules, some contractual and some regulatory. In electricity, all potential market players understood the need to "design" the spot markets around the technological characteristics of the electricity system that govern the reliable, physical delivery of power. But within this framework, there was a good deal of debate in the mid-1990s (and since) over, among other things, definitions of market products, offer requirements, pricing mechanisms, the relationship of forward and spot markets, and the role of system operators. Moreover, the Federal Power Act required further rules to uphold the "just and reasonable" standard. Some of this debate was intellectual, and many initial decisions were made in "stakeholder" group settings. Not surprisingly, however, the move toward regulatory reform also prompted efforts at rent seeking through market design.

All potential market players obviously had some interest in influencing market design. Two groups were particularly influential. The first group consisted of the incumbent regulated monopoly utilities. Initially, they focused, in many key states, on ensuring that regulated retail rates would allow them to recover stranded costs if they exited the generation business.[7] Once this phase of regulatory reform was over, the restructured utilities turned to a new phase of attempting to influence market design—keeping wholesale power prices low. In some parts of the country, they found common ground with consumer advocates who were trying to keep wholesale energy pricing controlled through market rules. The second group active in rent seeking, the nascent power traders such as Enron, sought to establish market rules and procedures that they would find beneficial when conducting spatial and temporal arbitrage. In general, they also sought to minimize regulatory limits on product pricing.

Although often highly technical in nature, the market design debates are possibly the most interesting part of the restructuring process. In analyzing these debates, it is important to stress that market design in the United States has developed a distinctly regional character (although some regions have converged in design over time, in response to technical and economic lessons of experience). In particular, regional prerogatives have so far dominated federal policy objectives in the two regions where retail electricity costs are generally lower than elsewhere in the country: the Pacific Northwest and the Southeast. In the former, policymakers have been particularly reluctant to allow changes in market design, fearing that the outcome will be higher prices. In both regions, state regulators and large incumbent utilities are wary of losing control to federal regulators.

In addition, it is worth remembering that the complicated and uncertain nature of the design process overwhelmed all sides involved to some degree. Very little has happened exactly as anticipated by any party. A notable example in the mid-1990s was the legislature in California, which attempted to satisfy all interests when drawing up new regulations but in so doing created an inefficient market design that took years to reform. In part for these reasons, the dust has not yet settled on the politics and economics of electricity market design.

Key Elements of Wholesale Electricity Regulatory Reform

The FERC has used a number of policy and regulatory levers to facilitate market competition and encourage efficiency: open access, market expansion, efficient market designs, and mitigation of market power. Our discussion focuses on the development of the wholesale market, with only a few references to state regulatory decisions.[8]

Open Access

The foundation of robust competition in the electricity markets, as in other privately owned network industries (such as telecommunications or natural gas), is open access to the network. Following several years of development, the FERC issued landmark policy in this regard in 1996, through Orders 888 and 889.[9] Order 888 required utilities to set nondiscriminatory and nonpreferential rates for transmission service, and Order 889 improved transparency by requiring firms to post their available transmission capacity on the Internet.

Order 888 did not require the industry to follow a particular type of market organization or to adopt specific market pricing rules. Rather, the order encompassed (a) the transmission systems operated to support the organized, or "centralized," markets for power then under consideration in California and the northeastern U.S. power pools, and (b) those that remained under the control and operation of individual utilities. Further, within the category of organized markets, the FERC was not ready to choose a specific design. Instead, Order 888 provided the principles for an independent system operator (ISO). As the name suggests, an ISO is an entity, typically a nonprofit regulated organization, that acts as a third-party operator of the transmission system and hence allocates all transmission capacity to prospective users. Its purpose is to separate ownership and control of the transmission grid, thus greatly increasing the effectiveness of the open-access regime.[10] The first major steps in organizing ISOs with centralized markets were taken in California (1997) and in the three power pools of the eastern United States: PJM, named after the states of Pennsylvania, New Jersey, and Maryland but including several other states (1997); New England (1999); and New York (1999).

Outside the ISOs, open access has had a more ambiguous track record. Use of the transmission system has greatly increased as a result of the open-access rules. Problems have emerged largely in the way vertically integrated utilities manage the availability of their transmission capacity.[11] There has been persistent concern about and some evidence of discriminatory behavior in the allocation of such capacity to other users of the grid. In 2005, the FERC proposed to reform Order 888 in part to address such issues. The upshot, then, is that open access in electricity transmission requires market rules and seems destined to require regulatory oversight for some time to come.

Market Scope

By the late 1990s, while trading of bulk power had expanded, the markets remained quite balkanized. Outside the ISOs, as noted earlier, there were still barriers to trade and economic inefficiencies resulting from the manner in which vertically integrated utilities managed access to their networks and, regarding the larger utilities, some concern about their dominance of power markets in their service territories and surrounding areas. The ISOs themselves, while encompassing larger regions than most single utilities, were quite varied in geographical scope—some operated in only one state, others in more than one. And there were signs that the market designs in some ISOs, such as those in California, were problematic.

The next attempt to address the problems of open access and market development took place in 1999, when the FERC set forth Order 2000.[12]

The centerpiece of this order was the concept of the regional transmission organization (RTO), essentially an ISO with sufficient geographical scope to ensure that its boundaries, which were often artifacts of the utilities that had joined, were not interfering excessively with trade. (For that reason, the terms "ISO" and "RTO" will be used interchangeably from this point on.)

The crucial limitation of Order 2000 was that RTO formation was voluntary. Immediately following its issuance, RTO planning committees sprang up in most parts of the country that did not yet have organized markets. But when the California market crisis began brewing in late 2000, the RTO concept met with growing political resistance in some regions, particularly in the Northwest and Southeast. Elsewhere, the process of centralizing power markets continued. Since 2000, ISOs with auction markets have been established in the Midwest (through the expansion of PJM westward in 2004 and the start of the Midwest ISO in 2005) and are planned for some southern and central states (the Southwest Power Pool, planned for 2007).

Market Design

Open access to transmission and sufficient market scope facilitate the development of competitive wholesale and retail markets. While policymakers initially thought that on these foundations market institutions and rules would arise in a reasonably straightforward fashion through regional consensus, they have instead proven to be contentious and at times difficult to formulate and implement. Since the start of the academic and policy debate over the revival of competitive electricity markets, an overarching design question has been how to reconcile power system operations, which must remain largely centralized (that is, under the control of a utility or an ISO), with the organization of liberalized power markets.[13] This leads to many subsidiary questions. How should spot electricity services be defined and priced, and how many products are needed to provide sufficiently "complete" markets?[14] Should centralized regional auctions be the primary form of spot market organization? How should transmission usage be priced and transmission property rights allocated? Even less well understood initially, but increasingly central over time, was the introduction into the designs of essentially regulatory requirements, such as targets for resource adequacy (or installed capacity) and rules to mitigate market power.

The FERC initially played a limited role in these debates. As noted earlier, Order 888 did not require the formation of ISOs.[15] Where ISOs did form in the mid- to late 1990s, the commission with minor modification approved different market designs in almost every case. At the time, there was no consensus on the best design. But by the end of the 1990s, there was a growing perception at the commission that some ISO market designs were unworkable, notably California's. However, there was still no strong empirical evidence of market design failure in any region. Hence Order 2000 supported an "open architecture" for RTOs and did not require a standardized design.

In 2002, following the California crisis, the FERC, under new political leadership, proposed a "standard market design" for the United States that essentially combined the best practices from the eastern ISO markets.[16] Many aspects of the proposal were well received, but others were not. In particular, some southern utilities, which had never formed ISOs, resisted the pressure to follow the ISO model and surrender control over transmission scheduling and spot energy pricing. Northwestern utilities and public commissions, still reeling from the regional effects of the California crisis and seeking to protect access to their low-cost public hydropower, were similarly loath to enter a new phase of market development. Under mounting congressional pressure, the commission soon emphasized that it would defer to regional preferences on market design, although it would apply principles and lessons learned to ensure that efficient designs emerged. But by 2005, the commission had formally set aside the concept of national standardization. Nevertheless, about two-thirds of the U.S. power sector has adopted or is moving toward a market design that is consistent with the standard market design proposal. We turn now to the key design debates.

ISOs AND FORWARD MARKETS: CENTRALIZATION VERSUS DECENTRALIZATION. Much of the design debate in the United States in the early to mid-1990s was encapsulated, somewhat inaccurately, by the terms "centralized" and "decentralized."[17] The crux of this debate concerned whether, given the nature of power system technology, liberalized electricity markets could achieve economic efficiency without a relatively high degree of centralized hierarchical coordination, detailed market rules, and possibly some administratively determined prices. Proponents of centralized market models answered this question essentially in the negative: the owners and operators of private generators would not have the technological capability—particularly informational and system control—to create an economically efficient (and perhaps reliable) interface between forward financial transactions and the physical operations of the grid in the short time frames needed (hours, minutes, and even seconds). Instead, a centralized, but independent market operator, such as an ISO, was needed to operate both the spot markets and the transmission system simultaneously. Before the establishment of the U.S. markets, the best-understood power market with such centralized features was the market in England and Wales, in operation since 1990; the designs proposed in California and elsewhere in the early 1990s were often variations on its (evolving) rules.

As an alternative to the centralized market designs, prospective merchant suppliers such as Enron propounded a more decentralized vision, in which private entities would form largely unregulated forward power exchanges (similar to other organized commodity exchanges) separate from an ISO.[18] The bulk of power trading would take place within these exchanges, and ISOs would subsequently largely be limited to adjusting the forward energy positions through a voluntary bidding process, such as for congestion management during the operating day.

California established a version of the decentralized market model in 1998. On the other side of the country, versions of the centralized model were established in PJM in 1998–99 and in New York in 1999 (and subsequently in the other eastern and midwestern ISO markets). Following the California crisis, the mood shifted away from the decentralized design.[19] California itself, under FERC guidance, has completed but not yet implemented a redesign of its market along the principles that had prevailed in the eastern ISO markets.[20] However, while the intellectual debate appears to be largely settled as of this writing, regions of the country that did not form ISOs in the initial period of market development continue to resist centralized power markets.

SHORT-TERM GENERATION AUCTION MARKETS. The decision to establish centralized generation auction markets operated by ISOs in several regions is one of the major design and technological innovations resulting from the regulatory reforms. In general, the ISO operates two energy spot markets, a day-ahead market, which clears typically in the midafternoon before the operating day (and hence could be characterized as a forward market, although most spot trades clear in this market), and a real-time or "dispatch" market, which clears as often as every five minutes of the operating day. [21] Offers to sell and bids to buy wholesale power (denominated in dollars per megawatt-hour) must be submitted a few hours before the markets clear. Most of the physical market activity is on the selling end, as few buyers of power are currently "price-responsive"—that is, they simply buy at the clearing price, whatever that is. There is also a substantial quantity of what is called "virtual" buying and selling by arbitragers between day-ahead and real time, resulting in a convergence of market prices between these two markets. In terms of organization and pricing, the markets are auctions with uniform clearing prices for energy and additional payments for costs associated with starting up a generator (and other "nonconvexities" in the supply-offer curve) if needed to clear the market. Also, most ISOs use a pricing approach known as locational marginal pricing, in which spot prices reflect the effect of transmission congestion (and losses) in determining the marginal, price-setting offer or offers at each location on the network. Spot buyers pay the energy prices at their locations, and spot sellers are paid the prices at their locations. For the most part, the ISO is thereby able to manage the congestion on the system by adjusting the output of the generators in each minute of the day through locational pricing signals.

These vast regional markets, several consisting of tens of thousands of pricing points spread over the transmission network, represent an unprecedented realization of the early vision of spot markets for power.[22] At one level, they operate very well, allowing the regional market operator to capture the efficiency available through large-scale optimization of hundreds of supply offers and demand bids. But transmission markets have not always provided the equivalent ease of decisionmaking. Also, in the absence of a well-developed demand side, energy trading remains entangled in other market rules designed to improve efficiency and control market power, as discussed next.

TRANSMISSION PRICING AND PROPERTY RIGHTS. Because of the nature of power flows, transmission pricing and the assignment of tradable transmission property rights have long been recognized as among the most complicated technical problems for designers of competitive power markets.[23] In essence, electric power "flows" over the network according to laws of physics that determine how much flow takes place on each connected transmission line when power is injected at one point (such as a generator) and withdrawn at another point (such as a substation on the distribution network). All transmission lines have physical (or reliability) limits to the flow that they can accommodate, which creates an upper bound on their usage. These conditions create transmission congestion.

Congestion in this context means that too many parties are seeking to use a transmission line, and some method is needed to ration its usage to maintain reliability. In regions without ISOs, a typical bilateral contract to deliver power from one area to another requires a corresponding transmission contract whose actual flows may cross the territory of multiple utilities (who have typically sold rights to some of their transmission capacity to other parties and are using the rest to serve their own load and their own off-system sales). In this context, congestion is difficult to manage efficiently because these interconnected utilities have only administrative agreements as to who backs off the grid when it is congested (the transmission reservations are ranked in different priority classes); that is, there is no information on the value of the underlying power contracts nor typically on the marginal cost of congestion relief. Often there is also insufficient information on who is causing congestion. As a result, the prevailing approach is to have engineers monitor the state of the system and order physical curtailments of transmission usage when it appears that lines might get overloaded, regardless of the economic effects of such curtailments. Increased trade due to open access only increased the prevalence of such curtailments. In contrast, the concept of ISO markets, where the system operator now had centralized control of the grid over a large region, was seen as fertile ground for experimentation in more efficient congestion management. The basic objective of the various design proposals that emerged in the mid-1990s as the first ISOs were being developed was to ration scarce (congested) transmission capacity through prices.

Although arcane, the argument over transmission pricing and property rights that subsequently took place was as vociferous as the related debate over the role of the system operator in the markets. The initial design decisions roughly paralleled the outcome of the centralization issue: California tested a simplified zonal pricing approach that was preferred by market traders, whereas the eastern ISOs markets, after some zonal experiments, by and large adopted congestion pricing and associated transmission rights based on the locational marginal pricing model. Over time, experience proved the latter approach superior in efficiently managing congestion, although not without problems of its own, including some difficulty in exactly hedging the locational congestion charges over time using the available types of transmission rights. In addition, questions remain about whether the design stimulates sufficient transmission investment. In sum, the design of transmission markets continues to evolve, and the FERC remains engaged in this process.

RESOURCE ADEQUACY AND CAPACITY MARKETS. Before restructuring, state or regional regulatory bodies established requirements to ensure that vertically integrated utilities had a sufficient margin of generation under ownership or contract to cover some level of unanticipated demand in the coming year. These were called resource-adequacy or installed-capacity requirements. Typically, the capacity requirement was equal to some percent, usually in the range of 12 percent to 18 percent, over and above the utility or the power pool's annual peak load.

The advent of restructuring occasioned a good deal of debate over the merits of continuing the regulated capacity requirement and including a capacity product market alongside the energy market. As an alternative, critics of such mandatory requirements proposed an "energy-only" market in which energy prices would "spike" sufficiently to attract enough surplus generation capacity, as would be more typical of an "unregulated" commodity market. FERC's jurisdiction over state capacity requirements is probably limited, although it did ultimately have to approve designs for regional capacity markets for those ISOs that chose to implement them.

Given its jurisdictional constraints, the commission remained agnostic on this issue for many years, approving the initial California design without capacity requirements but also allowing the East Coast power pools (PJM, New York, and New England) to translate their historical regional capacity requirements into markets for capacity products. In the standard market design proposal, following the California crisis, which in part appeared to stem from inadequate generation resources within the state, the commission finally sought to make a resource adequacy requirement mandatory.[24] However, this was seen as an intrusion into state regulation and was one reason why several regions rebuffed the standard market design. Currently, the commission works with the different ISOs to refine designs for resource adequacy.

DEMAND-SIDE PARTICIPATION. The first phase of electricity restructuring focused on the design of generation and transmission markets. However, markets only function well when both buyers and sellers can express their preferences. The problem in this for electricity markets is the lack of price-responsive demand.[25] Its absence is not due to a shortcoming of the ISO wholesale energy auction markets: sufficiently flexible demand bids are easily accommodated in the ISO day-ahead markets, giving end-users time to react to anticipated prices, and five-minute wholesale spot prices are available in real time. Rather, as in the era of cost-based regulation, demand response has been suppressed by poor incentives flowing to retail customers via their continued regulated rate structures, and by cultural conditioning through decades of exposure to average prices. These circumstances are in turn responsible for the impetus behind several aspects of the extensive "design" of electricity markets, particularly in areas that blur the boundary between markets and regulation, such as capacity markets that in part correct for buyers' inability to adjust to unexpected spikes in demand and the spot offer caps discussed in the next section that protect buyers from high prices.

LESSONS OF MARKET DESIGN. The FERC learned several important lessons from attempts at market design by itself and others. To begin with, inefficient market designs work sufficiently well in periods of excess supply, but can fail in periods when supply is tight. In any market design, the details matter; inefficiencies and opportunities to exercise market power will present themselves and must be addressed in a timely fashion. The commission also found that regional preferences trumped the goal of national standardization. In changing course over 2003–05, it affirmed that regions of the country should be able to address their own regulatory, economic, and social characteristics when designing markets. As of this writing, this basic posture seems likely to prevail in the coming years.

Monitoring and Mitigating Generation Market Power

Market power is the ability of a supplier (or buyer) of a product to raise (or lower) the market price above (or below) the competitive price. There was not much question that in the transition from the era of monopoly regulation, the new electricity markets could be particularly prone to generation market power.[26] This is due to several factors. Storage of power is not cost-effective. Entry can be difficult in parts of the country. In some areas, markets are concentrated, particularly under certain conditions. For example, because of transmission congestion in some locations, it is not unusual to have few sellers for many hours of the year, including those of peak demand. Moreover, short-term demand for electricity is largely inelastic. As was later seen, poor market designs themselves can increase market power when suppliers learn how to manipulate the rules.

The Federal Power Act's "just and reasonable" standard requires that market-based rates be granted only to suppliers without significant market power.[27] Only Congress can repeal this requirement, and it has not done so for wholesale electricity markets. The policy problem, then, is how to meet this requirement without excessive regulation of supplier behavior. Beginning in the late 1980s, as part of its granting of market-based rates, the FERC required prospective wholesale power market suppliers (and merger applicants) to pass market power reviews. In the mid-1990s, after rejecting arguments that existing antitrust laws and methods would be sufficient to meet the just and reasonable standard, it grappled with how to adapt such tests to the era of electricity restructuring and to the two different types of wholesale markets that were being developed, those under ISOs and those outside ISOs.

Outside the ISOs, the FERC has followed a largely standardized, although ever-evolving, approach to the screening and mitigation of generation market power. Using various market power measurements as initial screens—including measures of market share and more recently market concentration and pivotal supplier tests—the commission has progressively made it more difficult for large dominant suppliers to sell their surplus power at market prices without some type of offer cap.[28]

In the ISOs, a different type of market-power screening and mitigation began to evolve. Centralized ISO auctions allowed for the instantaneous participation of potential wholesale suppliers from larger regions than were possible before open access. If the generation capacity within the ISO boundaries was considered a geographic market, it was initially expected that market concentration would be low and hence market power would be greatly diluted.[29] However, the hourly spot pricing introduced by ISOs highlighted the market-dividing effect of transmission congestion and the lack of price-responsive spot demand. These factors could result in substantial market power when system supply is tight generally or when transmission capacity limits the import of power to a particular location that otherwise has few sellers, often cities or towns, called a load pocket. Within a few years, all the ISO markets, with FERC approval, had imposed offer caps on spot suppliers. The standard rule is to impose a spot offer cap of $1,000 per megawatt-hour (currently $400 per megawatt-hour in California) outside the locations affected by transmission congestion. Inside the load pockets, the offer caps tend to be more restrictive, being designed to prevent price spikes in excess of efficient scarcity prices whenever the pocket is congested.

When regulators establish offer price caps, it is typically only through experience that they determine whether such caps are too restrictive or not restrictive enough (which has become a political issue as well as a matter of economic efficiency). When the caps appear too loose, as was the case in California during the price spikes, they were progressively tightened until prices subsided. In the eastern ISOs, a more persistent issue has been offer capping that is too restrictive to allow certain generators to recover long-term fixed costs through market prices, although such a determination is almost always contested. One method is to relax the offer price restrictions to allow generators that are persistently offer-capped more leeway to increase their offer prices. Another method is to create proxy "demand curves" for the energy auction during shortages; that is, the ISO automatically establishes a high price when power is running short. These demand curves are known ahead of time and allow generators to recover scarcity rents without having to raise their offer prices well above marginal cost while also encouraging buyers to prepare for high-price periods. Experiments with both these types of rule changes and others are under way in the ISO markets. For the most part, however, they are politically controversial and remain works in progress.

Case Study of Market Failure: The California Crisis and Enron's Trading Strategies

Market liberalization in California was an attempt to lower the high rates charged by the state's investor-owned utilities, resulting in part from nuclear-plant cost overruns in the billions and expensive long-term PURPA contracts. State regulators presented an initial proposal for a market design in 1994, and for the next two years much of the California debate, which became more political and vitriolic than elsewhere in the country, centered on whether to create essentially centralized or decentralized markets. Two of the three California investor-owned utilities initially supported the "poolco" model: a centralized market with an auction for spot power and locational marginal pricing. Marketers and traders (including Enron) proposed versions of a "bilateral" market: a decentralized market with competing exchanges for forward power based on zonal pricing and an ISO that was restricted to a minimal real-time market function and transmission scheduling.

In 1996 the California legislature propounded a restructuring law (Assembly Bill 1890) that attempted to incorporate elements of the different proposals. Among other things, the law gave retail customers the option to choose a new retail supplier or retain their existing utility supplier under a capped rate reduction that was frozen for four years, established provisions for recovery of utility stranded costs, required the investor-owned utilities to divest about half of their fossil generation units (they voluntarily sold off most of the remainder), and created a market organization consisting of an ISO that would manage the transmission system and procure ancillary services and real-time energy, and a separate Power Exchange (PX) that would hold day-ahead and hour-ahead energy auctions.[30] Other parties were also allowed to organize forward exchanges, but the three large investor-owned utilities were required both to offer their remaining generation capacity and to purchase all their power hourly through the PX for five years, after which the forward exchanges would be in true competition. Hence rather than locking in the benefits of their divestiture through long-term contracts, they were required to take the risk of the spot market in return for the stranded cost-recovery mechanism.[31]

This arrangement was unique to California. In terms of market power mitigation, there were initially no offer caps in the PX market, only an offer cap of $250 per megawatt-hour on energy in the ISO market, which would also serve as a de facto limit to the PX market price (this cap was later raised to $750 per megawatt-hour before being lowered subsequent to the California price spikes). In essence, then, California chose to combine features of both centralized and decentralized markets, as the result of a process characterized as "a series of compromises made by design committees including interest group representatives, drawing on bits and pieces of alternative models."[32] Arguably, the marketers and traders were on the winning side of most of the compromises in the wholesale market design debates, while retail consumers were the (temporary) victors in the retail market rate caps.

The design flaws in the California market were well known conceptually, and some had been advised against by FERC staff and others before the market's launch.[33] These flaws included zonal energy pricing that shifted costs to buyers in the zone and inefficient procedures for adjusting the PX day-ahead auction results for purposes of ISO congestion management. But after considerable political pressure, the commission decided to defer to the state government's wishes.[34] Once the market began operating, many of these flaws emerged and were patched through additional rules. There were also many incidents of market gaming, with one well-known scheduling incident purposely engineered by Enron to test the market flaws and the political/organizational response.[35] In early 2000 these persistent problems led the commission to begin pushing the ISO to redesign the market along more efficient principles.[36]

Why was the California market able to sputter forward from 1997 to 2000 despite so many design flaws? At the time, generation capacity in the West was sufficient (in relation to demand) to keep prices low and hide the price effect of market inefficiencies. In 2000, however, generation supply grew short because of reductions in hydro availability resulting from a drought in the Pacific Northwest. At that point, a series of developments that combined scarcity of supply with market manipulation was set in motion. Wholesale market prices "spiked" to the market cap for long periods of time.

The details of the California crisis, its ripples throughout the West, and the FERC's regulatory responses have been examined in great detail elsewhere.[37] By general consensus, the California utilities' exposure to the spot market, combined with the freeze on retail rates, greatly increased the financial impact of the crisis. The commission's subsequent investigations, along with the analysis of other parties, showed that market manipulation, such as inflation of gas market price indices and various transmission scheduling practices, and the exercise of generation market power through economic and physical with-holding exacerbated these market conditions (although debate continues over the exact effect).[38] Moreover, in 2001, under pressure to act, the state of California and other parties entered into high-priced long-term contracts during the price spikes that were soon above market prices.[39] As parties sued for refunds, investigations and refund proceedings dragged on for several years.

Since the crisis, the California ISO has engaged in a significant effort with FERC support and guidance to redesign the wholesale power market, adopting, at the time of this writing, most of the market organization and pricing features of the East Coast U.S. markets, such as the PJM market discussed next. However, the commission is not able to address structural problems, such as the probability of drought again diminishing hydro availability and the barriers to generation and transmission entry in California.[40] As in other regions of the country, state regulators will have to fashion a combination of market and regulatory solutions tailored to California's electricity infrastructure needs.

Enron and Electric Power Markets

To many observers, the rise and fall of Enron was emblematic of the failures of regulatory reform in electricity markets. The Enron story is, of course, much broader than its trading activities in the power sector; its corporate philosophy and its manipulation and cooptation of its financiers and accountants have been explored in some detail.[41] The focus here is on two questions of interest to the analysis of electricity regulatory reform in the United States (and elsewhere). First, was Enron (and similar companies) able to influence the reform process to advance its own interests or did it reap the unintended consequences of design errors made by others? Second, was Enron's ability to game the California market a special case, or were other ISO markets equally vulnerable?

Enron was influential among electricity policymakers in the mid-1990s because it was a major player in the recently liberalized natural gas markets and many observers anticipated that success in gas would carry over to electricity. Moreover, at the time, the new merchant and financial firms were widely touted as the future of power generation and trading. Regulated vertically integrated utilities were not known for innovation or efficiency. In contrast, the new traders and arbitragers hired the best from the utilities and brought in academics and in-house modelers to develop their risk-management strategies. Hence the viewpoints of these potential new market entrants were given a good deal of weight, even as their visions of market design were subject to critique.[42]

As the first competitive U.S. power market was being designed in California, in about 1994–96, Enron presented its views on a design that would create a fertile ground for its forward trading activities. Over this period, Enron strategists and consultants were also developing its "asset-lite" approach to financial trading, which further affected its notion of an appropriate market design. Enron did own a few generators (outside California), but most of its power business was devoted to forward financial trading and to establishing itself as a market maker in energy (and many other commodities) through its Internet-based trading platform, Enron On-line. Enron understood the value of being a first mover in this nascent business sector and of being able to influence price indexes (that is, to affect the published estimates of forward prices against which the bulk of forward trades would clear). In addition, Enron sought to influence the design of spot markets to benefit forward trading. If centralized power markets were designed efficiently, to keep transaction costs low and simplify the relationship between the forward and spot markets (when power would go to physical delivery), then the business of power marketing would be a more competitive and hence lower-margin business. It was thus in Enron's interest to promote market designs that increased the potential for arbitrage while inhibiting the ISO from establishing its own efficient dispatch as a basis for spot pricing.

In California, one objective appears to have been to make the state-mandated PX market as inefficient as possible in order to allow competing exchanges (such as Enron On-line) to eventually displace it.[43] Enron and others further advocated transmission property rights and the zonal congestion pricing that were adopted (initially) in California, and that would result in a subsidy from zonal buyers to the sellers. Despite this maneuvering, had the California crisis not unfolded, Enron's ventures in power marketing would likely have failed (as did most of its other ventures of the period) or simply shrunk to a smaller scale. Interestingly, Enron claims to have lost money in California before the price spikes.[44] In 2000, however, the situation in California changed; Enron had correctly anticipated the supply shortage and was poised to make significant revenues.[45] At this time, Enron was best known for its creative efforts to take advantage of the flaws in California's market, especially features of the transmission scheduling process, to raise market prices.[46] Of course, many other suppliers also engaged in market manipulation and in exercising market power during this period.

After the California crisis, policymakers were forced to ask whether other regional market designs, such as those in the eastern United States, were vulnerable to Enron-style gaming. The FERC addressed this topic in its rule for a standard market design proposed in 2002.[47] It concluded that most of the scheduling games that Enron and others devised to create spatial and temporal arbitrage opportunities in California would either not be allowed or would not yield the same economic results under the locational marginal pricing and scheduling rules of the standard market design (and hence under the similar designs of the eastern ISO markets, such as PJM). Moreover, no other region of the country exposed its wholesale buyers to the spot market through mandate as California did.

Regardless of the actual causes, the political result of the Enron affair, in conjunction with the California crisis, strengthened resistance to market reforms in most parts of the United States that had lagged behind California and the northeastern states. This contributed to the failure of the FERC's proposed standard market design, although the commission continued to work with California to implement a market redesign along similar lines.[48] The Enron investigations also led directly to additional market rules: notably a new set of "behavioral rules" seeking to control illegal behavior after the fact.[49]

Case Study of Organized Market Success: PJM

The relative success of the ISO markets in the eastern United States was essential to the continuation of the regulatory reform process once the California crisis unfolded. These markets also experienced many start-up problems associated with market design and implementation. However, most were soluble within a reasonable time frame and, more important, did not cause significant financial transfers through the markets. This section focuses on PJM, although there are many lessons to be learned from the other eastern ISO markets.

PJM began operations as a power pool in 1927 (with three utilities). By the mid-1990s, its eleven member utilities had years of experience sharing surplus spot energy on a cost-based, "split-the-savings" basis and centrally redispatching the system to accommodate scheduling of transmission service. As already noted, in 1996–97, PJM debated aspects of the "centralized" versus "decentralized" market design that roiled California, focusing in particular on whether to simplify market-based congestion pricing for the purposes of forward trading. In 1997, under the influence of Enron and other marketers (which had the support of one of the incumbent utilities), PJM in fact instituted a zonal pricing design but quickly found that it created poor incentives for transmission scheduling across the system. Unlike California, PJM immediately suspended zonal pricing and began dispatching the system with cost-based offers using locational marginal pricing, the first such implementation in the United States. Market participants could "self-schedule" their own resources or buy through the spot market. Financial transmission rights were allocated to the market participants to hedge the resulting marginal congestion charges. No restrictions were placed on forward energy contracting. Also unlike California, PJM carried over its regional capacity requirement to the ISO market, obliging buyers to meet their requirement either through their own generation or through purchases in a centralized capacity market. Generators that qualify for status as "capacity resources," which account for the great majority of PJM capacity, are required to offer all their surplus capacity into the ISO's energy markets.

The bid-based PJM auction for real-time spot energy formally began in April 1999.[50] Suppliers were allowed to submit offers for start-up, minimum load level, and energy. The rules for mitigating market power were simple: PJM instituted an absolute offer price cap of $1,000 per megawatt-hour, and any unit that was dispatched to a higher level of output because of transmission congestion had its offer price capped at short-term variable cost plus 10 percent.[51] The supplier was then paid the market-clearing price at its location. PJM requires that suppliers submit daily variable costs in the event that they are capped. PJM then added new market features and products incrementally over the following years, such as a day-ahead energy market, a regulation market, and an operating reserve market.

Although PJM has faced its share of market problems, at least during the first decade of restructuring, it has been widely considered the most successful of the U.S. ISO markets. Empirical evidence suggests that the day-ahead and real-time energy markets have been competitive.[52] Spot prices in PJM often reach the hundreds of dollars per megawatt-hour during peak hours, but the averaged spot prices remain close to estimates of average marginal costs. Table 7-1 shows the calculated price-cost margin (the difference between the actual market price and a hypothetical simulated price that would have occurred in a perfectly competitive market) in PJM for 1999–2004 (in comparison with New England and California in the same period). Market participants have registered few complaints about the market with the FERC. When elements of the market design fail, or firms are found to be manipulating the market, PJM has generally moved quickly to curb manipulative practices and implement alternative rules.

A number of factors have contributed to this success. The history of centralized operations in the prior power pool and the development of a competent

Table 7-1. *Estimated Price-Cost Margins in U.S. ISO and RTO Energy Markets, 1999–2004*[a]

Market	1999	2000	2001	2002	2003	2004
California	−0.02 to 0.31 (PX)	−0.16 to 0.63 (PX)		0.2 to 0.4 (ISO)	0.14 to 0.23 (ISO)	0.01 to 0.23 (ISO)
New England	0.10[b]		−0.03 to 0.06	0.06 to 0.11	−0.04 to 0.09	−0.06 to 0.03
PJM	0.02[c]	0.04	0.02 to 0.09	0.02 to 0.11	0.03 to 0.12	0.03 to 0.08

Source: The California analysis is from Severin Borenstein, James Bushnell, and Frank A. Wolak, "Measuring Market Inefficiencies in California's Restructured Wholesale Electricity Market," *American Economic Review* 92, no. 5 (2002): 1376–1405; and California ISO annual reports on market issues and performance, 2002–05. An average for the year 2001 is not available in the public literature. The New England analysis appears in James Bushnell and Celeste Saravia, "An Empirical Assessment of the Competitiveness of the New England Electricity Market," CSEM WP 101 (University of California, Berkeley, Center for the Study of Energy Markets, February 2002); and ISO New England, Inc., annual markets reports, 2002–05. PJM analysis is from the PJM state of the market reports, 1990–2004. The ranges for PJM are the difference in the Lerner index between using marginal cost estimates (lower estimate) and marginal cost plus 10 percent estimates (higher estimate). The ranges for California before 2004 and New England reflect the difference in the Lerner index calculated using the same marginal cost offer stack but based on either the mean bid price submitted that would clear the market (lower estimate) or the market clearing price (higher estimate). Both of these clearing prices might be lower than the marginal cost of the marginal unit. The California ISO estimates for 2004 are the range of monthly average markups calculated using a "single-resource portfolio" methodology. A version of this table appears in Richard P. O'Neill and others, "Independent System Operators in the USA: History, Lessons Learned, and Prospects," in *Electricity Market Reform: An International Perspective*, edited by Fereidoon P. Sioshansi and Wolfgang Pfaffenberger (Oxford: Elsevier, 2006).
a. All values are load-weighted averages unless otherwise indicated.
b. May to December.
c. April to December.

management team in that process appear to have smoothed the way for market design decisions that avoided most of the mistakes of the California experience. Another important factor in retrospect was the continued vertical integration of many PJM companies.[53] This kept exposure to the spot market small while market experience was developed. At the same time, it did not inhibit the entry of new merchant generation and divestiture in the region.

All in all, the PJM transition to the competitive wholesale market was in many respects more conservative and measured than that of California, but the resulting price stability and record of management capability was important in building confidence in the market. In 2003 ISO New England terminated its own flawed initial market design (in operation since 1999) and simply adopted most of the PJM rules and much of its software. As another indicator of operational success, PJM undertook a major regional expansion in 2004, absorbing several large midwestern utilities.

Quantitative Analysis of Electricity Markets

Despite the sense that the design and implementation of electricity markets remains in evolution, there are positive quantitative indicators of market performance. For example, cost-benefit analyses of national or regional restructuring, although difficult to conduct accurately, have had similar general findings.[54] While start-up costs of ISOs that operate spot energy markets are roughly equal to the short-term benefits, the long-term benefit-cost ratio appears to be positive. Incentives to cut operational costs, yet to be implemented, have significant potential and are discussed in the concluding section.

Although typically not incorporated into the cost-benefit analyses just discussed, there is also empirical evidence that the market reforms have produced benefits in production efficiency. Evidence of the inefficiency under the prior cost-based regime can be found in the massive claims for stranded costs (approximately $200 billion) that utilities were allowed to recover in the transition to open access. Other evidence, from government statistics, indicates that U.S. nuclear plants increased their utilization capacity from 76.2 percent in 1996 to 90.5 percent in 2004, in part through performance incentives and competitive market opportunities.[55] The utilization of investor-owned utility coal power plants in ISO regions of the eastern United States has also apparently improved, with cost savings on the order of 2 to 3 percent.[56] Investor-owned utility plants in restructured states have reduced their labor and non-fuel expenses by about 5 percent compared with investor-owned utility plants in states that did not restructure.[57]

Any gains in economic efficiency due to restructuring are highly susceptible to being eliminated by the exercise of market power. Although there is some debate over the methodology for estimating market power, the general conclusion is that, with the possible exception of California during the price spikes, market power in the ISO markets has for the most part been well controlled (see table 7-1), and in some cases possibly overcontrolled (as in some of the "load pockets" described earlier).

Lessons Learned and Some Further Steps to Successful Restructuring

In the United States, the electricity markets have not been "deregulated" but rather have been subject to regulatory reforms that promote competition through open transmission access, market expansion, and efficient market design, while constraining market power under the Federal Power Act's "just and reasonable" standard. In our view, the overlay of market rules is not simply a residue of unnecessary regulation but is a needed framework for the transition of the electricity industry from the market structures and cultural norms of the prior era of cost-based franchised monopoly regulation into the period of market competition.

This transition to well-functioning markets is likely to be measured in decades for a number of reasons. Although open access to the transmission grid is the foundation of robust competition in generation services, the development of open access remains a work in progress. And while market designs have advanced in the ISO regions, providing for short-term pricing signals, they remain incomplete and subject to further development, particularly in providing incentives for investment. Moreover, artificial operational boundaries remain. At the same time, greater interest in and implementation of coordination between system operators, not to mention advances in metering and communication technology, are paving the way to increased competition across ever-larger regions. Market design is also intimately related to methods of mitigating power in the generation market, through which the FERC will continue to seek a balance between inhibiting market power abuse and not dampening the price increases that would be due to true supply scarcity.

Another important policy goal is to improve the efficiency and innovative capability of the ISOs. In their start-up phase, these organizations have been funded through charges to market participants, with little attention to efficiency. Unlike traditional regulated utilities, these organizations are market operators and information conduits, and their asset base is human capital and information technology. New incentive approaches must take that into account.

A final factor, and one that is hard to analyze quantitatively, is the somewhat complicated nature of the ISO markets, particularly for newer, smaller participants with limited human resources. Among the attributes of these regional markets are multiple products sold variously through hourly, daily, monthly, and multimonth auctions; thousands of pricing points for energy and congestion; and thousands of pages of technical manuals and business rules. All of these features potentially contribute to efficient economic decisions but are daunting to some. A number of parties are currently urging that the regulatory reform process reverse course in large degree, perhaps returning to regulated, vertically integrated utilities in the regions where divestiture has taken place, or at least to simpler, if less efficient, market designs, instead of the fairly complicated ISO market designs. These parties include large industrial buyers and smaller transmission-dependent utilities that were previously supportive of the effort to promote open access and competitive regional markets. In the near term, the FERC, in part under the guidance of the Energy Policy Act of 2005, is taking steps to address the concerns of these parties. For example, it is requiring ISOs to provide long-term transmission rights that provide them with more stable hedges against congestion charges. Time will tell how smoothly such market actors can adapt to the market designs. The push to establish ISO markets throughout the country has certainly waned. Whether it will gather steam again will depend in part on how clearly market participants perceive the benefits of centralized wholesale market designs.

Notes

1. The FERC has limited authority over municipal, state, or federally owned generating and transmission facilities. Also, with the exception of hydropower projects, the FERC has no jurisdiction over the construction or maintenance of power-generating plants and, until recently, over transmission lines. These come under state and local jurisdiction. However, the Energy Policy Act of 2005 increased the FERC's ability to require siting of transmission lines, particularly in critical infrastructure corridors. Texas is the only state that is not subject, over most of its territory, to federal regulation of wholesale power; however, Texas has undertaken wholesale and retail competition on its own.

2. Retail competition allows industrial and residential customers to choose between competing retail suppliers. Most states have rules specifying conditions under which the regulated suppliers become providers of last resort.

3. For example, by 2000 the states of California, Connecticut, Maine, New Hampshire, and Rhode Island, all of which were undertaking retail competition, had passed laws requiring utilities to divest generation assets.

4. In this context, "independent" generally means that the supplier is independent of the vertically integrated utility that it may be selling to. Merchant means that the supplier is entirely reliant on market revenues (that is, its assets are not under any form of cost-of-service regulation).

5. The just and reasonable standard is a legal standard of fairness that essentially requires judgment by the regulator based on the evidence. For a commonly cited Supreme Court ruling on the application of this standard affecting FERC rate making, see *Federal Power Com'n v. Hope Natural Gas Co.*, 320 U.S. 591 (1944).

6. Federal Energy Regulatory Commission (FERC), "Promoting Wholesale Competition through Open Access Non-Discriminatory Transmission Services by Public Utilities; Recovery of Stranded Costs by Public Utilities and Transmitting Utilities," Order 888, FERC Stats. & Regs., par. 31,036 (April 24, 1996); Federal Energy Regulatory Commission (FERC), "Open Access Same-Time Information System (formerly Real-Time Information Networks) and Standards of Conduct," Order 889, 75 FERC, par. 61,078 (April 24, 1996).

7. In the 1990s, the incumbents in many key states faced the prospect of significant stranded costs in generation, as state regulators were beginning to conduct prudency reviews of their investments, particularly for nuclear plants. Consequently, getting out of the generation business was being seen as a plausible financial strategy.

8. Some of the regulatory issues important to the understanding of the markets will not be addressed extensively here, including the relationship of the electric industry's reliability standards and the markets.

9. FERC, Order 888; FERC, Order 889.

10. A largely equivalent arrangement from the perspective of transmission users could be achieved via a regulated transmission company that owned and operated the grid but owned no generation. This was the arrangement established in England and Wales in 1990 through privatization. In the mid- and late 1990s, many parties in the United States lobbied for such transmission companies to form across large regions of the grid. But they never managed to aggregate more than a few utilities in a few states.

11. See, for example, FERC, "Standard Market Design and Structure, Notice of Proposed Rulemaking," 18 CFR Part 35, Docket RM01-12-000 (September 2002), app. C. Note that there have been some transmission-only utilities outside the ISOs that presumably had better incentives regarding transmission access.

12. FERC, "Regional Transmission Organizations," Order 2000, 89 FERC, par. 61,285 (December 20, 1999).

13. Two seminal contributions before the mid-1990s were Paul L. Joskow and Richard Schmalensee, *Markets for Power: An Analysis of Electric Utility Deregulation* (Cambridge, Mass.: MIT Press, 1983); and Fred C. Schweppe and others, *Spot Pricing of Electricity* (Boston: Kluwer Academic, 1988).

14. "Complete markets" in this context means that all potential market value embodied in the electric power system, particularly generation units and transmission facilities, is priced through a market.

15. FERC, Order 888, p. 279.

16. FERC, "Standard Market Design and Structure, Notice of Proposed Rulemaking."

17. An alternative characterization is "integrated" for the former and "unbundled" for the latter. See, for example, Robert Wilson, "Architecture of Power Markets," *Econometrica* 70, no. 4 (2002), p. 5. In the early 1990s, other terms used were "poolco" for the former and "bilateral" markets for the latter. See, for example, William W. Hogan, "An Efficient Bilateral Market Needs a Pool—Comments on the 'Blue Book' Regarding Competitive Wholesale Electric Markets: Role, Structure and Efficacy," California Public Utilities Commission Hearings (San Francisco, August 4, 1994) (http://ksghome.harvard.edu/~whogan/).

18. The term "merchant" is defined in n. 4.

19. See, for example, Wilson, "Architecture of Power Markets."

20. FERC, "Order on the California Comprehensive Market Redesign Proposal," 100 FERC 61, 060 (July 2002).

21. In addition to energy, the ISO markets include products called "ancillary services," notably operating reserves, which is unused capacity on available generators that is held in reserve in the event of an unplanned outage of a large generator or transmission facility, and regulation, which is output used for maintaining the second-by-second balance of

energy supply and demand. These ancillary service markets are of much smaller financial consequence than wholesale energy and hence will not be discussed in this chapter.

22. See especially Schweppe and others, *Spot Pricing of Electricity.*

23. Hogan, "Contract Networks for Electric Power Transmission"; FERC, Order 888.

24. FERC, "Standard Market Design and Structure, Notice of Proposed Rulemaking."

25. Severin Borenstein, "The Long-Run Effects of Real-Time Electricity Pricing," Working Paper 133 (University of California, Berkeley, Center for the Study of Energy Markets, June 2004).

26. This was pointed out earlier in Joskow and Schmalansee, *Markets for Power.*

27. In *Federal Power Com'n* v. *Hope Natural Gas Co.,* the Supreme Court announced the principle that FERC is not bound to the use of any particular rate-making method, as long as the outcome is just and reasonable. The courts have subsequently approved the prices that result from well-functioning, competitive markets as just and reasonable. Commonly cited court opinions include the following: "When there is a competitive market the FERC may rely upon market-based prices . . . to assure a 'just and reasonable' result," *Elizabethtown Gas Co.* v. *FERC,* 10 F.3d 866, 870-71 (D.C. Cir. 1993). Also, "In a competitive market, where neither buyer nor seller has significant market power, it is rational to assume that the terms of their voluntary exchange are reasonable, and specifically to infer that the price is close to marginal cost, such that the seller makes only a normal return on its investment," *Tejas Power Corp.* v. *FERC,* 908 F.2d 998, 1004 (D.C. Cir. 1990).

28. The idea of the pivotal supplier screen is that in markets with no demand elasticity, any supplier that can put the market into deficit has significant market power over its residual demand, hence the ability to raise market prices. This screen would be less effective (and less needed) if the markets had sufficient demand elasticity.

29. See, for example, FERC, Order 888.

30. For detailed descriptions of the 1996 restructuring decisions, see, for example, Carl Blumstein, Lee S. Friedman, and Richard J. Green, "The History of Electricity Restructuring in California," Working Paper 103 (University of California, Berkeley, Center for the Study of Energy Markets, August 2002); and Paul L. Joskow, "California's Electricity Crisis," *Oxford Review of Economic Policy* 17, no. 3 (2001): 365–88.

31. Privately, some utilities admitted that relying on the spot market was a gamble based on forecasts of sufficient surplus capacity being available until these purchase requirements lapsed.

32. Joskow, "California's Electricity Crisis," p. 370.

33. Hogan, "An Efficient Bilateral Market Needs a Pool."

34. California A.B. 1890 received a lopsided majority in the legislature, and the commission received letters from the California congressional delegation endorsing the market design.

35. FERC, "Final Report on Price Manipulation in Western Markets Fact-Finding Investigation of Potential Manipulation of Electric and Natural Gas Prices," prepared by FERC, Docket PA02-2-000 (March 2003).

36. FERC, "Order Accepting for Filing in Part and Rejecting in Part Proposed Tariff Amendment and Directing Reevaluation of Approach to Addressing Intrazonal Congestion," 90 FERC, par. 61,006 (January 7, 2000).

37. See, for example, Blumstein and others, "The History of Electricity Restructuring in California"; Severin Borenstein, "The Trouble with Electricity Markets: Understanding California's Restructuring Disaster," *Journal of Economic Perspectives* 16, no. 1 (2002): 191–211; Scott M. Harvey and William W. Hogan, "On the Exercise of Market Power through Strategic Withholding in California" (Harvard University, John F. Kennedy School of Government, April 2001); Joskow, "California's Electricity Crisis"; Paul L. Joskow and Edward Kahn, "A Quantitative Analysis of Pricing Behavior in California's Wholesale Electricity Market during Summer 2000," *Energy Journal* 23, no. 4 (2002): 1–35.

38. There are many regulatory cases and a large literature on this topic that we will not review here. Of note, see FERC, "Order Establishing Prospective Mitigation and Monitoring Plan for the California Wholesale Electric Markets and Establishing an Investigation of Public Utility Rates in the Wholesale Western Energy Markets," 95 FERC, par. 61,115 (April 26, 2001); FERC, "Final Report on Price Manipulation in Western Markets Fact-Finding Investigation of Potential Manipulation of Electric and Natural Gas Prices"; Severin Borenstein, James Bushnell, and Frank A. Wolak, "Measuring Market Inefficiencies in California's Restructured Wholesale Electricity Market," *American Economic Review* 92, no. 5 (2002): 1376–1405; Joskow and Kahn, "A Quantitative Analysis of Pricing Behavior in California's Wholesale Electricity Market during Summer 2000."

39. However, by 2005, owing to increases in the price of natural gas, most of these contracts were "in the money."

40. In systems with significant amounts of hydropower, building generation reserves for dry years is politically difficult. Similar problems have occurred in Brazil, New Zealand, and Norway, as well as in the western United States. In addition, California is considered a hostile environment for the siting of fossil fuel generation.

41. Paul M. Healy and Krishna G. Palepu, "The Fall of Enron," *Journal of Economic Perspectives* 17, no. 2 (2003): 3–26; Bethany McLean and Peter Elkind, *The Smartest Guys in the Room: The Amazing Rise and Scandalous Fall of Enron* (New York: Portfolio/Viking Penguin, 2003).

42. Hogan, "An Efficient Bilateral Market Needs a Pool."

43. These market design objectives were fairly clear to market observers, but the regulatory bargains struck in the California legislature precluded rational intervention from the outside. See, for example, the analysis in Steven Stoft, "What Should a Power Marketer Want?" *Electricity Journal* 10 (June 1997): 34–45.

44. See the testimony of Douglas Bohi, FERC Docket EL03-180-000 (May 13, 2005).

45. McLean and Elkind, *The Smartest Guys in the Room.*

46. See, for example, FERC, "Final Report on Price Manipulation in Western Markets Fact-Finding Investigation."

47. FERC, "Standard Market Design and Structure, Notice of Proposed Rulemaking," app. C.

48. As an ironic twist to this story, in the last months of its existence, some of Enron's traders began to be supportive of PJM's locational pricing and its high-volume trading hubs.

49. FERC, "Investigation of Terms and Conditions of Public Utility Market-Based Rate Authorizations, Order Amending Market-Based Rate Tariffs and Authorizations," 105 FERC, par. 61,218 (November 17, 2003).

50. PJM, "State of the Market Report, 1999" (PJM Interconnection, L.L.C., Market Monitoring Unit, June 2000) (www.pjm.com).

51. This rule, which can cap the spot prices charged by generators in load pockets at near- to short-term variable cost for many hours of the year, has been controversial. Recently, the FERC has required PJM to loosen the rule to allow such intermittently operated generators to recover their long-term fixed costs.

52. See PJM state of the market reports, 1999–2004; Erin T. Mansur, "Vertical Integration in Restructured Electricity Markets: Measuring Market Efficiency and Firm Conduct," Working Paper 117 (University of California, Berkeley, Center for the Study of Energy Markets, October 2003).

53. Some argue that vertical integration is a stronger explanatory variable than market design for why PJM was more successful than California. See James Bushnell, Erin T. Mansur, and Celeste Saravia, "Vertical Arrangements, Market Structure, and Competition: An Analysis of Restructured U.S. Electricity Markets," Working Paper 126 (University of California, Berkeley, Center for the Study of Energy Markets, February 2005).

54. See, for example, the survey of RTO cost-benefit analyses found in FERC, "Staff Report on Cost Ranges for the Development and Operation of a Day One Regional Transmission Organization," Docket PL04-16-000 (October 2004).

55. The data are available from the Energy Information Agency of the U.S. Department of Energy. See www.eia.doe.gov.

56. Stratford Douglas, "Utilization Rates of Coal-Fired Power Plants in the Eastern U.S. and the Efficiency of Electricity Market Reforms" (West Virginia University, Department of Economics, August 2004).

57. Kira Markiewicz, Nancy L. Rose, and Catherine Wolfram, "Has Restructuring Improved Operating Efficiency at U.S. Electricity Generating Plants?" Working Paper 135 (University of California, Berkeley, Center for the Study of Energy Markets, July 2004). Note that 1 percent savings in the U.S. markets translates into more than $1 billion a year.

8

The Perils of Market Making: The Case of British Pension Reform

ALAN M. JACOBS AND STEVEN TELES

In 1986 the government of Margaret Thatcher launched one of the most radical social policy reforms ever enacted in an economically advanced welfare state. In a comprehensive overhaul of British pension arrangements, the Conservative Party made deep cuts in public retirement benefits and allowed workers to opt out of public or employer-provided schemes into personal savings accounts. It went beyond what is ordinarily understood as privatization, challenging *all* collective modes of provision—state and occupational—with a form of personal self-provision. Responsibility for and control over the provision of retirement income would pass from governments, corporations, and trade unions into the hands of the individual.

By the mid-1990s, Thatcher's pension reform had caused a massive—and expensive—policy disaster. In the "misselling" scandal, overzealous pension retailers lured hundreds of thousands of unsophisticated customers into

We would like to thank the many readers who provided feedback on prior drafts of this chapter. Among them are Eugene Bardach, Melissa Bass, Martha Derthick, John Hills, Mark Kleiman, Theodore Marmor, Lawrence Mead, and Graham Wilson. We would also like to thank the participants in the conference "The Politics and Economics of the Market" at Brandeis University in January 2005 for their helpful comments. Special thanks go to Martin Levin, who invited us to take part in the project. We are grateful for the able research assistance provided by Samuel Dewey, Nico Dragojlovic, and Frank Hangler.

"personal pensions" that made them worse off than their existing arrangements. Misselling and low rates of personal savings not only increased pensioner insecurity but, in an ultimate irony, foiled its architects' attempt to roll back collectivism. By 1995, largely in response to misselling, the ancient self-regulatory framework by which the financial services industry had been governed for centuries was displaced by a centralized regime of state oversight and a staggering burden of rules and regulations. By the time New Labour came to power in 1997, the British government was, to an unprecedented degree, dictating what financial services could be sold and how to sell them—and, by implication, constraining consumer choice. The state had actually rolled *forward* into economic domains ruled until then by market forces.

In our view, British pension privatization backfired so badly because of three factors: causal complexity, decisionmakers' cognitive biases, and the pressures of democratic accountability. These forces reflect an underlying logic that tends to govern ambitious projects of privatization and liberalization. One notable feature of such endeavors is their inherent complexity. Privatizing public services or state-owned firms or liberalizing monopolistic industries often means constructing a market where none existed before, requiring a shift not only in ownership but also in regulatory structure, tax rules, and possibly public subsidies. Multiple simultaneous changes create an enormous degree of causal complexity, overwhelming the capacity of decisionmakers for comprehensively rational calculation. Second, in the face of this daunting complexity, policymakers usually turn to a set of cognitive shortcuts—including ideology—that greatly simplify the decisionmaking process. At the same time, these shortcuts introduce systematic biases into the design process, increasing the likelihood of undesired effects. Third, as constituents feel the painful consequences of miscalculation, elected politicians will try to limit the damage and compensate the losers—drawing, naturally, on the power of the state to do so. As the government reacts to crisis under the voter's watchful eye, a market-making project may, paradoxically, culminate in an expansion of state activity that equals (or even exceeds) its initial retreat.

We want to underline at the outset two observations that we believe are fundamental to understanding pro-market policies. First, market creation entails not merely a *negative* choice to get the state out of the way, but an affirmative act of *policy design*. All markets exist within institutional structures shaped by public policy: with any decision to decollectivize, privatize, or deregulate, policymakers must necessarily make a host of additional choices about how to configure, and perhaps even direct, the new market.

These choices are not simply dictated by an objective, self-evident logic of the "invisible hand": they are *political* decisions among alternatives—and will have major, and imperfectly foreseeable, consequences for market dynamics.

Second, markets develop *over a substantial period of time*. When markets succeed, they do so through slow processes of competitive selection, learning, and strategic adjustment by producers, consumers, and public officials. Meanwhile, the dynamics of policy feedback—political responses to initial reform outcomes—often determine whether the market-makers' vision ever materializes. In other words, the success of a market design often hangs not just on its immediate and direct social effects but also on the responses of subsequent governments to those effects. For those interested in assessing market outcomes, there is thus no substitute for tracing economic and political dynamics unfolding over time.[1]

Though a single case, pension privatization in Britain provides an excellent laboratory in which to study the challenges and ironies of market making. The British government in the 1980s was led by politicians deeply committed to markets, with towering and disciplined legislative majorities in one of the most centralized polities in the democratic world. Given these advantages, the effort failed not for lack of will or favorable political conditions; failure was much more likely a result of features intrinsic to the logic of the enterprise. Lessons drawn from Thatcher's Britain should thus point to obstacles likely to confront market-builders in other democratic contexts as well. Those obstacles cannot be understood without first examining the Thatcher government's goals in creating the new pensions market.

The Goals of British Market Making

What did Thatcher's government hope to achieve? When the Conservatives turned their attention to pensions in the mid-1980s, the British system was an amalgam of two public tiers: a basic, flat-rate pension and the State Earnings Related Pension Scheme (SERPS) added in 1978. A degree of privatization existed from the start, as individuals with occupational pensions provided by their employers were allowed to opt out of SERPS. Despite being privately owned, occupational pensions at the time shared three key features with public arrangements: like a public program, occupational pensions pooled risk, rather than assigning it individually; and with that risk borne by employers, these schemes did nothing to connect members' interests to, or foster engagement with, financial markets. The 1986 Social Security Act made four major changes to British pensions policy. First, it allowed all individuals to opt out of

SERPS into an "approved personal pension," creating a second alternative to the state system. Second, it gave a financial bonus to those who switched to personal pensions. Third, it ensured individual choice among options by forbidding employers to make membership in their occupational pension a condition of employment. Fourth, it cut SERPS benefits deeply.[2]

These moves to expand the market's role in Britain's pensions regime were motivated by a desire to reshape the country's political economy and electoral politics. One powerful stimulus for reform was fiscal.[3] Already the largest item in the state budget and expected to expand substantially in coming decades, social security was a major focus of the government's drive for spending control. The privatization project was also motivated by a critique of private occupational pensions. Employer-provided pensions penalized those who changed jobs in midcareer, weakening their effectiveness as instruments of retirement security and impeding labor mobility.[4] Moreover, with Labour Party groups mooting proposals to expand trade union control of pension funds, occupational schemes seemed to threaten the autonomy of financial capital, providing the Left leverage over the economy that it could not obtain electorally at the time.

Closest to the hearts of the most avid privatizers was the hope that individual retirement vehicles would help build a "nation of capitalists." According to an influential report by the Thatcherite Centre for Policy Studies, "At present the law actually results in a continuing shift of capital from the personal to the corporate sector—and for most people today ownership is ownership at second hand, and as such, is not ownership in the *motivational sense*."[5] Individual workers might effectively *be* owners of capital, but unless they held capital directly, they would not *feel* themselves to be so. Locating pensions savings at the individual level would reduce the psychology of mass dependence and, even more important, would give individual savers a greater stake in the country's economic prosperity.[6] When national industries were privatized, the effect was limited to those wealthy enough to buy shares. In contrast, the entire working population participated in either SERPS or an occupational pension. Linking retirement incomes to asset values would, it was hoped, blur the line between labor and capital, leading ordinary workers to think more like capitalists and, consequently, to vote Tory.

Ministers envisioned individual workers saving for their own retirement by making prudent investment decisions in well-functioning financial markets, with state and other providers of collective security retreating from the field. For reasons that should appear in a wide range of contexts, this vision was difficult to realize in practice.

The Perils of Market Making

Conservatives have long stressed the risks of unintended consequences that attend state intervention. But unintended consequences can also bedevil projects designed to shrink the role of the state, owing to the role of causal complexity and cognition in the initial policy design choices of market-making governments. In addition, certain fundamental features of democratic politics make it difficult for market projects to survive rounds of policy feedback in recognizable form.

Step One: Policy Design

All policymaking involves tinkering with imperfectly understood social, economic, or natural systems, generating uncertainty and the potential for unintended consequences. That said, not all political projects are *equally* prone to unanticipated effects. At least four features of a policy change will influence decisionmakers' predictive capacity:

—*Scope of change:* The more parameters that decisionmakers change at a single stroke, the greater the uncertainty of the outcome. This is especially true when the success of one policy adjustment depends on the effects of another.[7]

—*Novelty of choice context:* Predicting policy consequences means assessing how organizations and individuals will respond to a new context. Modeling these responses is easiest when institutions and individuals are asked to make routine decisions under incrementally altered conditions, and hardest when they are asked to make unfamiliar choices within novel institutional settings.

—*Size of information gaps:* In addition to a model, predicting policy consequences requires reliable data about the state of the world, especially about the resources, preferences, beliefs, and practices of those whose choices will influence the outcome. The poorer the data, the greater the uncertainty of the result.

—*Bounds on choices:* In some reform contexts, individuals and organizations have a wider *range* of options than in others. The more diverse the actors' menu of choices, the greater the scope for those choices to interact in unforeseen ways.

The project of creating new markets is likely to be especially fraught with these vulnerabilities. One reason is that all markets are structured by a policy environment that includes a web of regulations of products and prices, producer-consumer interactions, and market entry; rules governing the tax treatment of transactions or profits, or both; and, sometimes, direct state subsidies to producers or consumers. Predicting how market actors will react to a change in just *one* of these parameters is difficult enough. When multiple simultaneous changes are made, policymakers must forecast not only how actors will respond to multiple new constraints and incentives but also how they will respond to *each other's* hard-to-predict adjustments to the new policy structures. Just as important may be the complex ways in which the new arrangements will interact with preexisting institutions and market conditions.

Equally important, markets for new products require consumers and providers to make novel choices—choices that will be difficult or impossible for governments to predict. When policymakers introduce a new class of good or service—one that is not a close substitute for any existing product—they will have little evidence to assist them in predicting consumer interest and competence. Stepping into the void of a new market, producers too will be making new decisions, about everything from the design to the marketing and pricing of a new kind of product.

Furthermore, policymakers will typically be fashioning new markets without some of the most important information in hand. Ironically, the yawning informational gaps that market making confronts lie at the core of the traditional case for markets. Advocates of laissez-faire over command-and-control solutions have long argued that key ingredients of the micro-economy are unobservable ex ante to state officials. Yet this claim for markets necessarily implies that market outcomes are highly unpredictable; it is precisely that uncertainty that gives markets their bite. If decentralized markets possess the informational virtues their advocates claim, then market making will be an inherently imprecise policy tool for achieving any *specific* social result. Finally, unless a new product market merely replaces old options, it will provide economic actors with an *expanded* menu of choice—thereby enlarging the scope for unexpected dynamics.

Market making thus presents policymakers with an enormous degree of causal complexity and uncertainty. What is known about the bounds of human cognition—even that of expert decisionmakers—suggests that policy framers are unable to deal with such complexity in comprehensive analytical terms.[8] Rather, they are likely to rely on a number of *shortcuts* in arriving at decisions. We draw attention to two especially powerful types of shortcuts: reliance on ideology and cognitive processes associated with the confirmation bias.

While ideology is politically ubiquitous, it is likely to play an especially important role in motivating projects of market making. One simple reason is that such projects are rarely politically attractive in the short term. When state provision or monopoly is replaced by market forces, voters are more likely to notice disruptions to their own current arrangements than the diffuse benefits of enhanced efficiency—which, in any case, will usually take longer to emerge.[9] The best-organized interests, meanwhile, will usually be those that benefit from the status quo, whether public sector unions or workers and firms in currently regulated industries. Most of the prospective beneficiaries of privatization and deregulation will be small, unknown, or yet to even emerge.[10] Market-based reform will thus rarely be a response to social demands for more markets per se: it is more likely to originate with ideologically motivated state actors themselves.[11]

New ideology, having initially motivated a project of market making, can also substantially simplify the task of policy design under uncertainty. First, ideology directs decisionmakers facing complex choices to a limited set of *policy tools* and *causal propositions* about how the world operates.[12] Second, preexisting ideas structure how actors process *information* in the course of decisionmaking. A wealth of psychological evidence indicates that individuals are systematically more likely to seek, weigh, and credit information that *supports* their prior beliefs. This "confirmation bias" leads even expert decisionmakers to avoid or discredit challenging evidence or cases, or to interpret them in ways that leave their prior beliefs intact.[13] Ideology thus acts not merely as a simplifying template but also as a convenient filter. One would thus expect politicians ideologically committed to market expansion to seek out evidence and precedents for action that illustrate the virtues of choice, competition, and private ownership—and to systematically underweight evidence of market dangers.

Even when those dangers *are* recognized, however, market-makers may have strategic reasons not to act to reduce them. Hedging against the risks of markets involves steep tradeoffs: any attempt to diminish the four risk factors listed earlier will almost automatically reduce market dynamism, blunting choice or competition and possibly discouraging firm entry. In short, caution could kill the market. What is more, a strategic logic will push proponents to err on the side of maximizing market activity. Since it carries short-term costs and is rarely demanded from below, market making's survival will depend on rapidly attracting support among voters and organized groups. The surest way to guarantee such support is to generate market activity—to spur individual and organizational investments in the new arrangement. To those worried about the project's durability, getting the market right may be less important than getting it going.

Both cognitive and strategic forces thus reduce the likelihood that the designers of new markets will insure against the market's potential risks. To this end, market-makers will often eschew regulatory constraints that might reduce the range of potential outcomes and avert the worst—even when the worst could be reasonably anticipated. In fact, market advocates can be expected to give the market a push, even subsidizing it in ways that may amplify the unpredictability.

Step Two: Policy Feedback

The problem of unintended consequences has a second dimension: any unwanted outcomes will emerge in the context of democratic political processes that bode especially poorly for market-makers' goals. That is because those policymakers who must respond to negative results will face strong incentives to begin dismantling or constricting the market. We base this claim on three simple observations about the character of accountability and decisionmaking in democracies.

First, public expectations of accountability are rigid and slow to change. According to Madsen Pirie, "Once the service is in the private sector, it is outside the direct area of government responsibility. Its costs no longer have a direct impact on taxation; its labour force no longer works for the state; and its level of service is determined by demand. In short, the government takes no more blame for its performance."[14] Wishful thinking, we would argue. When long financed or provided by the state, a good or service builds popular expectations around itself. While perceptions of "publicness" may soften as the market takes root, such commitments are likely to be sticky.

Second, incumbents in a democracy can rarely count on continued tenure in office or firmly bind the hands of their successors. Even if elements of a new market are irrevocable, future governments will possess tools for limiting its scope—especially the potent weapon of *regulation*. As Steven Vogel argues in chapter 2 of this volume, freer markets often require more rules. Note, too, that the original designers of a new market will, themselves, often fail to recognize this requirement. However, if this irony is not built into the reformers' original blueprint, then their successors may well construct it for them.

Third, democratic politics move faster than markets evolve. Markets work not because of brilliant decisionmaking by entrepreneurs but because failure is punished over time, and successful innovations survive. Even in the best case—when markets *do* ultimately deliver the outcomes their designers intend—the path to this equilibrium will be littered with constituents' interests.[15] In the meantime, politicians will face strong electoral pressures to use public authority to compensate losers and prevent further losses—that is, to bring the state back in, at the expense of market autonomy.

To summarize, market making is beset by cognitive and political challenges. The uncertainty of the enterprise and the ideological filter through which its advocates perceive it obscure its riskiness. The race against political time to entrench the new market creates further pressures to promote its expansion and eschew precautionary measures that might stunt its growth. In a democratic context, however, such a choice is always a gamble. If unintended consequences do emerge, tomorrow's government will face strong pressures to intervene. While elements of private ownership and competition may survive, the scope of state activity may ultimately return to—or even expand beyond—its pre-reform boundaries, blurring the lines between private market and public control.

Designing a New Pensions Market

In its quest for individualized ways of providing for retirement, how did the Thatcher government design the new market? To achieve its goals, the government needed to move workers out of collective pension arrangements, but these were extremely difficult to change. Winding down SERPS, for instance, would have carried large, short-term transition costs.[16] Even less conceivable was the idea of abolishing occupational pension schemes, which by the mid-1980s covered about half of the British workforce—partly as a result of prior state policies to encourage workers to opt out of SERPS. From the point of view of Thatcher's ministers, these occupational schemes, with their large pooled funds and restrictive exit conditions, were as important to reform as the public scheme.[17] But abolishing or withdrawing state support for these schemes would have imposed overwhelming costs on employers—a central component of the Tory political coalition. Mature private pension plans were deeply entrenched in the British political economy, and even a government as powerful as Thatcher's could not inflict a measure this punishing on business.

Reformers would therefore have to build their plans around these schemes' continued existence. While they could not abolish occupational pensions, the government could—and did—loosen their grip on employees. The 1986 reform forbade employers to *compel* workers to join their occupational scheme, and it allowed all workers to leave their company's plan for a personal pension. While a pragmatic compromise, placing the two regimes side by side made the market far more complex than replacement would have. Personal pensions would have to supplant occupational schemes by *competing* with them (and SERPS) for customers. Workers, in turn, would have to make a choice between two hard-to-compare options—a defined-*benefit* occupational pension, and a defined-*contribution* personal pension. This interaction between changed policy instruments and the market environment in which they were embedded set the stage for the misselling scandal.

Moreover, the market that policymakers hoped to use *did not yet exist:* there was as yet no market of individualized retirement savings vehicles for most British workers to opt into. Thus the reform proposal contemplated not merely enhancing the right of individuals to choose but creating an entirely new choice. To summon this new market into existence, ministers subsidized it by giving holders of personal pensions a rebate on their National Insurance (NI) contributions and by deferring taxes on their contributions into personal pensions (as was done under occupational schemes).

Getting this market going would not be easy. When the government first proposed creating the personal pension option, the reaction from providers of financial services was underwhelming. On one level, this was surprising, since this option would give the industry millions of potential customers. However, most firms were unconvinced that there was much profit to be reaped in managing countless small funds, given the administrative costs associated with them. The industry also feared, prophetically, that the scheme would encourage future government interference in the pensions market.[18]

Ministers found this reaction sobering: this was not an industry eager for the government to push back the boundaries of the state. And yet, as Secretary for Social Services Norman Fowler put it, "I needed to rely on the industry to deliver the goods."[19] Interestingly, ministers did *not* draw one obvious conclusion from this rebuff: that if the costs of provision exceeded a rational consumer's willingness to pay, then a true market for personal pensions could never emerge. On the contrary, rather than reconsider the project, British policymakers took market creation as a given and nonnegotiable goal.

With that objective fixed, ministers sought to make personal pensions even more attractive for consumers, thereby luring providers into the field. The government adopted two broad strategies of market shaping. First, they boosted personal pensions returns well beyond a market baseline. For instance, for younger workers who chose a personal pension over SERPS, state rebates would be *higher* than the actuarial value of SERPS. Concerned that even this advantage would be insufficient, Fowler insisted that all new personal pensions be granted an additional "incentive" worth 2 percent of a worker's insurable earnings for the first few years.[20] A switch from occupational to personal pensions would also yield immediate rewards: while workers were usually required to make contributions to employer schemes, they would not be required to make any out-of-pocket payments into their personal pension.

The government's second strategy of market promotion relied on persuasion rather than calculation. Workers entitled to generous retirement benefits from their current employer could be expected to approach an alternative, unfamiliar savings option with considerable caution. To help counteract consumer inertia, the government launched an aggressive advertising campaign that emphasized the benefits of a fully portable, individualized retirement option. Ads pictured citizens breaking the chains—literally—of collective pension schemes, proclaiming that "the right pension for you is now yours by right."[21] This campaign helped create a powerful "halo effect" around the new retirement vehicles.

To a degree, ministers did consider market risks. While the pension reform bill was being prepared and considered, the government was simultaneously writing a bill to reform the financial sector, including firms that would sell personal pensions.[22] The Financial Services Bill imposed broad obligations on salespeople's interactions with customers. They were required to obtain enough information about customers to assess whether a given product made sense for them ("know your customer"), recommend only those products that did ("offer best advice"), disclose their own interests, and state rates of return and charges.[23] The rules thus focused on creating the right informational environment for consumer choice.

Particularly striking, however, is what the government did not regulate in detail: the character of the product sold. Most consequentially, ministers chose not to regulate the size and structure of the new pensions' fees. The government's information-based rules left the responsibility for prudent long-term decisionmaking in the hands of the consumer—even as the new market's design created powerful short-term incentives for workers to leave their current arrangements. Moreover, compared with product rules, point-of-sale regulations set an extremely high informational bar for *enforcement,* requiring a structure to oversee the behavior of thousands of individual salespeople. This was not a task for which the British financial regulatory apparatus was equipped. The combination proved explosive.

The Misselling Scandal: Causes and Consequences

While the 1986 Social Security Act certainly has its defenders, it led in only a few years to one of the greatest policy debacles of recent British history: the "misselling scandal."[24] British pension expert David Blake sums up the basic facts thus:

> Between 1988 and 1993, 500,000 members of occupational pension schemes had transferred their assets to personal pension schemes [PPS] following high pressure sales tactics by agents of PPS providers. As many as 90 percent of those who transferred had been given inappropriate advice. Miners, teachers, nurses and police officers were among the main targets of the sales agents. Many of these people remained working for the same employer, but switched from a good occupational pension scheme offering an index-linked pension into a PPS towards which the employer did not contribute and which took 25 percent of the transfer value in commissions and charges. . . . As a result of public outcry, PPS providers have had to compensate those who had been given inappropriate advice to the tune of £13.5 billion.[25]

How did Britain go from advertisements showing people breaking free of their old pension arrangements to visions of older Britons demanding restitution from previously rock-solid financial companies? The misselling scandal was driven by a number of factors, including features of the 1986 act, changes in the evolving regulatory regime, and the internal structure of the financial industry.

Many observers cite the scandal as an object lesson in the dangers of *privatization*.[26] But, strictly speaking, those who contracted out of SERPS were well advised to do so, given the cuts being made in the program and the generous subsidies on offer. The misselling scandal focused most intensely on those who were previously in occupational pensions—that is, those *already* in private schemes. The disaster must thus be understood as a consequence of constructing a *new* market in personal pensions and of individualizing retirement options, rather than of privatization per se.

By itself, a personal pension scheme should not have been a terribly complex financial device. The complexity arose from individuals having to determine not only which was the best personal plan but also whether a personal pension was preferable to their existing occupational scheme. This was an intrinsically difficult decision, even for the financially sophisticated, given the difficulty of comparing collective, employer-provided pensions and individualized personal savings arrangements.

Most important, benefits in the two schemes were extremely hard to compare. Employer plans were usually defined-*benefit* schemes with payments based on years of service with a particular employer and final salary, often including death benefits for widows and dependents. That said, they were generally not fully portable across firms.[27] In contrast, a personal pension was a defined-contribution vehicle—the payout being purely a function of individual contributions based on lifetime earnings, charges, and market returns—and it *was* fully portable.

Even had all things been equal between the two, the choice would have been a complex function of factors such as risk preference, family structure, and expectations of continued employment with a single firm. But all was far from equal. On the one hand, the 2 percent rebate on NI contributions placed a thumb on the scale in favor of personal pensions. On the other hand, employers' own preferences tilted the scale back toward occupational schemes. As the major employer federation admitted during the reform debate, employers provide pensions "as a means of improving efficiency by helping recruit, motivate and *retain* the employees they require."[28] An occupational scheme was, therefore, purposely designed to be hard to walk away with. In fact, it almost never made long-term sense for individuals to move from a company scheme to a personal one and lose the employer contribution. But this net effect was far from transparent, and the enticement of the immediate bonus invited poor decisionmaking. The complexity and risks of the individual market were thus greatly increased by the government's attempt to promote radical change *alongside* the inherited occupational pension regime.

The effects of consumer overload were amplified by complex interactions with the broader financial services regime. As discussed earlier, pension reform took place at the same time as regulatory reform for financial services as a whole. While its goals were broad, the new Financial Services Act (FSA) was seen as a necessary element of the new personal pensions market. Not only did the FSA interact with pension reform in complex ways, but it also sat uncomfortably atop inflexible features of the existing financial services regime: the internal structure of firms and the competitive pressures under which they operated; the sophistication of individual market actors; and the capacities of governmental and quasi-governmental regulatory bodies.

The logic of the new FSA regulations was informational, to ensure that consumers had the necessary data to make prudent long-term choices. Yet in making financial providers the information conduits, the regulations assumed the probity of existing sellers. Indeed, policymakers at the time perceived the insurance industry in particular as a body of "conservative" professionals constrained by deeply embedded norms of client service, rather than as a group of salespeople motivated purely by financial gain. Under the assumption of a norm-driven industry, it made sense to instruct providers in quite general terms—to "know your customer" and "provide the best advice" as to whether switching into a personal scheme was appropriate for a particular individual.

Unfortunately, the FSA's effectiveness depended on features of corporate culture that were under substantial stress—and that the FSA itself was in unforeseen ways helping to disrupt. The new market opportunity, for instance, encouraged financial firms to quickly produce an enormous network of sales agents tied to their products.[29] One effect of this rush to hire was to exert strain on existing systems for training sales agents.[30] The new market's complexity made poor training a major liability. Determining whether a switch was right for the individual demanded detailed knowledge not just of the sales agent's product but also of the operation and services of occupational pensions. Acquiring this information was time-consuming and required specialized expertise. Moreover, few firms had experience managing a large and dispersed direct-sales force, and their existing compliance divisions had low status and limited competence.[31]

Thus as the reform came into effect, the firms expected to provide personal pensions were in flux and had weak internal systems to enforce whatever regulations the government had established. The new retail environment also weakened incentives to fulfill the FSA's obligations. Having taken on large new sales forces, product providers compensated retailers largely through commission—creating an incentive to sell, not provide balanced advice.[32] The FSA thus assigned providers a task that was irrational for their sales agents, putting pressure on already weak corporate compliance systems.

These problems were compounded by the actions of consumers, who rushed into personal pensions in unanticipated numbers. Whereas the government had predicted that 500,000 people would opt into a personal pension, the number within just a few years totaled *four million*.[33] This explosion in take-up was partly the result of the reform's short-term incentives, combined with aggressive state and provider advertising. Firms' promotion efforts included an unprecedented £7 million marketing campaign by Prudential.[34]

The speed of the market's growth had several important effects. As already noted, it spurred more hiring of sales agents, further stressing already frail training and compliance systems. In addition, the tempo of market growth far outpaced that of regulatory oversight. Regulators, moreover, were slow to uncover misselling activities because of a poor fit between their capacities and the nature of the problem. Britain's financial services regime was governed by self-regulatory bodies possessing modest analytical capacity and generally dependent upon firms' willingness to self-police. The resulting methods of collecting information caused the regime to develop an enormous blind spot. As Howard Davies, the head of the Financial Services Authority, explains, "Regulators tended to take, as the basis for their assessments, a sample of transactions from across a life office's whole range of business. Pension transfer and opt-out cases would not feature prominently in such a global sample."[35] Moreover, their focus on individual firms left the regulators better equipped to identify individual problems than systematic trends. As Julia Black and Richard Nobles have also noted, "The processes for standing back and taking a cross-industry approach to anything but the most blatant activities were limited."[36]

When the regulators did acquire better intelligence on the selling of personal pensions, the result was shocking. According to an early survey, "Only nine per cent of firms' files showed substantial compliance, . . . 85 per cent showed no evidence of alternative pension arrangements having been considered, and in only 23 percent of cases was there an adequate analysis supporting the recommendation."[37] Moreover, the resulting sales tactics seem to have had an enormous impact: one study found that of those customers who took out a personal pension, only 16 percent were "self-motivated," while 60 percent were swayed by a sales agent's advice.[38] Designed to police the "few bad apples" in fundamentally sound firms, the regulatory agencies were not prepared for widespread and systemic abuse in an entirely new line of business.

The Sources of Policy Error

What accounts for this policy disaster? One possible explanation is the deceptive nature of prior experience—specifically, the top financial providers' reputation for probity. As one senior civil servant closely involved with the planning of the 1986 act observed, "We didn't really see the misselling coming. We wrongly assumed that the whole of the pensions industry would maintain the standards of the best. There is a long tradition of service in the pensions industry."[39]

Though the information in the hands of decisionmakers was incomplete, this alone fails to explain the policy failure. In fact, the misselling disaster was far from unforeseen: its major elements were all publicly predicted by prominent actors during the decisionmaking process.

From the opposition's front benches in Parliament, Margaret Beckett foretold the disaster perhaps most concisely: "There is the danger that people may be misled into taking out personal pensions, without realizing the risks that they will incur."[40] It was also predicted *ahead of time* in Parliament and major newspapers that

—the new pension product, in comparison with occupational pensions and SERPS, would be nontransparent and too complex for consumers to adequately understand;[41]

—the administrative charges in particular would be excessive, not fully disclosed, and difficult for consumers to understand;[42]

—agents selling personal pensions would fail to represent their clients' best interests, present products in misleading ways, lack training, or sell too aggressively;[43]

—the 2 percent incentive and reduced contributions required for personal pensions, combined with lack of foresight or sophistication, would lead to massive exits from occupational or state pensions that are, over the long run, a better deal or more secure;[44]

–regulations requiring sales agents to provide information to consumers would be difficult to monitor and enforce;[45]

—there was tremendous uncertainty about the size of the population opting out;[46]

—individuals who imprudently chose to switch from existing arrangements to personal pensions would likely have inadequate pensions in old age; and[47]

—the new regulatory regime was an inadequate response to such risks, and specific additional measures were needed to provide independent advice, requirements for standardized presentation, or caps on fees, for example.[48]

Given that misselling was a scandal well foretold, why did ministers fail to adequately adjust? Their responses to these warnings suggest that an ideological commitment to markets served as a powerful filter of both causal complexity and new information. Most revealing are the statements made by Secretary for Social Services Norman Fowler, the reform's chief architect. When queried about the potential risks, Fowler gave a strikingly modest estimation of the problem's potential scale or the likelihood of its emergence. When a member of Parliament pointed out that "the implications of contracting out of SERPS are very complicated" and asked whether "individuals will be able to understand them," Fowler replied that he did not "see any reason why that should not be possible."[49] It is not just that Fowler's sense of the challenge was sharply at odds with much informed opinion. He also appears not to have given serious thought to what the state might do to mitigate the dangers. When pressed to explain his plans for aiding consumer choice, he indicated little clear direction: "The Government can provide information as far as that is concerned; I mean leaflets and so on. It is probably, I think, that organisations like the Occupational Pensions Advisory Service and the Consumers' Association will also want to bring forward more information of that kind."[50]

Fowler's remarks also reveal the theory of markets with which he was operating. He seems to have had high expectations for the capacity of competitive pressures to satisfy consumer preferences and to create the preconditions for rational decisionmaking. In particular, he assumed that competition itself would solve the informational problem in large part: "more providers," he said, would mean "better information."[51] Similarly, a multiplicity of contending providers would keep administrative fees low.[52]

Fowler also operated with extremely strong assumptions about consumer rationality, evident in his response to concerns that the proposed pension alternatives might entice individuals to opt, imprudently, out of their current arrangements:

I find it hard to believe that employees will be tempted out of a good occupational scheme just to take advantage not only of a modest incentive—2 per cent—but of a temporary incentive, because it lasts only for five years. Employees may have other reasons for preferring a personal pension, such as the expectation that they will frequently change their jobs. If they left an occupational scheme, they might be giving up the promise of pension contributions from their employer and they would have no statutory right of return to their employer's scheme. That is a matter that they will have to weigh in the balance.[53]

Notably, the long-term disadvantages of leaving a good occupational scheme were, for Fowler, all the more reason to believe that individuals would be unlikely to do so—and that this was not a danger for policy design to guard against. Comments by other Conservative members confirm that Fowler was not alone in his vision of the personal pensions market.[54]

Clues to the nature of ministers' information processing can be pieced together from the structure of the decisionmaking process as well as from politicians' statements. Fowler, for example, pointed to just two sources of lessons about the risks confronting consumers in the new pensions market. One was the U.S. experience with individual retirement accounts (IRAs). In a visit to the United States, Fowler had observed that competition among pension providers brought down administrative charges and was "entirely beneficial as far as the public is concerned."[55] What Fowler overlooked but is equally important is that price competition there was underwritten by a regulatory structure that *required* transparent charges in American mutual funds. What is more, American IRAs were a top-up to public and employer benefits, whereas the British were forcing consumers to choose *among* public, occupational, and personal pension products.

The other case study upon which the minister drew was closer to home: the 1985 Social Security Act, which enhanced the portability of British workers' occupational pension claims. Pointing to the success of the campaign to publicize portability rights, he argued that the complexity of the personal pension decision could be addressed through advertising.[56] Again, the analogy was a poor one, eliding the distinction between consumer tasks of sharply differing levels of complexity. That Fowler reached for such distant parallels to support his case suggests a marked search for confirmatory information.

Conversely, Fowler appears to have filtered *out* information that might have made the risks more apparent. Ministers' precommitment to a new personal pensions market was evident in their early deliberations. When Fowler convened an inquiry to consider reform options in 1983, he instructed the members to devise plans for personal pensions. The process was better suited to uncovering evidence for personal pensions than to scrutinizing their feasibility or weighing them against alternatives.[57] In addition, provider disinterest, far from discouraging the government, led it to redouble its market-making efforts. A civil servant involved in the process later recalled that officials had tried to highlight the risks of the new market, but that ministers did not want to come to terms with these risks in the process of policy design.[58]

Reformers also drew comforting, but overly sanguine, lessons from Britain's own experience with the provision of financial services. In fact, providers of financial services were already being criticized for their high administrative costs, inadequate disclosure, noncompliance with existing law, conflicts of interest, and "over aggressive selling of unsuitable pension policies."[59] Available information should have pointed to a need for tougher, prescriptive regulation—including rules on the type and presentation of fees— to make the personal pensions market work, rather than the "light-touch" point-of-sale regulation that the government chose.

To be clear, we do not contend that politicians ignored clear and obvious indicators of the likelihood and mammoth scale of the misselling scandal. The novelty and causal intricacy of the enterprise generated ambiguity around signals of danger, leaving them open to multiple interpretations.

Most dimly perceived (even by critics) were the ways in which tectonic shifts within the financial services industry itself, and the internal structures of firms, would interact with policy changes.

Yet it is hard to escape the conclusion that policymakers' interpretation of this uncertainty was distinctly biased toward the underestimation of consumer risk. Encouraging this interpretation, in addition to ideology, were signals that the market might have trouble getting off the ground. Given lukewarm provider reactions to an earlier version of the reform proposal, ministers worried that take-up would be too low and that caps on charges or tight rules might further deter firms from entering the market. In short, the regulatory tradeoff looked distinctly unappealing.

One further feature of the designers' mindset helps explain their choices. As one civil servant recounted, ministers believed that the time frame they were dealing with provided a substantial margin for trial and error. Because they were aiming to draw primarily younger workers into personal pensions, the politicians believed they would have time, before these workers retired, to sort out any problems that might emerge.[60] Of course, this is consistent with the view that any bumps in the road would be modest. What followed made a mockery of hopes that wrinkles could be ironed out later: policy adjustments did indeed follow these disastrous consequences—but not on the terms of the market-makers themselves.

Regulatory Feedback

The dramatic shift in the structure of pension provision was both more costly than reformers had expected and less conducive to their long-term goals. The reform drained far more from the budget in the short term than the chancellor expected, largely as a result of greater-than-anticipated uptake. These losses not only squeezed government finances in the first few years, but they also exceeded expected long-term savings from reduced public pension rolls.[61] Worse than the cost overruns, however, were the consequences of misselling, especially the likelihood of lower retirement incomes for workers who exited generous occupational schemes. Given that the government had sought to reroute, not reduce, flows of retirement income, this can only be considered a serious policy setback.

While less adequate pensions were an *unwanted* consequence, the *perverse* consequences were even more striking. Soon after the scandal broke, the public outcry provoked a chain of policy reactions that would restore and in some ways increase the state's role in pension provision and in financial markets.

The first was the Major government's Pensions Act of 1995,[62] which imposed enormous new regulations on the pensions industry and created a new authority (the Occupational Pensions Regulatory Authority) with sweeping investigative powers and the ability to seek both civil and criminal penalties for a wide variety of new offenses.[63] Where Thatcher's ministers hoped that competition and self-regulation would ensure a sound pensions market, their successors, though from their own party, were forced to eat away at ancient patterns of self-regulation and impose extensive new regulations.

These intrusions by the state went further with the Labour government's arrival in 1997. To the Conservatives' changes, Labour added a new Financial Services Authority that took over the responsibilities of the Securities and Investment Board, assumed the Bank of England's supervisory functions, and absorbed and effectively nationalized the long-standing self-regulatory organizations. For the first time in its history, Britain had a centralized state financial regulator. What is more, basic regulatory principles were called into question.[64] Prescriptive standards for financial products adopted during Labour's first few years reached well beyond Britain's regulatory tradition. The government's Individual Savings Accounts and Stakeholder Pensions (an alternative to personal pensions for low earners) incorporated standards that set maximum investment charges, banned front-end loaded charges, and required providers to offer access to small savers.[65] In addition, the Personal Investment Authority took a hard line on independent financial advisers, cutting the industry in half in the government's first two years.[66]

The most important consequence of these successive layers of regulatory feedback has been greater complexity. As the government-appointed Turner Commission recently reported, "The UK has the most complex pension system in the world. This reflects the impact of decisions made over the last few decades, each of which appeared to make sense at the time, but the cumulative effect of which has been to create bewildering complexity in the state system, in the private system, and in the interface between them."[67] In addition to making it even more difficult for unsophisticated savers to understand the market, this complexity has increased costs, constricted the supply of providers, and reduced returns for low-income investors.

By weakening public trust in financial markets, the misselling scandal also set back Tory ministers' mission of aligning the interests of average workers to those of capital. As the Turner Commission concluded, "The retail financial services industry has lost the trust of customers as a result of a sequence of misselling scandals and problems."[68] Pensions privatization further linked citizens to the state as their protector against exploitation in a market relationship inherently characterized by asymmetrical information. Surveys both at the end of the Conservatives' reign and more recently confirm that support for government social spending (including pensions) is strong, has increased since the 1986 Social Security Act, and continues to resemble continental European rather than American levels.[69]

It is important to note the precise nature of the perversity of policy feedback here. The Conservatives did rein in the *supply* of public expenditure, but not the *demand* for state intervention. When the new market went badly, governments were still held responsible, and new regulation was the logical response. While intending to expand the market, Thatcher's government set in motion a process through which Britain socialized a large part of its financial markets. It also remains to be seen whether state parsimony can survive the retirement of millions of workers on meager personal pensions and millions more on residual state benefits. While the Conservatives reduced the state's *actuarial* liabilities, they may have bequeathed to their successors a vast *political* liability that can only be discharged through an expansion of the conventional welfare state.

Conclusion

Thatcher's government began the reform process with significant advantages: ideological commitment, institutional authority, and unusually flexible policy structures. In these respects, Britain's 1986 pension reform is an ideal case for testing whether governments *can* successfully replace collective modes of provision with new markets. Within a decade, however, this ambitious reform damaged the state's fiscal outlook, made pensioners less secure, led to massive new state intrusion in financial markets, and diminished public trust in private vehicles of saving and investment.

On almost all counts, reform outcomes dashed market-makers' expectations. At their best, of course, markets produce outcomes that are hard for policymakers to predict ex ante. The sheer ambition of the government's project created enormous causal complexity by requiring multiple simultaneous changes in the choices, rules, and incentives economic actors faced. It is not surprising, therefore, that things did not go according to plan, nor is it especially revealing that the causes of disaster appear clear in retrospect. What *is* striking about the reform process is how prominent the danger signs were before the fact, and how little attention ministers paid to them, given that risk-reducing design choices were proposed at the time. The available record suggests that ministers' cognitive strategy for managing uncertainty led them to systematically underestimate the risks of market failure.

An ideology that emphasized the virtues of markets drew ministers to the endeavor in the first place. Once they turned to market design, this world-view simplified causal complexity by supplying a model of the economic world based on stylized assumptions about competitive pressures and individual rationality. In this model, a whole range of potential problems, from informational scarcity to administrative costs, appeared little more than grist for the competitive mill. The record suggests that ministers sought out and paid more attention to information that reinforced, rather than challenged, this worldview. Given their goals, the most worrying signals were those received from providers suggesting that the market might never emerge and thus that it needed a good push, not burdensome safeguards against hypothetical dangers.

The misselling scandal was certainly an undesired consequence, but the consequences most at odds with reformers' intentions were those that flowed from the reactions of later governments to policy disaster—especially the substantial socialization of the "private" pensions market. Once things went badly, it was impossible for any elected government, even a Conservative one, to let the market sort itself out. Even though mechanisms of pension provision had shifted, public expectations had barely moved: the government in power when misselling broke had to react with bold initiatives to correct market defects. It is in the nature of democratic politics that those who enact large reforms are rarely in a position to control their long-term evolution. In the slow, painful process of market making, unintended reactions by future politicians may be as consequential as unintended dynamics in the market itself.

This feature of the disaster also suggests the limits of "learning by doing" in a competitive political environment. By relying on competition to solve problems, Thatcher's ministers were implicitly taking a patient view, since markets only punish failure over time. They also seemed to believe that they would have time to make new policy adjustments in response to any trouble that arose. In a democratic context, there is much to be said for getting it right the first time. The problem is not merely that one's political opponents may get to make the future adjustments. As the Major government's responses make clear, even those who designed the reform may find themselves forced to respond to painful consequences in ways driven more by the logic of electoral accountability than by the original logic of privatization.

We do not mean to suggest that projects of market making are inevitably doomed to failure or perversity. In particular, we should emphasize that the same dynamics may not play out with such a vengeance when governments seek merely to expand the role of *already functioning* markets. The British case does, however, suggest a pattern that may play out across the life cycle of many kinds of market-based projects. It also suggests a couple of hypotheses about the factors that may make market mishaps more likely.

First, the role of strong ideational commitments suggests that the ideological ardor of governments of the right may make them less effective market-makers than those of the left. We note that some of the more successful cases of deregulation or privatization in this book relied on the consensus judgment of experts that the injection of markets into particular domains would lead to better outcomes. Social Security privatization in Britain, in contrast, was driven by a sweeping vision of social and political transformation. Ironically, "Third Way" politicians may, precisely because they lack a principled faith in markets (or a transformational social project), be more intellectually flexible and catholic in their tastes for information and advice. As a consequence, they may be more likely to insist on policy measures that will minimize the probability of unwanted outcomes—and of more extensive interventions down the road.

Second, this case suggests that centralized decisionmaking processes and complex policy changes may make for a volatile combination.[70] In a Westminster system, critics in the opposition parties have almost no capacity to force the government to take their concerns into account in the process of policy design. In contrast, a setting where multiple political parties share policymaking power may force policy framers to take a wider range of risk perceptions into account in their design choices.

Not so long ago, conservatives warned the Left about tampering with institutions based upon abstract theoretical schemes, going so far as to warn of a "law of unanticipated consequences": once something becomes rooted in people's expectations and way of life, government planners cannot know all the ramifications of tampering with it. What is more, they warned of the hazards of entrusting noble social goals to imperfect political decisionmakers armed with necessarily incomplete information. The evidence presented in this chapter suggests that unintended consequences are as great a danger to grand schemes that would shrink the state as to those that would extend its reach. Market making is an act of policy design, and there is no reason to assume that government officials will be better at structuring new markets than they are at engineering public programs. Our argument thus implies that conservatives would be wise to proceed with the same skepticism, caution, and epistemological modesty they have urged on others. It also suggests that they will be sorely tempted to ignore this advice.

Notes

1. Here we heed the more general advice to political analysts by Paul Pierson, *Politics in Time: History, Institutions, and Social Analysis* (Princeton University Press, 2004).

2. Nicholas Timmins, *The Five Giants* (London: Fontana, 1995), p. 402.

3. Steven Nesbitt, *British Pensions Policymaking in the 1980s* (Brookfield: Avebury, 1995), p. 41; United Kingdom Department of Health and Social Security, "Population, Pension Costs and Pensioners' Incomes: A Background Paper for the Inquiry into Provision for Retirement" (London: Her Majesty's Stationery Office, 1984) (www.bopcris.ac.uk/bop1984/ref4028.html).

4. Norman Fowler, *Ministers Decide: A Personal Memoir of the Thatcher Years* (London: Chapmans, 1991); Nesbitt, *British Pensions,* p. 64.

5. Centre for Policy Studies, "Personal and Portable Pensions—For All" (London, 1983).

6. Hiroshi Araki, "Ideas and Welfare: The Conservative Transformation of the British Pension Regime," *Journal of Social Policy* 29, no. 4 (2000): 599–621; Paul Lewis, "Consequences: Personal Pensions," BBC Radio 4, 1996.

7. On this point and the next two, we borrow from Arthur T. Denzau and Douglass C. North, "Shared Mental Models: Ideologies and Institutions," *Kyklos* 47, no. 1 (1994): 7–8; and Jeffrey L. Pressman and Aaron B. Wildavsky, *Implementation* (University of California Press, 1984).

8. Denzau and North, "Shared Mental Models: Ideologies and Institutions"; Herbert A. Simon, "Designing Organizations for an Information-Rich World," in *Computers, Communication, and the Public Interest,* edited by Martin Greenberger (Johns Hopkins University Press, 1971); Hillel J. Einhorn and Robin M. Hogarth, "Behavioral Decision Theory: Processes of Judgment and Choice," in *Decision Making: Descriptive, Normative, and Prescriptive Interactions,* edited by David E. Bell, Howard Raiffa, and Amos Tversky (Cambridge University Press, 1988).

9. R. Douglas Arnold, *The Logic of Congressional Action* (Yale University Press, 1990); R. Kent Weaver, "The Politics of Blame Avoidance," *Journal of Public Policy* 6, no. 4 (1986): 371–98.

10. Adam Przeworski, *Democracy and the Market: Political and Economic Reforms in Eastern Europe and Latin America* (Cambridge University Press, 1991); Susan C. Stokes, "Public Opinion and Market Reforms: The Limits of Economic Voting," *Comparative Political Studies* 29, no. 5 (1996): 499–519.

11. Barbara Geddes, "The Politics of Economic Liberalization," *Latin American Research Review* 30, no. 2 (1995): 195–214.

12. Mark Blyth, *Great Transformations: Economic Ideas and Institutional Change in the Twentieth Century* (Cambridge University Press, 2002), p. 32; Denzau and North, "Shared Mental Models: Ideologies and Institutions."

13. Raymond S. Nickerson, "Confirmation Bias: A Ubiquitous Phenomenon in Many Guises," *Review of General Psychology* 2, no. 2 (1998).

14. Madsen Pirie, *Privatization* (Aldershot, UK: Wildwood House, 1988), p. 54. Pirie was the head of Britain's Adam Smith Institute.

15. Przeworski, *Democracy and the Market;* Stokes, "Public Opinion and Market Reforms."

16. A result of having to continue paying pensions to those who had already contributed to the scheme while losing contribution revenues from current workers.

17. Fowler, *Ministers Decide.*

18. Ibid; Paul Pierson, *Dismantling the Welfare State? Reagan, Thatcher, and the Politics of Retrenchment* (Cambridge University Press, 1994), p. 62; Michael Prowse, "Why Few Wish to Join the Fowler Bandwagon," *Financial Times,* September 20, 1985, p. 20.

19. Fowler, *Ministers Decide.*

20. Nesbitt, *British Pensions,* pp. 92–93.

21. Quoted in Julia Black and Richard Nobles, "Personal Pensions Misselling: The Causes and Lessons of Regulatory Failure," *Modern Law Review* 61, no. 6 (1998): 796.

22. Ibid.

23. Ibid.

24. Daniel Finkelstein, "The Policy and Political Lessons of Britain's Success in Privatizing Social Security," A Special Report to the House Committee on Ways and Means, Committee Brief 30 (1997); Peter Lilley, *Winning the Welfare Debate* (London: Social Market Foundation, 1995).

25. David Blake, "The UK Pension System: Key Issues," *Pensions* 8, no. 4 (2003): 330–73.

26. Norma Cohen, "A Bloody Mess," *American Prospect* (2005) (www.prospect.org/web/page.ww?section=root&name=ViewWeb&articleId=8997 [January 11]).

27. Black and Nobles, "Personal Pensions Misselling."

28. Confederation of British Industry, "Pensions Policy for the Future" (London, 1984), p. 8.

29. This development was partly encouraged by FSA retailing rules.

30. Black and Nobles, "Personal Pensions Misselling," p. 798.

31. Ibid., p. 801.

32. Ibid., p. 802.

33. Richard Disney and Edward Whitehouse, "Personal Pensions and the Review of the Contracting-out Terms," *Fiscal Studies* 13, no. 1 (1992): 41.

34. David Blake, *Pension Schemes and Pension Funds in the United Kingdom* (Oxford University Press, 2003), p. 218.

35. Howard Davies, speech delivered to the National Association of Pensions Funds, Autumn Conference, November 20, 1997.

36. Black and Nobles, "Personal Pensions Misselling," p. 813.

37. Ibid., p. 793.

38. Financial Services Authority and Personal Investment Authority, "Response to the Consultation on Phase 2 of the Pensions Review" (London, 1999).

39. Strachan Heppell, former official at the Department of Health and Social Security, interview with author, Ingatestone, United Kingdom, August 14, 2001. Guy Fiegehen, senior civil servant, Department of Work and Pensions, confirmed that "most financial

institutions had a reputation for being very safe, very stodgy," in an interview with the author, London, June 18, 2001.

40. Margaret Beckett, shadow minister for Social Security in *Parliamentary Debates,* 6th ser., vol. 98 (1986), col. 78.

41. Notes 42–49 cite only a sample of the sources making the respective predictions. House of Commons Social Services Committee, "First Report: Reform of Social Security," HC 180 (1986), p. x; Michael Prowse, "CBI President Criticises Pensions Phase-out Plan," *Financial Times,* June 22, 1985, p. 20; Barry Riley, "Need to Keep Up Guard Recognised," *Financial Times,* February 1, 1986, Weekend, p. xi.

42. Ron Lewis, member of Parliament, in Minutes of Evidence taken January 22, 1986; "The Big Bang: Tell Sid It's Time for Him to Watch Out," *Guardian,* October 24, 1986; House of Commons Social Services Committee, "First Report: Reform of Social Security," p. 3; Barry Riley, "A Vital Test for Self-Regulation," *Financial Times,* January 23, 1986.

43. Barry Riley, "Focus on Investor Protection," *Financial Times,* January 26, 1985, p. 112; Eric Short, "Wanted: a System That Will Work," *Financial Times,* January 8, 1985, p. 111; Sue Ward, "Week-end Money (Pension Points): The Retirement Plan That Might Not Live Up to All Our Expectations," *Guardian,* January 25, 1986.

44. Beckett, *Parliamentary Debates,* vol. 98, cols. 78–80.

45. "The Big Bang."

46. House of Commons Social Services Committee, "First Report: Reform of Social Security," p. x. As the committee noted, the government's actuary himself said that "there is no basis for making a firm estimate of the likely increase."

47. Beckett, *Parliamentary Debates,* vol. 98, cols. 78–80 and vol. 102 (1986), col. 385. Richard Price, "Policy on Pensions," Letter to the Editor, *Financial Times,* May 3, 1986, p. 9; Eric Short, "CBI Condemns Plan for Pension Switch Bonus," *Financial Times,* April 21, 1986, p. 11.

48. Eric Short, "Meacher in Pledge to Repeal Government Changes to SERPS," *Financial Times,* March 19, 1986, p. 10. See also Labour amendments offered in House of Commons Standing Committee B, "Minutes of Proceedings on the Social Security Bill," HC 377 (1986).

49. Minutes of Evidence in House of Commons Social Services Committee, "First Report: Reform of Social Security," p. 3.

50. Minutes in ibid., p. 4.

51. Minutes in ibid.

52. Minutes in ibid., p. 3.

53. *Parliamentary Debates,* 6th ser., vol. 98 (1986), cols. 89–90.

54. Ibid., col. 78; and *Parliamentary Debates,* 6th ser., vol. 102 (1986), col. 384.

55. Minutes in House of Commons Social Services Committee, "First Report: Reform of Social Security," p. 3.

56. Ibid.

57. Nesbitt, *British Pensions,* pp. 76–79.

58. Fiegehen, interview.

59. Quotation from C. Veasey, "Insurance Salesmen," Letter to the Editor, *Financial Times,* September 11, 1985, p. 115. See also Barry Riley, "Battle Joined on Legislation Front," *Financial Times,* April 14, 1986, p. 117.

60. Fiegehen, interview.

61. Richard Disney, Carl Emmerson, and Matthew Wakefield, "Pension Reform and Saving in Britain," *Oxford Review of Economic Policy* 17, no. 1 (2001): 90.

62. The act was also a response to Robert Maxwell's theft from his companies' pension schemes.

63. Belinda Benney, *A Guide to the Pensions Act 1995* (London: Butterworths, 1995), pp. 8–16; David Simpson, *Regulating Pensions: Too Many Rules, Too Little Competition?* (London: Institute of Economic Affairs, 1996), p. 32.

64. George Graham, "Treasury May Redraft Clauses in Bill," *Financial Times,* March 6, 1999, p. 6.

65. HM Treasury, "CAT Standards for Individual Savings Accounts" (London: Her Majesty's Stationery Office, 1998).

66. Jean Eaglesham, "Shape Up—or Ship Out: Broker Funds," *Financial Times,* February 13, 1999, p. 7.

67. Pensions Commission, "Pensions: Challenges and Choices" (London: Her Majesty's Stationery Office, 2004), p. 210.

68. Ibid., p. 214.

69. John Hills, "Following or Leading Public Opinion? Social Security Policy and Public Attitudes since 1997," *Fiscal Studies* 23, no. 4 (2002): 539–58; Max Kaase and Kenneth Newton, "What People Expect from the State: *Plus ça change,*" in *British and European Social Attitudes. How Britain Differs: The 15th Report,* edited by Roger Jowell and others (Aldershot, UK: Ashgate, 1998), p. 49. Karlyn Bowman, "Opinion Pulse: European Views," *American Enterprise,* December 2002, pp. 61–62.

70. This argument is supported by the British poll tax experience. David Butler, Andrew Adonis, and Tony Travers, *Failure in British Government: The Politics of the Poll Tax* (Oxford University Press, 1994).

9

A Market for Knowledge?
Competition in American Education

FREDERICK M. HESS

For more than a decade, market-oriented education reformers have touted the ability of competition to improve American K–12 education and wring inefficiencies and indulgent practices out of higher education. While arguing that competition will nonetheless promote quality, efficiency, and innovation, these advocates have sought to avoid the blunt, self-interested language of markets.

The result has been a strange politics of half-hearted debate. Proponents of deregulation have hesitated to use the instrumental language of markets. When proposals to expand school choice or competition among colleges have been adopted by public officials, they have typically been scrubbed of references to efficiency, productivity, winners and losers, or entrepreneurship. Even the champions of reform have opted for the gentler language of "choice"—while paying homage to the societal mission of schooling and its value as a public good. This has made for some astonishing, or astonishingly inept, efforts at market making. At the K–12 level, for instance, champions of competition have chosen to ignore questions about existing incentives for schools or managers, or the manner in which collective bargaining agreements restrict the ability of schools to respond to competition. In the world of higher education, reformers have sometimes simultaneously called for seemingly contradictory policies, such as establishing price controls, increasing subsidies for students, and promoting competition.

In the context of deregulatory politics, it is vital to understand that American education is not a regulated system in any conventional sense. K–12 schooling is, quite simply, a government-operated system with a small private sector. Higher education is a highly subsidized system dominated by publicly operated institutions, but with only modest regulation of the prices or services in private institutions. As for "deregulation," most such policy is not concerned with reducing government restrictions on private entities but with encouraging publicly managed entities to act "as if" they were private entities. These realities of the education sector have seldom been recognized by proponents and opponents of market-based reform, whose debates rest on the unstated assumption that publicly governed schools and colleges will behave like traditional profit-seeking firms when confronted with students empowered to attend the school of their choice.

Of course, higher education already exhibits a significant degree of competition due to funding systems, career structure, and access to resources. Major colleges and universities engage in fierce competition to enhance their prestige, attract the most talented students, acquire research support, and collect athletic accomplishments. A much-discussed 2002 analysis concluded that "high prestige universities . . . increasingly find themselves in a virtual 'arms race' with each other, constantly scrambling for higher rankings, better students, better faculty, winning athletic teams, and more research funding."[1] Community colleges and smaller state institutions compete in the legislative arena with one another and with other services for state funds.

In K–12 schooling, there is substantially less competition and much more ambivalence about whether schools and educators should be subject to competition. Nonetheless, teachers compete to win positions in advantaged districts, superintendents and principals vie for the career-making accolades showered upon innovators, school districts compete with private firms to provide tutoring under the federal No Child Left Behind Act (NCLB), and principals eagerly explain how they contend for students who could attend other schools. More obviously, for-profit firms have always competed to supply K–12 schools with academic products and services such as testing, textbooks, curricula, professional development, and instructional supplies.

In short, rather than suggest that competition does not exist in education, it is more accurate for proponents of market reform to argue that education is currently subjected to *inadequate* or *unhealthy* competitive pressures, and that market-based reform will yield more constructive dynamics. This, however, places a particular burden upon reformers. If the problem is that existing competition is unproductive or toothless, then simply promoting increased choice among schools or colleges is an insufficient solution. It becomes paramount for reformers to embrace changes that will trump existing pressures, alter the rules of the game, and rationalize behavior in the intended manner.

Education has two purposes: a "private" purpose and a "public" purpose. Education is a "private good" to the extent that individuals benefit from the skills and training produced by schooling and is a "public good" insofar as one is learning skills, dispositions, or values that make for a better citizen and neighbor. It is generally agreed that the public content of schooling is highest in the elementary grades and declines through secondary schooling and higher education, though there is no objective way to determine the size of the public component at any particular grade level. To the extent that education is a private matter, proponents of choice-based reform contend that public officials should regulate with a light hand and should not privilege state-run institutions. Those who see schooling as primarily a public good, meanwhile, argue that the state should oversee its provision and ensure its quality.

Insofar as elementary and secondary schooling is a "public good," states and local school districts provide all children with a free K–12 education. Because postsecondary education is seen as much more of a "private good," students and their families are expected to pay for it—although states and the federal government subsidize colleges and universities and provide students with extensive grants and loans. The resulting arrangements buffer institutions from the choices students make and limit the ability of students and families to shop for schools. In education, state subsidies and rules defining an acceptable product shape consumer behavior. Producers operate in accord with state mandates; under stringent requirements for permissible operations, staffing, and responsibilities; and on the basis of the need to attract public funds.

In both K–12 and postsecondary education, a persistent difficulty for market proponents has been the disparity between the rhetoric and reality of competition. Confusingly, there has been a tendency to conflate two very different dynamics and call them both "competition": one is the unleashing of self-interested incentives to compel public providers to improve, and the other is a loosening of restraints that hobble nontraditional and private providers.

Significantly, the most influential volume penned on educational competition, *Politics, Markets and America's Schools,* quietly failed to grapple with the central question of whether student choice would suffice to create effective competition.[2] In that volume, political scientists John Chubb and Terry

Moe used a national study of school performance to argue that autonomy and freedom from bureaucratic rulemaking enabled private K–12 schools to outperform their public counterparts. However, nowhere in the volume, despite an explicit assertion that policymakers should consider school vouchers a possible "panacea" for K–12 schooling, did the authors argue that these private schools compel public institutions to better serve students.[3] In short, even those scholars cited by proponents of educational competition have often paid limited attention to how or why educational competition works. Claims on behalf of the peculiarly designed public school choice and supplemental service provisions of NCLB have suffered from the same lack of clarity regarding the ways and means of competition.

It is vital to distinguish between competition intended to force public school systems, colleges, or universities to change in desirable ways and competition intended to permit new providers to emerge and thrive. This distinction yields two theories of change. The most straightforward way to unleash competition is to make it relatively simple for private providers to receive public funding for their educational services. If the accompanying regulation does not erect immense barriers to entry, this kind of *displacement* can yield immense change whether or not existing institutions respond productively. The alternative course is to use the threat from private providers and changes in public agency funding to compel a productive *public sector response,* trusting that self-interest will drive public schools, colleges, and universities to improve in response to competitive pressure. In contemporary policy debates, the rhetoric of public sector response is more common than that of displacement.

The Landscape of Education Competition

After health care, education constitutes the second largest sector of the American economy. In 2003–04, American taxpayers spent a total of $852 billion on education—$501 billion on K–12 and $351 billion on postsecondary—with 90 percent of the funding supplied by state and local governments.[4] In fiscal 2003, states devoted 33 percent of their spending to education.[5] Other than health care, there is no other sector in which improvements in quality or efficiency would have as large an impact on the public purse or on quality of life.

K–12 Education

Whereas American higher education features a diverse mix of private forprofit, private nonprofit, and public providers competing across geographic markets, K–12 schooling operates in a much more hidebound market. Public school districts enrolled 48.1 million students in 2003–04, just under 90 percent of the nation's 54 million K–12 students. Nonprofit institutions—primarily religiously affiliated—enrolled nearly all of the 6.3 million students in private schools.

All of the approximately 15,000 school districts across the country are nonprofit public entities. With a handful of exceptions, these districts derive more than 99 percent of their funding from tax revenues. While funding arrangements vary from state to state, in 2003–04 the majority of education funds were provided by the states, with local districts contributing about one-third of school expenditures and the federal government contributing about 10 percent. The national average per pupil expenditure in this period was $8,208, with the total cost (including construction and debt service) some 15 to 20 percent higher. Across states, average per pupil expenditures ranged from more than $12,000 in New York to less than $6,000 in Arizona and Utah.[6]

Public school principals and teachers are licensed in accordance with state credentialing rules. Although many districts employ large numbers of unlicensed educators, these individuals are typically regarded as stopgaps and are required to fulfill credentialing requirements or be replaced. Public school teachers and administrators are state employees and subject to relatively stringent state and local statutes, as well as contractual language that specifies pay scales and work conditions. In most states, teachers are tenured into their positions after two or three years, which makes it very difficult to remove them without an extended and often expensive process.

In private schooling, few of these conditions hold—though, for reasons of their own, private educators rarely use their advantages to maximize profitability or gain market shares. Private K–12 schools operate free from state regulations. They can hire without regard to licensure provisions, pay employees as they see fit, and readily remove or reward employees. In 1999–2000, the most recent year for which data are available, the Department of Education identified 25,138 private schools. Of those, just 21 percent charged $5,000 or more in annual tuition, while 41 percent charged less than $2,500.[7]

The private school sector illustrates some of the challenges confronting market reforms in education. As Teachers College professor Henry Levin noted in 2000, more than two dozen New York City schools charged annual tuition in excess of $20,000 and had extensive wait lists through good times and bad, yet sought neither to maximize revenues nor attract revenue-maximizing competitors.[8] In fact, most religious and secular schools heavily subsidize tuition with endowments, church funds, or similar sources of revenue. This makes for a peculiar marketplace, one in which key competitors to public provision are themselves unconcerned with profitability. The result is that many traditional private providers have little interest in exploiting market opportunities, maximizing revenues, or gaining market share—the objectives that market models typically assume when anticipating the nature and consequences of competition.

Perhaps surprising to those unfamiliar with schooling is that for-profit providers typically operate public schools rather than private schools, most often opening "charter" schools that have more independence than the typical public school. In 2003–04, there were 51 education management companies operating 463 schools and enrolling 200,403 students in 28 states and the District of Columbia. More than three-quarters of the schools were charter schools.[9]

Competitive forces are most evident in four areas of K–12 education, each a product of relatively recent changes to state or federal policy. First, somewhere between 1 and $1\frac{1}{2}$ percent of children are currently homeschooled. State laws rendered homeschooling illegal in nearly all states until the 1970s, when Christian groups spearheaded an effort to relax school attendance laws and ensure the right of parents to educate their children at home. Today, homeschooling is legal in all fifty states, operating under a variety of statutory restrictions. Estimates vary, but most place the homeschooling population at about 1 million. This has fostered a variety of opportunities for entrepreneurial providers, as families seek curricular materials and web-based instructional support.

Second, as of 2004, about 600,000 students were enrolled in 3,000 "charter schools" nationwide. These schools hold charters from state-designated entities that permit them to operate independently from the local school district. Charter school legislation, first enacted in Minnesota in 1991, funds schools with formulas based on enrollment, thus linking competitive performance to revenue. States fund charters to varying degrees, some at the same level as other public schools but many at a considerably reduced level. Only a few states offer charter schools substantial support when it comes to facilities and construction. As a result, entrepreneurs have encountered significant difficulty in getting charter schools started, often relying on philanthropic support and using third-rate facilities. In addition, public school districts and teachers unions have played a leading role in seeking to deny charter operators access to public capital for construction or facilities, have harassed them through legal and procedural means, and have supported caps on the number of permissible charter schools. In short, charter schools have developed amid pinched resources, inferior facilities, and political uncertainty.

Third, publicly funded school voucher programs, first enacted in Milwaukee in 1990, now operate in some cities (for example, Cleveland and Washington, D.C.) and on a limited statewide basis in Florida. Under voucher arrangements, the government provides individuals with a specified amount of money to be used toward tuition at any eligible provider. In each case, students are able to use the vouchers to attend private schools, including religious schools. Vouchers make the financial state of a school directly dependent on whether students enroll there, though most programs set per pupil funding at a substantially lower level than for local public schools. In 2003–04, the Milwaukee program enrolled more than 13,000 students and offered a maximum voucher of $5,882; Cleveland enrolled about 5,000 students and offered a maximum voucher of $2,700; and Florida's statewide voucher program for students in low-performing schools enrolled more than 600 students with a maximum voucher of about $4,600.

Fourth, the landmark No Child Left Behind Act of 2001 requires low-performing districts to use federal funds to create a competitive market for after-school tutoring services. More than 2,500 state-approved supplemental service providers are now competing for federal funds that average $800–$900 per eligible student. While many of the approved providers are school districts themselves or other nonprofits, a number of small for-profits and larger national for-profits, such as Platform Learning and Catapult Learning, are competing within this emerging sector. Harvard University business professor Clay Christensen has argued that most disruptive innovation tends to be pioneered by low-cost "down-market" providers who find ways to undercut established, pricey producers by delivering functional substitute products at dramatic savings.[10] Historically, the absence of for-profits, coupled with K–12 funding formulas and higher education subsidies, has stifled the emergence of cost-effective providers.

Outside of these new market niches where displacement is driving any evident change, public school systems have proven remarkably unresponsive to competition or shrinking student enrollment. This is due in part to state financing arrangements that buffer school districts from losing the full dollar amount associated with enrollment declines. For instance, from 1996 to 2004, Detroit public schools lost 35,000 of their 175,000 students to residential flight, charter schools, and private schooling. This 20 percent loss in district enrollment was accompanied by a real increase in total revenues and a double-digit percentage increase in total per pupil funding. Yet the district's refusal to close schools or cut personnel as enrollment declined led it to explore issuing bonds to help cover a $250 million shortfall in 2004–05 in lieu of imminent layoffs.[11]

Existing arrangements insulate educational leaders, administrators, and teachers from the consequences of their performance. Because individual teachers are not promoted or rewarded for exemplary performance, and because they do not face termination or demotion for poor performance, it is difficult for even determined leadership to spur employees to efforts beyond those they are disposed to put forth. And because neither school principals nor district superintendents are rewarded for attracting enrollment, they have little incentive to engage in controversial or unpopular measures to do so. Lacking the ability to readily assess, reward, or select subordinates, and in an environment where only the rarest school systems resort to layoffs, most principals and superintendents lack the means to answer market forces. In short, the flow of students into or out of public school systems has remarkably little impact on the administrators and teachers who staff those systems.

Higher Education

American higher education is generally regarded as the finest system of post-secondary education in the world, and scholars have boasted that it supplies two-thirds or more of the world's best research universities.[12] Nonetheless, in recent years concern with the spiraling costs of college tuition has triggered proposals for federal cost controls on colleges and universities that receive federal aid (which is nearly all of them). Reformers are hoping not so much that competition will improve quality but that it will help restrain costs— costs that consistently outpaced annual inflation by two to three percentage points during the twentieth century. The causes of these spiraling prices are complex, the most significant being that colleges and universities have not shared in societal gains in worker productivity.

The landscape of higher education is defined by heavy state and federal subsidies that distort purchasing behavior. Moreover, tuition continues to amount to only a small percentage of the actual cost of educating a student. Economist Gordon Winston has calculated that tuition at elite institutions amounts to well under half of the actual educational cost per student.[13] An array of subsidies, grants, and student loans helps students afford tuition while potentially undermining the incentive for institutions to be fiscally disciplined. In 2003–04, U.S. postsecondary students received a total of $122 billion in financial aid. The largest component, 45.5 percent, was provided by federal loans, while 19 percent was provided by institutions themselves.

In 2003–04, the combination of federal student aid and tax benefits averaged about $2,300 per student at two-year public colleges, more than $3,300 at public four-year institutions, and about $9,400 at private four-year institutions.[14] This amounted to half or more of either typical tuition at private institutions or in-state tuition at public institutions. In short, students were paying 50¢ on the dollar of the posted tuition. This disparity between what institutions collect and what students pay means colleges and universities may feel little pressure to control expenses or to compete on price.

Concerns about price inflation apply more to traditional four-year institutions than to the less prestigious strata of postsecondary education. Many casual observers are unaware of just how variegated American higher education is. In 2001–02, the most recent year for which data are available, the U.S. Department of Education reported that 9,256 postsecondary institutions offered training of some kind, while about 4,200 of these were recognized two-year or four-year degree-granting institutions. Of those, 2,364 were four-year colleges and universities, with about 600 public institutions educating nearly two-thirds of the 9.7 million four-year students. In the two-year sector, about 95 percent of the 6.3 million students enrolled were in public institutions. Meanwhile, among the 5,059 "noncollegiate" institutions (meaning those that did not issue two- or four-year degrees), more than three-quarters were for-profit entities.[15] Moreover, enrollment at for-profit colleges, while still constituting just 5 percent of total postsecondary enrollment, is growing at least three times faster than at traditional colleges, with revenues at for-profits growing as much as 30 percent a year.[16]

The world of research universities, major state institutions, and four-year colleges is marked today by fierce competition for students, faculty, athletic accomplishments, and research that will heighten an institution's reputation and prestige. University leaders are rewarded for boosting the prestige and prominence of their institutions, while success makes it successively easier to generate public and private revenue. Faculty and students benefit as well, though the benefits tend to be so diffuse that presidents and deans face fierce resistance when they try to strategically prune departments or reallocate resources. The result is that, except when under duress, colleges and universities tend to compete awkwardly, at half-speed, with leadership favoring visible gestures such as pursuing new research facilities or attracting National Merit Scholars over efforts to refashion curricula, departmental offerings, or faculty responsibilities.

Postsecondary faculty and administrators have often been attracted to the field by intrinsic incentives, leading them to resist changes deemed damaging to their academic prerogatives or lifestyles—even if such a stance hinders their "competitive position." A related complication is that prestige-driven competition is largely a zero-sum game, focusing on attracting key resources rather than enhancing productivity. The result is that much existing competition is little more than a reshuffling of faculty and students among schools.

Among four-year colleges and universities, the primary obstacle to cost containment is a management ethos that presumes it is undesirable to harness productivity advances by substituting technology for personnel. Given that prestige rests on attracting renowned faculty and allowing them sufficient time to write, conduct research, and engage in public activities, university leaders seeking to enhance the profile of their institutions have no incentive to increase faculty teaching obligations or the "efficiency" with which staff are used. Similarly, since smaller classes and opportunities for individualized attention are positive for reputation and recruiting, colleges have an incentive to avoid efforts to "streamline" staffing.

Unlike the prestige-minded and change-resistant world of four-year institutions, the world of two-year institutions has been radically altered in the past decade. The explosive growth of for-profit providers and the need to respond to this competitive challenge has prompted two-year colleges to aggressively pursue distance education, online courses, and cuts in faculty costs. Most significantly, the Apollo Group's for-profit University of Phoenix grew more than fourfold during the decade preceding 2004. Enrolling 213,000 students in 2004, both online and at its 150 "campus sites" and "learning centers," the university offered 646 credit-granting courses and 19 degrees that could be completed entirely online.

The University of Phoenix makes little or no effort to provide a traditional "liberal education." Instead, it specializes in convenience for students earning professionally useful degrees in areas such as retail management, health administration, teaching, e-business, criminal justice administration, and marketing. In response, public two-year colleges have been forced to compete with the options and convenience of for-profits, with the result that by 2002–03, 91.7 percent of two-year public institutions offered distance education. The comparable figure among two-year nonprofits was 18.1 percent.[17]

The growth of for-profit education has been slowed, however, by two federal provisions that are currently the subject of fierce debate. The "50 percent rule" prevents students from receiving federal aid if their institution enrolls more than 50 percent of students through distance education or offers more than 50 percent of its courses online. A second federal guideline permits colleges a free hand to refuse to issue transfer credit for courses taken elsewhere. Given the primacy of federal student aid in financing postsecondary schooling, the first measure has restricted the emergence of distance-based institutions. Arguing that established institutions have used their leeway to unreasonably limit the ability of students to utilize cheaper competitors, for-profit colleges have lobbied intensely to eliminate the 50 percent rule and require institutions to adopt more systematic, transparent rules for transfer credit.

American higher education encompasses two very different worlds. In the realm of four-year colleges and universities, most students are educated in public institutions, and the majority of private institutions are nonprofit, using expansive subsidies to provide an approximation of an ideal that includes liberal education, residential campuses, tenured professors, research facilities, and intramural sports and activities. Faculty and students are free to pursue multiple private and public purposes. On the other hand, in the larger world of two-year colleges, technical schools, and training programs, cheap public institutions that provide basic skills and vocational training are facing growing competition from small for-profits seeking to exploit a forgiving regulatory environment to deliver discrete training in a cost-effective and convenient manner.

Competition in K–12 and Higher Education

Across and within the worlds of K–12 and higher education, competition operates very differently, and efforts to promote it play out in unexpected ways. Both sectors have a significant public good component and are dominated by nonprofits with a structure of intrinsic and extrinsic rewards built largely on acquiring prestige and attracting higher-quality students. Beyond those broad similarities, educational competition is shaped by funding arrangements and the type of education being pursued.

On one hand, instruction in applied skills lends itself readily to commodification. Remedial tutoring services and training in vocational activities are straightforward, results are readily measured, and firms can construct focused delivery models that provide a reasonable rate of return. Because two-year institutions such as community colleges are particularly focused on vocational preparation, the less prestigious reaches of postsecondary education have proved particularly fertile ground for market forces. Similarly, low-prestige four-year institutions that provide a more vocational education have taken steps to manage costs by increasing faculty workloads and leaning more heavily on part-time faculty.

Meanwhile, broader and more experiential education does not fit as neatly into the classic market model. For instance, elementary schools and liberal arts colleges are expected to cultivate social behaviors, expose students to various skills and areas of interest, and provide a supportive atmosphere for development. They are not as readily judged on straightforward criteria and may find it difficult to boost profitability without sacrificing program elements deemed important to their mission. The prestige imperative means that four-year institutions have evinced limited interest in wringing out new efficiencies and can even push such institutions toward behaviors that increase costs and reduce productivity.

In K–12 schooling, the work most frequently cited by proponents of choice-based reform is the research of Harvard economist Caroline Hoxby and the Manhattan Institute's Jay Greene. In studying the effects of school vouchers and charter school programs on performance, Hoxby and Greene concluded that with the introduction of the programs, student achievement improved measurably in the public schools subjected to the most direct threats.[18] Greene found that low-performing Florida schools significantly improved their student test performance when the state threatened to issue vouchers to students in the lowest-performing schools. Greene's findings were consistent with data from other states that have introduced high-stakes tests. Schools subjected to concerted pressure of any kind tend to improve student test results as employees seek to avert sanctions—whether those sanctions are vouchers, a state takeover, or more intrusive district monitoring.

My own research, meanwhile, has suggested that a lack of meaningful incentives or consequences in existing school choice programs generally limits the scope and ambition of public agency response. In examinations of voucher programs in Milwaukee, Cleveland, and Edgewood, Texas, and of charter schooling in these locales and in Arizona, my colleagues and I found that competition provoked little substantive change. Except for a few Arizona districts that lost a quarter or more of their enrollment in a short period, public school systems responded with little more than symbolic appeals, advertising, and organizational add-ons.[19]

In vital ways, these findings are actually complementary to those of Greene and Hoxby. Competition does appear to have an impact on schooling, but its initial effects are modest and incremental and depend heavily on the structure of competition and the market context. At present, the research on the competitive effects of existing choice programs is too limited to be determinative, while the resulting analyses and policy recommendations fail to entertain any theory of how competition is likely to play out in public schools or colleges.

Competitive Response of Public Schools and Colleges

Markets work precisely because they are neither gentle nor forgiving. They are impersonal mechanisms that gain their power by harnessing self-interest and drawing on desire and fear. The power of the market lurks in the knowledge that even dominant firms may be only one innovation away from being overthrown, and that hungry garage inventors may be only one breakthrough away from success. It is the handful of entrepreneurs who take the chances and embrace the risk that drive innovation and growth, as with the entrepreneurs who have exploited new opportunities in vocational colleges or in services to homeschooling families.

Most individuals, however, are risk-averse, fearing losses much more than they value potential gains. Consequently, markets more typically work not by presenting opportunities, but by forcing resistant organizations to live in a constant state of low-level fear. There is little that is truly "voluntary" about responding to the fear of losing one's job or the desire for a promotion. The efforts of a single principal in the San Diego City Schools, a department chair at Penn State, or a manager at IBM or Disney are unlikely to have a significant impact on the bottom line or reputation of the larger organization. Accordingly, competitive models presuppose that these individuals will be primarily motivated not by a tenuous investment in aggregate outcomes, but by rewards and sanctions linked to their own work. This requires that organizations have leeway to select, terminate, reward, and sanction employees on the basis of performance—a state of affairs that does not apply to most of public K–12 schooling or four-year higher education.

Naturally, people seek to protect or insulate themselves from this relentless pressure. Investors and executives seek the security afforded by favorable government statute or by monopoly status. Employee unions seek ways to counter the pressures of the market and protect their members by restricting layoffs, curtailing the rights of employers to terminate workers, providing wage security, and limiting the monitoring and evaluation of workers. In the case of K–12 schooling, the nation's two teachers unions—the National Education Association and the American Federation of Teachers—have won statutory and collective bargaining language that protects employees from termination, standardizes compensation, restricts staffing, and otherwise minimizes uncertainty. At four-year institutions in higher education, tenure, limited unionization, and professional standards have combined to protect personnel in similar ways.

In the private sector, when competition is threatening enough—such as when American electronic manufacturers were met with an onslaught of Japanese competitors in the 1980s—it can bring these protective edifices crashing down. Firms either cast off inefficient rules and procedures or are overtaken by new providers.

However, the very nature of public organizations such as schools, colleges, and universities makes it possible to limit the effects of markets in two key ways. First, the market threat can be neutralized by political fiat. Public agencies are not threatened by bankruptcy in the same way that private firms are. Legislatures may require a public agency to begin competing against other entities, but they are free to buffer schools and colleges from the revenue losses that might attend a shrinking clientele. For instance, between 1990 and 2004, when Milwaukee lost nearly 15,000 students (more than 10 percent of its enrollment), per pupil spending in the district more than doubled. Of course, since public agencies depend on public revenue, and therefore on legislative sentiment, schools and colleges are not unconcerned with the loss of clients. However, without legislative action to base revenues strictly on student enrollment, schools and colleges are threatened less by revenue lost through consumer flight than by a loss of political support, whether due to a shrinking clientele or to steps that alienate friends and allies. This reality has crucial implications for leadership, especially when considering how public agencies will "compete."

Second, the incentives for officials in public school districts, colleges, or universities are fundamentally different from those for executives of private firms. Private firms are driven by investors anxiously watching profitability (or by owner-managers who have their own wealth riding on the future of the firm). When confronted by competitors, the overriding pressure to improve profitability propels executives to find new market opportunities, root out organizational inefficiencies, and pursue increased profitability. If executives do not take these steps, they risk being displaced by leaders who will. Now, economists inevitably find elements of the following discussion unsatisfying, pointing out that matters are more complicated than this analysis suggests. They are, of course, correct. However, the aim here is to show that "productivity-oriented" responses to competition differ from "political" ones.

Public organizations are, obviously, governed by public officials. Whereas private sector officials are judged by investors primarily on the basis of corporate profitability and growth, public officials are judged by more ambiguous criteria. Voters care little whether schools or colleges are attracting new clients (that is, boosting enrollment); thus officials are typically not rewarded for doing so.[20] Moreover, while voters naturally wish the government to operate efficiently, they rarely have clear measures to assess the efficiency of schools or colleges (though the growing prominence of test scores in the era of NCLB has begun to provide a more uniform, if imperfect, metric in K–12 schooling). What voters do care about is perceived quality of service, responsiveness, and evidence that the leadership is effective.

Because public school, college, and university leaders depend on the support of elected officials and the public, their effectiveness and future prospects turn on the breadth of their backing and on their ability to cultivate—or at least avoid provoking—influential and attentive constituencies. Key organized interests, especially teachers unions and civil rights groups, are invested in the rules that protect employees and ensure equitable service provision.

Given their environment, leaders have good reason to focus more on accommodating influential constituencies and assuaging public opinion than on pursuing new efficiencies. The notion that provosts or superintendents will hesitate to make painful decisions may appear to contradict existing scholarship regarding the desire of agency heads to accumulate and preserve bureaucratic "slack."[21] Slack refers to the extra resources and personnel that an official controls, and the accumulation of slack is a goal because it protects the official from changes in the environment, is a mark of prestige, and can provide power. In fact, there is no contradiction here. The desire to accumulate slack arises largely because extra resources permit officials to avoid hard choices and strengthen their positions, so they are able to more readily manage the disruptions due to competition or changes in policy. Nothing in the scholarship on bureaucratic slack has ever suggested that officials will imperil their position to collect slack—only that their default position is to seek more staff and resources. The experience of subjecting public agencies to competition suggests that officials are likely to deploy slack in an effort to dull the threat posed rather than respond aggressively in an effort to preserve slack.

Suggesting that public officials will hesitate to tackle inefficiencies is not to say they will ignore the challenges posed by competition. If market competition threatens to embarrass the organization or its community or increase local attention to services and their failings, the resulting air of crisis and scrutiny will press officials to provide a satisfactory response. Typically, political leaders are risk-averse and inclined to caution. There are times, though, when confronted with sufficient pressure, that inaction becomes costly. To do nothing in a crisis is to appear ineffectual; activity calms public concerns and positions leaders to claim credit for any perceived improvement.[22]

However, public schools, colleges, and universities are not well suited to act boldly. Public employees face extensive procedural requirements. Given substantial penalties for violating a statute and few rewards for effective performance, public servants have incentives to hew to procedural requirements—even when the requirements seem inefficient. Employees who respect these prosper, while entrepreneurs who violate norms or offend constituencies encounter difficulties. Consequently, when compelled to launch a public response to the threat of market competition, leaders are constricted in their course of action. One response is to enhance advertising and public outreach. These measures are cheap, are inoffensive, upset no routines, build public support, and can easily be tacked onto existing practices. A second, more interesting, response is the tendency of officials to relax procedures so as to permit the development of new programs and initiatives.

Even for managers in the private sector, it is arduous and unpleasant to undertake significant organizational changes. They do so only when they have to, relying upon their capacity to recruit and promote supportive managers, reward cooperative employees, monitor performance, and sanction or fire the uncooperative. Managers in public schools, colleges, and universities generally lack such tools. So, rather than forcing change upon their subordinates, they prefer reforms that allow entrepreneurial employees to step forward. The result is enhanced opportunities for principals to launch new specialty schools or university department chairs to pursue new programs. This solution avoids the conflicts provoked by coercion, while producing visible evidence of organizational change.

Unorthodox opportunities to provide new services appeal to entrepreneurial personalities, the same individuals marginalized in process-oriented public sector agencies. In fields such as education, these entrepreneurs are rarely motivated by self-interest as traditionally understood in economic discourse. Having forgone more lucrative opportunities of the private sector, they are frequently motivated by a sense of calling, intrinsic desire, or a desire for new challenges.

Competition-induced pressure can encourage influential constituencies to accept some relaxation of procedures, enabling entrepreneurs to punch small holes through regulatory barriers. Though inefficient practices are not rooted

out, new initiatives—such as new schools, departments, or hiring programs—may spring up beside existing practices. Pressured to provide a visible response, officials may chip holes in the regulations and procedures that
run like kudzu through public sector organizations. These holes permit
entrepreneurs to bypass traditional gatekeepers, creating new pockets of
reform and possibly starting to topple the existing edifice. It is also possible,
however, that the efforts will amount to nothing more than occasional weeds
growing limply through organizational cracks.

Public Sector Response in K–12: The Case of D.C. Vouchers

An example of how educational competition may work in ways other than
intended may be found in Washington, D.C. There, in early 2004, Congress
enacted the nation's most richly funded school voucher program, offering
vouchers of up to $7,500 to more than 1,000 students in D.C.'s public
schools. Proponents such as Representative Jeff Flake (R-Ariz.), who introduced the voucher program, rendered grand pronouncements about its likely
impact: "Not only will these scholarships help students who take advantage
of them, but they'll help the students who remain in the public school system
by freeing up resources and creating a competitive environment where both
public and private will thrive."[23] D.C. mayor Anthony Williams bragged that
"introducing choice and ensuring competition" would improve the schools
while holding the public schools "harmless."[24]

Williams's comment was telling. The D.C. voucher program did ensure
that the public schools would be held harmless. In a design compromise typical of most charter school and school voucher legislation, the program provided for the D.C. public school system to receive $13 million a year in addi-
tion to its current budget as a condition for potentially sending 1,000
students to private schools. In other words, the voucher program ensured
that the total size of the D.C. school budget would grow, while public school
enrollment declined. Despite the logical flaws in this kind of "market"
design, the rhetoric offered by Flake, Williams, and the program's other
champions mirrored arguments made a decade before in promoting D.C.
charter school legislation.

When charter school legislation passed in the District in 1995, grand
claims were made on its behalf. One charter proponent, Lex Towle of the
Appletree Institute, explained: "When you get a critical mass of good independent public schools, particularly in the inner city where they are most
important, that will help create the competition that will raise the level of

other public schools."[25] Critical mass ensued. By 2004 more than 20 percent of D.C. public school students were enrolled in charter schools. Yet after nine years of charter "competition," the U.S. Census Bureau reported that the District was spending more than $15,000 per student, but its system was still among the worst-achieving in the nation—wracked by scandal and plagued by managerial incompetence.

How can this be, given the basic tenets of market logic? Well, imagine if a Wal-Mart store manager were told that losing customers would have no impact on his salary, evaluation, or job security, while attracting new customers would require him to hire more employees, assume greater responsibilities, and erect a trailer in the parking lot to handle the added business—all without additional compensation or recognition. In such an environment, only the clueless would care much about "competing." The sensible manager's preference would be for a stable customer population (although the truth is, he would probably rather lose customers than gain them).

This is exactly how schools compete under the D.C. voucher program and in other voucher and charter plans nationwide. Consider the principal of an average elementary school in D.C. that was built to house 400 students and currently enrolls 375. What happens if that principal loses 75 students to charter schools or to the voucher program? Typically, three retiring teachers are not replaced, the school is less crowded, and the tiny amount of discretionary money that flowed to the school to support those students does not come in. In short, the principal's job gets a little easier. She earns the same salary and has the same professional prospects she would have otherwise, yet has fewer teachers to lead, fewer students to monitor, and a less crowded school.

Take the same school and assume that the principal reacts effectively to the incitement to increase enrollment, prompting the school to add seventy-five students. What happens? The principal takes on responsibility for three new teachers, must squeeze students into the last available classroom, adds two trailers out back to hold two additional classrooms, and crowds the school's cafeteria and corridors. This principal is now responsible for two teachers who are not happy about teaching all day in a trailer and fifty families that feel the same way about their child's classroom. In return for these headaches, the "successful" principal receives what? At best, a small pool of discretionary funds, typically amounting to less than $50 per student, more responsibilities, dissatisfied constituents, and no more recognition or pay.

The bottom line is that existing statutes, regulations, and personnel create difficulty for even aggressive, gifted reformers. The visibility of district officials, however, means that school systems cannot simply ignore the emergence of competition. The result is an incentive to forgo painful steps while focusing on symbolically potent appeals. The post-NCLB increase in attention to state test results is altering this calculus and increasing the importance of bottom-line performance, though the significance of the change is yet to be seen.

Five Wrinkles for Educational Competition

The effects of educational competition depend on several marketplace considerations that are a function of the educational process and the evolution of American education. Disagreement about the nature of effective schooling, a limited capacity among competitors, an incentive to enhance outcome quality by attracting desirable students, and the transaction costs implicit in switching schools all present particular challenges for educational markets.

Education as an Ambiguous Good

Producers have more incentive to attend to consumer preferences when consumers can easily evaluate products. In the case of educational venues such as traditional elementary schools, comprehensive high schools, or liberal arts colleges, disagreements about the nature of a quality education and the ambiguity of educational outcomes complicate evaluation. As University of California professor Liane Brouillette has noted, "Most people agree, at least in a general way, about what constitutes good health. Agreement on what constitutes a 'good' education is harder to come by."[26] While there are clear expectations for SAT preparation courses or literacy programs, there frequently is public disagreement about exactly what elementary schools, high schools, or colleges are expected to teach or look like. For instance, some urge schools to foster self-expression, while others call for more discipline and structure.

For providers seeking to fill a particular niche in a free market, such heterogeneity is more an opportunity than a concern. For public agencies charged with serving a broad public or a discrete geographic area, however, it can inhibit a coherent focus on productivity or strategy for improvement. In K–12, state accountability testing is forcing a consensus on the primacy of measured achievement in reading, language arts, and math that is far more uniform—and more similar to that in Europe or Japan—than has traditionally been the case in the United States.

Even when agreement about the goals of education is stipulated, however, there is concern that testing instruments and technology do not accurately measure school performance or instructional quality.[27] Particularly in the case of four-year colleges and graduate schools, murky measures of outcome and wide variation in student needs and abilities make it difficult to assess institutional productivity in any results-oriented fashion. Moreover, since education is ultimately a long-term endeavor whose benefits may not be fully evident for decades, there is always room to debate the utility of any short-term proxy.

In truth, clarity of service quality is often a function of how consumers *think* about quality and their willingness to define it on the basis of a few specified dimensions. This is particularly relevant in higher education. Most sophisticated observers argue that the relative quality of colleges or universities is difficult to judge, involves multiple factors, and depends on the student. Such nuanced cautions, while perhaps sensible, offer little practical guidance. As a result, various guides seek to rank institutions on specified criteria. While derided by experts, these rankings influence where students apply and have consequently prompted colleges to take steps calculated to boost their rankings. Defining quality on the basis of certain criteria encourages producers to focus on those criteria—regardless of disputes about what quality "truly" entails.

Constraints on Competitive Capacity

The competitive threat to traditional schools and colleges is partly a function of how many students can be educated by alternative providers or new ones that are likely to emerge. In K–12, private schools are generally much smaller than public schools and have a limited number of available seats, minimizing the number of students they can absorb. Existing private and charter schools are often hesitant to increase enrollment for fear of losing the sense of a tight-knit community. They also tend to be located in small buildings ill suited to expansion and lack the capital that would be required to expand their size. Although charter schooling did expand rapidly during the mid- and late 1990s and a handful of charter school operators are explicitly seeking continued growth, it is not clear whether the educator enthusiasm and charitable giving that helped launched new charters will operate on a scale necessary to sustain continued expansion.

Meaningful competition requires new schools to open or existing schools to expand. However, the development of future capacity is limited by various factors, primarily in K–12 schooling. First, most existing choice programs are funded less generously than district schools, and potential competitors are denied the kind of support for construction and facilities that public institutions enjoy. Second, many choice-related programs include strictures relating to admissions, staffing, or curricula that may dissuade possible operators. Third, in K–12 and in the world of traditional liberal education, most educators who want to open schools are motivated to do so because they have a vision of the school community they would like to create. These entrepreneurs prefer their communities to be relatively small, and few evince interest in "franchising."

In higher education, a variety of providers have emerged in the two-year and vocational segment, where the barriers to entry are fairly low. By contrast, the number of new, aggressive competitors in the four-year segment is very small, because of the considerable barriers there: the expense of providing the facilities expected by students and parents, the requirements for accreditation, the economics of service provision, and limited access to start-up capital.

Finally, the political opposition and legal uncertainty of choice-based reform can undermine the development of competitive capacity. Launching a new school or college, or expanding an existing one, requires an immense investment of resources and psychic energy. Investors and entrepreneurs are willing to make this commitment, but they want to be materially or emotionally compensated for their efforts. The fear of adverse political or legal action can reduce the number of investors willing to launch or expand schools.

The "Cherry-Picking" Temptation

The fact that education is a service "done to," rather than "provided for," a clientele has important implications for school operators. Unlike most producers, schools can make their performance appear much more impressive by adjusting the mix of their clientele.[28] They are able to do so precisely because they enhance the consumer's capacities rather than provide a defined product or service. It is difficult to assess the extent of such enhancement, however, so educational providers are often judged on the basis of a final product, such as test scores or graduation rates. This is true even though observers recognize that such outcomes are heavily influenced by factors beyond the control of the schools.

Schools and colleges can make themselves more attractive to consumers by accepting successful students and screening out those with difficulties. In a competitive marketplace, individual institutions have intrinsic and reputational incentives to pursue promising or high-performing students. The result is that elite K–12 schools and competitive four-year colleges engage in fierce efforts to maximize the quality of the student population. This does not mean that schools will necessarily seek to "cherry-pick" students—institutions may refuse to do so for moral or philosophical reasons—but the market will penalize schools that do not.

This phenomenon is not unique to education; it holds whenever an individual's experience is affected by the nature or identity of his or her fellow consumers. Hip restaurants and stylish resorts, selling ambiance as part of their appeal, strive to attract the "right" clientele. Because society is unconcerned about unequal access to nightspots or beach clubs, this behavior is typically not regarded as problematic—nor is the implication that only a limited number of providers will be elite. In the case of schooling, however, policymakers care deeply about equity and access. Educational choice programs therefore include eligibility and admissions provisions designed to limit "cherry-picking," simultaneously hindering the ability of producers to shape their product, target customers, or cater to client preferences.

Transaction Costs

Consumers are more likely to change goods when it is simple to procure the necessary information and arrange for service provision and transportation. They are less likely to do so if significant "switching costs" are involved. For example, changing schools may separate children from their friends, interfere with extracurricular activities, incur logistical or scheduling difficulties, or require students to adapt to new teachers and programs of instruction. If logistical constraints limit the number of families that can or will switch schools, the degree of competition is tempered.

This is a particular limitation for efforts to promote competition at the K–12 level in thinly populated communities or at the postsecondary level in states with a limited number of institutions. Obviously, transaction costs are less in the postsecondary environment, especially in web-based or vocational schooling, where there are fewer concerns about carefully assembled curricula, developmental issues, or tight-knit social circles. This helps explain why policy measures designed to foster competitive displacement have taken hold in the two-year college sector and in NCLB-style after-school tutoring programs. In communities where performance information is readily available, where choices are easy to access, and where logistical support is high, families are most likely to behave like active consumers.

Price Competition

Price competition necessitates incentives for low-cost providers. Currently in K–12, choice-based reforms such as charters, vouchers, and supplemental services require the state to send a specified amount of money to the student's new provider. The challenge in higher education is less stark since there is less emphasis on universal provision, though discomfort with low-cost higher education is still an important element of policy debates. As a consequence, providers have no incentive to provide low-cost service options. For-profit providers do have an incentive to cut their own costs, but neither for-profits nor nonprofits have an incentive to cut prices to attract customers if the state sets the per pupil payout at a specified minimum. It is not clear if there is a way around this problem without the risk of students investing less in schooling than the government prefers or without introducing concerns of inequity. Nonetheless, this is a challenge worth significant reflection.

The Politics of Education Competition

Most proposals to reform education through enhanced competition fail to wrestle seriously with what that course of action entails. In areas where competition is driving change, providers have exploited new opportunities to offer narrowly defined services and displace existing public agencies. Efforts to compel public schools, colleges, and universities to respond through market-based measures have enjoyed less success. There is a stark difference between reforms that create new room for nonpublic operators and those that harness competition to force public providers to change. Ambivalence regarding this distinction is at the heart of market-based reform. On one hand, reformers highlight the need for competition to challenge insulated institutions, unleash entrepreneurial energies, focus attention on productivity, and create incentives to find efficiencies. On the other hand, they hesitate to violate established notions of educational decorum, worry that vulnerable students may be harmed by marketplace dislocations, feel uncertain about for-profit educators, and prefer a "kinder, gentler" competitive regime.

Proponents of educational competition have proceeded with studied inattention to the central truth of market-based reform. Competition requires that producers have incentives to address consumer demands in ways that promote performance and productivity. However, this is precisely where public agencies, especially those with high levels of public support, can pursue rules and regulations that stifle potential competitors and buffer themselves from the consequences of competition. When asked to compete with private providers, public providers have significant incentive to choke off entry, lobby for protections, and satisfy constituents with symbolic gestures, while using the resulting slack to avoid structural changes that competition intends to force. Incentives of this nature suppress the pressures driving the technology of change. Labor-saving or efficiency-enhancing advances such as distance learning, web-based instruction, and automated assessment are adopted more slowly, unevenly, and with less attention to cost-savings than would otherwise be the case. Intellectual support for these efforts is provided by academics and policymakers who argue that schooling should not be analogous to the provision of other goods, and that insulating schools from incipient competition is sensible policy rather than indulgence.[29]

Although the public might be expected to support efficiency-minded proposals intended to control costs, there is no evidence of a constituency for cost-effectiveness—at least at the K–12 level. For instance, after-inflation school spending has tripled in the past forty years, while student performance has essentially remained stagnant. Nonetheless, rather than express any concerns about productivity, public opinion has consistently supported increased spending, and a plurality of the public routinely says that a lack of money is the greatest single challenge facing schools. While some observers trace undisciplined spending to the influence that teachers unions exert on school boards, the reality is that President George W. Bush increased federal spending on K–12 education more rapidly than any previous president—and was criticized primarily for not spending enough. Ultimately, the centrality of education to American notions of opportunity and meritocracy, sensitivity to questions of educational access and equity, and the public's abiding affection for educators and local institutions make it inordinately difficult to promote radical policy change in this area or to rally support on behalf of productivity or cost containment.

Not surprisingly, Americans are highly sensitive to any risk their schools face, have faith in the ideal of public schooling, express a high rate of satisfaction with their local school, and are averse to proposals for radical change.[30] Hence they are uncomfortable with importing into education the "creative destruction" that is the signature of market-driven improvement. Regarding public education as a shared national faith and their local schools and colleges with sentimental eyes, Americans are hesitant about the kind of ongoing opening, closing, and franchising that open competition implies. There is also much ambivalence about embracing a new breed of educators who are expansionist, profit seeking, or focused on cost-efficiencies, especially when it cannot be proven that they will be more effective than traditional educators. In fact, efforts to import new educators through "radical" new programs such as Teach for America and New Leaders for New Schools are actually *more* mission driven than traditional training programs and seek individuals focused single-mindedly on equity and social betterment. Given the hesitance of both the public and reformers regarding market-based school reform, political efforts to promote specific deregulatory measures—such as relaxing the licensure of teachers and administrators, allowing money to follow students more readily from school to school, or instituting more flexible compensation—might ultimately prove to have a more dramatic effect on educational provision than proposals for choice-based reform.

Such a prediction is tenuous, however, and depends on how the politics of choice evolve. Today, the strongest popular support for educational choice is found among those who are worst served by the present system: African Americans and the urban poor. The vision of school choice embraced by these communities has nothing to do with a commitment to free markets; it is a much more prosaic concern for gaining access to improved educational options. Such concerns make for a constituency that cares little about regulatory burdens or heightened productivity. In fact, many advocates of "public school choice" and similar measures also embrace an aggressive regulatory presence. Meanwhile, it is white-collar suburbanites who are most reticent about radical education reform. The reasons for these stances are unsurprising. Suburbanites have already invested in buying homes in communities with good schools, while urban families feel trapped in cities with low-performing schools. However, these stances are at odds with the suburban affinity for "market-based" solutions and the urban skepticism about "deregulation." An unusual political alliance has often resulted, in which Republican legislators from suburbs join grass-roots black figures from central cities to promote choice-based reforms, while black officeholders and Democrat legislators stand opposed. It is not yet clear whether Republicans will ultimately use choice-based reform to help win the allegiance of a new generation of black officials, whether Democrats will oppose school choice to help recapture suburban voters, or how long the present stalemate might continue.

These political calculations matter greatly for program design and for educational competition. One concern of black officials is that the limitations imposed on existing voucher programs, such as admissions lotteries and eligibility criteria, might be weakened or eliminated if small-scale programs become national policy. This makes them highly receptive to bureaucratic rules and oversight designed to minimize potential inequities. Neither the proponents nor the opponents of choice-based reform are particularly concerned with "creative destruction" or the requirements of dynamic markets. Conservative reformers who are committed to market-based reform, through the dictates of political convenience as well as a lack of considered attention to the requirements of market making, have sought to put black and urban faces out front while minimizing divisive talk about what it takes to make education truly competitive.

The same triumph of ideology over coherence has frequently marked the efforts of market enthusiasts to hold up American higher education as a model, arguing its preeminence in the world is due to the proliferation of available choices. Unfortunately, there is little meaningful evidence on which to declare that American higher education—as a whole—is or is not the best in the world. Meanwhile, the claim that "competition" in any conventional sense is responsible for the successes of American higher education is a tenuous one. American higher education boasts pockets of excellence and provides an expansive and diverse set of heavily subsidized choices. But that claim is far different from arguing that its successes are due to competitive pressures that lead it to control costs, improve quality, or boost productivity. The point here is not that competition has failed in higher education, but that it has never even been promoted in a coherent or familiar fashion.

In both K–12 and higher education, the sectors are dominated by public-operated, democratically governed providers. These organizations are bound by contracts, statutes, and public officials eager to placate influential constituencies. Consequently, "deregulation" or consumer choice—absent moves to transfer control and responsibility for public entities to profit-seeking management—is likely to yield only the faintest market imperatives. This reality has been routinely, and conveniently, overlooked by progressives who regard choice as a mechanism for promoting social equity and by conservatives seeking to make school choice as palatable as possible. Even when buffeted by consumer choice, as in higher education, nonprofit and publicly governed educational institutions have good structural, organizational, and political incentives to compete on bases other than cost or productivity. The ascendance of efficiency-conscious competition in education is not merely a question of deregulating but may well require the introduction of a degree of privatization that the public appears disposed to reject. Of course, such a determination necessarily precedes the more nuanced attention to the political economy of regulation that is thoughtfully portrayed in the companion chapters of this volume.

In the end, "deregulating" a marketplace can mean very different things, depending on the sector, the politics, and the context. Thatcherite reform in Great Britain consisted of dismantling state monopolies and creating competitive markets. Deregulation of the airline and trucking industries was a matter of the government making it easier for firms to pursue profit-driven agendas. In education, not even the most ardent champions of markets wish to see the government dismantle its system of schools. Meanwhile, the vast majority of non-state providers—in both K–12 and higher education—are nonprofit institutions, in which concerns about culture, comfort, and prestige, for example, often take precedence over the imperatives of maximizing revenues or minimizing costs. Exactly how deregulation will proceed in such an environment is unclear. How will it impel a public that regards educational expenditure as a rough proxy for quality to endorse cost-effectiveness? And how will it spur publicly managed schools to compete as if they were private sector organizations or encourage nonprofits to behave more like profit-maximizing firms? If the success of market-based reform ultimately hinges upon the entry and expansion of for-profits, precious little consideration has been devoted to either desirable regulatory measures or the political implications. Given that markets do not implement themselves but depend on the rules of the game and the fidelity with which their rules are monitored and maintained, this inattention leaves unclear what meaningful educational deregulation would even look like.

The abiding American faith in markets and in public institutions comes to a head in the case of schooling, where strong and passionate defenders of existing public institutions exist. But higher education and, to a lesser extent, K–12 education are being gradually modified by changes in technology and society. How these changes will be accentuated or accelerated by efforts to promote educational competition may well turn on whether the nascent political alliance for school choice deepens and expands into an alliance for expansive choice-based reform. However, even this alliance is focused more on limited and controlled forms of school choice than on educational competition. Ultimately, the fate of educational markets may be dimmed by the reality that there exists a powerful constituency for equity in American education and no such similar constituency for efficiency.

Notes

1. John Immerwahr, *Meeting the Competition: College and University Presidents, Faculty, and State Legislators View the New Competitive Academic Arena* (New York: Public Agenda, 2002).

2. John Chubb and Terry Moe, *Politics, Markets and America's Schools* (Brookings, 1990).

3. The full context for the discussion of vouchers as a possible panacea reads, "Without being too literal about it, we think reformers would do well to entertain the notion that choice is a panacea . . . choice is not like other reforms and should not be combined with them as part of a reformist strategy for improving America's public schools. Choice . . . has the capacity all by itself to bring about the kind of transformation that, for years, reformers have been seeking to engineer in myriad other ways." Ibid., p. 217.

4. U.S. Department of Education, "10 Facts about K–12 Education Funding" (2004) (www.ed.gov/about/overview/fed/10facts/10facts.pdf).

5. National Association of State Budget Officers, "State Expenditure Report" (2003) (www.nasbo.org/Publications/PDFs/2003ExpendReport.pdf).

6. National Education Association, "Rankings and Estimates" (Fall 2004) (www.nea.org/edstats/images/04rankings-update.pdf).

7. National Center for Education Statistics, *Digest of Education Statistics* (2002), table 61 (on the period 1999–2000).

8. Henry Levin, "Bear Market," *Education Matters* 1, no. 1 (2001): 6–15.

9. Alex Molnar, Glen Wilson, and Daniel Allen, *Profiles of For-Profit Education Management Companies: Sixth Annual Report, 2003–2004* (Arizona State University, February 2004).

10. Clayton M. Christensen, *The Innovator's Dilemma* (Harvard Business School Press, 1997); Clayton M. Christensen and Michael E. Raynor, *The Innovator's Solution* (Harvard Business School Press, 2003).

11. John Gehring, "Detroit Schools Facing Massive Cuts, Layoffs," *Education Week,* December 1, 2004, p. 5.

12. See Henry Rosovsky, *The University: An Owner's Manual* (New York: Norton, 1990).

13. Gordon Winston, "Subsidies, Hierarchies, and Peers: The Awkward Economics of Higher Education," *Journal of Economic Perspectives* 13 (January/February 1994): 1–22.

14. College Board, "Trends in College Pricing 2004" (www.collegeboard.com/prod_downloads/press/cost04/041264TrendsPricing2004_FINAL.pdf).

15. National Center for Education Statistics, *Digest of Education Statistics* (2003), table 5.

16. Goldie Blymenstyk, "For-Profit Colleges Attract a Gold Rush of Investors," *Chronicle of Higher Education,* March 14, 2003, p. A25.

17. *Chronicle of Higher Education, Almanac 2004–05,* p. 14.

18. See Caroline M. Hoxby, "Rising Tide," *Education Next* 1 (Winter 2001): 68; Caroline M. Hoxby, "School Choice and School Productivity (Or, Could School Choice Be a Tide That Lifts All Boats?)," Working Paper 8873 (Cambridge, Mass.: National Bureau of Economic Research, April 2002); Jay P. Greene, *An Evaluation of the Florida A-Plus Accountability and School Choice Program* (New York: Manhattan Institute, 2001); Jay P. Greene, Paul E. Peterson, and Du Jiangtao, "Effectiveness of School Choice: The Milwaukee Experiment," *Education and Urban Society* 31, no. 2 (1999): 190–213.

19. See, for instance, Frederick M. Hess, *Revolution at the Margins: The Impact of Competition on Urban School Systems* (Brookings, 2002); Frederick M. Hess and Patrick J. McGuinn, "Muffled by the Din: The Competitive Noneffects of the Cleveland Voucher Program," *Teachers College Record* 104, no. 4 (2002): 727–64; Frederick M. Hess, Robert Maranto, and Scott Milliman, "Little Districts in Big Trouble: How Four Arizona School Systems Responded to Charter Competition," *Teachers College Record* 103, no. 6 (2001): 1102–24; Frederick M. Hess, Robert Maranto, and Scott Milliman, "Coping with Competition: The Impact of Charter Schooling on Public School Outreach in Arizona," *Policy Studies Journal* 29, no. 3 (2001): 388–404.

20. Policymakers could choose to reward public agency officials for attracting clients, but such incentives are generally considered to be at odds with the larger mission of public

agencies. For a brief survey of the ethical dimension of this question, see John J. DiIulio Jr., ed., *Deregulating the Public Service: Can Government Be Improved?* (Brookings, 1994).

21. For further reading, see Nitin Nohria and Ranjay Gulati, "Is Slack Good or Bad for Innovation?" *Academy of Management Journal* 39, no. 5 (1996): 1245–64; John L. Foster, "Innovation in Governmental Structures: Minnesota School District Reorganization," *American Journal of Political Science* 14 (August 1975): 455–74; Mark Schneider and Paul Teske, "Toward a Theory of the Political Entrepreneur: Evidence from Local Government," *American Political Science Review* 86 (September 1992): 737–47.

22. See Murray Edelman, *The Symbolic Uses of Politics* (University of Illinois Press, 1972); Deborah Stone, *Policy Paradox: The Art of Political Decision Making* (New York: W. W. Norton, 1997).

23. Representative Jeff Flake, "D.C. Parents Deserve the Right to Choose Where Their Kids Go to School," press release, May 9, 2003.

24. "Mayor Defends Voucher Stance, Accountability Policy," *Washington Post,* July 17, 2003, D.C. Extra, p. T7.

25. Frederick M. Hess, "Without Competition, School Choice Is Not Enough," *On the Issues,* May 1, 2004 (www.aei.org/publications/pubID.20491/pub_detail.asp).

26. Liane Brouillette, *A Geology of School Reform: The Successive Restructuring of a School District* (State University of New York Press, 1996), p. 2.

27. For critiques of simple, standardized outcome assessments, see Mary M. Kennedy, "Approximations to Indicators of Student Outcomes," *Educational Evaluation and Policy Analysis* 21 (Winter 1999): 345–63; or Robert L. Linn, "Assessments and Accountability," *Educational Researcher* 29, no. 2 (2000): 4–16.

28. See Dennis Epple and Richard Romano, "Competition between Private and Public Schools, Vouchers, and Peer-Group Effects," *American Economic Review* 88 (March 1998): 33–62.

29. See Larry Cuban, *The Blackboard and the Bottom Line: Why Schools Can't Be Businesses* (Harvard University Press, 2004).

30. Terry M. Moe, *Schools, Vouchers, and the American Public* (Brookings, 2002).

PART III

Political Sustainability

10

Regulation, the Market, and Interest Group Cohesion: Why Airlines Were Not Reregulated

MICHAEL E. LEVINE

W hen policy analysts contemplate regulatory change, they commonly focus on how it will affect their desired state of the world. Few ask whether one can even "get there from here" or can stay there if one does make it. If they do consider this question at all, they tend to assign it to "politics" and treat it nonsystematically. To address this question seriously, however, one needs a framework—a theory— that can be used to predict whether a regulatory change could occur and, if it occurred, could persist. Most policy analysts have such a theory in mind, whether or not they know it. Some believe that a government acts to make outcomes more efficient or "fairer." Others think that "it's all politics" and concentrate on the impact of politics on the institutions they are analyzing. They often confuse the normative question, "What would be the best outcome?" with the positive question, "What outcome can I predict we will get?"[1]

Michael E. Levine © 2007

I have received helpful comments from Stephen Choi, Clayton Gillette, Jerry Mashaw, Alan Schwartz and participants in the New York University Faculty Workshop. Martin Levin was a particularly helpful editor. Excellent research assistance was provided by David Wise and Annemarie Zell. I am also grateful to Jamie Baker and Pakhi Eder of J. P. Morgan and Company for valuable assistance in compiling data. Remaining errors and infelicities are, regrettably, my own.

215

An appropriate framework for the inquiries and case studies in this volume is one that addresses the positive question. No proposed rearrangement of markets and regulatory institutions would be worth pursuing if one knew in advance that it was impossible to implement or would be quickly undone, as in the case of the 1986 U.S. tax reforms or various attempts to reform agricultural subsidies and quotas. The success or failure of any attempt at regulatory change clearly depends on recognizing and addressing, through institutional design, the present and future political forces that will aid, obstruct, or shape its implementation and operation. That exercise, in turn, can benefit from the lessons of history, arrived at through the examination of particular cases and application to other cases.

The Economic Theory Challenged

In the past thirty-five years or so, the only hypothesis exposed to rigorous specification and serious testing has been the "economic theory of regulation."[2] Although it has received wide, if grudging, acceptance among economists, this theory, in its pure form, fails to account for both the adoption and the persistence of airline deregulation. This difficulty, first highlighted in an earlier Brookings volume addressing the deregulations of the 1970s and 1980s, has been confirmed by subsequent events. Clearly, the theory now needs to be modified, to take into account the information that has emerged after thirty years of experience with airline deregulation.[3]

According to the economic theory of regulation, the main purpose of regulation is to create rents or to transfer them from politically weak interest groups to politically stronger groups. Which group is "politically stronger" usually depends on an increasingly concentrated impact and low organization costs. Furthermore, regulation is generally instituted or exercised to entrench existing firms and to promote special interests at the expense of the consuming public. In this view, the aspect of political strength that determines the regulatory regime is the ability to help regulators gain utility—that is, continued or enhanced power or a valuable post-government position. That ability is manifested in activities such as organizing votes or contributing resources to help win elections or otherwise influence whoever is in a position to appoint or elect regulators and retain them, or in making a well-known practice of employing former regulators on attractive terms. Given that large sums of money can be at stake, it is often supposed and occasionally demonstrated that the "support" reaches beyond what is legal. Typically, the theory predicts that the probability a public policy that creates or transfers rents will be adopted is directly proportional to the degree of organizational efficiency (the ratio of outcome benefits to the costs of organizing to achieve them) of the policy's potential beneficiaries in comparison with those potentially harmed by it.

But airline deregulation principally benefited poorly organized consumers and was adopted over the opposition of a relatively small and well-organized group of regulated airlines. And it has persisted despite spectacularly negative impacts on organized labor, management, investors, the largest firms in the industry, and assorted other interests. This is not to say that deregulation has been inefficient—by stripping the industry of government protection it allowed creative destruction and provided enormous benefits to the public, unorganized labor, some municipalities, and a few new entrant entrepreneurs.[4] Yet a conventional ex ante calculus would have suggested that the beneficiaries were too expensive to organize and the individual impacts too little (especially since monopoly rents were greatly reduced and hence not available for distribution) to dominate regulatory politics under the economic theory of regulation. Under the circumstances, several commentators have wondered whether it is time to revive a public interest theory of regulation abandoned since 1960 or so.

The Economic Theory Enriched

Despite the number of substantial losers as well as winners, some might describe the outcome of airline deregulation as a normative victory for an idea-driven, consumer-oriented "public interest." Any number of labor union members, investors, lenders, airline management, and municipalities that lost cross-subsidized service of large aircraft or that invested in airline facilities that had to be abandoned later would be willing to quarrel with that assessment. The central reason is that it is almost impossible to specify a priori precisely what is normatively justifiable, despite some heroic efforts in that direction. Be that as it may, the economic theory of regulation purports to be a positive, not normative, theory, and it is my task here to try to explain the airline deregulation outcome (an initial destruction of concentrated benefits that persists and resists reversal) in positive terms using a version of the economic theory.

I believe that both the deregulation and lack of reregulation of the airline industry can be explained by modifying the economic theory of regulation:

—First, one must define more precisely what is meant by special interests and their opposites. To do this, I abandon "public interest" as a positive rather than normative concept and instead posit a "general interest" that can be defined a priori in positive terms, as distinct from a "public interest" that for the most part denotes the preferences of the commentator rather than the polity.

—Second, I add to the theory's standard transaction and organization costs the information and monitoring costs that are pervasive in any real-world economic or political environment and that have been the linchpin of the new organizational economics. This modification, explained in detail elsewhere, explicitly takes into account (a) the "slack" that shields regulators from scrutiny or influence by the general electorate and (b) the constraints introduced by the reduction or disappearance of slack through the mechanism of a short public agenda of widely publicized issues.[5]

Slack occurs when information and monitoring costs shield the actions of a regulator from being observed by a rational electorate.[6] The economic theory of regulation must implicitly rely on the existence of slack in order to be operative. After all, if all actions by regulators could be perfectly observed and understood and voted on, no regulator in a democratic system would be allowed to introduce a policy that left a general polity (an electorate acting through its ordinarily accepted aggregation rules) worse off than before. Thus it is necessary to impose relatively high monitoring and organizing costs on the public or on institutional barriers that insulate regulators from influence by the general electorate in order to benefit special interests at the expense of the general polity or to enforce unpopular ideological views.

Slack arises because members of a polity ordinarily find the information necessary to monitor public officials too expensive to be worth acquiring or organizing to act upon. In the presence of slack, self-regarding regulators can "sell" policies to special interests in return for career support (help in achieving reelection, reappointment, or post-regulatory employment).[7] Alternatively, other-regarding regulators can pursue policies that they believe to be efficient or morally desirable but that they know would not be supported by the electorate. In the absence of slack, only policies that would be approved by the electorate can prevail, and these will not always be efficient and will often be morally dubious (as are dairy price supports) or worse (as is segregation).[8]

Slack disappears when the issues addressed by and actions of the regulator become the subject of such intense public scrutiny that the costs to a citizen of becoming informed on a matter drop to nearly zero and are therefore noticed by a rational electorate. Issues that are so publicized become part of the "public agenda," the set of issues that are so widely discussed in the media and elsewhere that no member of the polity can easily remain unaware of them. The presence or absence of an issue on the public agenda profoundly affects whether policies can be adopted that put at a disadvantage or displease whatever coalition of the polity is necessary to win an election. The public agenda for any polity is very limited at any given time, usually consisting of no more than a handful of pervasively discussed and highly salient issues. Even the fact of being directly represented on a ballot does not ordinarily make either a candidate or an issue part of the public agenda.[9]

Note, too, that putting an issue on the public agenda does not automatically lead to less or even better regulation. The existence or absence of slack does not automatically map into "good" or "bad" rent seeking in general. When a problem hits the headlines, "doing something about it" may be the general interest (*not* "public interest") result, but the "something," or even the doing of it at all, will not necessarily lead to more efficient or fairer outcomes. It will simply tend to lead to an outcome of which an informed polity approves. As in the case of rent control, public agenda issues may even involve rent creation and transfer, although in that case the theory says that the transfer will be to a broad subset of the general public but with a deadweight loss. Putting an issue on the public agenda simply makes it much harder (in principle, impossible) to generate private rents at the expense of a dominant voting coalition. Much regulation of "hot" issues (public agenda issues) imposes private costs on nondominant groups that exceed the benefits conferred on the public groups supporting it. This regulation might not be adopted if there was slack and the private groups could invest unseen in defending themselves.

So one has to distinguish the outcome of the airline case from possible outcomes in general. Airline regulation and, as of now, any possible reregulation requires a transfer of benefits under cover of slack from a dominant voting majority to an organized minority. "Freeing" of the industry made the firms' interests so diverse that it has so far been impossible to organize a potentially effective industry coalition (still a nondominant subset of the polity and therefore a "special interest" position, in this hypothesis) around a position that will not be opposed effectively by the rest of the polity or another subset, even if all this is going on behind the slack curtain.

If one believes that airline regulation was created to decrease competition and thereby create and distribute monopoly rents, then the likelihood of deregulation would be inversely proportional to the degree of competition and consumer benefit that deregulation would introduce, given the original incidence of benefits and costs and political salience.[10] Airlines were well organized as they sought regulation to greatly reduce competition among themselves, and the general public (most of which did not fly) was little affected and even less interested. As time went on and airlines responded to regulatory incentives, airlines became even more alike and airline interests became even better organized, and they and their co-participants (lenders, labor unions, small communities with strong political support, and, to a somewhat lesser extent, aircraft manufacturers) made relationship-specific investments that they needed to protect. It was thought that the potential benefits of deregulation would be quite large but would be widely dispersed among air travelers and conferred on firms not in existence or workers not yet hired.[11] As a result, the public, policy entrepreneurs, and journalists all ignored academic calls for deregulation.

Consequently, when new proposals for airline deregulation emerged in the 1960s, virtually no observers applying the economic theory predicted deregulation as the outcome, and the matter was ignored politically for almost a decade.[12] Very few have used the theory even in hindsight to explain what happened.[13] The government adopted a policy that destroyed the value of Civil Aeronautics Board (CAB) certificates (including their value as implicit loan collateral), destroyed the ability of airlines to suppress or greatly delay fare competition by concerted action through the CAB, ended a forty-year de facto moratorium on entry by new firms offering scheduled service in dense or long-haul markets, dramatically revised the route network (making some facilities and fleets obsolete), reduced or eliminated the incentive to maintain cross-subsidized service to smaller communities, and exposed to competitive pressure labor contracts that were well above the market in wages and work rules.[14] Why, then, was the industry deregulated?

The Enriched Theory Applied to Deregulation

Since the story of airline deregulation has been recounted at length elsewhere, only the critical details need to be reviewed here.[15] This industry was deregulated owing to the coincidence of several factors: First, the country was experiencing high inflation, which focused public attention on anything that promised lower prices. Second, several academic analyses supported deregulation as a policy that would lower prices to benefit the consuming public and so could be translated into something newsworthy for the media and striking for policy entrepreneurs. Third, the political ideology (of the Ford administration) engaged Republicans, and jockeying between Jimmy Carter and Edward Kennedy in anticipation of the 1980 presidential election garnered the support of centrist Democrats. Fourth, sleazy relationships given unfavorable publicity and an atmosphere of suspicion related to Watergate made many uneasy about widespread direct contact between the regulators and the industry and sensitive to even a whiff of scandal. Several congressional hearings ensued, along with an explosion of media coverage, and placed the issue on the public agenda, thus dramatically lowering information and organization costs to the consuming public. And fifth, results in the less-regulated intrastate California and Texas markets made it possible to project a favorable outcome to the traveling public if economic regulation were eliminated. Hence the issue became politically salient and generally popular, thus eliminating the veil of slack that had protected the industry and its regulators from public scrutiny.

As mentioned, the political competition between Senator Edward Kennedy and Governor Jimmy Carter at this time helped eliminate slack, as did the widely reported activity and statements of Alfred E. Kahn, chairman of the CAB in the Carter administration. An intellectually powerful, attractive, and mediagenic advocate of deregulation, Kahn had advocated airline deregulation in an academic treatise on the economics of regulation, testified before Congress, lobbied the White House, engaged the industry in debate, and was very accessible to the media. Kahn's charisma was supported by the work of the staff he assembled, which included, in addition to myself (I was in charge of the regulatory staffs, with jurisdiction over rates, routes, and interfirm agreements, domestic and international), Darius Gaskins (an innovative and energetic chief economist, later chairman of the Interstate Commerce Commission) and Philip J. Bakes (congressional staff member turned CAB general counsel), along with the voting and intellectual support of member Elizabeth E. Bailey, as well as the important other-branch engagement of then professor and now Justice Stephen Breyer as a Senate staff member and Mary Schuman (now Mary Boies) of the White House domestic policy staff. The often disputatious and always articulate interaction of Kahn, Bailey, Bakes, Gaskins, and Levine was displayed in public on a weekly basis owing to the adoption of "sunshine" rules exposing agency internal decisionmaking processes. What was sometimes called the "greatest regulatory show in Washington" (admittedly not a high bar to surmount) attracted media and industry attention and further contributed to the collapse of slack.

The issue and its proponents became prominent subjects of the print and broadcast media, and the lower fares and new airlines promised by deregulation seemed attractive to the very large segment of the population by then familiar with and attracted to air travel as a result of the widely publicized introduction of jets. They wished to fly or fly more often but were deterred by the cost of tickets. That it was cheaper to fly in California or Texas than in CAB-regulated markets was publicized through congressional hearings, news reports, CAB staff reports, and widely publicized academic commentary. Airline deregulation generated so much publicity that members of the public

almost had to exert effort not to be aware of it or informed about the arguments over it. With the disappearance of slack, the industry came under
overwhelming public pressure, to which first President Carter and ultimately
Congress responded with the Airline Deregulation Act of 1978 and the
International Air Transportation Competition Act of 1980, which deregulated the airlines.

These statutes had a huge financial and structural impact on the industry:
Of eleven trunklines (legacy airlines) that existed at the time of airline deregulation, at least three (Braniff, Eastern, and Pan American) were liquidated
through asset sales and then bankruptcy. Two or three disappeared less directly:
National was absorbed by and then liquidated with Pan Am, Western was
absorbed by Delta, and bankrupt TWA merged with American and was then
almost immediately liquidated. Only five of the eleven—American, Continental, Delta, Northwest, and United—are still flying. Delta and Northwest are
now in bankruptcy reorganization, and United has recently emerged from one.
Continental has been through bankruptcy reorganization twice, American
seems likely ultimately to follow suit, and it is easy to imagine circumstances
that will force those that have emerged to go through the process again. Of the
ten regional airlines existing at the time of deregulation, two were liquidated,
three were formed into a mainline operation (US Airways) that has emerged
from bankruptcy reorganization for the second time, three more were first
merged then later absorbed by Northwest, and another was merged into a
trunkline that was then liquidated (Ozark into TWA). Of the Alaskan and
Hawaiian airlines, only Alaska has survived without bankruptcy reorganization.

Deregulation generated numerous "poster children"—former intrastate
carriers and new start-ups that grew to a significant size.[16] A few have become
major airlines, such as Southwest, JetBlue, Frontier, and AirTran, but most
have disappeared without a trace, some after very short lives, including
among many Midway, People Express (nominally merged with Continental
in bankruptcy), Air Florida, Altair, Pride Air, Air One, and Columbia Air.[17] A
few were merged into legacy airlines and absorbed (PSA, New York Air, Air
California, Reno Air). America West has been reorganized in bankruptcy
twice and has now merged with twice-bankrupt US Airways. Time will tell
about a few of the more recent start-up attempts (JetBlue, Frontier, AirTran).
Only Southwest has thrived (it is now the fourth largest domestic airline) and
endured for any substantial period of time without falling back on the bankruptcy laws or a major financial "workout."

All this bankruptcy reorganization and liquidation, merger activity, and
transformation has wreaked havoc on various segments of the industry: creditors

have seen their security impaired and unsecured bonds repudiated, share-holders have been wiped out, and, most dramatically, unionized employees have lost all the security, above-market wages, and special benefits that they enjoyed under contracts of the regulated era. Tens of thousands of such employees have lost their jobs. Those still on the job remain there at considerable personal cost, especially where their high-paying and work-rule-protected jobs have been replaced by lower-paying and more demanding ones. Some civic interests lost their airline service. Others built facilities to accommodate airlines that ultimately disappeared or reorganized their route network to reduce service to the city, leaving the facilities abandoned and their operators holding a bag of debt when the airlines repudiated their obligations in bankruptcy. From time to time, "scandals" have erupted over stranded passengers, flight delays, denied boardings, passengers snowbound on aircraft within sight of the terminal, lost baggage, fewer amenities, and all-round poor customer service. Such lapses receive extensive media coverage, which puts pressure on politicians to "do something." High fares in some hub markets and on some business-oriented routes also draw media attention, not to mention intense passenger resentment. This in turn generates widely reported anti-airline political posturing on the part of elected officials and airline executives.

The Enriched Theory Applied to Reregulation

Given this history, why has airline deregulation persisted? Public policies are created at the intersection of interests, institutions, ideology, and information. Even in the formal world of social choice theory, an equilibrium condition chosen from among several core possibilities may be difficult to restore once it has been changed.[18] Policy, too, is difficult to change. It cannot be made instantaneously, without political friction, or without much time and effort. In the case of real-world regulation, the forces at play are not only interests and organization costs but also political institutions that mischaracterize or conceal information and that limit alternatives at any given moment.[19]

However, interests are in a constant state of flux, as people and organizations adapt over time and invest in responses to current policies. Furthermore, ideologies change as theoreticians, politicians, and events interact over time. All policies are created, applied, and changed through political institutions that facilitate some expressions of interest and ideology and suppress or impede others. These may change over time as well, along with the polity's level of information as issues move on and off the public agenda. Finally, to the extent that policy-affecting individuals are independent actors rather than merely role-playing products of the forces around them, changes in the cast of characters can also profoundly affect the outcome of the policy drama.

Why hasn't a coalition of the aggrieved organized some form of reregulation to protect or restore their rents or quasi rents? The economic theory of regulation would seem at first blush to suggest that airline deregulation should have been stifled by some combination of creditors, civic interests, unions, and other groups inducing legislators or agencies to reregulate the industry, either returning it to the status quo ante or imposing on it various uneconomic requirements designed to generate or protect economic rents or quasi rents created by regime-specific investments.[20] Yet Congress and the executive branch have by and large resisted and refrained from doing so. The industry has continued to operate with freedom over pricing, routes, and services; over success and failure; and over the use of labor, pension, and bankruptcy laws to rearrange its contractual commitments to employees, aircraft suppliers, and infrastructure providers.

Careful econometric analysis says that airline deregulation has been successful for the most part in that social benefits have vastly exceeded costs.[21] This is clearly an important aspect of the airline story but seems insufficient as a political explanation and certainly is not in itself an explanation under the economic theory of regulation, which predicts the victory of inefficient rent-creating policies over efficient policies that benefit the less organized or less informed.[22] The economic theory explains regulation as a device used to impose inefficiencies that create and transfer monopoly rents. If, after the airline industry became regulated in 1938, it developed solid constituencies that opposed change and then were increasingly discomfited when change occurred, why have they not been able to reorganize to achieve reregulation and minimize or eliminate the costs that deregulation imposed on them? What explains the persistence of deregulation as a public success for many and a concentrated private disaster for a potentially influential few?

First, and perhaps most important, what had been an almost unanimous coalition of perceived industry interests changed over time as new firms entered and old firms adapted in different ways to the pressures of new competition. In 1938, when the Civil Aeronautics Act was passed, and again in the 1975–77 period, when deregulation was proposed, the large airlines were unanimous in their preferred policy—regulation by the CAB. This unity ended when United Airlines broke ranks in 1977, although there continued to be widespread, nearly unanimous industry opposition to deregulation until the passage of the Airline Deregulation Act became a certainty in the late summer of 1978.[23] Admittedly, this opposition began to weaken as the

CAB took actions that made the board less valuable to certificated incumbents in that they promoted competition and ended protection in regard to both entry and pricing. As one industry official told me after we issued the instituting order in the *Oakland Service Case* proposing to allow service to Oakland by any airline that wanted to offer it: "If this is the sort of thing you intend to do, who needs you?" (To which I answered, "Precisely.")

Today, there is no longer an "industry position" on most matters of regulation and perhaps no "industry" at all in its historical sense. The airline industry is now a much more heterogeneous collection of firms than it was in 1978. Successful and struggling new entrants have emerged, and what in the way of government policy will protect or destroy quasi rents varies from firm to firm, whether a new entrant or a "legacy" carrier.

Under the deregulated regime, the legacy carriers themselves face widely differing financial and strategic situations and therefore differ greatly in their policy preferences. As noted earlier, almost all have been or are going through bankruptcy reorganization. As a result, they are pursuing diverse new strategies, shedding, modifying, or intensifying various commitments and investments in different ways. In addition to other changes, one or two (Continental and US Airways) have used bankruptcy laws to drive down labor costs to levels close to those of mature low-cost carriers (LCCs) like Southwest.[24] Others are still trying to do so. United has tried and failed. Meanwhile, American Airlines is still operating with labor contracts specific to, left over from, or heavily influenced by the regulated era that continue to make its unit costs uncompetitive. Continental and American have legacy fleet and infrastructure commitments that will probably require bankruptcy to reform. Most significant, American, Delta, and Northwest (and Continental, though it first eliminated then reestablished an extensively modified plan through its two previous bankruptcies) bear the regulatory-era burden of defined-benefit pension plans, which LCCs do not have, and these will have to be addressed through bankruptcy or legislation.[25] United and US Airways have already terminated theirs in bankruptcy (repudiated them and turned them over to the Pension Guarantee Insurance Corporation [PGIC], a government entity). Others are attempting to "freeze" them (honor old defined-benefit obligations but refuse to take on new ones). All are searching for new strategies that will enable them to succeed in competition with LCCs. None has the assurance of continuity that came with a CAB certificate before 1978.

Under these circumstances, government policies that would best promote profit vary widely among airlines. Southwest, which is well financed and has low unit costs, would be perfectly happy to see some of the legacy carriers liquidate and certainly has no interest in preserving the present survival-biased

Chapter 11 procedures.[26] JetBlue is in a similar situation. Two others concerned that Chapter 11 is keeping competitors alive, AirTran and Frontier, have complained that legacy airlines such as America West are pricing "below cost" to compete with them. They have demanded government action to limit legacy airline competitive responses to LCC initiatives, which would make it more difficult for the legacy airlines to defend themselves against displacement by LCCs. Delta and Northwest have not yet shed their defined-benefit pension plans in bankruptcy, as did U.S. Airways and United, but instead achieved legislation that requires them to freeze them in order to effectively refinance their funding obligations over a long period of time. The LCCs, United, and US Airways are indifferent or hostile to such remedies, since they no longer need it. American and Continental were at first indifferent, but became conditionally hostile (unless they were included) once the bill passed when it became clear that Delta and Northwest would have more favorable pension obligations than they would. They are now struggling to reopen legislation that has already been enacted, without the support of the others.[27] In short, airlines have championed their own relief needs while opposing those of others.

LCCs have also been unwilling to pay the market price for the "slots" (rights to land or take off) necessary to serve slot-controlled La Guardia and Reagan National airports, alleging that legacy airlines have conspired to keep them from purchasing these slots at "reasonable" prices. LCCs have therefore lobbied for government intervention to make slots available to them. Not surprisingly, legacy airlines have vigorously opposed such action. For them, portfolios of these slots represent important financial and competitive assets, often pledged as loan collateral (some to agencies of the U.S. government!). Southwest, which does not serve these airports, appears not to care. AirTran and Frontier, which operate hub-and-spoke systems serving New York and Washington, care very much.

These diverging interests and attitudes have a direct impact on the politics of reregulation. The Air Transport Association (ATA), historically the industry's most powerful trade association, requires unanimity among its members before it can take a position on legislation or regulation. Some of the LCCs (ATA, Southwest, and JetBlue) and all the surviving legacy airlines, whatever their condition, are members. Not surprisingly, the association has seldom reached a consensus on a regulatory issue since deregulation, and it is difficult to imagine a regime that would affect pricing, entry, service standards, or capacity that it could support. What it has been able to promote are transfers from public treasury funds to the industry such as the $5 billion in compensation for the Federal Aviation Administration's "ground-stop" following the terrorist attacks of September 11, 2001. The Air Transport Association is no longer the effective instrument to promote policy change that it was when it was formed during the Great Depression. This increases organization costs for any proponent of reregulatory policy change.

Municipalities also have evolved from a world in which they simply joined together to lobby the Civil Aeronautics Board for more service. Some municipalities, for example, made relationship- and regime-specific infrastructure investments on the basis of the intentions and success of particular airlines that are now readjusting fleets and route systems and turning to the bankruptcy laws to repudiate contractual obligations for assets they regard as unnecessary. These bankruptcies can leave the municipalities with indebtedness but no corresponding revenues. In extreme cases, airlines are liquidated with real consequences to the city at which they were based or maintained hubs. For example, TWA's de facto liquidation cost St. Louis service and jobs.

On the other hand, municipalities are also served by growing and successful new entrants or benefit from strategic realignments by legacy carriers and do not want to see those airlines inhibited. Some municipalities are conflicted. The proposed end of legislative limitations on the scope of service from close-in Love Airport has left the Dallas city government torn between its desire to promote low-fare service by Southwest from Love and its dependence on American Airlines' huge hub system at Dallas-Fort Worth International Airport.[28] The net result of all this is that now there is seldom one "municipal" or "airport" voice on policies that differentially affect particular airlines.

Customers are not of one mind, either. Some are sorry to see frequent and convenient legacy-line service disappear, such as that provided by the US Airways hub at Pittsburgh or at Philadelphia, now threatened by new competition from Southwest. On the other hand, some customers at Philadelphia have become fans of Southwest and worry less about the effects of its expansion on US Airways. Similarly, travelers from the Northeast or Midwest to Florida welcome the deregulated free-for-all, while those at Minot, North Dakota, worry about whether and how they will get service if Northwest goes into bankruptcy.

Unions opposed deregulation and served as a focus of efforts to prevent it. They have continued to seek protection from competitive labor markets. In the Airline Deregulation Act of 1978, they were promised public assistance if the number of workers employed in the industry shrank. That assistance never materialized because in fact airline industry employment has grown enormously since 1978. Unfortunately for the unions, the new employees have been largely nonunion workers. Even those who are union members, as at Southwest, are working under contracts and conditions vastly more productive than those at legacy airlines. As a result, the interests of new employees differ greatly from those of the traditional airline unions: with a strong desire to preserve growth opportunities for their firms, they do not wish either to halt the "deregulation movie" or rewind it to an earlier time.

This has been a problem since the early 1980s for those concerned about competitive freedom, but it has become particularly important in recent years, with the vast expansion in the LCCs' market share. Most of the first-generation new entrants (such as People Express and New York Air) died or were absorbed in the 1984–87 period. Likewise, most of the second-generation new entrants (Reno Air, Vanguard, and others) died or were absorbed in the 1990–93 period. Although there was a political constituency for low airfares, especially in the leisure segment of the market, there was much less pressure on business-type fares. As a result, by 1994 (after the 1990–93 shakeout), the "industry" market share of LCCs was still only a little more than 7.7 percent of passenger revenue and 13.7 percent of passengers. By 1998 the figures were not much higher: 10.9 percent and 17 percent, respectively. The most important nonlegacy Air Transport Association member initially was rapidly growing Southwest Airlines, which often broke with legacy airlines on policy matters, but by 2002 the association included AirTran, Jet-Blue, Frontier, and other LCCs. As of this writing, the LCCs have a growing market share of about 30 percent of passenger revenue and 37 percent of passengers, while the legacy airlines have been conspicuously unable to find a fare structure and level that they all are willing to accept.[29]

All this discord in the absence of "mediagenic" regulatory issues builds slack. The issue of regulation and competition rarely makes the news, let alone the public agenda, with the exception of local interest at hub cities that pay relatively high prices for the abundance of nonstop service they get. Service failures such as lost baggage and late departures and arrivals are covered by the media and occasionally merit government hearings, but those issues have failed to achieve a policy consensus comparable to the academic unanimity on deregulation that prevailed in the mid- to late 1970s.

Perhaps more interesting than any differences on particular issues is the fact that management at the legacy airlines has adapted or been selected to operate without many regulatory constraints and would find it costly to readapt to a regulatory regime. In other words, the management and people inside the major airlines have become a regime-specific interest group separate from shareholders. Even the weak cannot imagine a regulatory regime that could help them much in an era of legacy hub-and-spoke route structures (with mostly common costs in every city-pair market), concomitant price discrimination, and intense pressure from low-cost competitors. No one thinks it is politically imaginable that the LCCs will be prevented from offering low fares in any foreseeable regulatory regime.

Management has also made many investments in assets required under deregulation, from facilities to software to fleets. Deregulation has created pressure to exchange large aircraft for smaller ones to serve more fragmented markets, to adapt terminals to serve as hubs for connections, and to offer more choices of U.S. gateways for international service. So airlines have built or financially guaranteed terminals and maintenance hangers specifically adapted to these route structures, schedules, and fleet patterns. They also bought fleets of aircraft to fly these routes and use these facilities. And non-airline entities (such as those that locate corporate headquarters and factories) and suppliers (that design and build aircraft and equipment) have invested heavily as well.

Moreover, the proliferation of fares and the freedom to price-discriminate even under competition have stimulated huge investments in revenue-management software and the human capital to operate it.[30] This has forced even new entrants and other LCCs that formerly eschewed them to adopt the pricing strategy and make the investments, although their systems are often simpler and cheaper than those used by legacy airlines. The enormous growth and expansion in scope of the route system under deregulation has created many opportunities for complementary investments in hard assets and human capital, including the location of plants and offices by actors with no other connection to the industry. The development of hub-and-spoke systems to efficiently maximize system scope and of point-to-point airlines to minimize costs on the densest routes has created intense but divergent local constituencies. They have become a very important force for policy conservatism, almost like a spontaneous and uncoordinated version of those in many congressional districts that have won contracts for key defense systems. The current rash of bankruptcies and liquidations is putting some firm-specific investments in jeopardy (an enormous twelve-hangar maintenance center in Indianapolis built with public funding for United was partially re-leased to other users at very attractive prices), but making others even more precious.

Paradoxically, the only voices for reregulation have been some struggling new entrants and a couple of academics. One law professor is in favor of "enlightened" reregulation that would not have the defects of the old regime (what such a structure might look like is not made clear).[31] An emeritus New Dealer thinks that all unregulated competition, especially in infrastructure industries, is "wasteful."[32]

Some have also charged that deregulation has changed government institutions and bureaucratic incentives and capability in a way that makes political meddling more difficult. But this is largely illusory. The change in institutions has been subtle compared with the substantive change in regulation. If anything, airline regulators should have become more politically responsive to interest groups, not less. The Civil Aeronautics Board was nominally an "independent agency," constitutionally a "creature of Congress" staffed by civil servants and a few political appointees directed by a small cadre of congressionally confirmed bipartisan members serving fixed terms and ultimately operating under "sunshine" rules. The airlines now are regulated (to the extent regulation remains) by several hundred specialist staff members in the Office of the Secretary of Transportation, reporting to a politically appointed assistant secretary and through the political organization of the department to the secretary and ultimately the president under rules mandating much less process transparency than was imposed on the CAB as an independent agency.

As to the civil servants themselves, about half of the CAB's employees, including virtually all of those working on policy matters, went over to the Department of Transportation (DOT) and became the core of its airline group. Only now has its composition begun to change significantly as staff members retire. Even so, many of DOT's senior airline staff still have CAB backgrounds. The policy preferences of that group have not changed much over time. Without constraints from above, they remain enthusiastic about deregulation as long as there is a continuous and obvious flow of visible benefits—an oversupply of aircraft, a proliferation of entrants, and declining prices. They become worried about it when the opposite is the case: when the carrier population is in decline, the market is cyclically undersupplied pending new investment, and cyclical demand has turned around (allowing price increases on the reduced supply). While they have lacked the statutory power to reimpose the ancien régime, they retain considerable residual power over conditions of competition and agreements, especially in the international arena, and the important power to distribute valuable operating rights in limited-entry international markets. And from time to time they have expressed considerable interest in making proposals designed to "preserve" the advantages of deregulation by imposing new regulations that will encourage new entrants, keep a lid on pricing, or make the competitive process less "unfairly predatory." Some of these, such as the Computer Reservation System rules, served their intended purpose but persisted long after being rendered obsolete by the Internet. Others, such as the competition conduct rules proposed at the end of the Clinton administration, would have created a regulatory swamp from which deregulation would not have returned alive.

What is different from 1975–84 and earlier is that the department is officially and overtly part of the administration and thus explicitly subject to political and broad policy considerations. Before, the administration and even members of Congress were merely, if they chose to be, a "party" in CAB proceedings, in which their advice was made public. Now the only insulation from the executive branch lies in route awards in entry-restricted international markets and other adjudication functions (as defined by the Administrative Procedures Act). This creates slack that could support a coalition for reregulation, but that could also be "consumed" as ideological advertising for the Republican Party, behavior that can be used to appeal to a broad constituency or a Burkean minority. As an example, when the DOT staff started a policy proceeding in 1998 designed to limit incumbent competitive responses to new entry (a matter that might not have gone far in the Levine-Gaskins-Bailey days at the CAB but that was, surprisingly, explicitly supported by its most influential deregulation-era chairman, Alfred E. Kahn, and might have done better at an independent CAB somewhat insulated from administration politics), opposition came from many quarters to which the Republicans are responsive, and the matter was unceremoniously dropped when the Republicans took the presidency in 2001.[33]

In the same way, the CAB, then DOT, and, very publicly, Kahn became concerned about the Reagan administration's unwillingness to use the antitrust law aggressively with respect to mergers and industry structure, although the administration's policies for the deregulated airline industry were entirely consistent with those it pursued in other unregulated sectors. With a lingering attachment to traditional regulatory concerns, the staff appeared naive about the way both competitive airline markets and the new regulatory politics actually work.

First, it did not recognize the economics of scope and density that make it difficult to support more than one airline's hub at a city. Second and perhaps more important, to them competitive markets meant a kind of gentlemanly competition in which losers did not complain because winners did not play rough. This style has never existed in the business world without government enforcement, is widely regarded as protectionist and inefficient, and has disappeared even from modern sports, amateur and professional. In real-world business competition, competitors try to gain as strong a market position as possible and fight competitors wherever and however it seems worthwhile. If competitors disappear, so much the better. They do not observe Marquess of Queensberry rules but limit themselves only to the degree necessary to avoid antitrust prosecution. Antitrust prosecution is limited by law to preventing mergers that would create a monopoly or to thwarting deliberate attempts by single firms to achieve and maintain a monopoly. Fierce, unkind, and "ungentlemanly" efforts to take business away from competitors are explicitly permitted, even when fatalities occur.[34]

Further, the staff regards price discrimination as evidence of monopoly. But price discrimination is essential to the recovery of common costs in competitive markets.[35] Airline networks, like all networks, incur many costs in common to serve a diversity of customers. It is necessary to aggregate passenger trips in order to put together a group of passengers large enough to fill even the smallest aircraft that can provide service in most city-pair markets at competitive costs. Individual flights in hub-and-spoke systems carry passengers on many different itineraries, and even in systems that emphasize point-to-point service, flights carry passengers who attach widely varying value to a particular schedule or route.

Once airline pricing was freed from its regulatory straitjacket, price discrimination became pervasive in the system. It was and is necessary for survival in a competitive airline industry. But price discrimination is also a tool that can be used to establish, enforce, and maximize the value of a monopoly. Smaller competitors have complained bitterly as larger, higher-cost airlines have adjusted their mix of fares to keep passengers from defecting to new entrants that introduce lower fares reflecting their lower costs, especially when capacity is increased to accommodate passenger volumes stimulated by the new lower fares. Their cries of "foul" resonate especially strongly in the political arena when the new fares imposed on incumbents are promoted vigorously by them and then abandoned as soon as the new entrant exits the market. New entrant airlines have demanded regulatory intervention to prohibit or inhibit this behavior. But efforts to enforce "fair" competition deprive customers of low fares in the here and now; produce many unintended negative consequences when applied to firms whose costs, demands, and competitive alternatives are not and cannot be transparent to regulators without full reregulation and artificial accounting; have "chilling" effects on markets; and promote political distortions.

In this world, the choice is never between imperfect markets and perfect regulation, or between imperfect regulation and perfect markets. The choice is between imperfect markets and imperfect regulation. The antitrust laws now reflect this, but the losers are never enthusiastic about the outcomes or the methods used to reach them and can always cite some deficiency in the competitive or regulatory process that has brought them to the sad pass they find themselves in. Accepting that neither markets nor regulation are perfect, the interesting question presented by airline deregulation is why imperfect but freer markets were allowed to continue in the face of pressure from those significantly disadvantaged by them, and why there was not even more pressure to reimpose regulation, however imperfect.

Another factor accounting for the persistence of airline deregulation might be the changes both in received ideology and party alignment since 1980. Coupled with the institutional change, this means that actions undertaken both in the presence and absence of slack are different from those that obtained in the heyday of regulation. Of course, the liberal wing of the Democratic Party can always be counted on to press for regulation insofar as it retains, against all evidence, a sometimes hidden and sometimes overt belief that regulation almost always produces superior results to those achieved in imperfect markets. Also at any given moment, one will find industry, labor, and other political interests lobbying for this or that form of protectionist modification to deregulated competition to cure some impact they are suffering under the existing regime. At the same time, public and political faith in the efficacy of regulation as a way to lower prices or improve service has declined considerably over the past thirty years. The Republicans have been committed to that posture, although they do not always act on their word.[36]

The liberal wing of the Democratic Party has not controlled both the presidency and Congress since 1968. Since the airline deregulation of the late 1970s, the only Democratic president was a centrist. The party lost control of Congress in 1994 and regained it only recently, but its majority is narrow and includes many centrists. And, of course, the administration remains in Republican hands. Airline deregulation was initiated by the Ford administration but achieved by a centrist Democratic president and a Democratic Congress supported by scholars, think tanks, and policy entrepreneurs, many of whom were Democrats themselves. Any urge on the part of Democrats to backslide has been kept in check by the need to gain the support of Republicans, without much help from scholars, who generally continued to support the policy.

Although the Republican Party has been rhetorically committed to free markets for the period since deregulation, it has certainly demonstrated an ability to create and transfer rents when politics required it.[37] Hence the change in party alignment is not itself a full explanation of deregulation's persistence. Senator John McCain, who identifies himself as a conservative, market-oriented Republican, has nonetheless managed to manipulate policy to favor his Arizona constituents, often at the expense of the general public. As chairman of the Senate Commerce Committee, for example, he carved out an exception to the National Airport perimeter rule so as to allow America West to serve it nonstop from its Phoenix hub, while Delta's Salt Lake City hub and United's Denver hub continued to be excluded. He also helped to make slots at National available to America West without allowing existing airlines to use them to expand service. As the ultimate transfer, McCain helped persuade the Air Transport Stabilization Board to guarantee $380 million of $450 million in loans to keep America West afloat and then to permit it to use those proceeds to merge with US Airways. The market-oriented solution to each of these issues would have been to eliminate the perimeter rule, continue to permit slot purchases and sales or go to an auction or variable landing-fee system, and to leave America West to the tender mercies of private capital markets.

Ironically, Senator McCain achieved much of this while also appearing responsive to public pressures in the wake of various momentary public-agenda "scandals" related to delays, baggage mishandling, pricing, service failures, and such headline-grabbing incidents as Northwest's inability to get passengers off an aircraft trapped on the ground for six hours in a snowstorm at Detroit. He has done so by holding distracting hearings from time to time and threatening to reregulate the industry in various ways! The industry has responded with promises to do better (which usually also brought some political benefit to Senator McCain), and the issues receded into obscurity again.

I do not mean to single Senator McCain out for obloquy. Most, probably all, legislators have from time to time abandoned ideological commitments to do favors for constituents at the expense of the general interest. For example, consider the support by dairy-state Democrats of regulations that raise the price of milk to the urban poor who are nominally an important object of their concern. And the creation of mediagenic but ineffective events to gain publicity is part of every politician's repertoire. Rather, Senator McCain's performance on these issues despite his general track record as an independent legislator highlights the almost universal manipulation of slack by public officials for political ends.

General policy is certainly affected when the party in power changes, but this has not been the sole, or perhaps even most important, factor governing decisions regarding comprehensive reregulation of airlines. After all, there appears to be little or no constituency in the Democratic Party for price and entry reregulation, even in the face of the huge decline in rents captured by labor unions. The persistence of deregulation despite its negative impacts on well-organized constituencies is best explained by changes in the amount of slack, perceptions of the electorate that influence what they will support in the absence of slack, and the nature of the reward structure for regulatory actors.

The Interests Affected

Deregulation succeeded against industry opposition because it was supported by a coalition of assorted interests: consumer groups, academics who were able to provide concrete examples of lower fares with less regulation, a public disgusted with scandals, charismatic individual spokespersons, and politicians looking for an anti-inflation or pro–free market issue. All these interests excited a media blizzard that lasted for several years. At the moment that deregulation occurred, there is no doubt that much of the electorate was aware of the issue and that most in that group supported the policy. The Levine-Forrence model would explain airline deregulation as a "general interest" policy (a policy that benefited a majority of the polity), was "on the public agenda" (very prominently discussed in the media, so that the public was very well informed about its benefits and followed its fate at very low cost), had easily identified supporters and opponents ("slack" had been greatly diminished), and thus could be opposed only at a public official's peril.[38] Those were the days!

As the old song goes, "Everybody wants to go to heaven, but nobody wants to die." Everybody wants competition, but nobody likes competitive markets. Consumer groups wanted deregulation because they wanted more competition and lower prices, but they also wanted the government to prevent price discrimination, to lower prices at hubs, and to police competitive practices. Small communities wanted to benefit from more flights and lower fares but objected to the fact that the expense of serving thin markets would be reflected in deregulated fares and that more flights meant smaller propeller aircraft would be substituted for larger jets. Recognizing that it could not oppose deregulation successfully, organized labor was mollified for a time by the fact that the airlines at which it had contracts were expanding rapidly, thereby increasing dues-paying members. Later, labor was not so happy when the expanded union membership found it could not compete with the many new employees working at low-cost, nonunion airlines or under contracts that undercut theirs and thus forced their firms to reduce staff or even go bankrupt.

Aircraft manufacturers and lessors were thrilled by the expansion of the industry, then appalled as their airline customers became tougher purchasers and much worse credits. Big cities were happy with lower fares and more service but grew uneasy as airlines came and went, often leaving unpaid infrastructure commitments behind them. Cities without hubs found themselves one stop from everywhere but able to fly nonstop only to hubs, which made them unhappy. Those lucky enough to have hubs discovered that they paid higher fares for the abundance of nonstop service than did those who got worse service. Service lapses had occurred before deregulation, but the explosive growth in markets, coupled with the need to control costs to meet fare competition, meant that lapses happened more often and airlines often could not be as generous in dealing with them as in the good old days of regulation.

In short, deregulation generated markets that looked like other real-world, mostly competitive markets, warts and all. Groups that were by general inclination in favor of government intervention on behalf of consumers were as vocal about the lack of regulation as they were in other markets. They blamed the lack of competition, but they really meant that the market had not turned out to provide what they thought it should, or to be as civil and other-directed as they had hoped. Competitors bit, scratched, lied (a little), cheated (occasionally), and sometimes even stole. But that is the way it is out there in the competitive world. The aggregate results were attractive to consumers, but many instances were not. And as consumers consistently showed that they cared more about price than quality, the market gave them what they wanted, whereupon they became nostalgic for the service quality of the good old days (but wanted it at the new prices, of course).

New airlines found the real world frustrating as well. They thought they would be competing against dinosaurs en route to extinction, then discovered the dinosaurs were not down and out but fighting for their lives. Now it looked as though the deregulation that had given them the freedom to compete needed the active supervision of the Department of Transportation.

All this discontent was reported in the press, but there was nowhere near the unanimity of informed opinion that had supported deregulation in the first place as to whether these difficulties reflected serious problems with deregulation or justified a return to the old regime or major intervention. The public remained interested in airlines, perhaps because so many people had flown by then, but many other issues crowded it off the public agenda. When it did surface from time to time—because another bankruptcy had occurred, a hub had been abandoned by a major airline, or people were complaining about a service atrocity or fares—arguments and counterarguments flew back and forth and then the matter receded. Complaining to the DOT was not particularly helpful, since it had limited power to help. And the problem with complaining to Congress was that when hearings were held, Congress received conflicting advice from apparently respectable and equally politically salient sources.

In fact, the greatest pressure for the government to "do something" and the most frequent instances of oversight tended to arise over the kinds of issues that regulation can be least effective in addressing, such as quality of service and response to service emergencies. More addressable issues such as mergers and monopoly were handled first by the Department of Justice, then transferred to the Department of Transportation, then finally sent back to the Department of Justice, almost never making it onto the public agenda.[39] Even congressional hearings on these subjects were covered largely by the trade press and in the business pages.

To the extent that individuals are thought to make a difference by serving as catalysts for putting issues on the public agenda and reducing slack, the only individual in a position to affect airline regulation during this period who had the media power of an Edward Kennedy, a Gerald Ford or Jimmy Carter, or a Fred Kahn was Senator McCain. Although McCain intermittently looked into securing favorable government treatment for his Arizona constituent America West and into certain consumer issues (some of which, notably nonstop service from National Airport to Phoenix, affected him personally), he had an ideological distaste for regulation, no continuous interest in structural overhaul of the industry, and no source of consistent advice as to what that overhaul should consist of.

Thus on the critical dimension of information, the post-deregulation period was quite different from the circumstances of 1975–79. With industry regulation rarely on the public agenda, slack became the normal condition. Views about how to use this slack differed widely among various interests. Instead of being divided in a bipolar fashion between a nearly unanimous industry (and its unions) and almost everyone else, as in 1975–79, the industry itself was divided. Consumers were very happy with prices and generally willing to put up in sullen but not mutinous fashion with the service that went with those prices. Competition increased dramatically, if erratically, in the deregulated era. Ideology was more favorable to markets and less favorable to regulation.

Canada: The Other Side of the Coin

Heavily influenced by the widely publicized successes of airline deregulation south of its border, Canada decided to deregulate its airline market in the

National Transportation Act of 1987, which entered into law in 1988.[40] Subsequently, it privatized its national airline, Air Canada, which, with government encouragement, acquired failing Canadian Airlines in December 1999. Unlike any one airline in the United States, Air Canada emerged as a clearly dominant firm, with a domestic market share of about 73 percent in 2002 measured by seat kilometer (that is, one passenger carried one kilometer, the standard metric measure of business volume) and a domestic market seat share (the number of seats installed in its fleet, a measure of capacity) of 64 percent in 2002.[41] Though it experienced strong competition in certain markets from LCCs, especially Westjet, many travelers were dependent on its service, and it vigorously combated efforts to gain footholds in its market. However, its methods generated allegations of predatory pricing.

Whereas such complaints failed to win intervention in the United States, either in court under the antitrust laws or at the DOT, they met with some success in Canada.[42] Rather than press their case in the courts or in the Competition Tribunal under standard predatory pricing provisions, however, those concerned about Air Canada's dominant position and practices petitioned for legislation to restrict airline pricing. Bill C-26, passed in 1996, reimposed a form of regulation on the airline industry, particularly on Air Canada. Under its terms, the Canadian Transportation Agency is empowered to review prices on monopoly routes and to disallow and roll back any "unreasonable" fares.[43] But the government also took steps to ensure that Air Canada did not set prices too low by creating special provisions in the Competition Act addressing predatory pricing in the airline industry.[44]

What accounts for the different responses in Canada and the United States? First, the industry structure was different. The broad proliferation of business models and firms that emerged and survived in the United States, with multiple examples of each, had no counterpart in Canada. Although several LCCs sprang up and continue to be established, no other airline shared Air Canada's interests, and it chose to lower its costs through a bankruptcy that devolved the airline into a constellation of firms, all owned by Air Canada and each specializing in meeting a particular competitive threat. These firms might have had an interest in different and competing government policies but were of course coordinated in their political program. As a result, most attempts to start new airlines in Canada failed, and Air Canada's singular dominance created relatively low organizing costs for those seeking protection from it. Interests were easily aligned in Canada—fare ceilings protected consumers while fare floors protected competitors (at the expense of consumers), preventing monopoly but restricting competition.

Second, this was an easily understood and appealing news story. Periodic failures plus the constant drumbeat of warning from the only apparently viable low-fare competitor, Westjet, created a David-versus-Goliath scenario for the press, which portrayed Westjet as seeking help in defending the consumer from monopoly dominance. The result was reregulation.[45] Once the reregulation was established statutorily, slack reemerged, allowing Air Canada, with its ongoing contact with the Canadian Transport Agency and large stake in the outcome, to begin special interest lobbying when the political environment returned to "normal." In response, the agency recently proposed to relax its restrictions on Air Canada's pricing.[46]

This effort was helped by policy entrepreneurship. Pointing to evidence that, notwithstanding its problems, airline deregulation has brought benefits and has generated academic support for policy change, Air Canada has been able to persuade the government that its pricing policies should be left to the market. Furthermore, it has urged the government to focus attention on remaining monopolies in airports and other infrastructure that inhibit entry and raise costs (the lion's share of which are, of course, Air Canada's!). With respect to policy entrepreneurship, then, the Canadian case is not inconsistent with the U.S. case.

Is This a Testable Story?

One might object that there are a large number of "moving parts" in this explanation and wonder whether it could be empirically tested. It is beyond the scope of this essay to do so, but some appropriate tests can be suggested:

—One could study the news media for the period 1975–78 to measure the frequency, extent, and prominence (reflected by column inches, location on a front page or business page, TV news time, "teaser" status, and so on) of stories that mention the possibility of new regulation or deregulation and compare that period with any four-year period since. One could also consider the number of hearings devoted to deregulation or reregulation, perhaps weighted by congressional importance: Did the reviewing committee have regulatory jurisdiction? Was the hearing chaired by a mediagenic member? The purpose of such exercises would be to determine whether the issue had reached comparable "public agenda" status after deregulation. This would function as a measure of slack.

—If little slack was present, one could study past public opinion polls or conduct surveys to see whether service quality dominated price and schedule as determinants of consumer choice in an effort to measure political salience.

This would help to establish whether there was general support for regulation that might improve service quality but reduce competition and raise prices.

—To determine whether political entrepreneurs thought that price and entry regulation would attract general support, one could investigate which government hearings were concerned with reducing slack on issues related to price and entry regulation. To the extent that they were attempts to expose service failures and that the remedies discussed were essentially quality regulations with no restrictions on prices or entry, the hypothesis would tend to be confirmed. If, on the other hand, the hearings focused on ridding the industry of bad actors and installing minimum prices to eliminate cutthroat competition forcing quality cuts, the hypothesis would be disproved.

—Where slack could be found, one could study organized industry-wide attempts to resist deregulation or promote reregulation by the U.S. Air Transport Association. Did the ATA take a position on any regulatory issues after United broke ranks in 1977, for example? If so, were any of the issues on which it took a position related to competition? Evidence of industry unanimity or of ATA testimony in favor of restricting competition would tend to prove the hypothesis false.

—In the presence of slack, one could apply conventional measures of political support such as political action committee contributions and congressional representation to see whether any credible coalitions in favor of competition regulation had emerged. If deregulation remained in the face of both slack and a powerful coalition to reregulate, that would prove the hypothesis false.

—By way of a case study, one could examine the most comprehensive attempt to reregulate competition—the DOT's so-called guidelines for competitive behavior proposed in 1998–99 (which failed to be adopted)—to test any conclusions drawn from the foregoing investigations.

Conclusion

Deregulation survived in the airline industry despite drastic changes of fortune that it induced among its participants for reasons related to interests, institutions, ideology, and information. Market forces changed the shape of the industry in ways that were hard to anticipate politically, institutionally, contractually, and financially. Some new entrants became important to the system and provided more nonstop service to a number of medium-size cities that had regarded themselves as neglected. They could do this because they did not focus nonstop service mainly on the relatively few cities that had been developed as hubs by legacy airlines. All the LCCs tended to operate simpler fleets than those that legacy airlines had been forced to employ to serve diverse routes and to use smaller aircraft than were required by legacy airlines to amortize cockpit labor costs over many seats. LCCs were able to avoid many of the unproductive labor practices and fixed pension obligations that had grown up in the regulated oligopoly.

As firms diverged in character and firms and communities made specific asset commitments on the basis of the deregulated regime, interests too became more diverse. Under the tight oligopoly created by the Civil Aeronautics Board, airline interests had been fairly uniform, with the result that airlines were able to lobby the CAB and Congress for positions that were agreed on in trade associations or were a natural outgrowth of their circumstances. When market forces reshaped the industry, airlines could no longer sustain the contractual commitments to ground facilities, aircraft, labor unions, and other investments and relationships that had grown up under regulation. The resulting financial and political damage forced many to modify or nullify those commitments, often with the aid of the bankruptcy laws.

At the same time, airlines that could adapt to the new circumstances found opportunities for new and expanding business. Since they benefited from deregulation, they were opposed to regulatory responses designed to protect the older relationships and investments. Those that had benefited from firms, practices, and facilities adapted to the regulated era were unable to align their interests with those of the group benefiting from the new market freedom. Even among the latter group, the differences were marked enough to make it difficult to formulate and sustain a specific LCC position on airline issues.

With institutions changed as well, regulatory authorities became more responsive to the administration that happened to be in power. The ideology of the administrations themselves changed during the relevant period, in general becoming more hostile to regulation (if not necessarily to cash wealth transfers). And finally, what had for a time been an issue of pervasive public interest with overwhelming support on one side became part of the usual political cacophony of recommendation and counterrecommendation, with little eye-grabbing drama to support its presence on the public agenda for any extended period of time. Even airline bankruptcy reorganizations failed to disrupt service enough to capture the public's attention. All in all, the diversity of interests and the institutional inertia of the status quo have enabled airline deregulation to survive.

Many of the lessons observed here can be generalized. Perhaps the most interesting and important observation is that the existence and nature of regulation reinforces the stability of the regulatory regime in a kind of positive feedback loop. Regulatory regimes tend to emerge from circumstances that put most or all firms in the same boat and reduce their diversity of economic and political interests—persistent industry-wide economic pressures such as the Great Depression or shocks to the system such as disruptions, catastrophes, or scandals. Some of these circumstances reduce slack and some create it, but the resulting alignment of interests makes firms easier to organize and hence more effective in either lobbying the general public or exploiting slack to obtain protective regulation. Once a regulatory regime is put in place, firms adapt to it in order to maximize the benefits to be received from the regulators. In fact, the regulators themselves encourage this process so as to enhance the political stability of the regulated regime. For example, the CAB spent much of its forty years of regulatory history trying to make the trunklines more like each other by increasing the size of the smaller airlines and favoring them in the award of new routes. But once a change in circumstances creates deregulation, the firms diverge in character and interests as they pursue different strategies and seek different niches in the deregulated market. These different firms are harder to organize and align, and the industry loses political coherence and influence. In such circumstances, as in the case of U.S. airlines, the deregulated regime can withstand fragmented or disputed challenges by even very distressed interests.

Notes

1. Joskow and Noll have called this the "normative as positive theory" ("NPT") approach. See Paul L. Joskow and Roger G. Noll, "Regulation in Theory and Practice: An Overview," in *Studies in Public Regulation,* edited by Gary Fromm (MIT Press, 1981).

2. Also known as the "public choice" theory of regulation or the "government services" theory of regulation. It is usually distinguished from the "public interest" theory of regulation, which posits that regulation is brought about by public-spirited government actors (legislators or administrators) to serve as a public corrective for inefficiencies or injustices generated by market imperfections or the failure of market outcomes to conform to social norms. The theory is usually attributed to George Stigler. See his "The Theory of Economic Regulation," *Bell Journal of Economics and Management Science* 2, no. 1 (1971): 3–21. For alternate theories of regulation, see R. A. Posner, "Theories of Regulation," *Bell Journal of Economics and Management Science* 5 (Autumn 1974): 338–58.

3. See Sam Peltzman, "The Economic Theory after a Decade of Deregulation," and comments by Michael E. Levine and Roger G. Noll, *Brookings Papers on Economic Activity, Microeconomics* (1989), pp. 1–58.

4. Steven A. Morrison and Clifford Winston, "The Remaining Role for Government Policy in the Deregulated Airline Industry," in *Deregulation of Network Industries: What's Next?* edited by Sam Peltzman and Clifford Winston (AEI-Brookings Joint Center for Regulatory Studies, 2000).

5. Michael E. Levine and Jennifer L. Forrence, "Regulatory Capture, Public Interest, and the Public Agenda: Toward a Synthesis," *Journal of Law, Economics and Organization* 6 (Fall 1990, Special Issue): 167–98.

6. The term "slack" was first introduced into the political economy literature by J. H. Kalt and M. A. Zupan, "Capture and Ideology in the Economic Theory of Politics," *American Economic Review* 74 (June 1984): 279–300.

7. In fact, a general version of the economic theory of regulation makes slack in the political process the normal case and assumes that officials can optimize the amount of slack they experience. See S. P. Magee, W. A. Brock, and L. Young, *Black Hole Tariffs and Endogenous Policy Theory: Political Economy in General Equilibrium* (Cambridge University Press, 1989), chap. 18, "Optimal Obfuscation."

8. Ibid.; Kalt and Zupan, "Capture and Ideology in the Economic Theory of Politics." An inefficient result might be achieved in the absence of slack when economically efficient rents or quasi rents (that is, locational, scarcity, inframarginal, asset-specific rents) accrue to a relatively small and politically weak subclass or to individual firms outside the electorate determining the careers of the relevant regulators and are destroyed or transferred by inefficient policies to a general electorate. Residential rent control usually operates in this way, especially in jurisdictions like New York City that have a high percentage of tenant occupiers. And policies designed to disadvantage minorities, women, or "deviant" groups often are supported by the general polity.

9. See, for example, C. Haberman, "Beware: Voters Could Sway This Election," *New York Times,* September 2, 2005.

10. For a reasonable hypothesis, see Lucile Sheppard Keyes, *Federal Control of Entry into Air Transportation* (Harvard University Press, 1951).

11. Michael E. Levine, "Financial Implications of Regulatory Change in the Airline Industry," *Southern California Law Review* 49 (May 1976): 645–64.

12. Michael E. Levine, "Is Regulation Necessary? California Air Transportation and National Regulatory Policy," *Yale Law Journal* 74 (July 1965): 1416–47; William A. Jordan, *Airline Regulation in America: Effects and Imperfections* (Johns Hopkins Press, 1970).

13. The most conspicuous exception is Peltzman, "The Economic Theory after a Decade of Deregulation."

14. The CAB created no new "trunklines" (combination carriers of passengers and cargo with no categorical restrictions written into their certificates) between May 1938 (when sixteen airlines were "grandfathered" by the Civil Aeronautics Act of 1938) and 1978, although it did allow limited entry by firms with more specialized roles, such as operating regional (Hawaii and Alaska), nonscheduled, or charter service or with the primary objective of serving smaller markets (although they may have been permitted limited scheduled service in dense markets to cross-subsidize their obligated service in thin ones).

15. See Peltzman, "The Economic Theory after a Decade of Deregulation"; and Kalt and Zupan, "Capture and Ideology in the Economic Theory of Politics." Also, Martha Derthick and Paul J. Quirk, *The Politics of Deregulation* (Brookings, 1985); Stephen Breyer, *Regulation and Its Reform* (Harvard University Press, 1982), pp. 197–221; and

Barbara Sturken Peterson and James Glab, *Rapid Descent: Deregulation and the Shakeout in the Airlines* (New York: Simon & Schuster, 1994).

16. Federal economic regulatory jurisdiction extended only to airlines operating across state lines. Safety jurisdiction was plenary.

17. I have neglected to mention any number of smaller start-ups or the many financial reorganizations and changes in morphology of others. See, for example, T. A. Heppenheimer, *Turbulent Skies: The History of Commercial Aviation* (New York: John Wiley & Sons, 1995).

18. See A. Schwartz: "Statutory Interpretation, Capture and Tort Law: The Regulatory Compliance Defense," *American Law and Economics Review* 2 (Spring 2000): 26.

19. Magee and others, *Black Hole Tariffs*, chap. 18; K. A. Shepsle and B. R. Weingast, "Structure-Induced Equilibrium and Legislative Choice," *Public Choice* 37 (June 1981): 503.

20. O. E. Williamson, *The Economic Institutions of Capitalism: Firms, Markets, Relational Contracting* (New York: Free Press, 1985); David Besanko, David Dranove, and Mark Shanley, *The Economics of Strategy,* 3rd ed. (New York: John Wiley & Sons, 2003), pp. 128–32.

21. Steven A. Morrison and Clifford Winston, *The Evolution of the Airline Industry* (Brookings, 1995), pp. 6–7. See also Peltzman, "The Economic Theory after a Decade of Deregulation."

22. An odd version of the economic theory was proposed by Gary Becker, "Comment," *Journal of Law and Economics* 19 (August 1976): 245–48. According to Becker, the deadweight loss from inefficient regulation creates pressure for structures that dissipate less value, so that more benefits can be distributed to organized constituencies. Thus inefficient regulation is replaced by more efficient measures in a continuing process, of which airline deregulation is an example. Of course, this Panglossian version of regulatory theory does not explain how inefficient regulation arises in the first place or why all inefficient regulation does not ultimately wither away, to be replaced by an efficient regime, a manifestly false prediction.

23. Although it had initially joined in the regulated airline industry's opposition to deregulation, United, then the largest U.S. domestic airline, concluded in 1977 that network size mattered competitively, that its size meant that it was unlikely to get many new route awards in competitive proceedings (the CAB had a tendency to promote industry competitive "balance" through its route awards), and therefore that it could accept competition if deregulation would confer route entry freedom.

24. Airlines that have entered or risen to prominence since deregulation have come to be called LCCs.

25. Pension plans that guarantee a fixed monthly payment on retirement that is a function of length of service and previous compensation.

26. See especially the provisions that give a six-month exclusivity to existing management to put together a financial reorganization plan, usually extended many times to achieve a period as long as several years. United management's exclusivity was extended for more than three years. This produces rents for labor and particularly management that keep operating under some vestige of the nonviable arrangements while being protected from creditors, who are very much losers in the circumstances. Effective October 17,

2005, the law was changed to limit the exclusivity period to eighteen months; 11 U.S.C. 1121(d)(1), (2) (2005).

27. H.R. 4 Pension Protection Act of 2006. See *Aviation Daily,* October 11, 2006, item 6.

28. This dispute has been "settled" between American, Southwest, and Dallas by an agreement to grant Southwest a de facto monopoly on expanded service from Love Field, tempered only by two gates (out of twenty) assigned to American and two to Continental. U.S. House Committee on Transportation and Infrastructure Press Release 103, 2006; Wright Amendment Reform Act, HR 5830, 2006. American and Southwest, of course, have a concentrated common interest in keeping competitors out of the "neighborhood" at the expense of Dallas Metroplex consumers and were able to engage a senator (Kay Bailey Hutchison of Texas) to represent their local interests in a Congress with bigger fish to fry, a classic example of a local regulation that followed the economic theory in its enriched or original versions.

29. See, for example, Keith L. Alexander, "American Fare Cuts Presage Price War; Discounts Up to 85% on Florida Flights," *Washington Post,* November 19, 2004, p. E1.

30. Michael E. Levine, "Price Discrimination without Market Power," *Yale Journal on Regulation* 19 (Winter 2002): 1.

31. P. S. Dempsey and A. R. Goetz, "Regulatory Failure as Catalysts for Political Change: The Choice between Imperfect Regulation and Imperfect Competition," *Washington and Lee Law Review* 46 (Winter 1989): 1–40.

32. F. C. Thayer, *Rebuilding America, The Case for Economic Regulation* (New York: Praeger, 1984); F. C. Thayer, "Airline Regulation: The Case for a 'Public Utility' Approach," *Logistics and Transportation Review* (Vancouver) 18 (September 1982): 211–35.

33. 63 Fed. Reg. 17, 919-22 (April 10, 1998).

34. *Brooke Group Ltd.* v. *Brown & Williamson Tobacco Corp.,* 509 U.S. 209 (1993); *Matsushita Elec. Industrial Co.* v. *Zenith Radio,* 475 U.S. 574 (1986).

35. Levine, "Price Discrimination without Market Power."

36. Jonathan Weisman and Jim VandeHei, "Road Bill Reflects the Power of Pork, White House Drops Effort to Rein in Hill," *Washington Post,* August 11, 2005, p. A1.

37. See, for example, John J. Fialka, "White House Expresses Concern over Cost of Senate Energy Bill," *Wall Street Journal,* June 15, 2005, p. A4; "The Ethanol Party," Editorial, *Wall Street Journal,* May 26, 2005, p. A12; James A. Barnes, "Beating the Bushes for Earmarks," *National Journal,* February 10, 2001, p. 415.

38. Levine and Forrence, "Regulatory Capture, Public Interest, and the Public Agenda."

39. Except for a few specific issues, such as the grant of antitrust immunity for agreements between airlines in international service.

40. R.S. 1985, c. 28 (3rd Supp.). For many of the facts and most of the references in this section, I am indebted to Edward Iacobucci, Michael Trebilcock, and Ralph A. Winter, "The Political Economy of Deregulation in Canada," chap. 13 in this volume. The analysis and interpretive conclusions are my own, and those authors are in no way responsible for them.

41. Debra Ward, independent transition observer on airline restructuring, *Airline Restructuring in Canada: Final Report* (Ottawa, September 2002), p. 76.

42. *U.S.* v. *AMR Corp,* 335 F.3d 1109 (10th Cir. 2003), *aff'g* 140 F. Supp. 2d 1141 (D. Kan. 2001).

43. An Act Respecting the Oceans of Canada 1996, C. 31 (Bill C-26) (assented to December 18, 1996, ACT).

44. Competition Act, R.S., 1985, c. C-34, s. 1; R.S., 1985, c. 19 (2nd Supp.), s. 19. secs. 78, 79.

45. See Edward Iacobucci, "Public Choice Theory and Recent Developments in Canadian Competition Policy," in *Selected Topics in Corporate Litigation* (Kingston, Ont.: Queen's Annual Business Law Symposium, 2000/ 2001).

46. The Canada Transportation Act Review Panel, *Vision and Balance* (Ottawa, June 2001), recommended the elimination of this provision. In addition, the government has proposed changing course by eliminating all airline-specific provisions in the Competition Act. See Minister of Industry, "Minister of Industry Tables Amendments to Strengthen Competition Act," press release, November 2, 2004.

11

Reaching Competition despite Reform: When Technology Trumps (De)Regulation and the New "Old" Politics in Telecommunications Reform

ANDREW RICH

When President Bill Clinton signed the Telecommunications Act of 1996, all sides of the preceding debate claimed victory. It looked as though existing local and long-distance telephone companies along with cable television providers would be able to compete in one another's markets and new companies would be welcomed into each market with the regulatory advantages necessary to succeed. Just the week before, the law had passed in Congress with overwhelming majorities; only sixteen members of the House and five members of the Senate voted against the final conference report. The signing took place on February 8 in the Library of Congress—the first time such a ceremony was held there. It was a lavish affair, with Lily Tomlin playing telephone operator Ernestine and members of Congress crowding around the president as he signed his name to the new law. President Clinton enthusiastically remarked, "Today, with the stroke of a pen, our laws will catch up with our future. We will help to create an open marketplace where competition and innovation can move as quick as light."[1]

In 2007—more than a decade later—few continue to trumpet the new law as fostering terrific competition and innovation. In fact, few lawmakers talk publicly about it at all; if they do, it is rarely in glowing terms. The first sign of political peril associated with the Telecommunications Act was the defeat of the law's champion in the Senate, Republican Larry Pressler of South Dakota, in November 1996. Pressler, who had chaired the Senate Commerce Committee, which wrote much of the law, used the issue in his campaign, promising that greater competition would lower telephone and cable prices for his rural constituents. His Democratic opponent, arguing that these results were unlikely, won by two percentage points. Pressler, the only Senate incumbent to lose in 1996, was told by his pollster after the election that the telecommunication issue had cost him between 5 and 6 percent of the vote.

The suggestion that the new telecommunication law might not bring consumer prices down turned out to be more than just political rhetoric. The results have been mixed, with wire-line telecommunications prices in most markets falling, but overall consumer spending on telecommunications services generally increasing. To most observers, it has become clear that the Telecom Act did not represent real deregulation or provide a credible road to competition, as its supporters had predicted. In fact, the law has generated more rules and more conflict between industry and regulators than before. And in the sectors directly affected by the law, there has been more consolidation than competition. Telecommunications is a case where market-based structural reform led to more rather than fewer rules and to a competition structured by regulators rather than market forces. In sum, legislative reform has hampered the development of a competitive environment in the way envisioned by lawmakers when they took up the issue in the early 1990s.

Why this failure? Telecommunications reform seems to be a case of the triumph of "old politics" over "new." By old politics I mean the politics of entrenched interests. Telecommunications reform pitted two giant industry sectors—the long-distance companies and the "Baby Bells"—against one another. The stakes were enormous, and their strategies powerful, as both sides relied on their greatest assets: (1) the leverage of thousands of jobs at risk in the districts of members of Congress, and (2) highly developed and sophisticated lobbying operations in Washington that were prepared to influence the preferences of lawmakers. Moreover, all sides of the industry had deep pockets. In recent election cycles, the telecommunications industry has collectively contributed more to federal campaigns than just about any other industry. It has also spent more on lobbying—both before and after the Telecommunications Act passed—than any other industry. This financial leverage combined with the industry's success in maintaining a low public profile in the reform debate provided the "regulated" parties significant political power in influencing the course of that debate.

Initially, telecommunications reform was in step with the "new politics of public policy," which tied decisionmaking to particular ideas or philosophies of government that transcend the particular stakes of entrenched interests in a policy dispute.[2] The idea in this case was market-based reform, but its substance was eventually distorted and all but lost as the battle for telecommunications reform proceeded. The political priorities of the well-financed industries overpowered the philosophical commitments to market reform among some lawmakers. The new law that emerged from this intense policy fight lacked a true deregulatory spirit and would continue to be manipulated by dominant industries, especially in matters before the Federal Communications Commission (FCC). That political manipulation and the broader debate of the past twelve years are the subjects of this chapter.

On the surface, the 1996 Telecommunications Act held great promise for market-based reform. It was intended to follow in the tradition of federal deregulation of other industries in the 1980s—most notably airlines and trucking. But the substance and dynamic of the change turned out to be quite different for telecommunications. The outcome fell far short of what was achieved in other industries. Reflecting the urgings of most of the industries involved, the final 1996 Telecom Act established little more than rough parameters for deregulating and achieving competition in the telecommunications sector, set no date for abolishing regulatory hurdles to competition for the Baby Bells (much less for abolishing the regulators themselves), and left the details of the law's intentions and how it was to be implemented to the FCC and the courts. Although the FCC was responsible for sorting out most of the details and major provisions, every step in this direction was bound to be challenged by one party or another in the courts, which generally showed little deference to the regulators. Implementing the law thus became a long drawn-out process.

Interestingly, in the past five years competition and lower consumer prices have actually begun to emerge in telecommunications markets. But these phenomena are not due to any features of the Telecom Act or its implementation by the FCC. Rather, significant advancements in technology—particularly the growth of wireless phone service and, more recently, voice over Internet protocol (VoIP)—have challenged the sectors that were the focus of the Telecom Act, namely, the hard-wired local and long-distance operations. Not being subject to the Telecom Act, the new technologies have remained by and large unregulated, with a highly competitive market developing around them. As a result, the political and policy dynamics surrounding telecommunications have been reconfigured, not because of, but largely *in spite of* the actions of policymakers. Advances in technology have trumped the regulatory efforts of Congress and the FCC and opened the sector to market-based competition that policymakers failed to produce on their own.

The Context for Telecommunications Reform

During the 1980s and early 1990s, telecommunications reform gained most of its impetus from the persistent lobbying efforts of the industries affected. The list of these industries was long. In its final provisions, the Telecommunications Act of 1996 created substantial new business opportunities for local telephone companies (the Baby Bells or regional Bell operating companies, known as RBOCs), long-distance carriers (for example, AT&T, MCI, Sprint), and cable television companies to compete in one another's markets. With profound anxieties during the law's development about how it would provide such opportunities, these and an assortment of related industries— ranging from publishing, broadcast, and radio to burglar alarm and cellular operations—played an active role in lobbying over the legislation's content.

The economic stakes in the bill were great for a host of enormous industries, and the political stakes equally high for members of Congress as a consequence of unrelenting corporate pressure during negotiations. In the decade ending December 31, 1994, leading into the first round of debate over telecommunications reform, the communications industries contributed almost $40 million through political action committees and soft money to candidates and political parties.[3] The size of political contributions and the scope of lobbyists involved in telecommunications reform were enormous. The 1996 law was largely shaped below the radar screen of the general public, through political deals that sought to appease interested parties. Without the public's attention, the principal aim of key legislators was to find a compromise that balanced the short-term interests of all parties to the reform.

In the years leading up to the 1996 act, the American telecommunications industry was regulated by two entities: the 1934 Communications Act, much modified over time, and Judge Harold Greene, who was responsible for enforcing the consent decree over AT&T's 1984 divestiture of the RBOCs. Under the 1982 decree, put into effect in 1984, the Baby Bells, which were more or less monopoly providers of local phone service, were prohibited from offering long-distance or other information services and from manufacturing telecommunications products. Divested of the Baby Bells, AT&T was left as the dominant long-distance service provider as well as manufacturer of communications equipment in the United States, although with the emergence of rivals MCI and Sprint, the environment steadily became more competitive.

In the same year that the AT&T consent decree took effect, Congress passed legislation amending the 1934 Communications Act in a way that substantially reduced regulation of the cable industry. By 1984, 30 million Americans were cable subscribers, up from about 10 million a decade earlier.[4] The 1984 Cable Act, passed by Congress under pressure from the Reagan administration and the cable industry, eliminated virtually all regulation of cable rates at both the national and regional levels and at the same time blocked telephone companies from offering cable service within their geographic market areas. In the late 1980s, cable rates increased by 40 percent, fueling movement toward reregulation of the cable industry, which was approved by Congress and enacted over a veto by President George Bush in 1992. The new law made cable service subject once again to both federal and municipal rate regulation, with new, even stricter supervision by the FCC.

Faced with restrictive legislation, the Baby Bells, long-distance companies, and cable operators did what they could in a series of mergers, buyouts, and court cases to enter one another's business. However, the difficulties posed by the mixed regulatory environment, the realities of the new technologies, and the growing convergence of the telecommunications industries proved troublesome for market participants and regulators alike. Many previously unconvinced policymakers began to agree that further reform was indeed needed. By the latter half of 1993, the first round of comprehensive telecommunications reform legislation was being drafted in Congress, and the move toward enactment of the 1996 Telecommunications Act had begun in earnest.

Positioning for Advantage in Reform

The central issue of the telecommunications reform debate was the conditions under which the Baby Bells and long-distance carriers might be permitted to enter one another's markets. Without a radical change in thinking by Judge Greene, the Bell companies could not offer long-distance service unless it was sanctioned by Congress. The Baby Bells badly wanted this opportunity, so congressional action was a necessary first step.

Once the reform effort got under way, a number of other issues surfaced: universal service, cable regulation, foreign ownership bans, broadcast spectrum allocation, and regulation of material dealing with sex, violence, and pornography. As diverse as the issues were, they boiled down to two basic concerns: the appropriate market structure in telecommunications industries and the need for government regulation to accommodate that structure. Views on market structure were either monopolist or pro-competitive. Some thought the way to achieve either a fair and efficient monopoly or balanced and effective competition was to introduce more government regulation, while others wanted less regulation.[5]

By the early 1990s, however, few economists, lawyers, or members of the industries still favored a monopolistic structure for the telecommunications industries, particularly after seeing the success of competitive markets in other sectors. But what level of regulation was required to promote competition? This question was at the heart of most of the battles over telecommunications reform in the 1990s. Some pushed for complete deregulation of telecommunications industries, with full cross-ownership and unregulated customer fees. Others argued that existing asymmetries in size among potential telecommunication competitors, along with an obligation to ensure universal telephone service, called for substantial government regulation and supervision in creating and sustaining a competitive environment. These were the two main lines of thought before and after the Telecommunications Act was passed.

Moving to Legislation

In the fall of 1993, the first serious bills to address the reform of the telecommunications industries were introduced in the House. One was introduced by John Dingell (D-Mich.), chairman of the House Commerce Committee, and Jack Brooks (D-Tex.), chairman of the Judiciary Committee, long-time friends who were motivated by a desire to see Judge Greene relinquish authority over the Baby Bells. On the same day, a second bill was introduced by Ed Markey (D-Mass.), chairman of the Commerce Committee's telecommunications subcommittee, and Jack Fields (R-Tex.), his Republican counterpart. It aimed at creating a regulatory context for competition among telephone and cable service providers.

The two House bills set the stage for serious legislative progress in 1994. In February, Ernest Hollings (D-S.C.), chairman of the Commerce, Science, and Transportation Committee, joined the debate on the Senate side, introducing a bill with John Danforth (R-Mo.). Hollings was an AT&T ally. In its content, the Hollings-Danforth bill combined elements of both House bills but created higher hurdles for the RBOCs before they could extend service into cable, long distance, and manufacturing.

In both the House and the Senate, final debates required a negotiated compromise with the industry over permitting the RBOCs into long-distance service. The House passed telecommunications reform bills by overwhelming margins on June 28, 1994.[6] In the Senate, passage was not so easy. A version of the Hollings bill was approved by the Senate Commerce Committee on August 11, 1994. But Senator Robert Dole (R-Kans.), the Senate minority leader, had other plans for the bill. In late August, Dole entered the debate with his own draft alternative, which he began informally circulating among colleagues. Dole thought the Hollings bill created hurdles that were too onerous for the Bell companies to surmount before they could enter long-distance competition.

Dole never formally introduced his bill. It was intended merely to stop Hollings, who by early September was running out of time for Senate floor action before the October recess for the election. With a slim Democratic majority, Republicans could have filibustered or placed a hold on the legislation, which is what Dole threatened. As David Wilson, Dole's staff member on the issue, recalls, "We figured that we had 15 or 16 days' worth of cloture votes that we could, if we wanted, rake them over the coals with. So theoretically, there was not time for them to fool around with us. And, even though we were in the minority at the time, that is why they had to come to us and say, what's it going to take to get it out on the floor and take a vote."[7] Unwilling to compromise, on Friday, September 23, 1994, Chairman Hollings announced that there would be no telecommunications reform bill passed out of the Senate that year. He blamed Senator Dole, along with the Baby Bells, for preventing it.

With sweeping electoral victories in both the House and the Senate, the Republicans took control of the congressional agenda in January 1995, and while not a part of the House's Contract with America, telecommunications reform was one of the first issues out of the starting blocks in both chambers. Thomas Bliley (R-Va.) became chairman of the House Energy and Commerce Committee, and Larry Pressler (R-S.D.) took control of the Commerce Committee in the Senate.

The Senate was the first to act on telecommunications. Pressler knew that reform died the previous year because time had run out, so the goal he set was to have the Senate pass a telecommunications bill by Easter. Pressler held his first hearing on telecommunications reform on January 9, well before a bill was even ready for discussion. Following the hearing, he put a gag order on his staff, ordering them not to talk to lobbyists or journalists until a draft of reform legislation was complete. On the last day of January,

Pressler personally distributed actual draft legislation to every committee Democrat as well as the vice president. The Pressler bill was similar to the previous Hollings legislation in many respects, but it provided a three-year date-certain after which the Baby Bells could enter the long-distance market.

Given two weeks to comment on the Pressler draft, Democrats came back in the middle of February with their own alternative bill, also similar to the Hollings bill from the previous Congress. In negotiations that lasted through the first part of March, Pressler made significant concessions. He agreed to replace date-certain entry for the Baby Bells into long distance with fourteen competitive requirements for the Bell companies that came from Hollings— and were favored by the long-distance providers.[8] On March 23, the committee passed, by a vote of 17-2, a bill that deregulated the cable industries, lifted cross-ownership bans between the telephone and cable businesses, and enumerated the fourteen-point checklist for Baby Bell entry into long-distance service.

Senator Dole and his staff had been patient with Pressler all through his negotiations with Hollings and the Democrats. David Wilson, Dole's staffer, had sat in on the discussions leading up to the committee-approved bill, but, at Dole's insistence, he had refrained from trying to dictate the terms on which agreement should be made with Hollings. As the spring wore on, however, Dole decided he had to intervene. Before the bill headed for the Senate floor, he worked with Pressler on amendments that might make the legislation more deregulatory. Industry groups—particularly the Baby Bells—were directly involved in working with Wilson on the amendments.

The Dole amendment passed on the Senate floor and moved the bill in a more deregulatory direction.[9] After a week of debate, the amended bill passed the Senate by a vote of 81-8. It still included the fourteen-point checklist for Bell entry into long distance but included as well date-certain cable deregulation and provisions for cable and telephone competition.

In the House, Republican committee staff began conversations on a telecommunications bill the day after the election, but members did little more than hold preliminary talks in November because they were distracted in large part by the Contract with America. It was late May when the House Commerce Committee approved a bill favored by the long-distance industry by a vote of 38-5.[10] The full House did not take up telecommunications reform until the beginning of August, by which point the legislation under consideration had changed substantially.

Following its passage in committee, the House bill went through a vetting process by the House leadership. As had happened in the Senate, the House leadership considered the legislation too regulatory. At the urging of the Baby Bells, the leadership compelled the committee to accept a manager's amendment when the bill came to the floor, relieving the Baby Bells of certain competitive restrictions for entering long distance and bringing it closer to the amended bill that the Senate had passed.[11] After more than nine hours of debate that began close to midnight on August 3, the full House passed an amended telecommunications reform bill by a vote of 305-117. After a protracted conference committee process, the conference report was approved by both chambers on February 1, 1996, making way for the president's signing ceremony on February 8.

What Was Missing in the Debate?

Many members of Congress closely involved in the debate had a strong interest in achieving a deregulated, competitive market. But this interest was trumped by the concerns of the industries that would be affected. As a result, the final law fell short on a number of fronts where it might have provided for deregulation and market competition. The goal of the law, as described by the FCC on its website, is to let "anyone enter any communications business—to let any communications business compete in any market against any other."[12] In reality, the law permitted only limited competition to take place—and only after complicated hurdles had been jumped. The law provided no date-certain when restrictions on competition might be lifted; instead, it outlined steps that had to be taken by the incumbent firms—especially the Baby Bells—before they could compete in one another's markets.

Three important sets of actors were by and large absent from the narrative of how the Telecommunications Act came to pass: (1) the public interest community, (2) the president and vice president, and (3) the research community. An expanded role by any of the three might have changed the final law, making it different in content and perhaps more coherent. But for a variety of reasons, all three had only a small input—in contrast to Congress, which was in direct negotiation with the industries involved.

Public Interest Community

The consumer or public interest representatives who were vocal in the telecommunications reform debate were frequently called on to testify in Congress and to provide comments for journalists—but they had little substantive effect on the legislation. Three prominent activists from these groups were Gene Kimmelman of Consumers Union, Mark Cooper of the

Consumer Federation of America, and Andrew Schwartzman of the Media Access Project. Their principal concern was consumer rates, a subject on which each was outspoken. But they faced two obstacles, the first being the power of the dominant industries. No matter what public interest advocates said, reform was going to be resolved to satisfy the interests of the industries. For the reasons already discussed, the industries had the ear of key lawmakers. Second, the public interest community had a hard time making a credible case for reform's possible effects on consumer prices, leaving lawmakers confused as to the comparative benefits of different combinations of reform. Who offered consumers more—long-distance or local phone companies? What about cable? The public interest community did not do much to answer these questions or alleviate policymakers' confusion.

Though it had little influence on the basic competitive aspects of the reform, the public interest community did have some input in the universal service and decency provisions of the law. Members of Congress were easily persuaded that whatever else might change in telecommunications policy through reform, the federal commitment to subsidized wired phone service for all rural customers must be retained. Rural state senators and public interest group leaders helped Congress sort out these provisions. Likewise, members of Congress developed side proposals to protect children from adult material on television and the Internet. Family-focused interest groups helped Congress with these provisions.

The Clinton Administration

Whereas the public interest community had difficulty making itself heard, the president and, to a large extent, the vice president apparently decided not to engage much in the debate. For all of the credit that Vice President Al Gore might have deserved for his role in facilitating the development of the Internet and his outspokenness on telecommunications issues as a candidate, he took little part in negotiating features of the telecommunications act on behalf of the Clinton administration, which left most of the task to Congress. Since the process was dominated by Congress—with little effort by the president to insist on a coherent set of policies in the law—it is perhaps no surprise that the legislative debate became fragmented and greatly influenced by the industries.

Vice President Gore did give several speeches early on in the telecommunications reform debate, but by all accounts, he and the president left the negotiating of the legislation to Congress. In the summer of 1995, for example, he attended a meeting of House Democratic leaders to raise administration objections to two aspects of the bill: the repeal of broadcast ownership restrictions and the lack of a provision for the V-chip, a blocking device parents could use in controlling their children's viewing. Representative Markey sponsored amendments that addressed the White House concerns, both of which were approved by the House. Apart from voicing occasional concerns, however, Gore and the administration appeared to exert little pressure—and had little influence—on the final telecommunications reform law.[13]

The Research Community

Researchers, especially economists, also had limited influence in the telecom debate, which by 1994—two years before the Telecom Act passed—was already being shaped by old-fashioned interest-based politics. Facing enormous pressure from all the industries affected by the potential reform, Congress lost track of the intellectual merits of deregulation, which provided the original rationale and the continuing rhetorical justification for reform. The voices behind that intellectual rationale were drowned out in the debate as well.

By contrast, market-based ideas about deregulation had played a strong role in the move toward deregulation in the 1970s and 1980s, especially in the transportation and airline sectors. In an in-depth analysis of the political origins of airline and trucking deregulation, Martha Derthick and Paul Quirk illustrate that reform occurred following a convergence of academic and political evaluations in its favor: "Drawing upon both theory and empirical research, economists were convinced that much economic regulation in fundamentally competitive markets had large costs yet yielded no benefits, and their analysis reinforced the work of other disciplines that had criticized regulatory agencies as captives of the regulated industries."[14] Through the 1950s and 1960s, academic economists converged on the argument that price, entry, and exit regulations were generally inefficient and undesirable. In the 1970s, this research was turned into specific proposals, and policy experts strengthened policymakers' confidence in deregulation to the point that it "became a preferred style of policy choice in the nation's capital, espoused more or less automatically, even unthinkingly, by a wide range of officeholders and their critics and used by them as a guide to position taking."[15]

The deregulatory fervor of the 1970s and early 1980s helped propel the AT&T breakup in 1982, and it had some residual effects on telecommunications policy in the 1990s. But many of the same economists who had made their reputations by contributing quite credibly and independently to the deregulatory chorus at that time were, by the 1990s, paid consultants of telecommunications companies that were angling for reform.

During the two decades leading up to the Telecommunications Act of 1996, the Baby Bells, AT&T, and other telecommunications companies depended on expert economists to justify their case for a more favorable marketplace, both in affidavits and testimony before the FCC and in court. They hired experts at think tanks and universities to lend credibility to their filings and to make their case appealing.[16] As Bell South's Bob Blau explains it:

> There has to be a reason to get Congress to change a consent decree. And that reason ultimately has to go to the welfare of consumers, the economy. People have to be convinced of that. And so we, as well as the other side, use experts to help make our points. . . . It sort of raises the debate by adding some ideas and points of view that do, in fact, relate to the consumer and consumer welfare that need to get made and get factored and are, in fact, factored in by the policymakers.[17]

Henry Geller, a former assistant secretary of commerce in the Carter administration, sees it slightly differently: "It's almost like the *Mikado,* where there's a line about adding verisimilitude to an otherwise bald and unconvincing narrative. They're using the experts because they have to."[18] Geller certainly found them all "very bright" and "able" people who "really do believe" in their work. But, he added, "you've got to take everything they say with a ton of salt" and recognize that "nobody's going to pay attention. You're a hired gun. You wouldn't pay attention to their lawyer. Oh, you'd listen to his arguments, but you wouldn't be stroking your brow saying, I've just heard great truth. You'd say, I've just heard a great advocate."[19]

With many experts lacking independent credibility—and their expertise and ideas ignored anyway as the debate took on steam—the final considerations were around what the industries would accept. Their lawyers negotiated the terms of competition. And the role of lawyers—as opposed to that of economists—only increased as the new telecommunications law headed to the Federal Communications Commission for implementation.

Implementing Failed Reform

As written, the Telecommunications Act left a great many issues unresolved, which meant that the FCC had much of the responsibility for interpreting the new law. The commission set to work, using its authority to devise a complicated system of rules for entry for new telecommunications companies that required incumbent firms to make parts of their networks available to new entrants.[20] As one critic observed, the law itself contained "more than

100 pages of detailed legal mandates and prohibitions in an ill-advised attempt to micro-manage the transition to deregulation rather than cut the knot." But "the act call[ed] for more than ninety bureaucratic inquiries, evaluations, and rulings by the Federal Communications Commission as part of its implementation."[21] In his memoir, Reed Hundt, chairman of the FCC at the time, recalls his reaction upon reading the new law for the first time: "The conference committee compromises had produced a mountain of ambiguity that was generally tilted toward the local phone companies' advantage. But under principles of statutory authority, we had broad authority to exercise our discretion in writing the implementing regulations."[22] The FCC moved quickly and with an expectation that every decision it made would be second-guessed in the courts by whichever side lost. The industries that were to be affected by the new law recognized the potential for harm—or advantage—at the FCC. Each had its phalanx of lawyers ready to argue for and defend rules needed to promote its market advantage.

The FCC is a five-member commission, with each commissioner appointed for five-year terms. Commission membership must be split between the two political parties, with three members from one and two from the other and with their chairman appointed by the president. There have been four chairmen since the Telecommunications Act passed. The act promoted competition in local telephone service by requiring the Baby Bells to "unbundle" their networks of lines and switches, making them available for lease by new competitors. Lawmakers had concluded that it was not realistic for new entrants to emerge in the local phone markets if they had to lay new wires for service; the initial investments would be prohibitive. Moreover, interconnection among networks could become a problem. So the law required a process of regulated unbundling of the Baby Bell incumbent networks before the Baby Bells could enter other markets. This provision of the law became a major sticking point at the FCC—and the trouble that surrounded it reflected the conflicts that have become endemic to the implementation of the Telecom Act.

During the period of "forced competition" after the law was enacted, the Baby Bells remained subject to price regulation. But battles erupted over how to interpret the pricing requirements—both for service and for the leasing of the unbundled local networks—and how to decide when local telephone companies had done enough to merit entry into long-distance competition. Initially it was expected that local telephone companies would be permitted to enter the long-distance market after (1) the state public utility commission had certified that the company had opened its market to competition, (2) the

FCC and Department of Justice agreed that conditions had been satisfied to achieve competition in local markets, and (3) the FCC certified that local phone company entry into the long-distance market would be in the public interest—each a significant hurdle.

In fact, in the years since the Telecommunications Act became law, the FCC has written three sets of rules for structuring the unbundling of the local markets, all of which have been challenged in the federal district court. So far, federal judges have struck down two. For their part, the Baby Bells have pursued expensive—and slow—litigation of most core elements of the Telecom Act, thereby delaying implementation of most of its provisions.

One might say the act breathed new life into the FCC. Far from giving birth to unfettered deregulation, it set the parameters for the FCC to become centrally involved in negotiating the relationships among telecommunications companies. As Adam Thierer, now a telecommunications analyst at the libertarian Cato Institute and a critic of the FCC's implementation of the law, observed, the law's "vaguely worded phrases about the need to encourage competition" gave little indication of how this was to be done:

> The law delegated broad authority to the FCC to carry it out. But the one thing that was clear was that this was not cold turkey deregulation. The law didn't say, as previous deregulatory initiatives did, that on this date all of these rules and regulations will cease to exist. So it cannot be labeled deregulation, strictly defined. What it can be labeled, I think, is managed competition, which is a bit of an oxymoron, of course. Or, . . . "deregulatory industrial policy"—which is to say it's deregulation with an asterisk that says okay, we believe we are going to liberalize these markets, but we're going to guide the process. We're going to have our hands on it at each juncture to make sure it unfolds the way we think is "fair." Well . . . if you allow for that sort for meddling, meddle they will. And indeed that's exactly what the FCC did.[23]

Following enactment of the telecom legislation, expenditures by the FCC rose by about one-third and stayed at permanently higher levels in the ensuing years. The FCC's regulatory output grew as well. The number of pages of the *FCC Record*—which compiles FCC decisions, proposed rulemakings, and adjudications—tripled after 1996, from fewer than an average 10,000 pages a year to close to 25,000 pages a year.[24] By October 1997, the FCC had issued 184 reports, orders, public notices, and other official documents associated with the new law.[25] It appeared that deregulation had "permanently increased the inputs and outputs of the FCC . . . that a one percent increase in real expenditures for the FCC would produce about a nine percent increase in output."[26]

Increased activity at the FCC also appears to have led to increased political activity at the telecommunications firms: between 1994 and 1998 membership in the Federal Communications Bar Association rose by 73 percent, reflecting significant new interest in helping the telecommunication firms in legal disputes.[27] Of course, this was a period in which the telecommunications industry was expanding, which may help to account for the increase in membership. In view of the economies of scale as a business grows, however, the growth of firms in itself does not explain the increase in the ranks of lawyers working on telecommunications issues.[28]

Before 1996, many political observers suggested that members of Congress had drawn out the time it took to achieve reform so as to maximize the number of campaign contributions they could obtain from telecommunications firms. Evidence of spending since the reform passed suggests that they need not have worried. Between 1998 and September 2004, telephone companies alone contributed $60.5 million to federal campaigns, more than the amount the entire telecommunications industry contributed to campaigns in the decade preceding reform. Contributions of telecommunications companies combined (telephone, cable, and broadcast) over the 1998–2004 period totaled $145.6 million.

Perhaps more remarkable, over roughly the same period the industry spent nearly $1 billion on lobbying. Of this amount, $498 million came from telephone companies, $222.3 million from broadcasters, and $119.9 million from cable television providers.[29] This spending appears to have surpassed all other industries in lobbying expenditures during this period.

In February 2003, the FCC announced the third set of policy revisions requiring the RBOCs to offer unbundled services to competitors. FCC policies were subject to triennial review for rulemaking, a process that purportedly included extensive research and analysis of market trends. The commission passed this third set by a vote of 3-2 but reported little research and analysis in support of its recommendations. The FCC voted on a "term sheet" rather than an actual draft order, suggesting to some that its decisions rested on a political—rather than policy—rationale. Greg Sidak, a leading telecommunications economist, complained that the decision of the FCC, which was established "to be an expert independent agency," reflected "neither expertise nor independence": "The commissioners could not be sure what they were voting for, and their statements accompanying the decision radiated politics. The possible dimensions of political struggle in the Triennial Review are multiple . . . [including] the personal ambitions of Commissioner Martin versus those of Chairman Powell; and, even though they seem far fetched, White House concerns about the ramifications of unbundling and TELRIC pricing for the 2004 presidential election."[30] Sidak questioned, "Why should Congress delegate the making of transparently political decisions concerning telecommunications to a body whose comparative advantage is not supposed to be politics?"[31]

In fact, by most accounts, Congress intentionally left the difficult telecom reform issues to the FCC (and, less intentionally, the courts). And it did so knowing full well that the FCC is a political body. Most members of Congress still view the law as a deregulatory and pro-competitive instrument. Members of the FCC complain that its ambiguities required their interventions, however complicated or frustrating those interventions might have been to the various parties involved. In fact, as a leading critic of the FCC's handling of the Telecom Act has pointed out, "Congress invited them to manage competition, and they did so with a vengeance."[32] In previous rounds of deregulation, several industries were opened to competition without increasing regulation, the commissions regulating them were abolished, rate regulation all but disappeared, and firms were not required to sell their services or lease their facilities to rivals at regulated prices. In this case, "by contrast, legislators viewed a large part of the distribution network in telecommunications as a natural monopoly. As a result, the 1996 act instructed regulators to determine which incumbent-carrier facilities should be made available to entrants and to establish the cost basis for wholesale rates for such facilities, two issues that have tied up the regulators and the courts for most of the past nine years."[33] In 2006 the FCC is still negotiating and making rules about the Telecommunications Act.

Lessons from Telecommunications Reform

The power of ideas—ideas about the merits of deregulating markets and opening sectors to competition—that have been powerful in so many policy debates over the past two decades lost steam in the debate over telecommunications, with the "new" politics of public policy giving way to the "old." Although the deregulatory impulse motivated the first push toward reform, the battle over accomplishing competitive markets in telecommunications took a different course because the segments affected—long distance and local service—were competing head to head. By contrast, the debate over redistributing power in the airline and trucking industries had pitted the industries collectively on one side and the government on the other.

In telecommunications, the question was not so much what power the government should retain but rather what advantage each industry segment should retain. With a focus on this question, the industries took control of the debate, forming alliances with members of Congress that crossed party lines. As a result, final preferences on reform had much more to do with keeping jobs in members' districts, contributions to members' campaigns, and the effectiveness of strategic lobbying of members than with the impulse to carry out reform in a way that follows the "right" ideas (however defined). Aside from providing the basic rationale for pursing reform, market-based ideas—and the economists who might have promoted them—played little substantive role in the law's final development and passage.

In an environment where policymaking was largely controlled by the industries with stakes in it, lawmakers lost sight of (and in some cases, lost interest in) how best to accomplish competition and deregulation. Each side of the industry effectively articulated a different scenario for how to promote competition—and prevent the tyranny of the incumbent firms. As a consequence, rank-and-file members of Congress were bombarded with conflicting information on which to base their policy judgments. In the face of this confusion, they had even greater reason to fall back on their political preferences for one or the other industry in deciding which to support in the legislation (and what level of support to provide). Moreover, the confusing rhetoric led members to believe that the changes being made late in the debate over the Telecom Act would not detract from the generally deregulatory, pro-competitive thrust of the bill—and that the details would be worked out by the FCC, anyway.

But the vague and complicated nature of the final Telecom Act made the FCC's task difficult. The aggressive and pro-regulatory preferences of the FCC itself affected the law's implementation as well. The agency is quite limited in its ability to challenge the expertise of the industries it regulates. Few FCC commissioners are deeply knowledgeable about the intricacies of the industries and the way technological change might affect them, which means the FCC is not a thoroughly independent expert bureau. There are few independent sources of expertise in any case, as most of the knowledgeable economists work for one part of the industry or another. In sum, a debate that began anchored in the "new" politics of policymaking—a politics based on ideas—quickly fell back into the "old" politics, dominated by the self-interested industries.

Interestingly, competition has started to emerge in telecommunications—in spite of (rather than because of) the 1996 act and its effects to the contrary. That is to say, segments of the telecommunications industry directly affected by the new law have not experienced high levels of competition. Furthermore, new companies have not succeeded in offering local telephone service; instead, several of the Baby Bells have merged, consolidating their businesses. There have been delays in Bell entry into long distance. And the incumbent long-distance carriers—most notably, AT&T—have seen their markets and corporate prospects shrink to a shadow of their former selves. Even so, competition has effectively emerged in other telecom markets.

Although the Telecom Act imposed more rather than fewer rules on the industries affected by the law, the law did not, in fact, have an impact on all segments of the industry. Most important, Congress and the FCC chose not to regulate (and, in some instances, were prevented from regulating) the wireless market, and, so far, they have chosen not to place regulation on voice over Internet technology as well. These alternatives for telecommunications—especially wireless operations—have challenged the hard-wired segment and created competition where it otherwise would not exist.

Technology has overtaken the policymaking process and created market-based competition where lawmakers and regulators did not. Regulators have stayed out of the new markets, in large part because these markets have no dominant incumbents flexing their political muscle in Washington. Competition has emerged and prices have been forced down.[34] There appears to be a significant lag between when new telecommunications firms develop market share and when they develop political power in Washington. Likewise, a lag occurs between the loss of market share (most notably by AT&T) and the loss of political power in Washington.

Nevertheless, new developments in telecommunications—and the impulse by regulators so far to stay out of them—suggest that market-based competition might have a chance in the future. Members of Congress are talking about revisiting telecommunications reform in the coming years, but no one is clear about what that exercise might entail. Many close observers of the industry believe congressional action is unlikely. That leaves it to the new sectors in telecommunications—wireless and voice over Internet, in particular—to build a political constituency in Washington that protects them and other segments of the telecommunications market from the same fate as their wire-line predecessors.

Notes

1. Dan Carney, "Telecommunications: Indecency Provision Attacked as Clinton Signs Bill," *Congressional Quarterly Weekly Report,* February 10, 1996, p. 359.

2. See Marc K. Landy and Martin A. Levin, eds., *The New Politics of Public Policy* (Johns Hopkins University Press, 1995).

3. "Robber Barons of the '90s," *Common Cause Report* (June 1995). According to the FCC, the seven individual Bell companies combined spent $64 million on state and federal lobbying in 1993, up from $41 million in 1992. Mike Mills, "The New Kings of Capitol Hill," *Washington Post,* April 23, 1995, p. H1.

4. *Television and Cable Factbook, 1995* (Washington: Warren Publishing, 1995), as cited in Robert W. Crandall and Harold Furchtgott-Roth, *Cable TV: Regulation or Competition?* (Brookings, 1996), p. 5.

5. Eli M. Noam, "Beyond Telecommunications Liberalization: Past Performance, Present Hype, and Future Direction," in *The New Information Infrastructure: Strategies for U.S. Policy,* edited by William J. Drake (New York: Twentieth Century Fund Press, 1995).

6. On committee passage, see "Bill Advances in House on Telecom," *New York Times,* March 17, 1994, p. D2. The Brooks-Dingell bill (HR3626) passed 423-5, and the Markey-Fields bill (HR3636) passed 423-4. See "House Passed Telecommunications Legislation by Big Margins," *Communications Daily,* June 29, 1994, p. 1.

7. David Wilson, telecommunications aide to Senator Robert Dole, interview, Washington, May 6, 1999.

8. Kirk Victor, "Will the Real Chairman Please Stand Up?" *National Journal,* April 8, 1995, p. 892.

9. A number of side issues gained public attention during the course of debate, some far more than the core competition issues in the bills. Most notably, Senator James Exon (D-Nebr.) introduced a controversial amendment banning pornography from the Internet. The amendment passed and was part of the final legislation (although overturned in part by the Supreme Court in 1997).

10. "House Commerce Panel Passes Telecom Bill," *Communications Daily,* May 26, 1995, p. 1.

11. Kirk Victor, "How Bliley's Bell Was Rung," *National Journal,* July 22, 1995, pp. 1892–93.

12. See www.fcc.gov/telecom.html.

13. Although Gore delayed the process a bit, it is notable that he did not have substantial influence over the legislation for much of the debate. As the *National Journal* reported in April 1995, "Gore is surely unhappy at the growing perception that for all his pronouncements on the importance of the information superhighway, he's had little noticeable impact on the legislative process." Kirk Victor, "Will the Real Chairman Please Stand Up?" *National Journal,* April 8, 1995, p. 892.

14. Martha Derthick and Paul J. Quirk, eds., *The Politics of Deregulation* (Brookings, 1985) p. 238.

15. Ibid., p. 35.

16. See Andrew Rich, *Think Tanks, Public Policy, and the Politics of Expertise* (Cambridge University Press, 2004).

17. Bob Blau, interview, May 6, 1999.

18. Henry Geller, interview, Washington, May 5, 1999.

19. Ibid.

20. The Supreme Court upheld the role of the FCC in interpreting the Telecommunication Act of 1996 in 2002, in its decision in *Verizon Communications Inc.* v. *FCC.* In particular, the court upheld the reasonableness of the FCC's pricing rules for unbundling parts of the existing networks.

21. W. Russell Neuman and others, *The Gordian Knot: Political Gridlock on the Information Highway* (Cambridge, Mass.: MIT Press, 1998), p. xiii.

22. Reed E. Hundt, *You Say You Want a Revolution: A Story of Information Age Politics* (Yale University Press, 2000) p. 154.

23. Adam Thierer, Cato Institute, interview, Washington, January 19, 2005.

24. J. Gregory Sidak, "The Failure of Good Intentions: The WorldCom Fraud and the Collapse of American Telecommunications after Deregulation," *Yale Journal of Regulation* 20 (Summer 2003): 211–12.

25. Martin Cave and Robert Crandall, *Telecommunications Liberalization on Two Sides of the Atlantic* (Washington: AEI-Brookings Joint Center for Regulatory Studies, 2001), p. 11.

26. Sidak, "The Failure of Good Intentions," p. 212.

27. Ibid., p. 213.

28. See ibid.

29. John Dunbar, Daniel Lathrop, and Robert Morlino, "Networks of Influence: The Political Power of the Communications Industry" (Center for Public Integrity, October 2004).

30. Sidak, "The Failure of Good Intentions," pp. 224–25.

31. Ibid., p. 225.

32. Robert W. Crandall. *Competition and Chaos: U.S. Telecommunications since the 1996 Telecom Act* (Brookings, 2005), p. 1.

33. Ibid., pp. 2–3.

34. Ibid., *passim.*

12

The Day after *Market-Oriented Reform, or What Happens When Economists' Reform Ideas Meet Politics*

Eric M. Patashnik

For a capitalistic society with a massive stake in well-functioning markets, many Americans are surprisingly passive toward market efficiency. This is not because market forces are disconnected from politics and public authority. Just the opposite. The government defines property rights and provides the capacity to enforce them. The "free market" and the polity are joined at the hip.

Nonetheless, many politicians and citizens alike fail to appreciate the benefits of market efficiency. Indeed, it is almost as if "the market" were *politically invisible*. This lack of awareness stems from three factors. First, while the activities of many market participants are observable, the market is fundamentally a *social process* based on voluntary, self-regarding exchange. How the market performs its magical feats of social coordination in the absence of a central planner is subtle and mysterious to many people. Second, the market is often blamed for problems for which it bears only partial and indirect

Parts of this essay originally appeared, in somewhat different form, in Eric M. Patashnik, "After the Public Interest Prevails: The Political Sustainability of Policy Reform," *Governance,* April 2003, pp. 203–34. Support for this project was provided by the D&D, Earhart, and Smith Richardson Foundations.

responsibility. For example, many people believe that the market creates gross economic inequalities. In truth, the market process of quid pro quo exchange simply *permits* inequalities in talent, ambition, education, inherited wealth, and dumb luck to yield unequal outcomes. Although the market does not automatically remove extant social inequalities, it is not solely responsible for most of them.[1] Third, and most important, the market lacks a reliable constituency. Efficient markets are a kind of public good. They benefit the nation as a whole. Yet precisely because of this feature, market participants, including corporations with strong profit motives, have a strong incentive to focus on their own narrow goals, leaving the promotion of market efficiency to others.

To be sure, the basic legitimacy of market capitalism is better accepted today than it was in the 1950s, owing to the collapse of centralized state planning and the strong performance of the U.S. economy. Market capitalism looks more attractive when it has no credible institutional rival and times are relatively good.

While political support for markets may have improved, market efficiency arguably remains an underrepresented interest in American politics, even in an era when politicians of both parties feel compelled to sing the market's praises. Market efficiency is frequently confused with the wholesale shedding of vital public functions or with the satisfaction of corporate demands for subsidies and inducements. *Pareto-optimality and crony capitalism are not the same thing.* Ironically, business actors are often the worst culprits when it comes to resisting market-enhancing policies. That is why many excellent suggestions for Pareto-improving, market-oriented reforms—such as deregulation, the creation of new marketable goods, and the elimination of grossly inefficient subsidies—remain to be implemented.[2] Meanwhile, other useful ideas from economists for creating, freeing, and facilitating markets may simply be ignored by the politicians.[3]

It has long been a staple of social science theory that concentrated business interests seeking to preserve rents and escape competition will triumph in clashes with the broader public. When the benefits of a market-oriented reform, such as pro-competitive deregulation, are concentrated yet the costs diffused, the actors who benefit from existing policy inefficiencies will have a strong incentive to mobilize. In contrast, the more diffuse group (for example, consumers, taxpayers) that would profit from the freeing of market forces will for the most part be passive and unaware of what they stand to gain.[4]

What is remarkable is that sweeping, market-oriented reforms *have* been adopted in the United States. Leading examples include the deregulation of the trucking and airline industries. These shifts in economic arrangements were fought tooth and nail by the groups that benefited from long-standing governmental barriers to market competition. Yet Congress mustered the political courage to impose costs on narrow clienteles in order to free market forces and serve a larger public interest.

Unfortunately, the passage of bold, market-oriented reforms is no guarantee that reform goals will be achieved. For one thing, their targets are the problems of the day before yesterday, whereas their success depends on what will occur tomorrow. For another, the politicians who enacted the reforms will not be in office forever. They may be replaced by officials with different economic goals and agendas. Markets are also inherently disruptive. They create losers as well as winners. Furthermore, market-oriented reforms can be undone by their unintended consequences or even unraveled deliberately by their creators. A politician who curbs inefficient, incumbent-protecting economic regulations at one moment may decide to restore them later. Despite all these drawbacks, market-oriented reforms *can* become durable. More than a quarter century after Congress repealed the federal regulations that promoted the interests of powerful lobbies such as the American Trucking Association and the Teamsters over those of ordinary consumers, for example, the U.S. trucking industry remains highly competitive.

This chapter examines what happens the day *after* economists' reform ideas become law. Why are some market-oriented reforms quickly reversed or eroded while others are successfully consolidated? The answer: their ultimate fate depends upon *politics*. Durable market-oriented reforms do more than destroy an existing policy subsystem. They generate a self-reinforcing process in which the identities and organizational affiliations of relevant interests change and key economic actors adapt to the new regime. In sum, durable market-oriented reform *reconfigures* political dynamics.

This outcome can be demonstrated for three canonical reforms in the United States: airline deregulation, the Tax Reform Act of 1986, and the "Freedom to Farm" agricultural reform. All three sought to promote private economic competition, but their strategies differed. Airline reform relied on deregulation—the removal of price and entry regulations in a competitive industry. Tax reform closed a myriad of narrow tax breaks that artificially distorted wage, price, and profit signals, with a view to making the allocation of resources more efficient. The Freedom to Farm law provided for deregulation coupled with the scaling back of inefficient supply-side subsidies. All three reforms represented the surprising triumph of policy expertise and economic efficiency over the demands of narrow special interests. However, only airline deregulation can be said to have been durable. Tax reform has largely been eroded, while agricultural reform has had a mixed fate. These complex patterns can be attributed to institutional shifts and policy feedback effects.

Good Economics versus Good Politics

Good economics does not automatically translate into good politics. "Let's eliminate deadweight losses" is rarely a winning campaign slogan. Yet bold market-oriented reforms *have* been adopted on numerous occasions.[5] How did these stunning reform victories take place? Recent political science literature highlights three political conditions that generally must obtain for such economically efficient policies to be adopted.[6] These conditions presume the existence of key reform actors such as public interest groups, coalition leaders, and the media.

First, experts' reform prescriptions must be linked to salient public issues. In the case of airline deregulation, policy entrepreneurs such as Senator Ted Kennedy (D-Mass.) linked pro-competitive deregulation to voters' fears of runaway inflation.[7] Second, lawmakers must be insulated from the political blame associated with imposing losses. This often requires skillful manipulation of the institutional setting in which policy decisions are made.[8] And third, reformers must be willing to make tactical concessions in order to build a winning political coalition. In the tax reform case, Senate Finance Committee chairman Bob Packwood (R-Ore.) doled out "transition rules"— special preferences that exempt certain groups from the new tax law—to hold the reform coalition together.[9]

In other words, the adoption of market-oriented reforms is *not* a political impossibility. Indeed, dramatic changes in the American political system over the past several decades—including the displacement of "iron triangles" by more fluid "issue networks"—have arguably made inefficient policies more vulnerable to challenge than they were previously.[10] Yet these secular trends do not guarantee that any given market reform will stick. It is one thing to get efficiency-enhancing reforms adopted. It is quite another to ensure the durability of the reforms over the long haul.

The Political Durability Problem

After market-oriented reform, governance should become less particularistic and more incentive-based, competitive, and rational. But reform does *not* extract public policy from ultimate dependence on the political process. All market-oriented reforms require, at a bare minimum, rules and legal frameworks to support them. Some reforms, such as the establishment of a new market for tradable permits to control acid rain emissions, require the government to create new property rights and help stimulate trading. In short, the government's role *changes* after reform, but government does not disappear.

Because government is inevitable after reform, politics is inescapable. Market-based reforms frequently offer low per capita benefits to many people. These are ideal conditions for the emergence of "free-rider" problems.[11] The intended beneficiaries of the reforms will generally face more difficult burdens of collective action than will the interests that would profit from the reforms' unraveling. In sum, market-oriented reforms, especially those that involve the withdrawal of inefficient subsidies, may collapse for the same reasons they are unlikely to be enacted in the first place. Rather than a one-shot static affair, market-oriented reform must be seen as a *dynamic process* in which forces seeking to maintain or protect a reform may be opposed by forces seeking to undo it.

In addition to always being "up for grabs," reforms may follow different paths after enactment. They do so because reform is an unfolding historical process unleashed by the willingness and ability of policymakers to promote or frustrate a particular line of policy development.[12] Two factors, in particular, govern that line of development: the extent to which *political structures* propel a reform forward and protect it from inhospitable policy change, and the *policy feedback effects* that the reforms may generate among relevant social actors.

Political Structures

While current policymakers always retain the legal authority to revise existing laws, a policy reform may promote its own survival if its passage coincides with structural changes that nurture it and disable potential opponents. Structural changes may promote reform durability in three (overlapping) ways. First, they may damage or dislodge the bureaucratic or regulatory institutions responsible for the policy outputs being targeted for change. The reworking of state capacities is often essential to prevent "iron-triangle" relationships inimical to the larger public interest from simply reproducing themselves after reforms are adopted. Second, changes in political structures may alter the transaction costs of enacting certain kinds of legislation.[13] In particular, such changes will promote reform durability if they increase the transaction costs to lawmakers of distributing subsidies or other particularistic benefits to narrow well-heeled groups. Third, the chances of durability increase if a reform shifts control over a given policy area to a governmental venue in which pro-reform coalitions enjoy privileged access.

Policy Feedbacks

As noted earlier, a reform's line of development is also affected by policy feedback, which confirms that reform is fundamentally a *dynamic* process.[14] Reforms are consolidated not because they are "frozen in place" but rather because they become self-reinforcing, with subsequent policy changes channeled in a particular direction.[15] A critical yet thorny task is to determine what circumstances affect the prospects for subsequent revisions and what kinds of revisions will be more or less likely under different circumstances.[16] Scholars have begun to make good progress on this problem by elaborating the feedback processes involved.[17]

One such process is the way reform shapes the *identities and organizational affiliations of relevant social actors*.[18] Those affiliations can be either relatively stable, with little change in the identities and constellation of relevant organizations following the reform's enactment, or quite fluid, with an ever-changing constellation of groups pressing agendas and forging coalitions in the wake of the reform's adoption. A second important feedback process is the effect of the reform on social actors' *investments*. After the reforms, relevant social interests can make extensive commitments on the expectation that the reform will stay in place. This suggests a process of increasing returns in which groups develop assets that are specific to the new policy regime.[19] Alternatively, key groups may fail to develop an economic stake in the reform's survival. The reform does not change the interests of relevant groups, and complementary public or private investments are not made. In sum, reforms may generate path dependence, but it is an empirical question whether they actually do so.[20]

The possibilities can be represented by a simple two-by-two matrix in which both the stability of group identities and the level of commitments vary (figure 12-1). Four distinct reform paths can be specified. First, when affected groups fail to make significant investments on the expectation that the reform will not be maintained and new interests do not emerge as important players, there is a high probability of *reversal*. Policymakers will face strong pressures from the dominant group to restore the status quo ante. Second, when the reform fails to prompt major investments in maintaining it but the organizational environment is fluid, the reform is likely to face *erosion*. In this case, policymakers will seek to satisfy the demands of a multiplicity of different groups, hence will adopt new policies that undermine or

Figure 12-1. *Post-Adoption Dynamics of Policy Reform*

Group investments	*Stability of group identities and affiliations*	
Modest Social actors fail to make large-scale investments; organizational adaptations to the reform are minimal	*REVERSAL* Repeal of the reform; return to status quo ante *Example: effort to retrench agricultural subsidies*	*EROSION* Undermining of reform projects through subsequent adoption of new laws with antithetical goals *Example: Tax Reform Act of 1986*
Extensive Groups make large-scale, often highly specific investments based on the expectation that the reform will continue	*ENTRENCHMENT* Consolidation of the reform unaccompanied by major shifts in group affiliations *Example: deregulation of acreage controls and farmers' planting decisions*	*RECONFIGURATION* Reform produces a major shift in political dynamics; patterns of policymaking fundamentally change *Example: airline deregulation*

contradict prior reform objectives and leave the reform project in shambles. This process is akin to what other scholars have termed "layering."[21] Third, reforms will, by contrast, be *entrenched* when the identities and affiliation of relevant groups remain basically stable but key actors make large-scale investments on the basis of the reform's expected maintenance. Fourth, political dynamics will be *reconfigured* when a reform leads to the emergence of new groups and interests whose presence in a given sector induces all organizational actors to invest heavily in ways complementary to the reform's continuation.

Three Case Studies

The limits and possibilities of reform sustainability can be illustrated by the post-adoption dynamics of recent market-oriented reform in three sectors of the U.S. economy: airlines, taxes, and agriculture. The post-reform line of development has differed in all three cases: the subsidy-curbing component of agricultural reform has been reversed, but the deregulatory aspect has been entrenched; tax reform has been seriously eroded; and only airline deregulation has succeeded in thoroughly reconfiguring political dynamics.

Agricultural Reform

Economists have long been critical of U.S. agricultural policy. Since the New Deal, the federal government has tightly regulated how farm owners could use their land in exchange for crop subsidies. Between 1973 and 1996, the U.S. government guaranteed farmers "deficiency payments" equal to the difference between a politically determined price level (called the "target price") and the average nationwide market price actually received by farmers. Congress typically fixed target prices well above the free market level. At the same time that it was subsidizing farmers, the government sought to discourage agricultural *overproduction*. When commodity stocks were deemed too large, the secretary of agriculture, under certain conditions, was required to impose an annual acreage-reduction program. The effect of these production limits was to shift some of the costs of farm programs from taxpayers to consumers. The government also placed a safety net under farmers by providing "loan deficiency payments" whenever market prices in their particular county fell below a certain threshold.

Agricultural subsidies did not come cheap. Deficiency payments alone cost the American taxpayer $30 billion between 1991 and 1995. These payments could not be justified on equity grounds. Though farmers were once relatively poor, the average farm household now has an income slightly above that of the average U.S. household.[22] In addition to imposing costs on taxpayers, traditional federal agricultural programs generated very large economic inefficiencies. The major source of deadweight losses was the opportunity costs of idled cropland under the acreage-reduction program—a pure waste of valuable resources.

In 1996 Congress responded to experts' criticisms of these policies by enacting the most sweeping agricultural reform in modern history—the Federal Agriculture Improvement and Reform (FAIR) Act.[23] Dubbed the Freedom to Farm Act, FAIR sought to move agriculture away from government subsidies and toward the market. The landmark measure contained two main features. First, it sought to retrench federal farm subsidies. The reform replaced deficiency payments with a fixed seven-year schedule of "market transition payments," which started at $5.7 billion in 1996 and then declined to $4.0 billion in 2002. Second, the reform sought to deregulate the agricultural sector. It scrapped annual acreage set-asides. No longer would good land sit idle. In addition, the reform gave farmers "planting flexibility." Instead of having to produce certain crops in specific quantities or on speci- fied acres, farmers were given the freedom to determine what crops they would raise.

An unusual alignment of the political and economic stars permitted FAIR's passage. In an era of large budget deficits, the on-budget costs of farm subsidy programs made them an obvious retrenchment target. When the 1994 elections gave Republicans majority control of Congress for the first time since the 1950s, the new leadership was eager to demonstrate its com- mitment to free market principles and dramatic policy change. In February 1995, Congress passed a budget measure calling for $13.4 billion in farm program cutbacks over seven years (in relation to a budget baseline that assumed rising government payments over this period due to expected declines in crop prices). The House Agriculture Committee attempted to achieve these budget savings through mere programmatic tinkering, where- upon House Speaker Newt Gingrich transferred authority for commodity programs to the House Budget Committee—a policy venue more amenable to structural reform of agriculture programs.[24]

Contrary to expectations, 1996 turned out to be a time of remarkable *prosperity* for agriculture. Farm cash income was up sharply. Most farmers could have expected to receive little federal assistance under the traditional deficiency payments system. As a result, the transition payment schedule contained in the reform proposal—which was not revised to reflect the recent improvement in market conditions—promised a massive near-term windfall to farmers. Strategic leaders were willing to sign off on this deal to weaken clientele opposition and smooth the way for the enactment of a per- manent reform.[25] The question left unanswered when FAIR was signed into law was whether Congress would keep its promise to wean farmers off gov- ernment support if the agriculture economy took another unexpected turn and commodity prices fell. It did not take long to find out the answer.

Beginning in 1998, U.S. commodity prices plummeted. Farmers were partly insulated from the effects of this market decline because they retained access to the federal loan program. Nonetheless, agriculture lobbyists aggres- sively demanded new direct assistance from the federal government to pro- tect farmers' total income. In a stunning reversal of public policy, Congress and President Bill Clinton willingly met these clientele demands, doling out more than $25 billion in "emergency" payments to agriculture since 1998 in addition to the FAIR transition payments (which were themselves boosted). By treating these new farm payments as "emergency spending," Congress was able to circumvent tough budget enforcement rules. Instead of declining steadily after 1996 as called for in the FAIR schedule, federal farm aid actually increased rapidly over the next several years. "The farmer," one journalist presciently wrote after the measure passed, "is a self-reliant, independent creature—on Mars. In America, if the farm economy crashes and crop prices collapse, look for farmers and their friends in Congress to seek old-style, price-sensitive subsidies on top of the new ones."[26]

In May 2002, President George W. Bush signed a ten-year farm bill (passed with strong bipartisan majorities in both chambers) that replaced the emergency aid Congress had been authorizing on an ad hoc basis each year since 1996 with a new countercyclical payment program based on crop prices, ending the pretence that policymakers were serious about weaning farmers off subsidies. During the 2000 presidential campaign, Bush had repeatedly praised FAIR's free market principles. But the Bush administration concluded it could not risk a veto of the farm bill in an election year in which partisan control of Congress was at stake.[27] The 2002 farm bill was estimated to cost $190 billion over the decade, some $83 billion more than the cost of continuing existing agricultural programs. Payments for grain and cotton farms were increased by 66 percent. The 2002 farm measure also restored price supports for wool and mohair and provided new subsidies to certain dairy farmers. "The bill reforms our farm programs in a way that will not require the emergency expenditures of the past few years," said Charles Stenholm (D-Tex.), ranking minority member on the House Agriculture Committee. "The 1996 farm bill was a philosophical document written by the House committee leadership. It was an utter failure. It failed our farmers."

What the reform failed to do at base was change the incentives elected officials faced from the interest group environment. It did not increase the political transaction costs to Congress of providing farm subsides; hence the requisite institutional changes did not take place. Congress and the U.S. Department of Agriculture (USDA) still controlled the agriculture policy agenda. Farmers were not politically stigmatized or organizationally incapacitated.

Although the effort to retrench farm subsidies has in large part been reversed, the deregulation of farmers' market activities has stuck. Historically, farmers were required to plant certain crops in order to keep getting subsidies, but this constrained their ability to move back and forth between different crops in response to changes in market conditions. In addition, as noted earlier, the government imposed a mandatory annual acreage-reduction program that required subsidized farmers to idle portions of their land, thereby reducing commodity supplies and raising consumer prices. While these opportunity costs received little media attention, they seriously distorted the marketplace. With the termination of the USDA's acreage-reduction authority in 1996, the market experienced major improvements in efficiency. According to agricultural economist Bruce L. Gardner, annual deadweight losses due to federal agricultural policy declined from about $5.0 billion in 1987 to about $1.1 billion in 1999.[28]

Two factors have reinforced the durability of this change. First, the USDA was stripped of its legal authority to idle cropland. It is rare that such a venerable Washington agency loses power. This change signaled the credibility of the government's new regulatory posture. Second, and just as important, agricultural deregulation had massive effects on private sector investment decisions. Freed from government planting restrictions, wheat and barley growers in the Northern Plains states converted millions of acres to higher-value soybeans, a crop that was ineligible for assistance under farm programs of earlier years.[29] Other farmers did not change their crops but simply planted more. Such planting decisions, in turn, created huge ripple effects throughout the farm economy. Because farmers were devoting their land to more diverse crops and using their acreage more intensively, agricultural suppliers had to adjust their inventories of fertilizer, pesticides, and herbicides. These investment responses have created new alignments of groups with a stake in the continuation of the reform. Even lobbyists who pressed Congress to fund new countercyclical farm payments have pleaded with Congress not to bring back heavy-handed federal agricultural supply controls. In sum, while the federal government has not yet extracted itself from the farm subsidy business, it has significantly improved the efficiency of a key economic sector.

Tax Reform

Politicians love to deliver goodies through the tax code. The concentrated benefits of special tax provisions offer ample political credit-claiming opportunities while the diffuse costs all but guarantee the absence of focused opposition. But there is no free lunch. The proliferation of tax preferences distorts market signals and forces tax rates to be higher than they otherwise would be. It also creates complexities and gross inequities across taxpayers with similar incomes.

While the economic case for comprehensive tax reform is compelling, every particularistic tax provision has a constituency. The political imbalance between the unorganized public that would benefit from loophole closing and the entrenched interests that stand to lose is so great that tax reform bills are often said to have no chance of passage. But in 1986 Congress managed to beat the odds. The landmark Tax Reform Act of 1986 (TRA) eliminated more than $100 billion of targeted tax breaks in the name of tax simplification, fairness, and economic efficiency.[30] The TRA directly eliminated a number of business tax expenditures (including the investment tax credit, the capital gains exclusion, and consumer interest deductions) and reduced many others (such as accelerated depreciation for machinery and equipment). When the TRA was signed into law, some proclaimed the dawning of a new era of federal taxation. Key parties to the reform deal promised henceforth to keep their hands off the tax code. Ways and Means Committee chairman Dan Rostenkowski (D-Ill.) even said he would hang up a "Gone Fishing" sign on the committee room door.[31]

TRA held up well for a time. Between 1985 and 1990, tax expenditures fell from 8.10 to 5.70 percent of gross domestic product (GDP)—a decline of nearly 30 percent.[32] But tax policy dynamics soon shifted. By the early 1990s, a number of the legislative architects of the 1986 act were no longer in office and new policy issues had risen on the agenda. Although he served as vice president in the administration that signed TRA into law, George (Herbert Walker) Bush was never a committed tax reformer. Once president, Bush used the authority of his office to advocate business and investment tax preferences. For their part, House Democrats also began to abandon their commitment to tax reform, arguing that the nation's rising economic inequality warranted more attention to "tax fairness." Budget legislation enacted in both 1990 and 1993 expanded some existing tax preferences (including the earned income tax credit) and created a few new ones. The Taxpayer Relief Act of 1997 opened the floodgates. The new tax breaks contained in the 1997 bill were expected to cost the Treasury $275 billion over the first decade and "vastly higher amounts" in the out years.[33] By 2003 federal tax expenditures had climbed back to 6.5 percent of GDP—a bit higher than their (pre-reform) level in 1980. Between 1987 and 2005, Congress made more than 15,000 changes to the tax code.[34] Traditional tax policy principles, such as equal treatment of equals, efficiency, and simplification, took it "on the chin."[35]

Rather than reversing the TRA outright, recent policy changes have in the main *eroded* the reform. With the important exception of the tax preference for capital gains, the major business tax expenditures attacked in 1986 have not been restored. The erosion of TRA nonetheless occurred because politicians have created a slew of major new tax expenditures for *social purposes*. As a result of these policy changes, and economic and demographic factors, social tax expenditures increased to 5 percent of GDP in 1999.[36] Some of the social tax breaks enacted in the 1990s were targeted for fairly narrow groups, others for broad swaths of middle-class voters. The Clinton administration, which was committed to an activist social policy agenda, found it could generate far more political support for new tax breaks than for increases in direct expenditures.

The Tax Relief Act of 1997 introduced (among other changes) a tax break for a new individual retirement account (Roth IRA), created new tax credits for children, and provided for the deductibility of student loan payments. The Economic Growth and Tax Relief Reconciliation Act of 2001 continued the trend toward expanding social tax breaks by enlarging the child credit, softening the impact of the "marriage penalty," and creating additional tax breaks for retirement savings and education. The proliferation of social tax breaks greatly increased the tax code's complexity. Given the large number of overlapping tax incentives for higher education and retirement savings, for example, many ordinary taxpayers did not know which ones to take.

During George W. Bush's administration, new corporate tax breaks also began to creep back into the tax code. Bush's first several tax cuts focused on rate reductions, especially for upper-income households. In 2004, however, he signed into law the largest corporate tax cut in twenty years. The measure included $140 million in tax breaks over ten years for interests ranging from tackle-box makers, Native Alaskan whaling captains, and restaurant owners to Hollywood producers, makers of bows and arrows, NASCAR track owners, and importers of Chinese ceiling fans.[37]

In retrospect, the TRA was built on weak political foundations.[38] The bipartisan coalition that enacted it was a fragile one. Some liberal Democrats believed the reformed tax schedule was not progressive enough, while many conservative lawmakers thought it had achieved true reform with its rate reductions. With the tax rate hikes of 1990 and 1993, many conservatives agreed that the implicit exchange of tax breaks for lower rates had collapsed.

The TRA failed to generate the positive feedbacks required to fuel a self-sustaining dynamic in support of base broadening. No major constituency group was induced to make extensive long-term commitments on the basis of the reform's expected survival. Indeed, public reaction to the passage of the act was distinctly *negative*. According to a 1990 Gallup opinion survey, only 12 percent of the respondents thought the measure had made taxes less complicated. Just 9 percent said it had made the distribution of tax burdens more fair.[39]

The most important short-term constraint on the unraveling of tax reform was the federal budget deficit. Under the pay-as-you-go rules of the 1990 Budget Enforcement Act, new tax expenditures had to be financed through other tax changes or cutbacks in entitlement programs.[40] This budget enforcement regime probably did restrain the proliferation of tax breaks for a while. By 1997, however, the federal budget situation had brightened. By taking advantage of this fiscal improvement, and designing certain tax breaks to start small, policymakers were able to enact a number of major tax breaks while technically conforming to budget enforcement rules.

Ultimately, however, the TRA did little to reconfigure the political economy of federal taxation.[41] It did nothing to slow the proliferation of new groups seeking tax breaks from the federal government. Nor did it raise the political transaction costs of opening new loopholes. There was no change in policy venues, and the authority to shape tax legislation remained in the hands of Congress. More radical shifts in jurisdictional authority, such as the delegation of control over the tax code to an independent agency comparable to the Federal Reserve Board, were never actively considered.[42]

Airline Deregulation

A third striking case of Pareto-improving reform, airline deregulation, arose in response to large inefficiencies that had developed during almost forty years of government regulation.[43] Between 1938 and 1977, the U.S. domestic airline industry was heavily regulated by the Civil Aeronautics Board (CAB), which was created to restrict entry into the infant civil aviation industry and protect existing carriers from "destructive competition."[44] The CAB determined which firms were permitted to provide commercial airline service, regulated permitted travel routes, and set ticket prices. Fares were determined according to a simple average-cost formula that gave little weight to passenger volume and other route-specific factors. Though average air service quality was high, so too were ticket prices, rendering air travel too expensive for many American families. Airlines set fares especially high on long-distance and densely traveled routes in an attempt to generate subsidies for high-cost service to small cities.[45]

Despite the consensus among policy experts that CAB regulation imposed large costs on the traveling public, lawmakers were slow to embrace airline deregulation. But Senator Ted Kennedy (D-Mass.) recognized that deregulation could serve to advance the broader cause of "consumerism" and led well-publicized committee hearings on the issue in 1974–75. The political momentum behind deregulation increased during the Carter administration, stimulated by rising public concern about stagflation and government regulation. The CAB pushed the case of reform through bold administrative action. Overwhelmed by the external forces arrayed against it, and internally divided, the airline industry "underwent a political collapse."[46] By January 1985, the CAB itself had been abolished through a sunset provision in the law.

Airline deregulation, like any major policy change, has created both winners and losers. Some airline carriers have failed, prices have increased on some routes and decreased on others, and some areas of the nation have gained services while others have lost them.[47] Most policy experts believe, however, that deregulation in this instance has been a dramatic policy success, vastly improving the welfare of American consumers. To be sure, not every passenger has enjoyed low fares. During the 1990s, for example, business travelers who wished to purchase last-minute tickets and were unwilling to accept Saturday-night stayovers were routinely forced to pay high fares. But most passengers who were able to book flights in advance enjoyed favorable prices. In 1998, 80 percent of passengers (accounting for 85 percent of passenger miles) paid lower fares than they would have paid in the same economic environment under the old CAB regime.[48] Travelers also have had more flights to choose from. Although some have worried that deregulation might compromise safety, the number of fatal accidents on U.S. aircraft has continued to fall. Commercial air service today is what riding on a bus used to be—a relatively affordable, if hardly elegant, means of travel for ordinary American families.

While deregulation's net social benefits are substantial, the reform has not escaped political criticism.[49] Among the primary concerns are the industry's reconcentration, a general decline in service quality, and an increase in fares and discontinuation of flights serving certain small cities.

During the late 1970s and early 1980s, the market competition unleashed by deregulation forced sweeping changes in the airline industry. People Express, Air Florida, and other new carriers emerged to challenge the existing carriers. Since the mid-1980s, however, following the failure of many new carriers and the federal government's approval of many airline merger requests, industry concentration has increased. Even so, studies show that during the 1980s and 1990s airlines were far more competitive at the crucial route level—where airlines compete head to head—than they were before deregulation.[50] Some policymakers nonetheless feared that the major carriers were using "predatory practices" in an effort to stifle competition from new entrants. The Department of Transportation in 1998 drafted guidelines defining "unfair exclusionary" behavior that would be subject to challenge. But Congress took steps to delay implementation of the guidelines after the air carriers and some independent analysts criticized them as a misguided attempt to reregulate the industry.[51]

Policymakers have also been concerned about a general deterioration of service quality. Because of increases in passenger traffic, U.S. airports and planes became increasingly crowded during the 1990s, and flight delays and late arrivals occurred more often. Some frequent flyers, especially affluent business travelers, looked back on the era before deregulation with misty eyes, perhaps remembering the joys of being served by an attendant who was not hurried or of having an empty seat next to them on which to rest their briefcases. Congress in 1999 debated legislation to create a "passengers' bill of rights" to promote higher-quality service. The major air carriers reacted negatively to the proposal. In order to forestall its passage, the airline industry announced its own bill of rights—accompanied by large political contributions to key members of Congress.[52]

Policymakers have also expressed concern about soaring prices and declining air services in a number of small and medium-size communities around the nation. In Charleston, South Carolina, for example, fares have increased 20 percent since 1994. Jet service has plummeted 22 percent since 1978, outraging local residents. Congress has periodically debated legislation to bring more air service to smaller cities.

Despite extensive media coverage of the problems associated with the adjustment to a deregulated market, the federal government did not intervene very much in the industry during the 1980s and 1990s. For the most part, policymakers resisted the urge to reregulate the industry in order to supply concentrated benefits to specific groups or regions. Why has airline deregulation persisted? In his insightful chapter on airline deregulation in this volume, Michael E. Levine points to a reconfiguration of interests, institutions, and ideas. My comparative analysis of market-oriented policy reforms reinforces this conclusion. Indeed, the shifts in governance dynamics in the airline sector since 1978 become even clearer when they are compared with the post-reform trajectories of tax and agricultural policymaking.

The most important reason for the greater relative durability of airline deregulation is that it has changed the identities and affiliations of societal interests—a powerful example of the importance of policy feedback effects. In the aftermath of deregulation, the airline sector has consisted of far more economically heterogeneous interest groups. Carriers still seek to capture new rents through anticompetitive regulations, but now there is almost always an opposing airline to exert counter pressure. Since 1978, no powerful group has pushed for comprehensive reregulation of the industry. Deregulation has also encouraged actors to make long-term investments in new aircraft, scheduling tools, and other assets. "Fortress" hub operations have been constructed at major airports around the nation, and supporting industries and firms have grown up around them. Any effort to undo these changes would be massively disruptive not only for the airlines but also for their host cities. "You can't unscramble the egg," said Senator Jack C. Danforth in 1987. "We've set in motion forces that aren't going to be reversed."[53]

Second, the ideological context of policymaking has changed, becoming more market friendly on the whole. Overt support for reregulation of the airline industry declined noticeably after the GOP gained control over Congress in 1994, although individual Republican lawmakers continue to search for ways to deliver narrow benefits to favored aviation clienteles when no one is looking or behind the veil of symbolic issues such as passenger rights. More important, key legal doctrines shifted in a way that discouraged new governmental interventions. For example, the Supreme Court established a high barrier to proving predatory pricing cases.

Third, deregulation undercut the political infrastructure that maintained the old policy subsystem. This did not occur in the tax reform case, while in agriculture only part of the infrastructure (the Secretary of Agriculture's legal authority) was narrowed. The key institutional shift was the elimination of the CAB, whose central mission was to regulate airline routes and fares. Problems in the airline industry must now be resolved through the Departments of Justice and Transportation, both of which have many other issues on their agendas. Executive policymaking with respect to the airline industry has consequently become an ad hoc exercise. With the CAB gone, as Levine stresses in chapter 10, air transport policymaking is far more susceptible to broad political influences, including pressure from the growing number of economic actors heavily vested in the new system. Although some government officials would still like to reregulate airlines, they lack an institution to protect their political autonomy.

The reform's durability was also served by the relative timing of the legislation. The Airline Deregulation Act was passed in 1978, just two years before Ronald Reagan was elected president "with a firm commitment to reducing regulation."[54] The Reagan administration's influence allowed the deregulated market to take wing under the protection of sympathetic politicians. By the

1990s, the political climate had shifted, and the public concerns that had originally invited deregulation (such as inflation) had faded. By then, however, deregulation had already been in place for more than a decade, and the economic organization of the airline industry had been fundamentally transformed. In contrast, the relative timing of agricultural reform was (in retrospect) much less favorable. Just as farmers were being forced to adapt to the new policy regime, their cash incomes were declining, owing to an exogenous change in export market conditions.

Despite deregulation, the federal government remains a major player in the commercial airline sector. Six years after the terrorist attacks of September 11, 2001, forced a temporary suspension of flights across the nation, Congress passed a $15 billion assistance plan to rescue the airline industry. The speed with which Congress approved this generous aid package was a tribute not only to the economic importance of air travel but also to the political skill (and opportunism) of airline industry lobbyists, who extracted more money from taxpayers than the industry lost during the brief shutdown. While the suspension of flights was obviously damaging to the airline industry, the main cause of its economic troubles in 2001–02 was the national economic slowdown. The airline industry has *always* been a boom-and-bust affair. The most successful airlines accumulate large cash reserves during good times and then spend them down when the economy loses steam. When the economy turns south, struggling airlines may be taken over or go out of business. That kind of painful, but necessary, market adjustment was expected to occur before September 11, with no government rescue anticipated. Indeed, analysts argue that the legacy carriers need to go through one more painful round of cost-cutting and capacity-shedding if they are to survive in today's low-cost environment. One effect of the recent airline bailout may therefore have been to temporarily prop up carriers that otherwise would have been allowed to fail.[55] With the passage of the airline bailout and new airline security regulations, the federal government assumes its largest role in the industry since 1978. Five years after the terrorist attacks, however, policymakers' commitment to allowing market forces to determine ticket prices and control travel routes remains strong.

Lessons

This analysis of the sustainability of market-oriented reform suggests five important lessons. First, and most important, *reform is a political project.* As a result, the long-term durability of Pareto-improving, market-oriented reforms simply cannot be taken for granted. The organized interests that bear the costs of policy reform do not necessarily disappear after the reforms are passed, and they may be joined by new clienteles that would also profit from the reforms' unraveling. Sustaining market-oriented reforms against the threats of erosion and reversal may, if anything, be an even more challenging political task than winning the passage of these reforms in the first place.

Second, *durable reform does not merely change policy outputs; it reconfigures institutions and social behaviors.* Reforms are most likely to last when they upset existing coalitional alignments *and* cause relevant actors to adapt to a changed environment. To the extent that these kinds of investments and long-term commitments are not made, the social basis of any reform is bound to be weak.

Third, *the use of compensation or transition schemes to buy out reform opponents is a doubled-edged strategy.*[56] On the one hand, such payments may provide the political lubrication necessary for the reform's passage. On the other hand, the very act of providing the buyouts provides a reminder of the government's power to deliver particularistic benefits and encourages groups to continue looking to the government for material assistance. Hence reformers need to think carefully about policy design issues when compensation schemes are considered. The challenge is to craft mechanisms that credibly tie the provision of temporary economic assistance to the future maintenance of market forces and private competition.

Fourth, *all market-oriented reforms are not born equal: some inherit policy legacies that are far more conducive to sustaining reform than others.* Consider the contrasting fates of airline deregulation and tax reform. The crucial difference between the two is not only that they entailed different strategies (deregulation versus subsidy reductions) but also that they did not demand the same level of behavioral change from Congress. To maintain a relatively clean tax code after 1986, Congress would have had to permanently break with long-standing patterns of providing tax favors, thus forgoing the exercise of fiscal powers that members had long jealously guarded from the executive. By contrast, even *before* airline deregulation passed in 1978, Congress had already extricated itself from day-to-day control over the airline sector, by delegating decisionmaking authority to an independent bureaucracy (the CAB) that possessed far more policy discretion over industry entry and fares than the Internal Revenue Service has ever been given over major tax decisions. It is one thing for Congress to promote market forces and a level economic playing field in a sector where the most important government actors

286 Eric M. Patashnik

are civil servants. It is quite another to do so in a sector where elected officials themselves like to pull the policy strings.

Fifth, *durable market-oriented reform reframes the policy debate and changes the salience of issues on the agenda but does not eliminate social difficulties.* Witness the continuing painful adjustment to airline deregulation. Air carriers are facing bankruptcy, meal service on even long flights usually consists of a tiny package of pretzels, and flight delays are common. Despite these difficulties and petty annoyances, the air travel system still delivers social value. Tickets are relatively cheap, flying is no longer an elite experience, and the pressure on the commercial airline industry to shed inefficiencies and meet consumer demand is tremendous. As the late Aaron Wildavsky argued, progress in policymaking consists not of eliminating problems but rather of substituting lesser troubles for greater ones.[57] Durable reforms redefine the problems the policymakers attend to and the menu of alternatives they choose from. They delegitimate certain ideas and legitimate others. In sum, *durable reforms reconfigure institutions, interests, and ideas.*

Notes

1. Charles E. Lindblom, *Politics and Markets* (New York: Basic Books, 1977).

2. Roger G. Noll, *The Economics and Politics of the Slowdown in Regulatory Reform* (Washington: AEI-Brookings Joint Center for Regulatory Studies, 1999). As with any governmental intervention, of course, market-oriented reforms will only succeed if they are well designed. The collapse of California's electricity restructuring and competition program offers a striking example of what can go wrong when market incentives are misaligned.

3. Economists who seek to promote the public good are not *above* politics so much as *for* a particular brand of it. Lindblom, *Politics and Markets.*

4. Mancur Olson, *The Logic of Collective Action* (Harvard University Press, 1965); George Stigler, "The Theory of Economic Regulation," *Bell Journal of Economics and Management Science* 2, no. 1 (1971): 3–21. But see Gary Becker, "A Theory of Competition among Pressure Groups for Political Influence," *Quarterly Journal of Economics* 98, no. 3 (1983): 371–401.

5. See, for example, Martha Derthick and Paul J. Quirk, *The Politics of Deregulation* (Brookings, 1985); Marc K. Landy and Martin A. Levin, *The New Politics of Public Policy* (Johns Hopkins University Press, 1995); Gary Mucciaroni, *Reversals of Fortune: Public Policy and Private Interests* (Brookings, 1995).

6. Some claim that general interest reforms occur when there are exogenous shifts in economic factors such as technology or market structure that serve to increase the demand for reform among affected economic interests. See Thomas Hammond and Jack Knott, "The Deregulatory Snowball: Explaining Deregulation in the Financial Industry," *Journal of Politics* 50, no. 1 (1988): 3–30. Economic shocks can doubtless produce conditions conducive to reform, but they are rarely instrumental. See Paul J. Quirk, "In Defense of

the Politics of Ideas," *Journal of Politics* 50, no. 1 (1988): 31–41. There are often long lags between the onset of the economic changes and the passage of reform legislation, suggesting that political factors determined the reform's timing.

7. Derthick and Quirk, *The Politics of Deregulation.*

8. R. Douglas Arnold, *The Logic of Congressional Action* (Yale University Press, 1990).

9. Ibid.

10. Hugh Heclo, "Issue Networks and the Executive Establishment," in *The New American Political System,* edited by Anthony King (Washington: American Enterprise Institute, 1978), pp. 87–124.

11. Olson, *The Logic of Collective Action.*

12. Theda Skocpol, "The Origins of Social Policy in the United States," in *The Dynamics of American Politics,* edited by Lawrence C. Dodd and Calvin Jillson (Boulder, Colo.: Westview Press, 1994).

13. Avinash K. Dixit, *The Making of Economic Policy: A Transaction-Cost Politics Perspective* (Cambridge University Press, 1996).

14. Paul Pierson, *Dismantling the Welfare State: Reagan, Thatcher, and the Politics of Retrenchment* (Cambridge University Press, 1994); Skocpol, "The Origins of Social Policy in the United States"; Jacob S. Hacker, *The Divided Welfare State* (Cambridge University Press, 2002).

15. Paul Pierson, *Politics in Time* (Princeton University Press, 2004).

16. Ibid., esp. chap. 5.

17. See, for example, Jacob S. Hacker, "Privatizing Risk without Privatizing the Welfare State: The Hidden Politics of Welfare State Retrenchment in the United States," *American Political Science Review* 98, no. 2 (May 2004): 243–60.

18. Skocpol, "The Origins of Social Policy in the United States."

19. Pierson, *Politics in Time.*

20. See ibid.; Brian Arthur, *Increasing Returns and Path Dependence* (University of Michigan Press, 1994); Kathleen Thelen, "Historical Institutionalism in Comparative Politics," *American Review of Political Science* 2 (1999): 369–404; Hacker, *The Divided Welfare State.*

21. See, for example, Hacker, "Privatizing Risk without Privatizing the Welfare State."

22. Bruce L. Gardner, "Agriculture Relief Legislation in 1998: The Bell Tolls for Reform," *Regulation* 22, no. 1 (1999): 31–34.

23. Adam D. Sheingate, "Agriculture Retrenchment Revised: Issue Definition and Venue Change in the United States and European Union," *Governance* 13, no. 3 (July 2000): 335–63.

24. Ibid.

25. Jonathan Rauch, "Cash Crops," *National Journal,* May 4, 1996, pp. 978–81.

26. Ibid.

27. Daniel Sanger, "Reversing Course, Bush Signs Bill Raising Farm Subsidies," *New York Times,* May 14, 2002, p. AI16.

28. Bruce L. Gardner, "Agricultural Policy: Pre- and Post-FAIR Act Comparisons," Policy Analysis Report 01-01 (University of Maryland, Center for Agricultural and Natural Resource Policy, September 10, 2000).

29. Dan Morgan, "Farm Revolution Stops at Subsidies," *Washington Post,* October 3, 2004, p. A3.

30. Arnold, *The Logic of Congressional Action;* Daniel Shaviro, "Beyond Public Choice and the Public Interest: A Study of the Legislative Process as Illustrated by Tax Legislation in the 1980s," *University of Pennsylvania Law Review* 139, no. 1 (1990): 1–123; Timothy J. Conlan, David R. Beam, and Margaret T. Wrightson, "Policy Models and Political Change," in *The New Politics of Public Policy,* edited by Marc K. Landy and Martin A. Levin (Johns Hopkins University Press, 1995).

31. Fred S. McChesney, *Money for Nothing: Politicians, Rent Extraction, and Political Extortion* (Harvard University Press, 1997).

32. Eric J. Toder, "The Changing Role of Tax Expenditures: 1980–1999," in *Proceedings of the Ninety-First Annual Conference on Taxation* (Washington: National Tax Association, 1999).

33. Allen Schick, *The Federal Budget: Politics, Policy, Process,* rev. ed. (Brookings, 2000), p. 151.

34. President's Advisory Panel on Tax Reform, November 1, 2005, chaps. 2, 14 (www. taxreformpanel.gov/final-report/).

35. Eugene Steuerle, "Tax Policy from 1990 to 2001," in *American Economic Policy in the 1990s,* edited by Jeffery Frankel and Peter Orszag (Cambridge, Mass.: MIT Press, 2002), p. 140.

36. Toder, "The Changing Role of Tax Expenditures." While the 1986 act did not target any of the major existing social tax expenditures (such as the home mortgage interest deduction) for outright repeal, it decreased their economic value indirectly by lowering marginal tax rates. See Christopher Howard, *The Hidden Welfare State: Tax Expenditures and Social Policy in the United States* (Princeton University Press, 1997).

37. Jill Barshay, "Corporate Tax Bills, Stuffed, Scorned—and Supported," *Congressional Quarterly Weekly Report,* June 26, 2004, p. 1540; Jonathan Weisman, "President Signs Corporate Tax Legislation," *Washington Post,* October 23, 2004, p. A10.

38. See Michael J. Graetz, *The Decline and Fall of the Income Tax?* (New York: W. W. Norton, 1997).

39. Joel Slemrod and Jon Bakija, *Taxing Ourselves* (Cambridge, Mass.: MIT Press, 2000), p. 6.

40. Unlike farm subsidies provided in response to declining prices (see the previous section), tax expenditures could not be cast as "emergency spending" exempt from budget enforcement rules.

41. Conlan and others, "Policy Models and Political Change"; S. D. Pollack, *The Failure of U.S. Tax Policy: Revenue and Politics* (Pennsylvania State University Press, 1996).

42. On this reform idea, see John F. Witte, *The Politics and Development of the Federal Income Tax* (University of Wisconsin Press, 1985); Alan S. Blinder, "Is Government Too Political?" *Foreign Affairs,* November/December 1997, pp. 115–20.

43. Derthick and Quirk, *The Politics of Deregulation.*

44. James Q. Wilson, *Bureaucracy* (New York: Basic Books, 1989), p. 76.

45. Paul L. Joskow and Roger G. Noll, "Economic Regulation during the 1980s," in *Economic Policy in the 1980s,* edited by Martin Feldstein (Cambridge, Mass.: MIT Press, 1994).

46. Derthick and Quirk, *The Politics of Deregulation,* p. 245.

47. By generating a constant ebb and flow in the fortunes of various interests, business groups, and geographical regions, airline deregulation has inhibited the development of a

concentrated, permanently aggrieved political constituency with a stake in deregulation's repeal.

48. Steven A. Morrison, and Clifford Winston, "The Remaining Role for Government Policy in the Deregulated Airline Industry," in *Deregulation of Network Industries: What's Next?* edited by Sam Peltzman and Clifford Winston (Washington: AEI-Brookings Joint Center for Regulatory Studies, 2000).

49. John E. Robson, "Airline Deregulation: Twenty Years of Success and Counting," *Regulation* 21 (Spring 1998): 17–22; Robert Kuttner, *Everything for Sale* (University of Chicago Press, 1999).

50. Morrison and Winston, "The Remaining Role for Government Policy in the Deregulated Airline Industry."

51. Carole A. Shifrin, "Tough Policy Questions: A Deregulation Legacy," *International Air Transport* 149, no. 19 (1998): 50. In 1999 the Justice Department brought a predatory prices case against American Airlines, but a federal district court dismissed it.

52. Some analysts have argued that the deficiencies of the airline system demonstrate that deregulation did not go far enough, because it failed to root out inefficiencies in public airports and the federal air traffic control system. See Morrison and Winston, "The Remaining Role for Government Policy in the Deregulated Airline Industry."

53. Quoted in Paul Starobin, "Deregulation: New Doubts, Damage Control," *Congressional Quarterly Weekly Report,"* July 11, 1987, p. 1489.

54. Marc Allen Eisner, *Regulatory Politics in Transition,* 2nd ed. (Johns Hopkins University Press, 2000), p. 182.

55. Noam Schreiber, "Why Are We Bailing Out the Airlines?" *New Republic,* October 8, 2001; Leslie Wayne and Michael Moss, "Bailout Showed the Weight of a Mighty and Fast-Acting Lobby," *New York Times,* October 10, 2001, p. A1. The government board responsible for distributing funds took seriously its responsibility to taxpayers. Many applications from legacy carriers were rejected.

56. See Daniel Shaviro, *When Rules Change* (University of Chicago Press, 2000).

57. Aaron Wildavsky, *Speaking Truth to Power* (New Brunswick, N.J.: Transaction Books, 1979).

13

The Political Economy of Deregulation in Canada

EDWARD IACOBUCCI, MICHAEL TREBILCOCK, AND RALPH A. WINTER

This is an opportune time to review the current state of deregulation in Canadian markets for electricity, telephony, and airlines, and to compare it with the U.S. experience. Deregulation has been in place long enough and enough problems have arisen in the transition toward competition to draw a number of lessons from those markets. These problems include shortages and consumer intolerance to high prices in electricity markets, a slow (in relation to prior expectations) rate of entry of competitors into local telephone service, and bankruptcies in the airline industry, even in the case of the dominant domestic carrier, Air Canada. The industries are structurally similar—each composed of a network in which some services can be competitively supplied but others exhibit features of a natural monopoly—and thus the policy issues connected with the deregulation of each overlap considerably. These issues are of wide interest because the industries in which they occur have a prominent place both in the Canadian economy and in the deregulation movement there.

Our benchmark for the normative evaluation of government policy across these industries is the maximization of economic efficiency, as measured by the sum of benefits to consumers and to shareholders of firms in each industry. This objective requires elaboration in two respects. First, it might seem possible to increase consumer benefits and even total benefits by treating capital invested by incumbent firms under traditional regulation as a sunk cost and not requiring current prices to cover a fair return to that capital. We assume, however, that the government should not renege on the implicit regulatory compact it has with firms that invested capital under the original rate-of-return regulation. For the sake of long-run efficiency, the state's commitments must be credible. Second, a more subtle aspect of designing efficient government regulation is that one must, paradoxically, incorporate the inability of government to commit to the goal of efficiency in future regulatory policy. As a result, political constraints must be taken into account in the analysis.

In the current period of deregulation, the role of political constraints in developing industrial policy varies markedly across industries. In the deregulation of telephony, for example, political resistance has been weak, given the lower prices for long-distance calls and technologically induced lower prices for the average bundle of telephony services. Most consumers have unambiguously been better off after deregulation than they were before. In contrast, resistance in the electricity sector has been strong, among citizens and politicians alike. When a move to greater efficiency triggered a sharp rise in electricity prices in Ontario, political constraints led to major distortions in electricity prices. This resistance is puzzling from the perspective of traditional political economy thinking and a factor that must be dealt with in a successful transition to greater reliance on market forces.

The most important lesson for future regulatory policy is that political constraints must be factored into policy design. In electricity, for example, a solid commitment by the government never to intervene in constraining future price increases—were such a commitment possible—might attract enough generation capacity that political pressure for limiting price increases would not arise in the future. But the design of regulation today cannot pretend that a policy will be immune to future political pressure to protect particular groups from the shock of excessive prices. It must take politics seriously by incorporating the constraint of no future government commitment to an efficiency-maximizing policy designed today (often referred to as the problem of "time inconsistency"). A related and well-established problem is that even efficiency-enhancing policies may be politically infeasible if the policies also involve substantial transfers of wealth away from organized interest groups. Attempts at deregulation must anticipate political obstacles to reform even at the cost of some reduction in total efficiency. A less-than-ideal reform that is robust enough to resist future political pressures is better than an ideal reform that will not survive in the political arena.

Electricity

Only two Canadian jurisdictions—Ontario and Alberta—have attempted significant restructuring of the electricity sectors by moving from the traditional, vertically integrated, regulated monopoly paradigm to a competitive paradigm, at least in electricity generation. The Ontario case merits particularly close attention because it was unsuccessful. The story of reform in Ontario is one of establishing a market mechanism for electricity prices but ultimately failing to commit to the restructuring of the market.

Reform in Ontario was motivated in part by the faith in markets of a Conservative government elected in 1995 and in part by enormous growth in the debt of the government-owned electricity company at a time when the provincial budget deficit had risen to historically unprecedented levels. The incoming government vowed to eliminate this deficit. The debt was the result of the province's failed investment in nuclear energy, which incurred major cost overruns and left as many as eight of the province's twenty nuclear power plants out of service at the same time.[1] By the mid-1990s, electricity debt had reached one-third of the entire provincial government's debt. In tackling the issue, politicians seriously erred in promising lower electricity prices with electricity reform, when economic efficiency and fiscal demands clearly pointed to the need for higher prices. Meanwhile, the investment in generation failed to materialize, constraints on imports tightened, and overall demand increased, leaving consumers vulnerable to rapid price increases when the weather turned exceptionally hot in the summer of 2002, shortly after market opening. Responding to public outrage over high electricity prices, the government (retroactively) set a price ceiling between 4 and 5 cents per kilowatt-hour. This was at times less than half of the marginal cost of electricity (not to mention the contributions to the enormous costs of capital that regulated prices should provide). The upshot was shortages of electricity as well as a deepening of the government debt that had inspired reform in the first place. We believe this outcome was predictable and could have been avoided had reform been designed with the constraints imposed by politics in mind.

Before reform, electricity generation and transmission were in the hands of a government-owned monopoly, Ontario Hydro, while distribution was handled by municipality-owned companies. In response to Ontario Hydro's mounting debt problems, the government embarked upon a restructuring program beginning in the mid-1990s. However, debt continued to accumulate: by 1999 Ontario Hydro's provincially guaranteed debt was approximately

Can$38 billion against assets of only Can$17 billion, leaving a "stranded" debt of Can$21 billion.[2] Meanwhile, the price of electricity in Ontario was frozen for several years after a 30 percent climb in the early part of the decade.[3]

The framework for the reformed electricity market was set out in the Electricity Act of 1998.[4] The act established plans for a wholesale electricity market in Ontario, eventually opened in May 2002, and split Ontario Hydro into two companies, separating the transmission and generation components. These new firms, Hydro One and Ontario Power Generation (OPG), began their operations in 1999, still as fully state-owned entities. Hydro One then bought up a number of local distribution companies. While it is not clear what objectives a state-owned monopoly is likely to pursue, to preclude the possibility of OPG using its dominant position to exercise market power, OPG entered into a market power mitigation agreement (MPMA) with the government.[5] Under the agreement, the OPG became subject to a wholesale price cap and was also required to divest enough of its price-setting generating units to reach a level of 35 percent within three and a half years of market opening and to reduce its market share of total capacity to no more than 35 percent within ten years of market opening. In addition, Hydro One undertook to make best efforts to increase inter-tie capacity with neighboring jurisdictions by 50 percent within three years of market opening.[6]

Two government agencies oversee the province's electricity market: the Ontario Energy Board (OEB) and the Independent Electricity System Operator (IESO). The IESO operates the wholesale spot market and performs the dispatch function; its independent Market Surveillance Panel was assigned the task of monitoring market power abuses (now transferred to the OEB). Initially, OEB's primary function was to regulate the monopoly segments of the electricity market (that is, transmission and distribution rates), although it now also regulates retail electricity prices. Market rules developed by the Market Design Committee—a multistakeholder group charged with the task of "regulatory negotiation"(reg. neg.) and primarily administered by the IESO—run to hundreds of pages, a vastly more complex regulatory environment than existed before deregulation.

When the wholesale market for electricity opened in 2002, the wholesale price was initially about 3¢ per kilowatt-hour but doubled (on average) over the first year. In November 2002, in response to mounting public outrage at the high summer electricity prices, the Conservative government announced its intentions to reimburse consumers for the high prices of the summer and freeze retail prices until 2006; it also directed local utilities not to cut off service to customers who could not afford to pay their electricity bill. The Electricity Pricing, Conservation and Supply Act of December 9, 2002, lowered and froze the retail price of electricity at 4.3¢ per kilowatt-hour for low-volume and other designated consumers (that is, municipalities, universities and colleges, public and private schools, hospitals and registered charities), as well as for those who had signed fixed-price contracts with retailers.[7] The freeze covered approximately half of the province's total electricity consumption. Wholesale prices remained determined by market forces, with taxpayers footing the bill for the shortfall in retail revenues in relation to costs. Demand, of course, is governed by retail prices. With the price freeze, Ontario's experiment with competitive electricity markets was abruptly terminated after barely seven months.

Throughout the 1990s and beyond, domestic capacity declined and reliance on imports increased, creating what seemed profitable opportunities for private sector investment in generation. Little such investment occurred, however. Only two small new private generation projects became operational during the first year of the open market. The lack of private investment was due in large part to the two-year delay in market opening and uncertainty over the final rules governing the market. The delay was particularly costly because capital markets had lost confidence in the electricity sector following the California crisis of 2000–01 and the collapse of Enron in 2001–02. By the time the Ontario market opened in May 2002, investors had already come to view the North American electricity market as too risky and were deterred from investing in new generation capacity. Conditions within Ontario before the California crisis also kept private investment away. For one thing, investment was deterred by continued OPG ownership and control of most generation assets and the uncertain future status of nuclear units. For another, there were environmental constraints on the sale of OPG's coal-fired generation plants

Under policies established by a centrist Liberal government elected in 2004, Ontario consumers now pay somewhat higher government-administered electricity prices and greater prices for higher volumes. But the increases have been modest, all in the range of 4–6¢ per kilowatt-hour. The OEB has in addition released details for a "smart" meter, time-of-use price schedule with a commitment to install time-of-use meters in every home by 2010, and an interim target of 800,000 meters installed by 2007.[8]

The government has also established a new body called the Ontario Power Authority, whose function will be to contract with the private sector to build new generation capacity and reduce reliance on the (now distorted) spot market as a signal for new investment. The need for new capacity has become even more urgent now that the government has decided for environmental reasons to retire all of the province's coal-fired generation plants (approximately 25 percent of total provincial generation capacity) over the next several years.

As in other industries that have been deregulated, electricity liberalization has the potential to move prices closer to marginal cost. But in the Ontario case, the nature of the industry and regulatory status quo called for *higher* prices. With public ownership and regulation of the electricity industry, prices did not reflect cost (as already mentioned, prices were frozen for almost a decade before deregulation). Just as prices above marginal cost create social losses, since some consumers willing to pay the cost of a product are priced out of the market, prices below marginal cost do so as well, since resources are devoted to supplying consumers who do not value the product as much as it costs to produce that product. Liberalizing the market and allowing retail prices to rise not only creates efficient incentives to invest in generation and transmission capacity but also increases efficiency by eliminating value-reducing transactions at prices below cost. However, Ontario experienced strong political resistance to higher electricity prices, and the government responded by freezing prices at low rates. As a consequence, the Ontario government has been underwriting massive losses, there has been no significant investment in generation or transmission, and incentives for consumers to conserve on electricity consumption have been severely attenuated, exacerbating existing imbalances in supply and demand.

The reasons for such apparently intense political resistance to higher electricity prices are not immediately obvious. To the extent that Ontario consumers, as consumers, gain through lower electricity prices, on average they lose even more (since subsidized prices lead to an inefficient use of provincial resources) as taxpayers because higher taxes are necessary to deal with the debt generated by buying high and selling low.

Why would citizens prefer a system in which they lose on net? Three theories may shed some light on this question. First, to the extent that some individuals are relatively intensive electricity consumers yet relatively insignificant taxpayers, they could gain by an electricity subsidy paid out of general tax revenues. This does not seem to be a plausible explanation of the apparently widespread political resistance to higher electricity prices in Ontario, however. Second, consumers today might rationally anticipate that the subsidy would be paid out of tax revenues only in the future and thus they may not bear the full cost of the subsidy since they may not be taxpayers then.

This is also not a plausible explanation. The strong political support in recent years in Ontario and elsewhere in Canada for balanced budgets indicates that voters do not want high public debt. A third reason, bounded consumer rationality, seems the most plausible explanation of the political salience of an inefficient electricity regulatory system. While calculating the impact of an electricity bill on one's budget is straightforward, assessing the impact of a Can$700 million annual government expenditure from selling electricity below cost on any given consumer is complicated. The higher price of electricity has a salience and obviousness that potentially higher future taxes do not, and consumers will be influenced accordingly. Indeed, Ontario electricity consumers are accustomed to very low and stable prices because of the decade-long freeze that preceded attempts at deregulating. While they have grudgingly accepted volatile and increasing prices in similarly important industries such as petroleum and natural gas, they are used to consistent, low prices in electricity and resist any change to this situation.

The most obvious way to minimize political resistance to deregulation is to ensure that its benefits are well publicized. Admittedly, the benefits of pushing prices closer to marginal cost, particularly if this requires a sharp increase, are unlikely to be readily understood by consumers, who as individuals have little to gain from such an understanding. This problem was exacerbated in Ontario by the government's irresponsible claims that prices would fall following deregulation without mention of the conservation and budgetary benefits from higher prices.

Another strategy is to adopt policies that are irreversible, or at least very costly to reverse. Rather than attempt ex ante to persuade everybody of the benefits of deregulation, the government could commit to a course of action that in the longer term would be more likely to inform citizens of the benefits firsthand. In fact, some of the benefits of deregulation arise only if the government is firmly committed to adhering to its agenda (time consistency). For example, to create incentives for investment in electricity generation, private actors need to be assured that the government will not simply abandon floating electricity prices. Without such a commitment, generation capacity will not be built, prices will likely jump higher, and the government will be forced to do an about-face on deregulation.

A government can strengthen its commitment to deregulation in several ways. An important step is to privatize whatever government corporations are involved in the industry (as was done in the United Kingdom and the state of Victoria in Australia, two of the most successful electricity restructuring experiences). Provided that it does not simply turn a public monopoly into a private monopoly but establishes a competitive market structure, privatization creates a political constituency in favor of deregulation: the firms (and their workers) that have invested in competing in the liberalized market. Once this constituency is active, the government will face countervailing pressure not to renege on its deregulatory plans. In contrast, the performance of the old Ontario Hydro and its two commercial successor companies, culminating in the firing or resignations of their respective boards of directors and senior officers, invites little confidence in continuing public ownership and operation of this sector. Oddly, the Conservative government in Ontario embarked on a politically controversial and unsuccessful attempt to privatize Hydro One (the transmission grid)—a natural monopoly whether publicly or privately owned—yet failed to seriously pursue an aggressive strategy of privatization and divestiture of generation assets that was crucial to the political economy of sustainable deregulation.

Another way of committing to deregulation may be, paradoxically, to involve the state directly in the market, at least at its inception. If the government were to offer up-front incentives to build electric generation capacity, for example, it would protect private investors from future regulatory reversals in two ways: it would lower the private investment required to enter the market and thus lower the private cost of possible future changes in policy; and by contributing to the building of generation, the policy would keep prices lower and avoid future pressure to revisit deregulation. Similarly, generating firms could be paid directly or indirectly to maintain excess capacity in generation, which would reduce the chances of price spikes or blackouts and thus political opposition to deregulation; such a strategy has been used in the United Kingdom, Pennsylvania-New Jersey- Maryland (PJM), and elsewhere. Such state intervention is not part of the textbook economic ideal of market allocation. The market and the prospect of high prices should do the job of providing incentives to invest in generation. But in the face of anticipated political pressure because of higher prices, these kinds of commitments may operate as sensible second-best strategies. State involvement early on can, ironically, guard against inefficient, politically driven state involvement later.

Another technique for managing political opposition to deregulation is explicitly to compensate losers. In Alberta, for example, following the initiation of restructuring in 1995, average wholesale prices tripled in the years 1999 to 2000. Retail consumers were then paid rebates of Can$40 a month in 2001, funded from the proceeds of the auction of Power Purchase Agreements. It is important that such refunds be insensitive to quantities purchased; otherwise the expectation of refunds acts as a distortionary price decrease. The government adhered to its commitment to restructuring and, partly as a result, approximately 2500 megawatts of new generator capacity was added to the Alberta system between 1998 and 2002 and another 5200 megawatts of new generation is forecast for 2003–06.[9] In response, the average wholesale spot price in 2002 fell back almost to 1999 levels.

Efficient consumption might also be achieved by paying consumers for the amount they reduce their consumption in relation to some benchmark. Residential electricity rates in California are structured along these lines: consumers pay a lower rate for electricity up to a percentage of a benchmark for their residence, a higher marginal rate for a middle band of consumption, and a much higher marginal rate for electricity consumption beyond 130 percent of the benchmark amount. A similar alternative would be to continue to subsidize electricity consumption, but only up to some amount that covers basic residential electricity needs, with significantly higher prices for volumes consumed above this threshold, which would at least preserve conservation incentives at the margin (as the present Ontario government has partly done). Again, these alternatives are not as efficient as floating prices, since the regulator must assess the appropriate subsidies and benchmarks. But they avoid the absurd consumption incentives facing consumers paying prices well below cost for all their power, while managing political opposition by potentially lowering some electricity bills in relation to the status quo.

The performance of the electricity sector in Ontario since restructuring has been very disappointing. Elsewhere, results have varied, from success (at PJM in the United States, as well as in England and Wales and in Australia's state of Victoria) to similar disappointments, most notably in California. As pointed out in chapters 6 and 7 of this volume, the problems in California's restructuring had some sui generis characteristics: the market was poorly designed, with separate agencies administering the dispatch function and spot market; all transactions were forced through the spot market, with no chance of entering into forward physical or financial bilateral contracts; there were serious abuses of market power; a retail price cap forced utilities to absorb the difference between unregulated wholesale prices and regulated retail prices; and environmental constraints on investments in new generation and transmission capacity precluded effective supply-side responses to higher prices.

Like California, Ontario has weakly integrated regional markets, which the Federal Energy Regulatory Commission in the United States has had some success in ameliorating but the highly decentralized Canadian federal system has barely addressed.[10] In contrast to California, Ontario appears to have had nothing fundamentally defective in its market design, and the escalation in wholesale prices following market opening seems to have had no connection to abuse of market power. A more likely reason for Ontario's higher prices is that administered prices were set at inefficiently low levels for almost a decade before the restructuring. In addition, policy instability discouraged new private sector investment in the sector. This lack of investment has created a vicious circle dictating more rather than less government intervention to mitigate rising prices, further attenuating private sector interest in the sector.

The Ontario experience teaches that credible and politically sustainable regulatory commitments to effective restructuring are easily the most important determinant of success or failure, even if such commitments may require economically second-best policies to mitigate political economy impediments to effective restructuring. As Eric Patashnik insightfully argues in chapter 12, the political durability of deregulation initiatives depends on policies that reconfigure interests after deregulation so as to create new constituencies that will make significant investments in the new competitive regime. This political reality was never addressed by the Ontario government in initiating deregulation of the electricity sector.

Telecommunications

The forces that have shaped deregulation in Canadian telecommunications have been a blend of the "new politics of public policy," driven by the power and appeal of particular ideas or philosophies of government as to the social good, and the "old politics" of entrenched interests, lobbying, and policy enacted to transfer wealth to interest groups most successful in building political power.[11] To assess the impact of this blend, one needs to identify where and to what extent the social good or *efficiency* objective has been met, whether this objective is compromised by the power of interest groups, and why the boundary between efficient dimensions and distorted dimensions of deregulation falls where it does. As explained in the introduction to this chapter, "efficiency" refers here to the maximization of the sum of consumer benefits and shareholder profits subject to the regulatory compact allowing shareholders a fair rate of return on invested capital. This objective is met in unregulated competitive markets. While consumer benefits are maximized in competitive markets, however, firms earn only a fair rate of return, nothing more. Efficient regulation mimics this outcome of competitive markets.

We find that the performance of Canadian telephony regulation has changed markedly in recent years. Historically, Canadian telephony regulation has had a favorable record compared with that of the United States and other countries of the Organization for Economic Cooperation and Development (OECD). Even as recently as 2001–03, telephony prices were relatively low in Canada, despite the high costs imposed by geography (in this rapidly evolving market, these data can be described as historical evidence). As documented in detail in the March 2006 report of the Telecommunications Policy Review Panel, since then, however, the system has been failing to keep up with either the pace of deregulation required for maximum social benefits or the pace established in other countries. Ideas on how to improve telecom regulation can be drawn from a comparative analysis of regulation's performance, structure, and political economy in Canada and the United States. Its lessons will enable Canadian consumers to benefit fully from the enormous improvements in technology for the delivery of telephony services and strengthen the political economy of deregulation.

Until recently, Canadian telecom markets performed well by international standards. According to a study by SeaBoard Consulting Group based on purchasing power exchange rate, Canadian rates for a basic service bundle in the first quarter of 2003 were *less than two-thirds* of U.S. rates for a representative sample of cities.[12] Canadian telephony prices in 2001 (again based on purchasing power exchange rates) were reportedly the tenth lowest among thirty-two OECD countries in the residential sector and sixth lowest in the business sector.[13] In terms of the overall price level, then, Canadian telecom regulation performed quite well by international standards.

Of course, one must remember that international and U.S. standards are weak. As Andrew Rich notes in chapter 11, U.S. telecom regulatory reform has met only some of its objectives, with wire-line telecom prices in most markets falling but overall consumer spending on telecom services generally increasing. Telecom regulatory reform, in his view, has led to more rather than fewer rules, and the resulting law has hampered rather than helped efforts to build a competitive environment.

These features are characteristic of Canadian telephony markets as well: wire-line telecom prices have not fallen substantially for all services, total consumer spending on telecom services has increased, and the reform of telecom regulation has without question led to more rather than fewer rules. Our perspective on these specific facts is somewhat different, however. First, because the reform of telecom regulation eliminated or substantially reduced cross-subsidies (through "rate rebalancing"), previously subsidized prices (for local service, specifically) would be expected to rise. This is efficient. Second, an increase in total expenditure is a consequence of overall price decreases in a market where demand is elastic. Third, as discussed shortly, a move toward liberalization of markets requires a transitional period in which there are indeed more rules and more decisionmaking by the regulator.

Rich argues convincingly that U.S. telecom regulatory reform was in some ways designed to stifle competition. Regional Bell operating companies (RBOCs), for example, were not allowed to enter the long-distance market, and when they did gain entry, access was severely limited by a set of stringent requirements. The fault lay largely with the 1996 Telecommunications Act, which failed to set out a workable and firm commitment to the transition to competition in the United States owing to enormous lobbying efforts by the industries affected ("the World Series of lobbying," according to one news report). As a consequence, the parameters for deregulation were weakened. The Telecom Act, Rich points out, was a very complicated compromise, the details and implementation of which were left up to the Federal Communications Commission (FCC)—but the FCC's decisions were regularly challenged in the courts by one party or another. As Rich explains, the courts showed little deference to the regulators, with the result that deregulation became a slow, cumbersome, unpredictable, and inefficient process.

Perhaps because of the different political dynamics at play in parliamentary and congressional systems, the transition parameters set by Canada's Telecommunications Act of 1993 were much less detailed than those adopted in the United States. Their details and implementation were assigned to the Canadian Radio and Telecommunications Commission (CRTC). Where U.S. regulatory decisions are constantly challenged in the courts, however, CRTC decisions seldom face such challenges because of the deference paid to the commission in the courts, and because of the limited conditions for appealing its decisions to the federal cabinet. These challenges, when launched, are rarely successful. Hence the details of implementation of the law's provisions are essentially regulatory fiat in Canada, in contrast to the treatment in the United States. This makes for a more streamlined, less politicized system, although Canadian regulation has become very cumbersome in many respects, with long delays for the approval of rates (prior approval of rates is required) and intensive micro-managing of decisions by the regulator (for example, some decisions concern which prices should be regulated down to the fifth decimal place and which to the fourth decimal place).

In telecom deregulation, traditional rate-of-return rules were replaced in 1998 by price-cap rules—thereby allowing incumbent telecoms greater freedom in their decisions on service prices and quantities.[14] However, this switch greatly expanded the complexity and number of regulatory rules and decisions. Under rate-of-return regulation, prices of individual services are set by the regulator, outside the discretion of the regulated firm, at levels that in principle cover total costs, including a fair rate of return on invested capital. Price levels are reset after each rate hearing, which may be as often as every year. With prices matched to changing costs, the regulated firm has little incentive to engage in cost-saving innovation. In addition, this kind of regulation is completely unsuited to a market in which technology is rapidly evolving and more competitors are capable of supplying an increasing percentage of services. Incumbent local exchange carriers (ILECs), now in the second term of price-cap regulation, face four main sets of constraints on prices: ceilings on the index of prices within each of a number of service baskets (currently eight), ceilings on prices of certain individual services, unbundling restrictions and prices at which access to essential and near-essential assets must be offered to competitors, and price floors or imputation tests. The central constraint of price-cap regulation, the ceiling on an index of prices for a basket of services, was initially set at a level that covered costs, with a fair rate of return on invested capital. The allowed price index could then be increased in any year at the realized rate of inflation, I, minus the rate of real cost decrease (as predicted at the outset of the price-cap period), X. Hence the price cap is commonly described as "I minus X" regulation.

A second, more significant factor underlying the apparently strong overall price performance of Canadian telecom regulation is the link between initial price-cap levels and rate-of-return regulation. The political economy during rate-of-return regulation, which was quite different from that in the United States, also played an important role. Allowed rates of return in Canada for public utilities were in general substantially less than those in the United States. A key decision by Canada's National Energy Board in 1994, with an impact on rate-setting across all utilities, set the allowed rate of return on equity for low-risk utilities at three percentage points above long-term government interest rates—a risk premium below the risk premiums implicit in U.S. utility rate setting. In the framework of Sam Peltzman's political economy theory of regulation, where the regulator's objective function is a weighted average of firm profits and consumer welfare, Canadian regulators were somewhat more consumer oriented.[15] With the initial allowed price-cap parameters grounded in rate-of-return regulation, Canadian telephony prices were lower.

Although the overall cost of service is a prime consideration in assessing efficiency, *relative* prices need to be examined as well. Efficient relative prices reflect differences in the marginal costs of providing services and are free of cross-subsidies.[16] Before deregulation, telecom prices incorporated three cross-subsidies: local service was subsidized by excessive long-distance prices; residential rates were subsidized by business rates, and high-cost, rural service zones were subsidized in each province by low-cost rates through the established system of "postage stamp pricing." That is, consumers had universal access to telephone service at a common price irrespective of cost differences. An essential step in the transition toward competition has been to eliminate or vastly reduce two of these cross-subsidies, from long-distance and business rates. The tremendous decline in long-distance rates resulting from the *rebalancing* of rates and improvement in the costs of service delivery is the single most obvious change in telephony since the start of deregulation. But the subsidization of rural rates through postage stamp pricing continues.

The political economy questions are clear. Why is this subsidization so entrenched when it has been feasible to remove other roadblocks to competitive pricing? After all, eliminating subsidies to local exchange service has imposed huge costs on local exchange consumers, and price rationalization elsewhere (in electricity markets) has been strongly resisted in the deregulation forum. The critical issue here is which force will win in the battle of efficiency—the maximization of total social benefits versus private interest group politics.

Subsidies to high-cost rural service survived the move to efficiency for the same reason that enormous agricultural subsidies persist in virtually every developed economy. The benefits of these subsidies are concentrated among a small population, rural residents, whereas their costs are spread out across a large population. In telephony markets, consumers within the highest cost-rate bands are a small proportion of total consumers. In addition, rural voters are overrepresented. In the U.S. political system, this is because senators are allocated by state rather than by population, and in Canada it is because federal and provincial ridings are geographically defined. Politicians would lose rural votes if the subsidies were removed but would not gain significant urban votes since the subsidy would not be a significant political issue for any individual urban dweller. Subsidies to rural residents of many different kinds survive (including postage stamp pricing for other public utility services and for, well, postage stamps).

Why did the subsidy to local service rates *not* survive? The answer to this question is more subtle. When the CRTC held hearings on the "affordability" of higher local service rates, the negative impact of the removal of the subsidies on poorer consumers in particular was a significant concern. In traditional, full-rationality-based political economies in which consumers are assumed to be *fully aware* of the impact of any economic policy, the general trend toward lower rates driven by the strong and steady improvement in technology would be irrelevant: the subsidy's costs and benefits to individual citizens would not be substantially affected by the general downward trend in costs, and the outcome of lobbying efforts and simply political influence would remain the same. The successful elimination of the inefficient cross-subsidy is likely due to a combination of two factors that are not incorporated in the traditional political economy of government policy. First, as psychologists Daniel Kahneman and Amos Tversky have convincingly demonstrated, individuals tend to assess welfare in relation to the status quo and are highly averse to losses by this measure.[17] In the conventional theory of rational decisionmaking, the status quo does not play a special role in the evaluation of losses and gains. In the deregulation context, the loss from not gaining fully from the general decrease in telephony pricing is less important to individuals than a loss they might incur in relation to the level of welfare (or pricing) before the change in telecom regulation. A second and related factor is that individuals are simply less likely to keep track of, or be aware of, "what could have been" rather than losses that are actually incurred. If local exchange prices do not rise greatly, the fact that these prices would have fallen even more had the subsidy been maintained is less relevant politically because consumers and voters are less likely even to be aware of the fact.

As the foregoing discussion demonstrates, the relatively strong historical performance of Canadian telecom regulation and its consumer benefits can be traced to price-ceiling constraints, including price caps, and the more consumer-oriented regulation in Canada during the period of rate-of-return regulation for public utilities. A second set of price constraints in Canada's telecom market performed less well. These constraints consist of price *floors,* also called imputation tests because price levels are justified through the imputation of costs, including shares of joint costs. The most contentious of price floor constraints in Canada are imposed on ILEC offerings in the emerging voice over Internet protocol (VoIP) service market.

VoIP service is the closest substitute to local exchange service that has emerged in the telecom market, but it does not rely on ILEC assets (not even a phone line). The service operates over the Internet and from the customer's perspective is virtually identical to land-line service. In the United States and almost all other countries, the rates on VoIP service by any supplier are unregulated. In Canada, the CRTC imposed a price floor on any VoIP offering by an ILEC, but competitors have been free to set any price that they wish.

Regulated price floors are rarely in the interest of consumers, who prefer low prices to high prices. Why has the CRTC imposed this restraint? The purpose was to ensure that "the incumbent local exchange carriers—those with market power—cannot price their local VoIP services below cost to stifle competition."[18] The CRTC's justification, in other words, is that a more competitive (unconcentrated) market structure can be obtained when the lowest-cost suppliers are constrained against pricing too low.

This argument confuses a competitive market structure as an end in itself with a competitive structure as a *means* to achieving lower prices. It is low prices that matter to consumers. The commission believes that ILECs have the incentive to price below cost in order to protect their dominance in the market, and that this dominance works against the social interest. As a matter of economics, there is only one theory under which dominant firms have an inefficient and anticompetitive incentive to price below cost: predatory pricing. If for some reason entry into a market is temporary, or potential entrants are so intimidated by a low incumbent price response to entry that they would never again attempt entry, then an incumbent firm can rationally price below cost as a means of investment in the opportunity to raise prices well above competitive levels once potential entry has disappeared. The necessary conditions for this incentive are very rarely met as a matter of economics. There is not even a remote chance that the conditions are met in the market for VoIP service. This market already has dozens of suppliers in Canada, the costs of entry are very low, and any of the more than 1,100 suppliers worldwide could enter if incumbents attempted to raise prices above competitive levels in the future. In short, low VoIP prices by incumbents can only be viewed as a competitive response by ILECs—not an anticompetitive practice. Low prices are in consumers' interests. Fortunately, the CRTC's decision to regulate incumbents' VoIP prices has recently been reversed by Cabinet Order.

This is not the only decision on which the CRTC has erred by confusing low prices with suppression of competition. In regulating the ability of incumbent telcoms to offer promotions, for example, the commission prohibits promotions longer than six months on the basis that "promotions of too long a duration become perceived by consumers as being standard offers, thus compelling competitors in the market to react by changing their own standard offers."[19] This, of course, begs the question of why the compulsion to respond with lower prices should be regarded as *anti*competitive. Protecting competitors is not equivalent to protecting competition.

The CRTC's regulatory restrictions on pricing have gone beyond addressing concerns that prices are too high or (the more recent focus) too low to visiting the issue of price discrimination. The CRTC has frequently acted to limit variable pricing in telecom, in part in keeping with its statutory mandate to ensure that there is no unjust discrimination in relation to the provision of this service. But price discrimination is ubiquitous in the industrialized world: for example, airlines charge different fares for leisure and business travelers, and cinemas charge different ticket prices for old or young patrons. Where price discrimination increases the output of an industry, as it often does, this tends to be welfare enhancing and permits firms to recover fixed costs by charging higher prices to less elastic demanders than prices charged to more elastic demanders (which may be related much more closely to the marginal costs of serving the latter and which ensures that they will be served).[20]

Despite the conventional view in competition policy thinking and law that price discrimination is rarely problematic, which would apply equally well to telecom, the CRTC has acted vigorously to eliminate variable prices as a form of unjust price discrimination. From the perspective of competition policy or total economic welfare, discounts to subsets of customers through win-backs or promotions that are not available to other customers within the same class, or geographic price discrimination whereby incumbent carriers reduce rates on services in regions where they face competition but do not reduce rates on the same class of services in regions where they do not face competition, are benign. CRTC restrictions of this nature represent, once more, excessive intervention in the telecom marketplace.

In sum, CRTC policies on price floors are a misguided attempt to make telephony markets more competitive because they confuse the concept of a competitive market structure as a means to greater market efficiency and competitive market structure as an end in itself. These missteps on CRTC's part are related to the emergence of competitive suppliers as an interest group in itself. Having perhaps even more limited expertise than the FCC in the United States, the CRTC relies largely on companies, and some consumer groups, to provide evidence on and analysis of regulatory solutions that its staff assesses, rather than proactively engaging in substantial research itself. As a result, perhaps inevitably, the regulator is forced to balance the interests of three groups: consumers, ILECs, and competitive suppliers. In the case of price floors, the interest of competitors is directly opposed to that of consumers, not to mention total social welfare. This contrasts with the useful role private competitors can play in politically resisting reregulation of maximum prices, as discussed earlier with respect to electricity. Efficient regulation does not balance the interests of the various parties affected; it maximizes consumer welfare subject to the constraints that the regulatory compact imposes on incumbent monopolists. Competition ensures that firms will earn fair returns without requiring regulation to be biased in their favor.

Airlines

The early history of Canadian aviation is one of government participation in almost every conceivable way. From the 1930s on, the Canadian government regulated airline practices extensively, setting fares and service conditions, such as frequency of service and size of airplane, approving entry by new airlines only if there was an unambiguous need for the entrant's services, which the government rarely found, and requiring federal approval for participation on any given route.[21] The government also owned and operated all the airports in the country, as well as the air traffic control system. The government even owned the dominant carrier, Air Canada.[22]

Deregulation began in the early 1980s and made its real impact on Canadian aviation with the passage of the National Transportation Act in 1987, signed into law in 1988. Entry was substantially deregulated: potential entrants only needed to meet a "fit, willing, and able" standard, requiring insurance coverage, certified aircraft and pilots, and 75 percent Canadian ownership.[23] Exit restrictions were eased as well: airlines were only required to give 120 days' notice of their intention to abandon a route. Fare levels and conditions of service were completely deregulated in southern Canada, while regulation was eased but did not disappear in the north, where the government continued to oversee fares, exit, and entry until 1996. Another important liberalizing step was taken in 1988 when Air Canada was privatized.

By contrast, steps to liberalize the market to foreign competitors have been tentative at best. Apart from the "Open Skies" agreement signed with the United States in 1995, which permits Canadian and U.S. airlines to compete over routes between the countries, strict barriers to foreign participation remain. Foreigners cannot own more than 25 percent of any Canadian airline, thus eliminating the prospect of a foreign carrier buying or otherwise establishing a Canadian airline and competing with Air Canada. Moreover, foreign carriers are restricted from carrying passengers point to point within Canada (cabotage).

Just as in the United States, where allegations of predatory pricing in airlines have become common (see chapters 10 and 12), Canada has begun focusing regulatory attention on competitive conditions in the industry. Air Canada acquired Canadian Airlines in December 1999 and emerged as a clearly dominant firm in 2002, with a domestic market share of about

73 percent by seat kilometer and 64 percent by seat.[24] This dominance created concerns about Air Canada's conduct. Whereas allegations of predatory pricing have failed to stick in the United States, most prominently in the case of American Airlines, there has been success in advancing this argument in Canada.[25] But rather than litigating predation in the courts or before the Competition Tribunal under standard predatory pricing provisions, the Canadian approach has been to address airline pricing practices through legislation. Bill C-26 passed in 1996 reimposed a form of regulation on the airline industry, particularly Air Canada. For example, Bill C-26 empowers the Canadian Transportation Agency to review prices on monopoly routes and to disallow and roll back any "unreasonable" fares.[26] To ensure that Air Canada did not set prices too low, however, the government also created special provisions in the Competition Act empowering the Competition Bureau (under s. 104.1) to issue temporary cease and desist orders in the face of alleged predation by a dominant airline without prior review by the Competition Tribunal. The bureau also has the power to impose administrative monetary penalties of up to Can$15 million on any airline that has abused its dominant position. In the airline industry, as in telephony, the government has been concerned about low pricing, particularly selective price cuts by incumbent firms designed to match competitors' prices on some routes. Recently, however, the government has proposed changing course by eliminating all airline-specific provisions in the Competition Act.

Aside from regulating the airlines themselves, the state has participated extensively in the airport business. Canada has 726 airports, 24 of which hold "national" status, in that they account for 90 percent of all scheduled passenger and air cargo traffic.[27] The federal government originally owned and operated the airports, but pursuant to a recent privatization scheme, airports are now operated by nonprofit corporations whose boards of directors include municipal government nominees that lease airport facilities from the government. Increased direct oversight of airports, including price regulation, is contemplated in the recently proposed Canada Airports Act. In addition, the state operates the air traffic control system. The Canadian government recently relinquished direct control of air traffic to Nav Canada, which is a nonprofit corporation with representatives on its board from a variety of stakeholders, including airlines and labor unions.

Deregulation has clearly had a significant, favorable impact on the airline industry.[28] Since deregulation, and particularly in recent years, there has been a proliferation of low-fare, low-amenity service. WestJet has been the most successful provider of low-fare service, increasing its market share as measured by seat kilometer from 4 percent to 14 percent between 1999 and 2002.[29] In total, low-fare service reached 36 percent of the market by 2002.[30] As a recent newspaper account put it, discount airlines have "pretty well blanketed" Canada with discount flights and are increasingly entering cross-border routes.[31]

Airline deregulation in Canada has had some other effects as well: prices for air traffic control and airport services, such as landing and parking fees, have increased since the privatization of Nav Canada and airports. Nav Canada's fees doubled between 1997 and 1998.[32] Revenue at the eight largest airports increased by 9.7 percent in 2001, even while the total number of passengers did not change.[33] The Canada Transportation Act Review Panel expressed concern that the airports were exercising monopoly power in setting prices.[34]

In the case of airport performance, the problems stem from a *lack* of regulation. Airports, because of their geographical locations and costs, are often essential facilities. In such circumstances, the market will not generate competitive prices, and price regulation is more appropriate. In their laudable push to deregulate airlines, policymakers have neglected to regulate the natural monopoly elements that remain.

In other respects, the opposite is true: there remains too much regulation in airlines, though recent government proposals are paying some attention to this issue. Following the merger of Canadian Airlines and Air Canada, the federal government was reluctant to let competition run its course, relying instead on extremely interventionist predatory pricing policies, under which a near-bankrupt airline was assumed to be a dominant predator when it simply matched its competitors' prices. Just as in the telephony industry, where federal authorities restricted price-matching by incumbents, they opted for a dubious policy of keeping prices high in the short run through the threat of predatory pricing laws in order to keep prices competitive in the longer run. This is misguided policy. Matching prices is the essence of competition, and authorities should generally resist the temptation to assume that they can accurately determine when a matched price is predatory. It is encouraging that the minister of industry recently proposed repealing the airline-specific provisions in the Competition Act, although the law was never passed owing to a subsequent federal election. Relying on conventional approaches to predation in airlines, as is done in the United States, rather than adopting specific provisions in the Competition Act, would leave a near-bankrupt airline less susceptible to findings of predation.

At the same time, it is discouraging that the federal government has neglected to deregulate in an obvious way to address concerns about Air

Canada's possible dominance: that is, by opening the borders to foreign competition. Both the remaining restrictions on foreign competition and the (current) regulation of airline prices through predatory pricing law represent cases of the government doing too much, not too little.

What lessons can be drawn from the deregulatory experience in airlines? First, deregulation is not an either/or proposition. Policymakers should examine an industry to determine which sectors present natural monopoly problems and which do not. Deregulating airports was not sensible, whereas deregulating airlines was. Second, political considerations can dominate the deregulatory agenda. The political fallout from the merger of Air Canada and Canadian Airlines combined with the failure of some small airlines put political pressure on the federal government to appear to be doing something. The course of action it chose, predatory pricing reform, certainly appeased small rivals and avoided a costly course, truly open skies, for Air Canada and its rivals alike. However, this action was not in the public interest, but rather in the collective interest of the domestic airlines. As in the VoIP case, where the emergence of rival telecommunications firms created political pressure to protect competitors rather than competition, the pressure of rival airlines surely affected the government's decision to adopt the airline-specific predatory pricing regime.[35]

The reasons for the Canadian approach to airline predation become clearer when one examines Canadian competition law alongside U.S. law. In chapter 10, Michael Levine suggests that the fracturing of the U.S. industry created obstacles to antitrust reform, whereas in Canada, Air Canada was the clear focal point that motivated reform. The structure of antitrust law in the two jurisdictions undoubtedly contributed to the different outcomes. U.S. antitrust law relies on very general provisions that set out standards for the courts to apply in adjudicating antitrust disputes. Though Canadian competition law relies on standards to a considerable extent, of course, it relies more heavily on specific statutory provisions regarding various potentially anticompetitive practices. Since amending the Competition Act to include airline-specific provisions was not a difficult matter, it was more feasible for political actors to press for such a change. In contrast, the Sherman Act has had the same general approach to monopolization since 1890; lobbying for a legislative amendment to it (or the more recent but still general Robinson-Patman Act) would not have seemed as plausible a strategy as in Canada. As a consequence, predatory pricing policy in airlines has remained a matter for the courts in the United States, where rent-seeking lobbying is presumably less influential, whereas it became a legislative matter in Canada. With the greater potential influence of competitors in Canada, it is perhaps not surprising that predatory pricing claims have been more successful there than in the United States.

Appropriate deregulatory regimes are ones that commit the government to a sensible course of action even in the face of political fallout from future events. For example, if the government had been insulated from the influence of local political actors, such as competitors, it might have resisted the push for specific predatory pricing laws for airlines.[36] When embarking on privatization and deregulation, the government could have entered into an international agreement that skies would be inexorably opened over time to foreign competition. An international agreement to this effect would have benefited Canada not only by promoting competition but also by deterring the government from adopting politically motivated regulation in the future, such as the airlines' current predatory pricing rules.

Conclusions

Two kinds of considerations should influence the design of the deregulatory agenda. The first is economic. The desire for greater economic efficiency has undoubtedly inspired the path of deregulation. The second is political. In our view, political considerations have not received sufficient attention in the deregulation of markets, and this failing has in turn jeopardized the economic benefits of deregulation. Future attempts at deregulation must do better in anticipating potential political obstacles to reform, even at the cost of departing from "first-best" options, in order to keep the deregulation train on track. Put another way, policymakers should view deregulation as an exercise in maximizing social wealth subject to political constraints.

Managing the transition from regulation to the market in network industries such as electricity, telecommunications, and airlines is a complex task. Although liberalization offers clear economic gains, the optimal mix of regulation and free markets is not obvious. This makes it all the more important to anticipate political resistance to deregulation and design the boundaries of market and regulation with such political realities in mind. Choosing a less-than-perfect approach that allows the government to commit to deregulation is preferable to establishing a technically optimal but politically infeasible regime.

In the introduction to this volume, Marc Landy and Martin Levin compare the "old politics" of entrenched interest group dynamics with the "new politics" of ideas or philosophies that transcend special interests. We view deregulation as a blend of the old and the new politics. Canadian telecom regulation, for example, has in some resects been less vulnerable to the distortions of interest groups than its counterpart in the United States, but in other respects it has been more vulnerable, to the detriment of consumers and social welfare. At a theoretical level, all evidence suggests that even the traditional theory of the political economy of regulation, with its assumption of full rationality, needs to be revisited.[37] As the evidence on the deregulation experience suggests, two ideas, well-known to behavioral economists and psychologists, play a critical role in political economy, the first of which is that the status quo—status quo prices, in particular—play an essential role.[38] Thus in an industry such as telephony, it is possible to move toward efficiency and away from the distortions of cross-subsidies because rapidly evolving technology protects harmed groups from experiencing price increases over time. (The harmed groups are relatively insensitive to the fact that prices would be even lower had the subsidies been maintained.) In electricity, the status quo bias means that current prices act as a rigid benchmark from which any upward movement is politically very challenging, whatever its efficiency or distributional impacts. Second, distortions in electricity pricing hinge not on the relative powers of competing interest groups, the traditional source of price distortions, but on a failure of voting consumers to understand the tradeoff between greater efficiency (including lower government deficits) and lower current energy prices. The latter are immediate, more concrete, and more easily grasped by consumers. The political economy of regulation must, in short, be sensitive to the themes of behavioral economics.

Patterns of deregulation in the United States and elsewhere around the world in recent years have been attributed to many factors:[39] changes in ideology concerning the relationship between state and market; changes in politically salient interests; changes in technology, which introduce new participants or potential participants on the supply side of various markets and stimulate new configurations of customers on the demand side; new ideas about alternative welfare-maximizing policies; new institutional arrangements that influence what interests and ideas are privileged in particular policy domains or marginalized in subsequent public policy decisions; and the internationalization of markets that induce countries to follow liberalization policies implemented elsewhere so as not to lose international competitiveness on either the import or export sides.

With respect to the three sectors discussed in this chapter, technological change seems of little significance in the airline industry, of somewhat more but still limited significance in the electricity sector, and of central significance in the telecommunications sector. Internationalization of markets, in Canada's case, has been an influential factor in the deregulation of airlines and telecommunications. Ideology seems to have played a minor role, with the partial exception of electricity restructuring in Ontario. Ideas in conjunction with new institutional arrangements seem to have been an important factor in electricity restructuring. But in the end, standard public choice explanations of existing policy configurations do not provide adequate account of the sorts of forces that disrupt existing political equilibria and lead over time (often relatively short periods of time) to nonincremental policy changes.

Notes

1. Michael Trebilcock and Ron Daniels, "Electricity Restructuring: The Ontario Experience," *Canadian Business Law Journal* 22, no. 2 (2000): 163; Tom Adams, *From Promise to Crisis: Lessons for Atlantic Canada from Ontario's Electricity Liberalisation* (Halifax, N.S.: Atlantic Institute for Market Studies, November 2000), p. 9.

2. Ontario Electricity Financial Corporation, *Annual Report 2004* (Toronto).

3. Ontario, Ministry of Energy, Science and Technology, *Direction for Change: Charting a Course of Competitive Electricity and Jobs in Ontario* (Toronto: Queen's Printer Ontario, November 1997).

4. Electricity Act, 1998, S.O. 1998, c. 15, Sch. A.

5. Trebilcock and Daniels, "Electricity Restructuring," p. 170.

6. Ibid., p. 171.

7. Electricity Pricing, Conservation and Supply Act, 2002, S.O. 2002, c. 23.

8. For a critique of this plan, see Ahmad Faruqui and Stephen George, "Preventing Electrical Shocks: What Ontario and Other Provinces Should Learn about Smart Metering," Commentary 210 (Toronto: C. D. Howe Institute, April 2005).

9. Terry Daniel, Joseph Doucet, and Andre Plourde, "Electricity Industry Restructuring: The Alberta Experience," Working Paper (University of Alberta, School of Business, May 2001).

10. See Richard Pierce, Michael Trebilcock, and Evan Thomas, "Beyond Gridlock: The Case for Greater Integration of Regional Electricity Markets," Commentary 228 (Toronto: C. D. Howe Institute, March 2006).

11. Marc K. Landy and Martin A. Levin, eds., *The New Politics of Public Policy* (Johns Hopkins University Press, 1995); also Andrew Rich, chapter 11 in this volume.

12. SeaBoard Group, *Communications Pricing for Consumers: A Cross-National Survey* (www.seaboardgroup.com [May 2003]). The Canadian cities were Toronto, Winnipeg, Regina, Lethbridge, and Cornerbrook. The American cities were Chicago, Pasadena, Augusta, Tuscaloosa, Boston, Seattle, and Boise. This study's conclusion that Canadian rates were less than two-thirds of U.S. rates was identical whether the services priced were a basic basket of local and (some) long-distance services or a basket with more long-distance services and many options.

13. See OECD, *Regulatory Reform in Canada: Regulatory Reform in the Telecommunications Industry* (2002). In the OECD data, the prices of Canadian and U.S. services are much closer than more recent SeaBoard data suggest. See SeaBoard Group, *Communications Pricing for Consumers.*

14. "Price Cap Regulation and Related Issues," CRTC Decision 97-9 (May 1, 1997).

15. Sam Peltzman, "Toward a More General Theory of Regulation," *Journal of Law and Economics* 19 (August 1976): 211–40.

16. Since joint fixed costs must be covered, efficient relative prices will also reflect differences in elasticities of demand, from the theory of Ramsey pricing.

17. Daniel Kahneman and Amos Tversky, "Prospect Theory: An Analysis of Decisions under Risk," *Econometrica* 47 (March 1979): 313–27.

18. CRTC Telecom Decision, May 12, 2005.

19. CRTC 2005-25, par. 66.

20. See Michael Trebilcock and others, *The Law and Economics of Canadian Competition Policy* (University of Toronto Press, 2003), pp. 339–57.

21. See David Gillen, *The Future of Canada's Airline Industry: Frills, No-frills or Walmart,* draft manuscript (Calgary: Van Horne Institute, 2001), p. 20.

22. Ibid. p. 1. See also p. 12, where Gillen suggests that public ownership of Air Canada was probably more influential than regulation in shaping commercial aviation in Canada. In their study of the impact of regulation on airline performance around the world, Gonenc and Nicoletti rely on state ownership of airlines as an indicator of the degree of regulation in that country. Rauf Gonenc and Giuseppe Nicoletti, "Regulation, Market Structure and Performance in Air Passenger Transportation," *OECD Economic Studies* 32, no. 183 (2001).

23. Ibid., p. 25.

24. Debra Ward, independent transition observer on airline restructuring, *Airline Restructuring in Canada: Final Report* (Ottawa, September 2002), p. 76.

25. *United States* v. *AMR Corp.,* 335 F.3d 1109 (10th Cir. 2003), *aff'g* 140 F. Supp. 2d 1141 (D. Kan. 2001).

26. Canada Transportation Act Review Panel, *Vision and Balance* (Ottawa, June 2001), recommended the elimination of this provision (www.reviewcta-examenltc.gc.ca/english/pages/finalreport.htm).

27. Gillen, *The Future of Canada's Airline Industry,* p. 144.

28. For example, Lazar reports that fares—net of taxes, airport fees, and Nav Canada fees—have fallen since Air Canada acquired Canadian Airlines in 1999, likely because of the growth of discount airlines: Fred Lazar, *Turbulence in the Skies: Options for Making Canadian Airline Travel More Competitive,* Commentary 181 (Toronto: C. D. Howe Institute, April 2003).

29. Ward, *Airline Restructuring in Canada,* p. 76.

30. Ibid, p. 21.

31. Brent Jang, "West Jet Spreads Wings Further with Launch of Flights to U.S.," *Toronto Globe and Mail,* September 20, 2004, p. B4.

32. Gillen, *The Future of Canada's Airline Industry,* p. 43.

33. Lazar, *Turbulence in the Skies,* p. 7.

34. Canada Transportation Act Review Panel, *Vision and Balance,* p. 152.

35. See Edward Iacobucci, "Public Choice Theory and Recent Developments in Canadian Competition Policy" in *Selected Topics in Corporate Litigation,* Annual Business Law Symposium (Kingston, Ont.: Queen's University, 2000–01).

36. On the importance of reconfiguring political constituencies to preserve economic reforms, see Eric Patashnik's discussion in chapter 12 of this volume. While privatizing creates a constituency that would oppose inefficient reregulation of maximum prices as discussed in respect of electricity, private actors might also lobby for explicit or implicit price floors which will often be inefficient.

37. Peltzman, "Toward a More General Theory of Regulation."

38. Kahneman and Tversky, "Prospect Theory."

39. Michael Trebilcock, "Journeys across the Divides," in *The Origins of Law and Economics: Essays by the Founding Fathers,* edited by Francesco Parisi and Charles K. Rowley (Cheltenham, U.K.: Edward Elgar, 2005).

PART IV

Conclusion

14

Dishonest Corporatism: Who Guards the Guardians in an Age of Soft Law and Negotiated Regulation?

MARTIN SHAPIRO

The quest for an objective and neutral social science often leads scholars to ignore the dirty side of what they study or to call it by some innocuous name. Lying, cheating, and stealing become "principal-agent" problems or "transaction costs" or "strategic behavior." Sometimes, however, it is probably a good idea to call a spade a dirty shovel. Thus if they are examining government regulation of business enterprises, in the current gilded age it might be as well to openly recognize two central phenomena of the business world. First, the wonderful stock market–oriented U.S. economy is a machine that creates incentives for dishonesty among corporate managers and their attendant lawyers, accountants, and bankers that are so massive as to be almost beyond human comprehension and to have induced amazing corporate cheating, lying, and stealing. In chapter 4, John Cioffi deals with one of these phenomena, dishonest competition, and the legislation aimed at reducing it, the Sarbanes-Oxley Act of 2002. Second, admitting the propensity of all politicians, and indeed of all humans, to ignore inconvenient facts, the administration of George W. Bush may well be the first truly postmodern presidency, one that believes that all "facts" are merely social constructions that can be reconstructed and deconstructed at one's convenience, so that truth and falsehood in government is itself an artificial distinction.

Reluctant Regulators

To the second phenomenon, that is, dishonesty in government, should be added an aggravating circumstance. Most business regulation is done under more or less general statutes that delegate to administrative agencies the power to make and remake the supplementary, detailed laws (usually called rules or regulations) necessary to actually implement the policies announced in the statutes. Over the past several decades it has become progressively more difficult and time-consuming to make new rules and regulations and to unmake or modify existing ones. This "ossification" of rulemaking means that as Republicans and Democrats alternate in the presidency, each regime is confronted at least in the short run with legal obligations to implement regulatory rules made by the previous administration with which it disagrees. So here, too, wonderful machinery is in place producing incentives for lying and cheating, this time by government regulators as a stopgap until they can accomplish what they view is an electoral mandate to change those regulations.

One particularly notable aspect of recent regulator behavior is what has been widely billed as a "war on science." This rhetoric has been fueled in part by controversies over stem-cell research, creationism (also known as intelligent design), manned spaceflight, and government funding of product-oriented rather than "pure" research. In part, the issue is also regulation. Some of the regulatory statutes require that regulations be based on the best available science. In many agencies, politically appointed executives have customarily deferred to the findings and recommendations of their scientifically qualified subordinates. Where an administration is bent on reducing the scope and impact of regulation or substituting "value" concerns for scientific ones, the science is likely to be manipulated, distorted, or flatly ignored. Authorities may find particularly fruitful the claim that no scientific consensus exists that compels regulation or a particular regulation. That is to say, no matter what the real scientific consensus, some scientist can always be found on the other side. The propensity of the media to define journalistic objectivity as telling both sides of the story encourages regulatory combatants to manufacture a second side. Pro-regulatory forces may manipulate scientific calculations of very small risks into what appear to be findings of imminent disaster, again encouraged by media fascination with disaster scenarios. Lying about science, either passively by ignoring it or actively by misrepresenting it, is now one of the central forms of regulatory dishonesty.

Inheriting a very proactive regulatory regime that it believes to be fundamentally wrong-headed but difficult and time-consuming to change legally, and operating in an intellectual climate of malleable facts (see, I, too, can call a spade an excavation implement), the George W. Bush administration has labored under sore temptations to engage in regulatory lying and cheating. Thus a social science of regulatory politics, one of the principal concerns of this volume, ought to be prepared to openly acknowledge that a major part of its subject matter is potential dishonesty by both the regulators and the regulated.

An Age of Soft Law, Negotiation, and Regulatory Partnership

This dishonesty is particularly salient today because of changes in regulatory thinking and practice. Once upon a time, so the story goes, the capitalist regulatory state believed in command-and-control regulation. In search of health, safety, environmental, and consumer protection, it left ownership in private hands but, to a limited degree, intervened to tell private management that it was forbidden to do certain things or even that it must do certain things. A central theme of this volume is that such command-and-control regulation began to fall into disfavor for a number of reasons. It is awkward to try to achieve a positive goal, like a clean environment, only by telling people what they cannot do. For each prohibited action, they find some alternative that may be equally bad in terms of the desired end state. Command and control over the details of complex processes, over inputs and throughputs, creates enormous monitoring problems and costs that may be avoided by mandating only outputs or results, which may be more observable and easily measurable. And, in a legal and political system that greatly empowers private actors in relation to the government, government commands tend to engender private resistance and thus high enforcement costs. Government may get more bang for its regulatory buck by seeking voluntary compliance than by issuing commands that generate counterlobbying and lawsuits. This point is particularly important given that Congress typically enacts ambitious regulations and then appropriates small amounts of enforcement money.

As the rest of this volume so dramatically indicates, this move away from command and control is not adequately captured by the word "deregulation." Rather, this activity often consists of a search for other modes of regulation that seek to avoid or reduce the costs attendant on command-and-control regulation. By overseeing performance or output as opposed to a process, regulation eases monitoring problems and provides the regulated entity with flexibility in achieving regulatory goals.

Flexibility is maximized, and monitoring costs may be reduced. Most important, incentives are created for voluntary compliance. Negotiated rule-making, in which new regulatory rules emerge from a consensus of the regulated entities, regulators, and other interested parties, may generate faster and more voluntary compliance. The attractions of voluntary compliance also lead to the substitution of "soft" for hard law. The government may advise, assist, or "jaw-bone" the regulated parties rather than seek to command them. Or the government may delegate regulatory authority to the regulated and engage in regulatory partnerships with them. For instance, government safety inspectors may be withdrawn in favor of safety programs initiated and implemented by the management of the regulated companies, perhaps with worker participation and with more or less government monitoring of results. Or government implementers of regulations may simply be instructed to negotiate settlements of regulatory violations rather than insist on immediate and complete remediation or punishment. The consent decree in which the regulatory offender promises not to do in the future what it does not admit that it did in the past is an extreme example.

Transatlantic Migrations of Regulatory Theories and Styles

In the previous volume in this series, Martin A. Levin and I examined the degree to which regulatory ideas and devices flowed across the Atlantic in both directions and the utility on each side of watching developments on the other.[1] We found Europe and North America comparable in the dominance of and strains on pluralist democratic theory, demands for transparency and participation, and respect for and suspicion of technocratic decisionmaking. Through accidents of chronology, regulatory experiences, first on one side of the water and then on the other, serve as instructive harbingers for later transatlantic counterparts.

Not so very long ago, it was fashionable to find contrast in U.S. and European regulatory styles. The American style was supposedly arms-length, even adversarial, litigation-oriented law enforcement. The European style consisted of collegial, consultative, cooperative relationships between regulators and regulated leading to voluntary but perhaps less than full compliance. The American style was transparent because it was adversarial. The European style was necessarily opaque because confidentiality was a prerequisite of successful negotiations between regulator and regulated.

A historical dimension ought to be introduced into this transatlantic contrast, however. Most American regulatory legislation of both the Progressive and New Deal era imposed on some government agency not only the duty to regulate but also the duty to preserve the health of the particular industry regulated. For the most part, these regulatory tasks were assigned to bodies of technical experts who operated from the same technical perspectives as the experts employed by the regulated industries. Regulatory agencies were supposed to maintain close and continuous contact with the regulated in order to precisely command and control. To be practical and successful, process regulation required intimate knowledge of industrial processes. Where adjudication was required, it was to be done largely within the regulatory agencies under the guidance of agency experts. Even when judicial review occurred, courts were to defer to the expertise of the agencies. Indeed, in the typical capitalist-friendly style of the New Deal, regulatory administrators, employing the expertise they shared with the regulated, were to round off the rough edges of the necessarily crude regulatory provisions enacted by nonexpert legislatures.

Everyone is familiar with the great wave of denunciatory "capture" literature eventually generated by the regulatory intimacy initially treated as a virtue. The regulated had co-opted the regulators. Indeed, it was often argued that the very regulatory statutes themselves had been conspiracies to shield the regulated from competition and allow them to collect monopoly rents.

The capture literature and the more general pluralist political theory of the 1950s heralded a judicial development that ended whatever honeymoon there had been between regulators and regulated. Beginning in the 1960s, courts began to pay less and less deference to agency expertise. Judges were more and more suspicious of agency discretion and demanded more and more proof that the agencies were obeying the letter of the law. The so-called American style of regulation flourished. Judicial and congressional demands for transparency and maximum participation in regulatory processes backed by the very great broadening of access to the courts for nearly any interested party moved regulation from intimate negotiation between enterprise and government officers sharing common technical expertise to public courtroom shouting matches between participants whose sole and shared expertise was shouting.

At the height of this activity in America, in the 1980s and 1990s, a certain movement was occurring in Europe as well. With the collapse of socialist ideology, the fight was no longer over whether to control enterprises by nationalization or regulation. Former socialists, still called socialists, and the new "greens" necessarily became friends of regulation, given that it was the only game still on the table. Demands for transparency and maximum participation in regulatory processes began to pick up and were accelerated by a number of regulatory disasters and by the growing general distrust of government or "crisis of legitimacy" experienced in Europe. Government bureaucracies there, long prided for their neutral, objective expertise, were to varying degrees politicized in many states. Perhaps most important, as the locus of regulation shifted from national capitals to the more distant, transnational regulators of the European Union, the intimate national circles of government officials and corporate executives and their attendant experts started breaking up. When regulation moved to Brussels, the corporate suits had to begin hiring multinational lobbyists to speak to some Dutch or Italian bureaucrat they hardly knew. At this point the regulated enterprises themselves began to favor the very participation and transparency rules that would have destroyed their intimate lunches with their own national regulators in Paris or Rome but facilitated corporate influence in Brussels.

Transnational Regulation and the Worship of Technocracy

The European scene was more complex than that, of course, precisely because it had now become one of transnational regulation. Whenever regulation becomes transnational, the great fear is that national governments will seek to intervene to distort regulation in favor of their own national economic interests or those of national sectors or enterprises. The American Progressives had tried to get politics out of regulation through the so-called independent regulatory commissions. The politics the Progressives feared was party politics. At least during a long transition period, proponents of transnational regulation fear politics because, at least until transnational parties arise, the only politicians around are national politicians representing national rather than transnational interests. The politics that proponents of transnational regulation want to keep out of the regulatory process is the politics of national self-interest. French influence ought not to be allowed to distort the regulation of beer so as to favor wine or French beer over German beer. The response is to emphasize the technical, objective, expert nature of regulation and to push for regulation by circles of experts, drawn to be sure from their nation-state homes—for where else can they be drawn from—but sharing common expertise in physics or pharmacology that is by its very nature transnational.

Any transnational regulatory regime is likely to push toward relatively closed and shielded regulation by nonpolitical experts because what such regimes have most to fear is outbreaks of political conflict between their member nations. This push, however, runs against the push for maximum transparency and participation that has been widely felt in both Europe and the United States. Those favoring democratic regulation may be no more content with regulatory processes captured by technocrats than they are with such processes captured by the regulated. Moreover, regulation by experts has a marked tendency toward capture by the regulated because the experts employed by the regulated are likely to have very strong influence on the overall perspectives of the expert community of which both the government-employed and privately employed experts are members.

To these complexities must be added another. At least during the transition phase, new transnational regulatory regimes are likely to be highly influenced by, indeed often really composed of, networks of regulatory officials of the national government. The national regulatory organs are the existing depositories of regulatory expertise. Often they are the actual implementers of transnationally enunciated regulatory policies. In building transnational regulation, they are the "there" that is already there.

Such networks are difficult to assess. They may turn out to be highly technocratic communities of expert midlevel government bureaucrats whose shared expertise dampens allegiances to particular national interests. This may be true even when the network participants are high-level government officials who are political appointees or the new breed of politicized civil servants because such executives are often captured by their own expert agency staffs. To the extent that the networks are composed of politicized officials, however, the result may be that routine regulatory matters are handled technocratically, but something quite different happens when the regulated entity has a lot of political clout in one or more of the member states (see Eugene Bardach's discussion of this phenomenon in chapter 15). In any event, such networks earn that label largely because they operate more by informal, and thus relatively opaque, communication rather than by open, formal, arms-length, rule-bound negotiation. Indeed, their very virtue is supposed to be their ability to avoid episodic adversarial, nation-against-nation confrontation in favor of continuous, cooperative, transnational conversation.

Thus certain tendencies in the general reaction against command-and-control process regulation are rooted in the particular need of transnational regulatory regimes to shield themselves against self-serving, national, political pressures. Such regimes and their academic proponents tend to focus on substituting the technocratic legitimacy of networks of experts for democratic—that is, electoral—legitimacy. Emphasis on expert discretion, while not logically entailing or requiring cooperative relationships between expert regulators and the regulated, is highly compatible with a vision of regulatory "partnership." If the experts themselves are to interact by informal, continuous cooperation and persuasion rather than by adversarial legalized decisionmaking, why not adopt the same style between regulatory networks and the regulated? If the law to govern the relationships between transnational and national regulators is to be "soft law," why not soft law for regulator-regulated relations?

Thus developments on both sides of the Atlantic are generating a new intellectual vogue in regulatory techniques and styles that is an outgrowth of deliberation. This new means of elevating government regulation above and beyond angst about pluralistic politics used to carry the name "corporatism." And not coincidentally it emerged first among students and proponents of the European Union and other transnational regulatory regimes. Transnational regulation such as that practiced in the European Union needs some protection from adversarial, national interest-oriented politics, and the participating European states already have a tradition of nonadversarial regulatory implementation.

The Transatlantic Move from Deliberation to Corporatism: AKA Soft Law, Regulatory Partnership, Negotiated Regulation

In the older era of pluralist political theory, regulation came down to those groups that were more equal than others capturing the regulators and using them to collect monopoly rents. This root economic inefficiency of regulation was aggravated by a legal pluralism that armed every interested party with all sorts of transparency, participation, and litigation rights that encouraged resistance to, and drove up the costs of, both initiating and implementing regulation. The multiplicity of adversarial participants and the hard law that resulted robbed the regulated of flexibility in meeting public interest goals and the incentives to do so.

The most fashionable response to the evils of interest-oriented pluralism has been "deliberation." Theories of deliberative democracy and deliberative bureaucracy and deliberative regulation are all over the place. The evils of pluralism will be cured by the interested parties, all the lions and the lambs, sitting down together. Instead of struggling against one another, each seeking to maximize its own interests, they will reason together to arrive at the truly best outcome—which will not aggregate pluralist interests but transcend selfish interests. And as appealing as this vision is in a domestic arena, it is even more so in transnational arenas where pluralist hardball is very likely to lead to deadlock or mutual retaliation between national participants rather than even-interest aggregation, let alone the general good.

Translated to the specific arena of regulation, deliberation becomes corporatism. Regulators and regulated should deliberate intimately, in a nonadversarial way, to arrive at the best modes of implementing mutually beneficial programs. One way of putting this is that Americans should move to the traditional European style. But it should be remembered that there was a strong strain of such style in the Progressive and New Deal styles of regulation too, although it became submerged under adversarial pluralist American developments from the 1960s onward.

The call for corporatism synthesizes or represents a convergence of a number of regulatory tendencies in America and Europe, with intellectual developments on each side of the water seen as forcing those on the other. First and foremost, corporatism is a vehicle for summarizing all the unhappiness about command-and-control, process-constraining, adversarial, hard-law regulation. Substitute instead a cooperative dialogue between regulators and regulated that directs joint energies toward the flexible, innovative solution of problems and reduces regulatory resistance and thus the regulatory costs of monitoring and enforcement. Second, it concentrates decisionmaking in communities of experts, expert bureaucrats, and expert private managers, shielding regulatory implementation from pluralist politics and so allowing true deliberation. Third, through the same empowerment of networks of government and enterprise experts, transnational regulation is shielded from disruptive and economically irrational national political pressures. The thinness of transnational hierarchical institutions and enforceable laws naturally leads proponents of transnational regulation to informal, consensual practices.

The corporatism purveyed can, of course, be either of the Right or the Left; that is, it can either be limited to government and management officials or be broadened to include labor and even consumer interests. Left corporatism, however, runs the danger of turning into pluralism the more beneficiaries of regulation are added to the authorized corporatist participants. For the very elderly, the word "corporatism" itself may be a turnoff, but it need not be used. "Soft-law regulatory partnership" and the like sound nicer.

The Risks of Technocracy and Corporatism

Corporatism, by whatever name, as an extension of deliberation, becomes a sweetness-and-light alternative to self-interested pluralism cum adversarial legalism. Modern regulatory problems are overwhelmingly complex, high-tech problems, and the technology is always rapidly changing. Inevitably those engaged at the frontiers of the technology know the most about it and are in the best position to deal with it, and they are in the enterprises not in the government. What better way to deal with such problems than through an alliance of management experts and government experts deliberating themselves into best decisions?

One response to the corporatist hymn is that resorting to technocracy does not wring out the dirty politics and leave the regulation clean. Instead, it creates illusions of objective, consensual, rational deliberative results by privileging the narrower range of preferences to be found in whatever community of experts gains control over a particular regulatory sphere rather than the broader, more conflictual range of interests actually present in that sphere. Unless corporatism allows everyone into the corporation, thus turning itself back into pluralism, almost by definition it assigns public policy-making to a set of persons with a range of interests and preferences smaller than and different from the sum of the full set of interests at play. Is this cloaking of expert managers and expert government officials in the priestly robes of deliberators really a move away from pluralist democracy?

My question here, however, is a somewhat different one. How attractive is corporatism if one presupposes that both the government and enterprise participants will be dishonest? And currently, in the United States, why should this not be presupposed? (I leave the recent episodes of corruption in the Unied Nations and the European Union and speculation about the ethics displayed by the multinationals to others more knowledgeable than myself.) The exposés of corporate dishonesty and dishonesty among the professions that serve U.S. corporations may be part of media hype, but their revelations are just as likely to be the tip of the iceberg, given the tremendous incentives to cheat currently at play. As for the government, it is controlled by persons with strong ideological incentives to subvert the regulatory regimes in place and a demonstrated inclination to vigorously distort and ignore truth and to circumvent procedures favoring transparency and full participation. To argue that the Bush administration has been no more prone to such urges than previous ones may or may not be correct but is hardly reassuring. Do Americans want regulatory partnerships and confidential, consensual regulatory conversations and discretionary rounding-off of statutory hard edges if they fear that many of these moves will end up looking like criminal conspiracies? Indeed, are they not likely to move to the most extreme form of adversarial legalism, criminal prosecution, when faced with dishonest corporatism, as the recent flurry of federal and state prosecutions suggest?

Railroad safety regulation is a nice little illustration of regulatory partnership. Adversary legalism would have an army of federal inspectors out issuing citations and levying fines every time the most trivial violation of a detailed set of operational specifications occurred. The Bush administration instead is practicing regulatory partnership, with government regulators and railroad management agreeing on a general and flexible safety improvement plan that will be implemented by the railroad itself under general government monitoring of overall performance. For the railroad, every deferral of safety expenditure is a favorable increment to the current bottom line and thus to the current stock price. And to some in railroad management—for example, at Union Pacific, which was finding it hard just to get its container freight off the docks and across the country in any reasonable time—safety is unlikely to attract the highest or most skilled level of management attention. Quite apart from the entities they spend their vacations with, government regulators who strongly believe that railroads ought to mind their own business and the government its own, and the less involvement the better, and who are told that gentle persuasion is the best regulatory tool, are not likely to press management very hard. As a result, when the grade-crossing gate breaks down, it is not likely to get fixed very fast even if the hard-pressed railroad is pushing more and more trains past it each day.

Corruption is, of course, a risk or potential cost in all regulatory regimes. Prosecutors can be bribed. Command-and-control regulatory agencies can be captured. But where regulation is the product of muted conversation between managers with high incentives to deliver the best bottom line now and regulators who do not want to regulate, are regulatory costs, when underregulation is counted as a cost, likely to be less than under adversarial legalism? For those who want deregulation pure and simple, regulatory partnerships, soft law, and all that corporatism entails may be the next best thing to sub rosa regulatory erosion where open deregulation cannot be achieved. Most of the studies in this volume, however, appear to point to the feasibility of regulatory change rather than total deregulation. If one insists on adding the adjective "dishonest" to corporatism, are the desired regulatory changes actually changes in a corporatist direction? Should the growing, glowing talk of corporatism in the sphere of transnational regulation be allowed to infect domestic discussions? In the United States, corporatism may well end up as a kind of criminal conversation.

All this does not mean, of course, that every move away from command and control and adversarial legalism is a bad thing. Nor, of course, does it mean that conventional rules are foolproof safeguards against dishonesty. As noted in chapters 2 and 8, however, ill-chosen constitutional rules may create unintended incentives to corruption. It does mean that every such proposed move ought to be examined under the premise that in many instances both the regulator and the regulated may be operating in bad faith. No regulatory move made by the Bush administration was without a defensible, more-bang-for-the-regulatory-buck rationale in terms of incentives to voluntary compliance, ease of monitoring, and tapping of private sector know-how and flexibility. Those that depend upon the joint discretion of regulators and regulated, however, may lose in real compliance and monitoring more than what they gain in flexibility, voluntarism, and in eliciting the skills of the regulated. Discretion is harder to monitor than yes or no obedience to black-letter rules. Black-letter rules have so many drawbacks, including their own monitoring difficulties, that one may wish to consider alternatives. But regulatory partnerships depending on the joint discretion of regulators who do not want to regulate and regulatees who wish to escape the costs of regulation are not an attractive alternative. What they are likely to achieve is unmonitorable, voluntary, flexible, highly skilled noncompliance.

At least for the present, every time Americans are tempted to use the devices of corporatism, they ought to add the qualifier "dishonest" before considering them the best solution to regulatory problems. And just because no other port in transnational regulation may be readily available does not mean that corporatist international style should be allowed to influence U.S. national costume.

Note

1. Martin A. Levin and Martin Shapiro, eds., *Transatlantic Poicymaking in an Age of Austerity* (Georgetown University Press, 2004).

15

Why Deregulation Succeeds or Fails

Eugene Bardach

The chapters in this volume demonstrate the great range of outcomes following deregulation efforts. There seem to be about as many pathetic failures as stirring successes. This fact raises an obvious question. Once deregulation is decided upon, what conditions make for success or failure?

Certainly, the relevant conditions are numerous. A striking one emerging from cases in this volume relates to the stakes for government or policymakers in undertaking deregulation or in designing post-deregulatory markets: when the stakes are high, their actions often lead, directly or indirectly, to failure. Ironically, these actions usually occur as a byproduct of a government's efforts to do good.

What Is "Success"?

Before turning to the empirical analysis, let me define "success." The short answer is "utility" or "welfare" maximization. Nonutilitarian considerations are important in other contexts, to be sure; but for policy issues in the domain of deregulation and those addressed in this volume, utilitarianism is adequate. The more important, and potentially controversial, point is that I do not include the satisfaction of provider interests in my definition. Thus if

Table 15-1. *When Government Has Higher Stakes, the Results Are Worse*

Result	Relatively low stakes	Relatively high stakes
Relatively successful	Airlines (U.S. and Canada) Canada telephony Railroads Agriculture: planting restrictions	PJM electricity
Relatively unsuccessful		Agriculture: subsidies School choice (U.S.)* California electricity Canada telephony price floors Ontario electricity British pensions Telecommunications (U.S.)*

deregulation causes regulators to lose their jobs, or public school teachers to experience slower salary increases in the face of competition from voucher or charter schools, I do not count these results against the success of deregulation.

Post-deregulation improvements (or diminutions) in utility should be assessed against two benchmarks. The first is the level known or assumed for the state of the world before deregulation. The second is the state of the world if deregulation had lived up to its potential rather than being blocked or thwarted in some way. The two rows in table 15-1 indicate my assessment of the relatively successful and unsuccessful cases discussed in this book; an asterisk marks the cases in which the second comparison weighed more heavily in my eyes than the first comparison.

Classifying Cases

The coverage of this book—the "politics and economics of the market"—is somewhat broader than the central topic here. I focus more narrowly on those cases featuring some sort of pro-competitive deregulation, with or without significant market design in its wake. I have omitted the cases in which government policy does not follow deregulation, as in Sarbanes-Oxley or tax reform (see chapters 4 and 12, respectively); those in which welfare state retrenchment, although about government relationship to markets, is about providing transfers or some form of insurance (chapter 5); and those in which changes in the liability law do affect markets but either are not engineered legislatively or are not deregulatory (chapters 3 and 4).[1]

In trying to classify the cases, I rely mainly on what the chapters relate, although I occasionally draw on external information as well. I also take modest interpretive license if the chapter author did not provide all the facts on which one would ideally base a classification.

Classifying Cases with Regard to Success

In the world of "network" industries, as chapters 6 and 10 make very clear, airline and railroad deregulation were successes; and as chapter 13 shows, airline and telephony deregulation succeeded in Canada. There is no need to summarize their conclusions here. Electricity deregulation in the northeast quadrant has also been successful in most instances; the one most fully described in chapter 7 is PJM.

Agriculture I divided into two parts: subsidies and planting restrictions. Although a policy begun in 1996 to withdraw subsidies was reversed in 2002, other key deregulatory features of the Federal Agriculture Improvement and Reform Act (FAIR) have stuck: no requirements to idle land, and no more constraints on farmers' prerogative to plant certain crops. This deregulation has avoided almost $4 billion a year in losses to the economy due to allocative distortions. Hence I count the crop decisions element of agriculture deregulation as a relative success.

Consider now the failures. If the FAIR act was a deregulatory success for agriculture in 1996, the subsidy program re-created on an even larger scale in 2002 was a clear failure. In the case of school choice, the possible effects on public schools, which might be supposed to respond to competition, appear to be relatively little (chapter 9). California's experiment in electricity deregulation ended with the bankruptcy or near-bankruptcy of two of California's investor-owned utilities and extremely high electricity rates for consumers, locked in for ten years. When it became apparent that the utilities' customers might switch to alternative power suppliers in the deregulated marketplace, the state legislature passed a law forbidding them to do so.[2] Ontario's short-lived effort at electricity deregulation was just as bad, though it was citizens in their role as taxpayers rather than ratepayers who would be obliged to pay up.

The list of failures would also have to include the Telecommunications Act of 1996: hundreds of millions were spent on lobbying and litigation and on running an expanded Federal Communications Commission (FCC), yet the stalemate over crucial details was still unresolved and the marketplace unimproved for consumers (chapter 11). In Canada, while most of the effort to deregulate telephony worked well, the regulatory commission made a mess of trying to perfect deregulation using price floors for certain services (chapter 13). And the British experiment in privatizing pensions that began in 1986 failed in at least two of its three objectives: protecting the public purse and reducing collectivism in the public sphere; it did increase labor mobility in the private sphere (chapter 8). The Pensions Act of 1995, passed largely in response to the "misselling" (fraudulent or nearly fraudulent representations) of private pensions initiated by the 1986 reform, imposed unprecedented regulation on the private pensions market. Moreover, the failure will grow, and become more apparent, as retirees discover their economic straits.

Classifying Cases with Regard to Stakes

As I said earlier, when governments or policymakers have high stakes in the outcome of deregulation, the prospects of success are worse than when they do not. This is shown by the clustering of cases along the main diagonal in table 15-1. But the idea of "stakes" in the outcome and its application to the cases at hand require elaboration.

The stakes for governmental actors are of four kinds. One is relatively straightforward: the material and psychological benefits associated with government employment. It sometimes happens that marketization introduces new competitors to face off against public providers, as in the case of charter or voucher schools (chapter 9); and in such cases, there is a threat to job security and income. In some cases, as in public education, there are also psychological stakes having to do with professional and civic identity.[3]

A second kind is budgetary. When a government subsidizes one or more parties in a market that the government itself regulates, it has a financial stake in how well that market works. The notable example here is British pension reform (chapter 8). If "personal pensions" are to substitute in the long run for government pensions, the private pensions industry had better be able to perform.

Third, stakes may be ideological. These relate to efforts to (1) implement a competitive-market ideology and (2) demonstrate the general principle that, in varied senses, this ideology can work better than the more statist or collectivist alternative. British pension reform is once again an exemplary case.

Fourth, there are "reputational" stakes in being seen to be doing a competent job of deregulation or, more commonly, not being blamed for doing an incompetent job. While all deregulatory policies present such stakes, of course, some do so more than others. These pertain to post-deregulation markets in which policymakers feel they have a continuing responsibility to make adjustments in the name of fairness or consumer protection or some other such value or symbol.

Consider the eight cases grouped as "relatively high stakes." School choice, as already noted, is a good example of a threat to employment stakes, while British pensions represent a budgetary and ideological threat. The stakes are also high in deregulating electricity because the government has a heavy burden to prove that a deregulated system can deliver reliable and reasonably priced electricity after decades in which consumers have been conditioned to the necessity of market regulation. In addition, the government has a continuing role in overseeing access to transmission facilities, which are a natural monopoly.

In U.S. telecommunications, before the FCC phase, the case was mainly about a struggle among industry titans brokered by Congress. Had the story ended with passage of the Telecommunications Act, I would have classified this as a low-stakes case. However, as chapter 11 makes clear, the act resolved very little. It left serious policy decisions to the FCC, which had an inclination to "meddle" in the name of fairness and other values. I see here significant reputational stakes. The efforts to deregulate telecommunications in Britain point to the same issues (chapter 2).

Agriculture subsidies are in the high-stakes category simply because they cost the federal treasury so much: Congress showered $10 billion to $20 billion on farmers during the eras when FAIR and the 2002 farm bill were debated and passed (chapter 12). If the government could disengage from agricultural markets, the savings would be noticeable, even in the federal budget.

As for the entities facing lower stakes, airline deregulators had only reputation at stake in the post-deregulation world. And even there the threat was limited because they had little continuing operational responsibility. The only politically significant distributional impact the deregulated market might produce was loss of service to small communities.[4] They designed a buffering provision for such cases, but it proved to be little needed.[5] Apart from that, regulators were prepared to let the gains and losses of the new competitive marketplace fall where they might. The same was largely true in the railroads case; petitioning for a rate adjustment by the Surface Transportation Board was a remedy in theory but not in practice, owing to high transaction costs. More broadly, policymakers were prepared to see shipping rates go up generally and were surprised when they actually fell (chapter 6). In the agriculture sector, the cessation of planting restrictions seems to carry relatively low risk for governmental actors in general, though I am making an inferential leap from what is said in chapter 12.

Discussion

The correlation between governmental stakes and policy results shown in table 15-1 may or may not reflect causality. Deregulation and market design are such complex and multifaceted exercises that their success or failure clearly depends on multiple factors. If a process involving governmental stakeholders has *some* role in impeding successful market design, though, what exactly might that role be? What might be the underlying dynamics?

Protectionism

The one clear case in table 15-1 of government protecting its own against market competition, arguably to the detriment of the public, is that of public school districts in regard to vouchers and charter schools. The dynamics of protectionism, as analyzed by Frederick Hess in chapter 9, are subtle. They include a large element of moral self-justification by individuals and "advertising, public outreach, and public relations" by the public institution. They also entail, among other mechanisms, buffering the public institution against competitive losses and giving permission to typically marginalized "entrepreneurial personalities" to launch visible new specialty schools or other such projects. This amounts, says Hess, to "punch[ing] small holes through regulatory barriers."

A rather different protectionist dynamic occurs in the case of agriculture. Here the public "employees" in question are members of Congress. In 2002 the favorable economic situation that had encouraged deregulation in 1996 had reversed itself. Many members of Congress believed their reelection might hinge on heaping subsidies on the farmers in their districts once again.

The More Interests and the Longer the Process, the More Trouble

Deregulated markets differ substantially with regard to the need for continuing—call it "second-phase"—government intervention, "need" meaning that the government could play a welfare-increasing role rather than simply leave the market to itself. It is likely that a desire to enhance welfare played at least a moderately important role in keeping the government involved in the design of the post-deregulation markets. In the cases here, there might have been three quite different welfare-increasing rationales for its continuing involvement once competitive deregulation was begun: ambiguous or incomplete property rights, residual natural monopoly, and externalities and information asymmetries. These last two categories often give rise to what is called social regulation.[6]

But however benign the motivation, the longer that second-phase intervention continues, the longer it remains a target for rent seeking and other such distorting forces. As explained in chapter 4, the challenge of designing a social regulation regime is to ensure that investors obtain appropriate financial and other information about publicly held corporations. This is a very standard design challenge in markets with asymmetric information, that is, where sellers have more information than buyers. Solving the asymmetric information problem was only one of several challenges for the U.K. pension reformers trying to shift workers out of public and nonportable private pensions and into portable pensions (chapter 8). They also had to structure the tax incentives and regulatory constraints correctly so as to induce workers to make the shift.

Some imperfections require more regulatory persistence than others. The tasks of optimizing telecommunications and electricity markets were (and are) seemingly relentless. In both cases, access to the transmission network was historically in the hands of local or regional monopolists, and these networks have natural-monopoly characteristics. Centralized decisionmaking, by the government or by its partial agent such as a regional transmission organization, was required in order to prevent anticompetitive exclusion from the network. Although the continuing governmental role affords opportunities for rent-seeking interventions, whether these are successful depends on the shrewdness of regulators and other policymakers: thus in table 15-1, PJM electricity is counted a success, whereas telecommunications and California electricity are not.

Good design or good luck may have protected other markets from second-phase interventions. Consider safety regulation in the post-deregulation airline industry. It is possible that airline deregulation required increased safety regulation, as the incentives increased for airlines, especially marginal ones, to cut corners on safety (chapter 2). Nevertheless, this was a relatively self-contained effort, an incremental increase in a safety-regulation system that was already in place and functioning reasonably well. It presented no handhold for strategies intended to reregulate the industry.

Railroad deregulation did afford some such handholds, but they were small. "Captive shippers" subject to monopolistically high rates could in principle appeal to the Surface Transportation Board (STB) for relief, but in fact have been frozen out owing to the case-preparation costs. The STB and the Civil Aeronautics Board (CAB) successor group, both in the U.S. Department of Transportation, were set up to oversee residual competitiveness issues in the newly deregulated markets. They might have become sources of continued intervention and may indeed have been motivated to intervene (chapter 10), except for the constraint of being responsible to the executive branch, which the Republicans controlled.

Ideologically Based Incompetence

The ideology of Britain's pension reformers—although antistatist rather than more narrowly antiregulatory—blinded them to the substantial perils of market making (chapter 8). Britain's robust system of employer pensions was eroded not only by pension reform but also by tax incentives to switch to private pensions whose effects the government planners did not predict, an initially anemic set of private pension sellers, a subsequently turbocharged set of sellers not above misrepresenting their products, and a population of buyers ill-equipped to negotiate the complex choices among pension alternatives. The Conservative government flatfootedly walked straight into all these hazards. The result of Conservative incompetence was to create conditions that subsequently led to a Labor initiative ten years later to, arguably, overregulate the private pensions market.[7]

The Canadian Radio and Telecommunications Commission (CRTC) also acted incompetently, but here it was because of a misguided theory of market creation, one that relied on a price floor for voice over Internet protocol (VoIP) services. As pointed out in chapter 13, the CRTC should have worried not about the distribution of market shares among competitors but about the competitive dynamics of forcing prices ever downward.

Blame-Avoidance

Another dynamic worth mentioning arises from trying to avoid blame. In the initial electricity deregulation legislation in California, the utilities sought to have ratepayers pay for the billions of dollars of "stranded costs" attributable to failed or incompetent construction of generating facilities; the state legislature agreed on the condition that the utilities accept a cap on retail rates. As wholesale power rates soared well above the retail rate cap, the policy (for this and other reasons) became untenable. The electric utilities were going broke, caught between rising wholesale prices and capped retail rates. Neither the governor nor the legislature nor the state Public Utilities Commission could admit that the retail cap invented by their prior policy design was a mistake and should be lifted; nor could they face up to imposing a sudden and massive financial burden on consumers.

The "solution" instead was for the state to become the wholesale power buyer for the utilities, in which capacity it signed long-term contracts at prices estimated to be more than 50 percent above expected future spot prices. "In part, the high prices spread over many years were a way for the state to hide astronomical prices it was implicitly going to pay for power during summer 2001 and 2002."[8]

Practical Implications?

I have argued that the most harmful condition for phase-two politics is for the government or policymakers to have relatively high stakes in the outcome. However, there may be at least four ways in which this condition can be avoided, minimized, or at least managed: shrink or neutralize the bureaucracy, absorb moral casualties, get most of it right the first time, and create countervailing constituencies.

Shrinking or Neutralizing the Bureaucracy

As noted in chapter 12, the reversibility of deregulatory reform helps to destroy the key institutional strongholds of protectionism, such as the CAB before airline deregulation and an important chunk of the Department of Agriculture before the 1996 FAIR act. The argument may be extended: destroying such bureaucratic niches also limits the capacity of important governmental stakeholders to intervene detrimentally in phase-two politics. Changing the bureaucratic niche can also help. In the railroad and airline cases, as mentioned earlier, the bureaucracies that succeeded the CAB and the Interstate Commerce Commission were constrained by the larger bureaucratic and political institutions (Department of Transportation and the White House) from intervening once again.

Absorbing Moral Casualties

Like all significant social transitions, deregulation typically has winners and losers. One need feel no sympathy for some of those losers, such as farmers grown rich off governmentally induced price manipulations. Others might seem more deserving, such as farmers thrown unprotected into the clutches of railroad monopolies or workers suddenly obliged to make investment choices they previously had no desire and little competence to make. The government's desire to buffer the deserving victims of deregulatory transitions is morally admirable as well as politically prudent. But buffering policies typically create opportunities for meddling of all kinds, including the revival of rent seeking. Hence it may be desirable to limit such policies. The preventable but unprevented losses of innocent parties may be the price for insulating an admittedly imperfect market from forces that would create even more costly imperfections. As Michael Levine writes in chapter 10, "In this world, the choice is never between imperfect markets and perfect regulation, or imperfect regulation and perfect markets. The choice is between imperfect markets and imperfect regulation."

On the other hand, in some cases it may be worthwhile to try to design buffering policies that do not permanently interfere with competitive pricing in the long run. Flat-sum rebates could be given to electricity consumers should prices drastically increase after deregulation, as was done in Alberta (chapter 13).

Getting Most of It Right the First Time

The second phase of deregulatory policymaking can be constrained simply by reducing the problems created by or left over from the first phase. Given the uncertainties and complexities of the world, this is not easy. The rhetorical fog created by rent-seekers certainly makes matters worse. They are as ready to claim they are helping to restore markets, should deregulation be in vogue, as they are to manage them should regulation be the watchword. But their idea of restoring markets is to structure certain critical relationships in ways favorable to their own interests. Enron, for instance, advocated (successfully) in the California electricity deregulation case for pricing and property rights arrangements that would be of advantage to forward traders such as itself, even though these would have made the new electricity market less beneficial for consumers (chapter 7). The Telecommunications Act of 1996 turned into a struggle between the long-distance carriers and the Baby Bells over the terms of access into each other's markets, a struggle that continued during implementation of the act by the FCC. Each party to the struggle claimed, with the support of its own academic experts, that it was the true spearhead of competition (chapter 11).

Nevertheless, it may be possible to deflect problems caused by sheer ideological blindness of the sort observed in the British pensions case. Preventable, too, may be short-sighted redistributional moves such as California's freezing of retail electricity rates while it was deregulating wholesale rates (chapter 6).

Creating Countervailing Constituencies

If it is impossible to prevent continued governmental meddling, it may be possible to create new constituencies to oppose it, such as new airlines and new farm interests (chapter 12). Or government corporations in the electricity sector could be privatized, to create a set of investors and workers with a stake in pressuring government "not to renege on its deregulatory plans" (chapter 13).

Conclusion

These ideas for reducing phase-two problems are but a few of many other possibilities. They are based on my interpretations of data to be found in the chapters in this volume. But those data have not been selected with an eye to developing or testing ideas about mitigating strategies; nor are the cases in this book more than a modest fraction of all the deregulatory cases that might have been tapped. Obviously, a great deal of research remains to be done.

I am a little more confident of the proposition that when government or policymakers have high stakes in deregulation or in intervening in phase-two markets, their actions often lead, directly or indirectly, to failure. This is not because the evidence is so rich or supportive but because the proposition is but an application of the more general theory that the process of government is vulnerable to a variety of hazards such as rent seeking, ideological zealotry, legalism, slow-paced bureaucracy, and the "piling on" of objectives and agendas.[9] These hazards lie in wait even when policymakers and administrators attempt, in good faith and generally with at least moderate competence, to use government to promote the public interest—as I believe was true for all of the cases discussed in this chapter.

Notes

1. I also omit the case of thrift institutions deregulation discussed by Jonathan Macey in chapter 3. This omission deserves explanation, since on the surface it looks similar to other cases of deregulation in sectors such as railroads or electricity. This is not, however, a case of deregulating an industry in order to create competition, nor of designing a regulatory scheme to offset market imperfections. In fact, there was ample competition in the overall banking sector, and even within the thrift subsector. The main reforms, allowing the thrifts to pay more interest and to diversify portfolios beyond housing, were done not mainly to increase competition but to help the industry avert insolvencies. Deregulatory ideology was certainly part of the motivation for policy changes during this period, but it was by no means the main part. The thrifts were lending long (long-term mortgages) and borrowing short and in the late 1970s were unable to compete with other financial institutions that were permitted to offer much higher interest rates. Congress and the Federal Home Loan Bank Board (FHLBB) simply had to find ways to help the industry out. It was technically difficult to do so because that involved finding the right balance between continued solvency-oriented restrictions and removal of sufficient restrictions to help the

most troubled thrifts become profitable. Moreover, the prospects for profitability are a subjective matter, and much of what Congress and the FHLBB did was not unreasonable, even if ultimately unsuccessful and in hindsight seemingly foolish. Macey correctly points to the ease with which both scrupulous and unscrupulous S&L managers could, and did, profitably externalize risks onto the public while retaining profits for themselves. But this absurdity was created not so much because competitive-markets ideology blinded Congress and regulators to the risks but because the historical regulatory framework plus the interest rate environment suddenly, and unfortunately, combined to force even well-run thrifts into bankruptcy or perilously close to it. Congress also failed to provide the various regulatory institutions with enough manpower to enforce appropriate regulations against the unscrupulous thrifts.

2. Severin Borenstein, "The Trouble with Electricity Markets: Understanding California's Restructuring Disaster," *Journal of Economic Perspectives* 16, no. 1 (2002): 191–211.

3. But note that I do not include the stakes here for regulatory bureaucrats whose careers might be jeopardized by their loss of power and function. That is a transitional effect, and the stakes I refer to here are only those that persist after deregulation has occurred.

4. Post-deregulation protection was also offered to the unions in the event of layoffs (chapter 10), but these did not occur.

5. Dorothy Robyn, *Braking the Special Interests: Trucking Deregulation and the Politics of Policy Reform* (University of Chicago Press, 1987), p. 160.

6. There is no reason to assume a priori that a newly deregulated competitive market would or would not benefit from additional intervention of this latter type.

7. Ideologically based incompetence is not the only kind of incompetence. Consider deregulation of the California electricity markets (chapter 7). Managing a competitive market in electricity is tricky under the best of circumstances, and many design decisions did not, in the mid-1990s, have simple and obvious right answers. Yet it was clearly a mistake for the California legislature to cap retail rates while allowing wholesale rates to float with the market. Whether through better luck or higher competence, the PJM designers, by contrast, avoided such problems.

8. Borenstein, "The Trouble with Electricity Markets," p. 209.

9. Eugene Bardach, *The Implementation Game: What Happens after a Bill Becomes a Law* (Cambridge, Mass.: MIT Press, 1977).

16

Concluding Thoughts: How the Whole Is Greater than the Sum of Its Parts

PETER H. SCHUCK

The task of summarizing the lessons of the preceding chapters is both challenging and alluring—challenging because the experiences and phenomena they discuss are dauntingly complex, and alluring because the arguments are so rich and suggestive. Since the specific lessons of each case study have already been made clear, it remains for me to explain why the whole of this volume is greater than the sum of its parts. I mean to identify the general patterns and principles common to all of them, and to call attention to certain factors (noted by the authors or otherwise evident to me) that may limit the reach of these generalizations.

The Complexity of Analytical Concepts

The first question to raise, then, is what do the policies studied in this volume have in common? All are instances of "deregulation" or "liberalization," in the sense that their policymakers' ostensible goal was to reduce government controls over a particular activity and allow market forces to operate under fewer legal constraints. But my phrase "policymakers' ostensible goal" raises three additional questions: (1) is there a discrete, identifiable set of policymakers? (2) is the goal they publicly embrace their real one, and (3) do they have more than one goal? Fortunately, each of the case studies addresses these questions and provides penetrating answers to them.

As noted in Marc Landy and Martin Levin's introduction, however, it is more accurate and fruitful to think of the policymakers as being engaged in "market design." After all, the government is not simply removing legal controls and then getting out of the way but is self-consciously fashioning (or as Eric Patashnik puts it, reconfiguring) markets so that they exhibit particular and contingent features. But calling it market design must not obscure the fact that markets exhibit certain features that the designers can neither contrive (for example, human striving) nor alter (for example, the law of supply and demand). Market design is political in every sense: it is highly partisan, requires side payments and other forms of compromise and coalition building, involves ideological struggle, and reflects deeply con-tested normative and empirical assessments of the competing claims of indi-viduals and communities.

These case studies render other familiar concepts in political economy both ambiguous and variable. Martin Shapiro, for example, distinguishes between "soft" and "hard" law. He sees soft law as a fluid, tentative, corpo-ratist project of delegated power and negotiation among well-organized inter-ests—a project, he thinks, that is peculiarly susceptible to corruption and rent seeking. Hard law, for Shapiro, consists of enforceable rules that can be applied more or less predictably and fairly to a variety of situations. Market design confounds the traditional distinctions between government and mar-ket, and between public and private. Market designers must blend these familiar categories into unexpected combinations, which in turn deprive these concepts of their customary boundaries and meanings.

Our authors use an array of analytical categories to help parse these com-plexities. Both Patashnik and Jacob Hacker present matrices that yield pre-dictions about the particular forms and political durability of market design policies. In contrast, most of the other analytical categories are essentially descriptive and taxonomic. By calling attention to the different aspects of these policies and sharpening otherwise-suppressed normative issues, these categories help to clarify one's thinking about these policies and issues. Hacker, for example, distinguishes three ways in which policymakers may retrench on previous welfare state commitments. Steven Vogel's four varieties of "reregulation" serve to underscore the important point, recurrent in our studies, that policy reform efforts often produce more regulation, not less. He also proposes five related categories of marketization techniques. Michael Levine (revealing an incisive eye for "i") contends that interests, institutions, ideology, and information explain the survival of airline deregulation in the face of the drastic changes that beset the industry in the last quarter-century. Alan Jacobs and Steven Teles distinguish market making and market adapting as two quite different genres of market design.

The Impetus for Market Design

Not surprisingly, different motivations and conditions propelled the market design efforts examined in this volume. After all, these efforts vary greatly in their policy domains and in the importance of their specific contexts. Moreover, as Hacker cautions, the ambition of explaining change constitutes the "soft underbelly" of the social sciences, which suggests the need for realistic expectations: social scientists are likely to be far better at identifying disparate factors associated with reform than at distilling those factors into broadly applicable causal theories.

Even so, I am struck by the fact that market design in these very different domains is driven by some common factors. Even more interesting, certain factors, notably the quest for efficiency gains, are much more politically effective in some areas than in others. First, the commonalities. A *sense of crisis* clearly helps to propel the reform project, raising its political salience. As John Cioffi shows, the tide of private litigation that engulfed the securities industry and corporate issuers engendered a sharp congressional reaction that led to far-reaching legal changes in 1995 and 1998. The collapse of Enron, WorldCom, and other major corporations in the wake of corporate scandals impelled Congress to enact the Sarbanes-Oxley law. Sometimes, however, the crisis is not immediate or even certain to occur, yet policy entrepreneurs can sometimes persuade the relevant political actors that crisis is indeed looming and that decisive and radical reform is needed. The Jacobs-Teles account shows how the Thatcher government used public fears to redesign the British pension system. And sometimes, as Jon Macey explains in his study of banking deregulation, the reform may cause the crisis rather than the other way around.

Macey's analysis highlights another common driver of reform: rent seeking by existing firms. He shows that deregulatory policies created large windfalls for many financial institutions. Indeed, all of our case studies seem to support the unsurprising proposition that market design efforts are products of self-interested jockeying for position among competitors in the market and among politicians. This is also the theme of Andrew Rich's analysis of congressional redesign of the telecommunications market. In his account, no sense of crisis existed and none was created. Instead, the principal forces propelling reform were a fierce struggle within and across industries for market dominance in the face of rapidly changing technology, and the politicians' need to propitiate the combatants, which were major sources of campaign funds and public opinion. Richard O'Neill and Udi Helman's review of the redesign of California's electricity market finds that Enron's desire to maximize churning and transaction costs gave it a huge market advantage. And a number of the studies show that rent seeking can drive the particular *form* that market design takes even when other factors propelled the market design itself. Indeed, it is fair to say that rent seeking plays an important role in every one of the policy domains reviewed here.

In some of these cases, a pro-market *ideology* was the primary motivation both for a policy of liberalization and, sometimes, for that policy's persistence even after its failure became apparent. The reform of the British pension system is the clearest example of this. Patashnik's account of the 1986 tax reform also emphasizes the influence of ideology and ideas—in this case those of economists. Here he converges with Levine, who credits economic theory with a major role in airline deregulation. In other cases—again, telecommunications is exemplary—ideology seems to have had little to do with fueling the reform, perhaps because ideology simultaneously pointed in a number of different policy directions, which is one measure of the complexity and opacity of a particular policy environment.

Often, it is *government budgetary pressures* that drive the campaign for market redesign, as in the far-reaching health and pension reforms analyzed by Hacker. In some instances, the impetus for market design lies in the quest for potential *efficiency gains*—and the struggle is over who will garner those gains. This motive need not be the same as the desire to relieve government budgetary pressures. After all, efficiency may benefit private interests for the most part, and at times can be pursued without triggering the kinds of political conflicts that budgetary policies entail. As Darius Gaskins points out, the lure of greater efficiency primarily motivated deregulation in the freight railroad and electric utility industries.

As just mentioned, however, efficiency goals do not always drive market design. Indeed, several of our authors—Patashnik most emphatically—insist that efficiency has little or no political constituency, in part because it is a public good that cannot be appropriated privately. Frederick Hess, in his study of competition-oriented reforms in public education, sees a powerful constituency for equity (which the constituents define in anticompetitive ways), but none for efficiency. I disagree. Politicians responsive to taxpayer concerns must be attentive to the social costs and benefits of policies, as are other interests that must act on the assumption that a public budget is a zero-sum (sometimes, a negative-sum) game. Precisely because producer groups and public employee unions engage in rent seeking, they have a strong interest in limiting rent seeking by others so that they can claim more of the budget for themselves. In the 1980s and 1990s, this competitive rent seeking drove policymakers to adopt budget and tax rules that generally required every new tax cut or expenditure to be offset by other tax revenues or spending reductions. (Why and how these desirable rules fell into desuetude would itself be a story worth telling. The new Democratic Congress may seek to restore them.)

The Relation between Market Design and Rules

As Steven Vogel points out, the relationship between government and the market, between a regime of enforceable rules and one of voluntary exchange, is obscure for two reasons. First, the interpenetration of rules and markets is so extensive and subtle that the distinction seems to melt away conceptually. Second, the relationship between them takes Protean forms. These obscurities, it seems, are endemic to the contemporary political economy.

Despite such obscurities, most of our case studies find that effective market design—even when seeking deregulation and increased competition—requires lots of rules, perhaps even more rules than before. I say "perhaps" because I am less convinced than some of our authors seem to be that, as Vogel puts it, the result of market design is "freer markets and more rules." I certainly agree that the evidence presented here demonstrates that *many* rules are needed if freer markets are sought. Whether there are *more* rules, however, is an empirical question—one, moreover, that should be relatively easy to answer. Is there any a priori reason to expect more rules? For anyone familiar with the mountains of statutory and regulatory provisions governing the old Interstate Commerce Commission and Civil Aeronautics Board (to pick only two examples), the answer to this question is probably no.

The more interesting and important question, however, is *which kinds* of rules are essential for market design. I glean from our case studies at least eight market design rule types, and others surely exist.

—Even the most unregulated markets need rules in order to define property rights, proscribe force and fraud, and establish certain legal remedies. Landy and Levin refer to these as "market-framing" rules.

—"Market-perfecting rules" (such as antitrust law, information requirements, and taxes on externalities) may be needed to remedy the market defects that competition cannot cure and may even magnify.

—"Log-rolling rules" may be needed to make the consequences of market design politically acceptable. In the airlines case discussed by Patashnik and by Levine, for example, Congress had to provide side payments in the form of regional and other subsidies to those interests whose opposition had to be neutralized in order for the reform to be adopted.

—"Incumbent-restraining rules" may be necessary in order to encourage new or more robust competition in the (re-)designed market. This asymmetric regulation, as Vogel calls it, is exemplified in the telecommunications case analyzed by Andrew Rich. As Rich's chapter also shows, however, incumbent-protecting rules are probably more common when politicians turn to market design, as studies of the design of electoral districts and campaign finance schemes have clearly demonstrated.

—"Activity-suppressing rules" may be imposed on everyone, not just incumbents, in order to reduce the level of a competitive activity viewed as a threat to the market. For example, the 1995 reform of private securities litigation was intended to limit "strike suits."

—"Social regulation rules" may be imposed as an adjunct to economic deregulation where policymakers fear that the intensified competition unleashed by the market design will threaten health, safety, environmental, and other values.

—An analogous fear may prompt policymakers to adopt "risk substitution rules." Macey shows, for example, that when market designers decided to jettison certain traditional kinds of competition-suppressing regulation such as market segmentation and interest rate ceilings, they strengthened other kinds of rules such as expanded deposit insurance and higher minimum capital requirements.

—Market designers may impose "market-constructing" rules intended to create new trading schemes that can improve regulatory programs.

The Politics of Reregulation

Often market design not only produces more rules but actually engenders a thoroughgoing reregulation of the activity. British pension reform is a particularly dramatic example of the dynamic leading to reregulation because the government's privatization effort began with such political and economic advantages that one would have predicted a relatively easy success and durability. In the event, however, a series of policy errors, official misjudgments, ideological blinders, private sector scandals, and feedback loops produced a policy disaster that created an irresistible public demand for reregulation. Other revealing instances of reregulation are the gradual evisceration of the 1986 tax reform and the sequence of corporate reform legislation. These examples suggest the importance of crises, policy innovations, partisan competition, informational feedbacks, and public backlashes to the prospects for reregulation. Politicians seeking to exploit these conditions are sometimes swamped and even undone by them—a process that Cioffi characterizes as "punctuated change within powerful, implicit, and largely unchallenged constraints." Less grandly, one might think of it as policy ebb and flow, action and reaction, cycling and recycling.

Indeed, reregulation (or stricter regulation) appears to be so common that, as in the case of the dog that didn't bark, the more interesting story is when (and why) a market design manages to survive challenges rather than being overthrown by reregulation. Deregulation's durability is what Levine means to account for in the airlines case. Rather than rest his explanation on the vast benefits that deregulation has generated, he emphasizes the heterogeneous interests and policy preferences that have developed in the post-deregulation period—not only among the carriers themselves but also among municipalities, customers, and industry employees. Another factor sustaining a market design is the path dependency created by large investments in deregulation-specific assets by the carriers and by its customers and suppliers. A reform's ability to reduce the regulatory slack that had sustained the prereform regulatory regime constitutes another barrier to reregulation.

Policy Inertia and Innovation

To Levine's useful list of the factors tending to stymie reregulation efforts, I would add a more general but common one: policy inertia. This is a condition on which the case studies in this volume shed some interesting and somewhat surprising light.

In the view of many students of American politics, U.S. policymaking and constitutional systems were designed (or operate) to frustrate or at least slow policy change except during periods when a widespread sense of crisis either exists or can be created. This notion, our cases strongly suggest, is far too simple, although its has some merit when one compares American political institutions with more highly centralized ones like the Westminster system. The market design initiatives presented in this volume—and indeed the reregulations that sometimes ensued—show that the relatively fragmented, inertial American system can nonetheless produce far-reaching policy changes under certain conditions. Whether these changes can be politically sustained, of course, is a separate question, but our case studies present important examples of enduring, politically popular, market-enhancing reforms.

Harder to answer is the normative question of whether, or under which circumstances, this inertial policy structure is a good thing. Our authors seem divided, at least with respect to their specific policy areas. Hacker laments policy "stickiness" in health and pension policy because it enables the old welfare state to avoid making the adaptations to the new risk profile necessitated by changing social conditions and needs. Instead, he argues, this inertia encourages policymakers to pursue the ineffective and inequitable strategies of policy drift, conversion, and layering. In the banking system, Macey notes, habitual policy errors are caused by the vested interests that coagulate around the status quo, the moral hazard that an embedded dual regulatory apparatus encourages state regulators to inflict on federal policies, and the rent seeking facilitated by a complacent inertia.

But some of our authors seem to think better of this inertia. Levine, for example, finds that it has sustained an innovative policy of deregulation, producing great benefits for consumers, communities, and the more nimble carriers. Patashnik, concluding that special interests readily subverted the 1986 tax reform, would have preferred to see *more* policy inertia once that reform was in place. Jacobs and Teles imply (without directly discussing the U.S. case) that the centralized Westminster system, in contrast to the highly fragmented, inertial American one, made it too easy for the Thatcher government to make serious pension policy errors and then to persist on this misguided, ideologically reflexive path, ignoring for too long the evidence of failure. Centralized governing institutions, they find, do not mix well with far-reaching, complex, error-prone policy changes.

Conclusion

What all of our authors demonstrate—in admirable detail and across a broad range of regulatory domains—is that politics pervades not only the forms of market design permitted by the struggle between policy innovation and political inertia but also the substantive content of these reforms. At the core of this struggle are interests, incentives, institutions, and ideas. The market constitutes, simultaneously, a tempting target for reform, a valuable policy instrument, and a powerful constraint that may defeat or distort the best-laid plans of policymakers. As these cases demonstrate, the market and the body of rules called the law—like other contentious couples—are unable to live with or without each other.

Beyond this important generalization, however, each of these case studies reveals a stubborn singularity. Some of the market designs have proved to be both enduring and, from a public interest perspective, quite successful, whereas others have been utter and dismal failures. The surface and air transportation deregulations are examples of the former, while the latter is illustrated by the efforts to reform agricultural subsidies and to create a private British pension system. The campaign to institute school choice so far falls somewhere in between but, alas, closer to the failure end of the spectrum.

Eugene Bardach's analysis, which focuses on the stakes of government officials in promoting or blocking reform, provides one useful way to understand and explain these different outcomes. But it also reveals some of the sources of this singularity, so frustrating to the social scientists fondly known as lumpers, who yearn for theoretical elegance and predictive power, but reassuring to splitters (like me), who tend instead to see diversity, distinctions, and messiness almost everywhere. Suppose, for example, that one wants to predict whether a health policy reform such as the new Medicare Part D, which seeks to use market competition among private insurers to provide better service and lower drug costs to seniors, will endure and (what is not the same thing) succeed. In making such a prediction, where should one look?

The answer, surely, is that one must look at many things. A telling thing, says Bardach, is the stakes for government actors, but (careful and subtle analyst that he is) he identifies at least four kinds of stakes: material and psychological self-interest, budgetary factors, ideology, and reputation. In the Medicare Part D case, I suspect, some of these stakes point in different directions: the ideological commitments of Bush administration officials would seem to favor the program's emphasis on private insurers, their budgetary concerns might favor the generally lower administrative costs of administering the program though conventional Medicare channels, and their reputational concerns might cut either way. For Shapiro, an essential consideration is whether the program is so corporatist that it induces corruption, dissimulation, cheating, and rent seeking, but he seems to acknowledge that such risks must be balanced against the disadvantages of command-and-control regulation. Moreover, that balance will likely be struck differently in every case, depending on many contingent factors. As Hess shows, unions often hijack efforts to introduce more family choice into public education, but in the airlines, notes Levine, it was possible to adopt a successful market design notwithstanding the power of the unions representing airline employees. Iacobucci and his colleagues describe successful deregulations in Canada of some of the same industries that in the United States were able to defeat the regulatory reformers' hopes. And so on.

Where does this leave policymakers, analysts, and theoreticians? The answer: without powerful predictive formulas, but with a much keener sense of the complexity of the political economy of regulatory reform, and a far more nuanced and sophisticated understanding of the conditions that are associated with successful and unsuccessful market designs. New legal rules, it is now clear, are essential to the political and economic success of market-oriented reforms that are usually promoted as a relief from rules. Political struggle is obviously a precondition not merely for the adoption of these reforms but for their survival amid the inevitable pressures for reregulation. And a satisfying explanation of public policy outcomes depends on many factors that are difficult to characterize and highly specific to the individual case. Once again, the splitters win.

To return to the book's central findings outlined in the introduction by Marc Landy and Martin Levin, three points bear revisiting. First, pro-competitive market designs appear to work best when limited to relatively simple objectives of market framing and reducing market imperfections. Second, macro policies that establish the broad framework of attitudes toward risk and the impact of moral hazard may be more influential in sustaining competitive markets than "micro" intrusions into this or that specific market. And third, policy designers cannot afford the luxury of considering themselves apolitical engineers or technicians. They must also act as statesmanlike policy entrepreneurs. They must predict the probable lines of political attack on their pro-competitive policies, do everything in their power to make their policy designs impervious to and resilient in the face of that assault, and sell their policies to a justifiably skeptical, risk-averse public.

Contributors

Eugene Bardach
University of California–Berkeley

John W. Cioffi
University of California–Riverside

Darius Gaskins
Norbridge, Inc.

Jacob S. Hacker
Yale University

Udi Helman
Federal Energy Regulatory Commission

Frederick M. Hess
American Enterprise Institute

Edward Iacobucci
University of Toronto

Alan M. Jacobs
University of British Columbia

Marc K. Landy
Boston College

Martin A. Levin
Brandeis University

Michael E. Levine
New York University School of Law

Jonathan R. Macey
Yale Law School

Richard O'Neill
Federal Energy Regulatory Commission

Eric M. Patashnik
University of Virginia

Andrew Rich
City College of New York

Peter H. Schuck
Yale University

Martin Shapiro
University of California–Berkeley
School of Law

Steven Teles
Yale University

Michael Trebilcock
University of Toronto

Steven Vogel
University of California–Berkeley

Ralph A. Winter
University of British Columbia

Index